Understanding and Managing Organizational Behavior

A Developmental Perspective

The Irwin Series in Management and The Behavioral Sciences

L. L. Cummings and E. Kirby Warren   *Consulting Editors*

Understanding and Managing Organizational Behavior

A Developmental Perspective

W. Alan Randolph
University of South Carolina

1985

Homewood, Illinois 60430

The diagram on the cover is our symbol for the levels of
organizational behavior and the developmental perspective. The four
moving balls represent the four levels—individuals, interpersonal
relationships, work groups, and organizations. The plane on which
they move represents the developmental perspective of viewing the
levels in terms of their past, present, and future. Over time, individuals grow; interpersonal relationships evolve; work groups develop;
and organizations change. You will see this diagram throughout the
book as a reminder of the four levels and the developmental perspective.

ISBN 0-256-03231-9

Library of Congress Catalog Card No. 84–81265

Printed in the United States of America

2 3 4 5 6 7 8 9 0 K 2 1 0 9 8 7

Dedicated with love to my wife
Ruth Anne
and my children
Ashley, Shannon, and Elizabeth

Preface

If you had asked me several years ago if I wanted to write a textbook on Organizational Behavior, I would have said absolutely not. There are so many books on the market, and writing a book seemed like such a monumental task. But then I went to the Organizational Behavior Teaching Conference at Harvard University in 1981 and led with Barry Posner and Andrew Pettigrew a session on teaching organizational behavior from a developmental perspective (that is, with a focus on the past, present, and future). The response to the idea was overwhelmingly positive from the 65 to 70 people who attended the session. But we all left a little disappointed that there were no texts which utilized this perspective, since it seemed to provide a framework to both integrate and make more useful the concepts typically covered in an organizational behavior course. My interest was peaked, and I decided to give some more thought to writing a text based on the developmental perspective.

You are now beginning to read the result of my efforts over the last three and a half years to produce such a text. My goals in writing the book have been to try to use the developmental perspective to: (1) help tie together the concepts and theories usually provided in an organizational behavior course, (2) help you better understand the concepts and theories that relate to effective management, and (3) make it easier for you as a manager to use these ideas to make you a better manager.

In a sense, the book is designed to teach you *about* management—hence the word *understanding* in the title. And most organizational behavior textbooks share this goal. But many books do not try to teach you *how* to manage, and this book is also designed with that goal in mind—hence the word *managing* in the title. I believe it is important for you to learn both *about management* and *how to manage,* and this book is an attempt to help you do both.

Thus, for example, I not only explore 10 commonly mentioned theories of motivation, but I also use the developmental perspective to help tie them together into a framework that can be helpful to you as a manager. Toward this goal of usefulness, I also have used three other devices. First, there is a case, the Home Computers case, that unfolds throughout the book. In almost every chapter, you will learn more about the Home Computers company and its employees, as I use the case to help you learn to apply the concepts and theories of the chapter. The case also helps to integrate the material from chapter to chapter, since in discussing it in one chapter we can refer back to discussions from earlier chapters. Student reaction to the case has been very favorable; they find it helpful in understanding and applying the concepts from each chapter.

The second device I have used to aid in understanding applications of the material is excerpts from *The Wall Street Journal* and other popular outlets. These excerpts are integrated into the text as examples to show you how the material being discussed applies to everyday events in the world around you. Again, the reaction from students has been very favorable; they find that these examples help the concepts come alive.

The third device is to supply at the end of a number of the chapters questionnaires that relate to the concepts from the chapters. By completing and scoring these questionnaires, you gain a feel for how your behavior can be explained using the concepts from the course. These questionnaires can be used to help you learn about the people you work with and thus help you be a better manager.

The bottom line of these ideas is that this book is written for you, the students who will read it. In addition to the two devices described above, I have also highlighted in boldface type some of the key points in each chapter, and have provided a more detailed chapter summary than is often found in textbooks. Furthermore, I have tried to explain complicated concepts in as simple a fashion as possible. My style of writing is to try to talk to you just as I might if we were in the classroom together discussing and trying to understand and use organizational behavior concepts and theories. Over the years of writing this book, my students have helped me achieve this goal.

The field of organizational behavior is at a point where a great deal is known about the nature of individuals, interpersonal relationships, work groups, and intergroup relationships. The challenge is to share this knowledge in a way that will help you become a more effective manager. If you will work with me as you read this book, I believe you will come away with a better understanding of organizational behavior and with the knowledge of how to be a better manager.

Acknowledgments

As with any book of this kind, there are a number of people who deserve thanks for their efforts at pulling it off. Larry Cummings and Kirby Warren, consulting editors for Irwin, provided encouragement, support, and some thought-provoking suggestions as I progressed from one draft to the next. The reviewers deserve a tremendous thanks for a job well done. In particular, the three people who probably deserve the largest thanks in terms of feedback on the chapters are Kim Cameron now at The University of Michigan, Greg Moorhead at Arizona State University, and Barry Posner at the University of Santa Clara. These three people reviewed every chapter of the book and provided detailed suggestions for improvement. While I did not always listen to them, their ideas provided a great deal of food for thought and helped me avoid certain errors in the book. In addition, a number of other people provided feedback on various batches of chapters, and they too deserve a note of thanks for providing many useful comments. Included are: Jim McFillen at Bowling Green State University, John Anstey at the University of Nebraska at Omaha, Kent Zimmerman at James Madison University, Jim McElroy at Iowa State University, Gabe Buntzman at Western Kentucky University, Linda Neider at the University of Miami, and Roy Glenn at Boise State University.

Here at the University of South Carolina, I owe thanks to Dean Jim Kane, Associate Dean Jim Hilton, and my department head, Joe Ullman, for providing the kind of atmosphere that makes a project like this book possible. Further, I would like to thank my colleague, Ed Cornelius, for having a number of his MBA students read and react to the book. Their feedback combined with that from my MBA and undergraduate students has been very helpful in making the book readable and helpful to students who want to become better managers. Another great help to me in writing the book has been my graduate assistant, Mary Anne Watson; she reacted to the various chapters and did a large share of preparing the Instructor's Manual that accompanies this book. Finally, several secretaries had a hand in preparing figures, tables, and the Instructor's Manual; I appreciate the help of Frances Donnelly, Sidney Rauch, and Kathy Fine.

And the last group to thank, but certainly not the least, is my family who endured a long process and provided much moral support throughout. My wife, Ruth Anne, was always there with flowers, champagne, a hug, or a word of encouragement—she always seemed to know which one was appropriate. In addition, she read every chapter, gave me feedback, and heard me discuss the book until she sometimes grew tired of it. My two oldest daughters, Ashley (eight) and Shannon (five), showed a surprising amount of interest in the book. Often as I sat in the study at my computer, they would come in to ask what I was doing and if they could see the book in the library when it was finished. I even heard them on occasion telling their friends about the book their Daddy was writing. Finally, my youngest child, Elizabeth, literally grew with the project. She was born in October 1982, shortly after I began writing the book, and she took many a morning nap on the bed in the study while I worked away at the computer. Now she runs in and wants to sit in my lap while I work. I cannot thank them all enough for their love and support, and for that reason I dedicate the book to them.

Indeed, I cannot thank enough all the people who helped in making this project a reality. I only hope that you will find the book useful as you try to understand and manage organizational behavior. Good luck!

W. Alan Randolph

Contents

Two-Factor Theory. Social Facilitation Theory. Process Theories of Motivation: *Expectancy Theory. Operant Conditioning. Equity Theory. Locke's Goal-Setting Theory.* Job Design and Motivation: *History of Job Design Concerns. Hackman's Core Dimensions Model. Motivation at Home Computers.* Applying the Theories to Home Computers: *Content Theories. Process Theories. Job-Design Theory.*

Understanding and Managing Organizational Behavior
A Developmental Perspective

- *Deter*
  Det
- *Changes*

Developmental
Approach.

3 levels

Dynamic
Environmental
Influences

Organizations

Work Groups

Interpersonal
Relationships

small
grp.

Individuals

Past

Present

Future

Change
Develop
Evolve
Grow

Organizational Behavior as Seen from a Developmental Perspective

Chap: 1

- what is Development Approach?
- what is Analytic Framework of Book?

An early researcher of organizations once said that we can neither live with nor without organizations.[1] Indeed, we depend upon organizations for most of the goods and services necessary for our survival and also for the leisure aspects of our lives. We have been influenced by and involved in organizations since our birth (for example, the hospital where we were born, our family, schools, clubs, and current jobs). Organizations have made our high standard of living possible, but they have also enhanced the stresses and tribulations of modern life. You probably hope to have a successful career working in and managing in one or more work organizations. Therefore, a question of paramount interest is how to be effective in an organization.

Chapter 1 begins to answer this question by introducing both the levels of organizational behavior and the developmental perspective. In it we develop an analytical framework consisting of four levels of organizational behavior —individuals, interpersonal relationships, work groups, and organizations. These levels then form the major sections of this book and are key aspects for an effective manager to understand and manage. Once we have the levels defined, we then overlay the developmental perspective to make the framework more useful to you as a manager.

Chapter 2 then brings this developmental perspective

A Developmental Framework for Studying Organizations

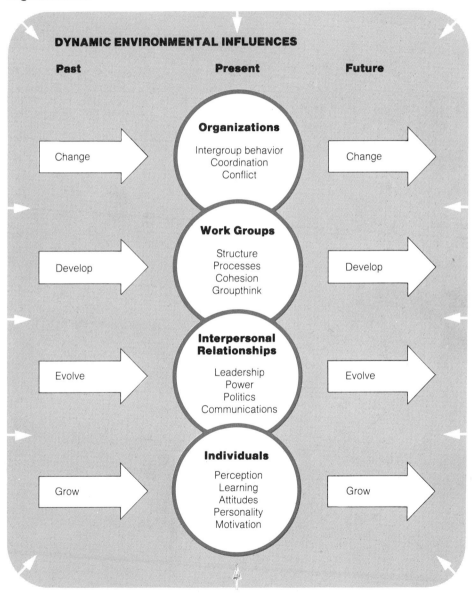

DYNAMIC ENVIRONMENTAL INFLUENCES

Past	Present	Future

Organizations
Intergroup behavior
Coordination
Conflict

Change → ← Change

Work Groups
Structure
Processes
Cohesion
Groupthink

Develop → ← Develop

Interpersonal Relationships
Leadership
Power
Politics
Communications

Evolve → ← Evolve

Individuals
Perception
Learning
Attitudes
Personality
Motivation

Grow → ← Grow

— supplemental list
not Kossen & Zitt to Ring.

down to a personal level. We discuss the career aspects of a manager's job by focusing on how different skills are needed at different phases of your career. We also explore the key stages of a working career and the key factors in the changing role of a manager over a career. As we get into the book, it will be helpful if you reflect on personal experiences. By doing so, you will help us achieve a major goal of the book—that is, making the material really useful to you as a manager.

Notes

1. G. C. Homans, *The Human Group* (New York: Harcourt, Brace and World, 1950).

C H A P T E R   1

Organizations and People as Dynamic Beings

As we begin our quest to understand and manage organizational behavior, it is important to appreciate the two most critical aspects of concern—people and organizations. Let us begin by exploring the nature of organizations, since it is the behavior of people **in organizations** that is our concern.

The Nature of Organizations

Most simply defined, **an organization is an invention of people that is a goal-directed vehicle for coordinating a set of activities for individuals and groups**. Managing in an organization is defined as **working with and through other people and groups of people to accomplish the organization's goals**. The process of managing is difficult because of the interactive nature of the elements comprising any organization, whether it is a business, a hospital, a school, a union, or a club. There are at least five main elements of an organization system that constantly interact in determining organizational effectiveness:

1. The **task** chosen by the organization (that is, the product or service to be provided and the markets to be served)
2. The **technology** chosen to accomplish the task.
3. The **structure** chosen to define jobs and interrelationships of people.
4. The **people** employed in the organization.
5. The **environment** in which the organization exists.[1]

As a manager, one of your critical challenges will be working with and through other people in the dynamic context that results from the interaction of task, technology, structure, and environment. Each of the five main elements of organizations represents a complex system that is brought to life through such processes as communications, decision making, goal implementation, and action plans. And in action, these elements are all interdependent with one another, and their interactions ultimately determine organizational effectiveness.

In this text, our primary focus is on the people element of organizations, within the context of the other four elements. This people aspect of organizations is what we mean when we use the term "organizational behavior." More specifically, **organizational behavior is the study of actions, feelings, and effectiveness of people in organizational settings**. Our focus is on what happens within individuals, between individuals (that is, interpersonal relations), within groups of people, and between groups of people (that is, intergroup relations). We want you to learn both to understand and manage organizational behavior, so you can be an effective manager.

In this endeavor to understand organizational behavior, we must also recognize that organizations are dynamic, developmental entities. That is, they change over time; they evolve from one state to another; and they may improve or decline in effectiveness. In other words, they are not static. And this dynamic nature applies both to the main organizational elements (task, technology, structure, people, and environment) and to the subdivisions under the people element (that is individuals, interpersonal relations, groups, and intergroup relations).

As we proceed through the text and the four subdivisions under people, we will use a developmental, dynamic, and change-oriented set of glasses for viewing and analyzing situations. By taking this time-based perspective we will be better able to understand why people and organizations operate as they do. Put another way, in order to understand why people and organizations behave the way they do **now**, we need to know something about their past history and development from past to present. We must also recognize that things will change as the future unfolds. Thus, our analysis must be continual if we are to effectively manage people in the present and the future. **This historical, evolving, and changing nature of people and organizations is what we mean when we use the term "developmental perspective."**

When we consider the dynamic nature of organizations and people, as well as the interactive nature of the elements of organizations, it is easy to see why understanding the behavior of people in organizations is a most difficult task. Learning how to be effective in an organizational context and how to manage the behavior of others in an organization is even more difficult. To illustrate why a developmental perspective will be helpful, consider the case that follows.

The Home Computers Case

Harvey Brown and his cousin, Bill Adams, decided, after several years of working for a large computer firm, to start their own computer manufacturing business. Following the entrepreneurial spirit that has characterized this country, they felt they could offer a computer that could be used in the homes of all Americans. Imagining huge sales of the computer, they set up business in Harvey's garage and basement in the fall of 1974. Today Home Computers enjoys sales of over $500 million, has offices from coast to coast, has 800 employees, and has three main divisions in the organization. But how did this happen? And what has happened to Harvey and Bill?

Back in the garage in the mid-1970s, Harvey and Bill, then in their mid-30s were quite energetic and highly motivated to put in long days. They worked through many failures and for over a year before they developed a prototype of their computer. There were many problems, not the least of which was a messy divorce for Bill. At the home show where they first demonstrated EZ1, the printer failed to work, and many people criticized the speed of the processor. Harvey and Bill did, however, manage to sell one computer to an older man who later became a source of financing for a revised and improved model. In fact, without Mr. Hearn's backing, Home Computers would have folded.

By early 1977, EZ2 was in the market, and at $1195 for the basic microcomputer unit, it received acceptance almost immediately. Sales demand was so great that Harvey and Bill leased a building to use for production and hired 16 employees. Now they had to be concerned not only with their own work habits and productivity, but also with the work habits and productivity of 16 other people. Questions of pay scales, fringe benefits, organizational structure, and a host of other business questions had to be addressed. Harvey and Bill quickly discovered that Bill's leadership style and motivational drives made him too overbearing for the employees, whereas Harvey was able to work well with them. To deal with this difference, Harvey became the production manager and Bill the sales manager.

This division of responsibility worked well for everyone concerned, and business prospered. Sales grew from 250 units in 1977 to 3,000 in 1980. Sales offices were opened in 14 locations around the country, and the number of employees grew to 500. Naturally, the organization also changed during this time period. An extensive sales division and full accounting department were added. Production expanded to include two plants to reduce distribution costs. Several layers of management hierarchy were added as Harvey became president and Bill became national sales vice president. Under Bill were three regional managers and a sales force of 45 people. A production vice president supervised the two plant managers, and each plant had approximately 200 employees.

But now Bill was not happy. The entrepreneurial flavor was gone from the company for him, and in 1981 he left to go into resort property development. Harvey decided to reorganize the sales division along product lines rather than geographic lines, since there were three distinct models of the Home Computers product, each with numerous options and special features.

One model was designed for home use; one model was better suited to schools and libraries; and the third model appealed to small business owners.

Business has continued to grow, and in 1983 Home Computers began to export to Canada and Europe. Also in 1983, an attempt to unionize the plant in Ohio failed by a narrow margin. But the closeness of the vote suggested to Harvey that his work force of 750 was not altogether happy with the Home Computers company. With the help of a consultant, Harvey has begun to explore the current situation and is finding numerous problems. Many employees feel the company has become too bureaucratic, with all decisions being made at the top. The spirit of a new organization has waned. A number of managers report personnel problems and problems of coordination between the various divisions. The friction between sales and production is especially noticeable. Production cannot keep pace with sales, and sales makes promises it knows cannot be kept.

These signs of decay are present despite the continuing rapid growth of the company. Sales have never been higher; Harvey is considering opening a new plant; and product requests are coming in from around the world. Harvey is unsure of what to do next, but he is certain of one thing: time will not stand still for him to conduct his analysis.

The Developmental Nature of Organizations

Imagine yourself in Harvey's position, or as one of the employees who has been around since the early years, or even as a new employee at Home Computers. Could you make sense of the many events that are simultaneously unfolding? What would you do now if you were Harvey? How would you begin to analyze this situation? To come close to understanding these events and learning what to do, we must draw on a number of organizational behavior theories and view them in a developmental perspective. In the remainder of this chapter, we will help you to understand what a developmental perspective is and why it is so important to you as a manager. We will then provide an analytical framework that is helpful in structuring the remaining chapters of the book. The framework deals with the four levels of analysis mentioned earlier—namely, people, interpersonal relationships, work groups, and intergroup relations. Each of these will be explored briefly in this chapter and in more detail in the chapters that follow. And we will also encounter the Home Computers case in the other chapters, as a vehicle for exploring the application of the theories we present.

Organizations and Change

As the Home Computers case illustrates, the name of the game in organizations is change. Like people, organizations are always evolving and developing, though their progression is less orderly. While we can view organizations such as Home Computers as passing through phases of birth, growth, maturity, and possibly decline, organizations—unlike people—can backtrack in their development. For example, an organization that is beginning to decline may introduce a new product line, begin a new marketing campaign, or implement other strategic decisions that can take it back to the growth stage. But an organization can easily move directly from birth to decline and failure, as the many small business failures each year attest.

It is important in understanding people and organizations to appreciate their dynamic, changing, and developmental nature. Neither people nor organizations suddenly appear on the spot in their present forms. They develop over time to their present state and then evolve into different states as the future unfolds. **Organizations and people exist within a time context, where their histories affect current perceptions of the world and where past decisions affect their current structure and processes.**

Some writers have likened this developmental perspective for studying organizations to using motion pictures, as compared to still pictures.[2] In still photos, one can get a clear picture of how things are at present and how they fit together to form the whole. Many theories in organizational behavior have been constructed in this fashion via crossectional research. That is, research data has been collected on a number of variables at only one point in time. Thus, we understand a great deal about critical relationships among organizationally relevant variables, but we do not always understand how to apply these relationships in dynamic settings. By viewing organizations as if through a motion picture lens we can gain an understanding of how the still picture came to be.

Imagine freezing a frame of a movie so that a group of people are sitting on the steps in front of a house. Looking at the still frame, we can determine who is on the top step, who is on the right or the left, and who is on the bottom step. But did they all come out of the house, or did some come from the yard? Was there some jockeying for the seated positions? By backing up the film and then running it forward, we can find answers to these and other questions. If we think about organizations as motion pictures, we can employ existing behavioral science theories in an analytical process that better portrays reality and that allows for an integrated view of events.

Analyzing Organizations Developmentally

What we are suggesting is that we use an analytical approach that is longitudinal in nature. If we look at the position of Harvey and Home Computers now in terms of the development of the organization since those days in the garage in the mid-1970s, we can better understand and see how to manage the present situation. Certainly, Harvey has changed since then. He has aged from his mid-30s to mid-40s. And as we shall discuss later in the book, there are important changes that occur in people from their 30s to their 40s. For one thing, Harvey is probably much more conscious of security issues. He may have children approaching college age. In short, he is a different person than he was in 1974, and he will continue to change.

Likewise, Home Computers is a very different company now than it was in the 1970s. Over its life, it has evolved from a struggling, small company to a successful and growing organization. During this time it has also evolved into an organization with a more complicated structure. Coordination and communication now involve the activities of many groups of people rather than just the activities of a few individuals. All is not rosy, as personnel and morale problems are becoming visible. Home Computers is thus showing signs of decline (or at least inefficiency), while it is still growing rapidly. To understand and manage this business, we need to look into: (1) the history of the company, (2) the previous decisions which affect the current state, and (3) the current developmental state of the people and the organization. By taking this approach, we can more effectively analyze Home Computers and decide what needs to be done. Things just do not occur in a time vacuum. In this book we will utilize an analytical framework that explicitly employs a time-based perspective in order to gain a better understanding of organizational life.

The Analytical Framework for This Text

The analytical framework we propose involves a diagnostic and predictive process that views issues in both an organizational and historical context. All topics are studied as they exist within an organization. For example, individuals are analyzed in the context of group and interpersonal relationships and within the structure of an entire organization and its environment. This organizational context is also embedded within a time dimension. All events are viewed in terms of their past, present, and future. This approach forces us to continually integrate topics and to review them at several points throughout the book. A more static application of theories would not encourage this integration. Nor would it be representative of the ever-changing way in which things occur in organizations. And since you, as a manager, must operate in a dynamic, organizational world, we want to provide you with a dynamic and developmental analytical framework which can help you apply the many organizational behavior theories.

The Four Levels of the Framework

The framework used in the text involves the four levels of organizational behavior, which are shown in Figure 1.1. The first level focuses on understanding the individual

**Figure 1.1
A Framework for
Studying
Organizations**

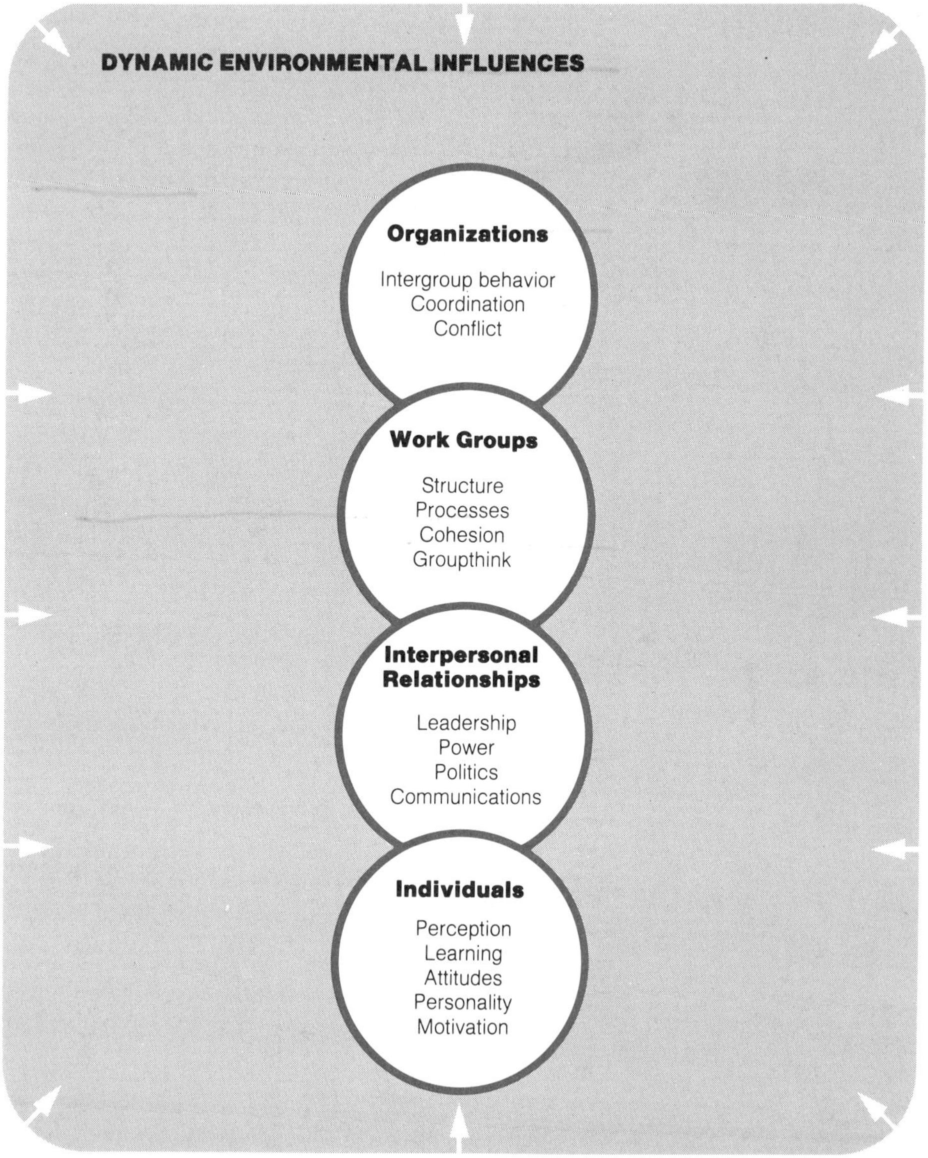

DYNAMIC ENVIRONMENTAL INFLUENCES

Organizations

Intergroup behavior
Coordination
Conflict

Work Groups

Structure
Processes
Cohesion
Groupthink

**Interpersonal
Relationships**

Leadership
Power
Politics
Communications

Individuals

Perception
Learning
Attitudes
Personality
Motivation

as a component in organizations. It deals with perception, learning, attitudes, personality, and motivation of individual organizational members. The second level builds upon the first and focuses on the interpersonal aspects of people working together in organizations. It deals with leadership and power relationships, as well as politics and communications among organizational members. The third level builds on the first two and focuses on the interplay between individuals and the organization structure. It deals with work teams in organizations and explores group structure and processes, and group cohesion and groupthink. The fourth level focuses on the interface between work teams in organizations, that is, the interplay between groups of people and the organization structure. It deals with intergroup conflict and coordination. All of these organizational behavior levels are embedded in the dynamic environmental influences which interact with an organization from the outside.

Figure 1.1 is also designed to show the interrelationships among individuals, interpersonal relationships, work groups, organizations, and the environment. All five of these elements interact to determine an organization's effectiveness. For example, who you are as an individual will affect your interpersonal relationships, effectiveness in a work group, and success in an organization. In return you will be affected by your work group, interpersonal relationships, and organization. Likewise, the interpersonal relationships of people influence work group effectiveness and organizational performance, as well as the individuals involved. And in return the group, the organization, and the individuals affect interpersonal relationships. As we work through the book one level at a time, it will be important for you to keep in mind that the other levels have a bearing on each topic we discuss. An organization exists with all four organizational behavior levels simultaneously interacting together and with the environment.

The Dynamic Dimension of the Framework

In addition to the four organizational behavior levels, there is also a dynamic dimension to our analytical framework, that is depicted in Figure 1.2. The arrows labeled "Past" and "Future" and located to the left and right

**Figure 1.2
A Developmental
Framework for
Studying
Organizations**

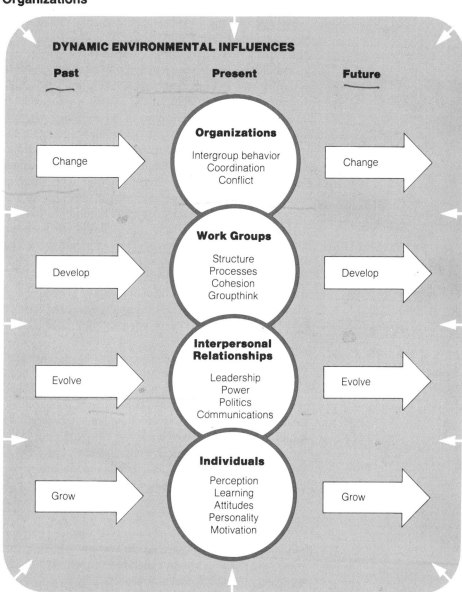

of the set of circles in the center of the figure are intended to show the developmental perspective. The key point here is that the four levels are always changing, and the interrelationships among the four levels are subject to influence by changes in any one of the four levels. In addition, all four levels are subject to changes in the environment, as well.

Just think about the recent environmental changes that have occurred in the United States. We have had a recession, then a revitalized economy, then concern over budget deficits—and who knows what will be next? Likewise, organizations change over time—they either grow and prosper or they decline and fail. Work groups also go through developmental stages, as do interpersonal relationships. Finally, individuals grow and change as the years pass. Thus, our analytical framework must acknowledge the dynamism of all four levels of organizational behavior. Let us now look briefly at the developmental aspects of the four levels, as a way of introducing you to the plan for this text. First we will explore the individual level, which is the focus of Section 2 of the book. Then we will look at interpersonal relationships, which are the focus of Section 3. Next, we will look at groups, followed by a look at organizations as a whole, which are the focus of Section 4. Finally, we will briefly explore environmental changes, even though they are not a major focus of this book.

Growth and Change in People

People who study organizations and managers in organizations agree that people are the basic building blocks in any organization—and also the source of many organizational problems. Managers often lament how nice it would be if the business could be run without people, still knowing that people are vital to the organization. Even the designers of sophisticated new machines and office equipment have learned that their designs must incorporate the concerns of the people who must use the equipment, as illustrated in Box 1.1. People are complex beings, and each person represents a unique character that will change over time. **To understand the employees in any organization and to understand ourselves, we must appreciate the developmental aspects of people**. Even if we can understand the people we manage right now, will we understand them tomorrow after they change? And if we are to really understand people in the present, we must know something about their past.

A number of recent books based on documented studies indicate that understanding a person's past helps us understand present behavior. In turn, this can help us direct work behavior in ways that are useful to the organization. People who come to work for any organization are "used products." We simply cannot purchase a new person as we can a new car, a new computer, or a new piece of machinery. Each person who is of employment age has had many years of experiences, contacts with many

---

Box 1.1
Human Factors Are
Stressed by Office-
Equipment Makers

New machines and office equipment aren't doing their job adequately if people have difficulty using them. So, increasingly, manufacturers are emphasizing human factors in the design of new products.

For all their sophistication, these systems still are operated by people, and the potential for catastrophe is great. Often, human adaptability is relied on to compensate for bad design, Mr. Hanes, an expert in human engineering, says. But in high stress situations, that adaptability lessens and human responses can make even fail-safe systems fail.

The March 1979 accident at the Three Mile Island nuclear power plant in Pennsylvania proves the point, Mr. Hanes says. The malfunction of a cooling system, which led to the shutdown of a reactor and the release of radioactivity, was blamed both on mechanical failure and on human error in assessing the damage and using controls to solve the problem. Mr. Hanes says the accident points up the need for human-factors engineering. "You just don't place new instruments in the control room without considering operating procedures and training."

Further, says Tom Stinnett, manager of man-machine design at Westinghouse's defense center in Baltimore, even a "good arrangement" of control-room dials and switches isn't enough to minimize human error because people can't keep up with messages the computer is spewing out. So, he says, the design of the controls must be thought of in terms of human ability.

By Susan Carey, *The Wall Street Journal,* June 11, 1982. Reprinted by permission of *The Wall Street Journal,* © Dow Jones & Company, Inc. 1982. All rights reserved.

groups, and training in a number of locations and topics. Burton White's book, *The First Three Years of Life*, suggests that a great deal of education has already transpired before a child reaches three years of age.[3] Social skills, attitudes, and intellectual abilities are well along in their development by the age of three. People, of course, do continue to develop beyond the age of three, but White argues that their degree of flexibility in lifestyle, intellectual capacity, attitudes, and so forth are significantly influenced by events that occur during those first three years. We will encounter these issues in detail in Chapter 3 as we discuss the perception process.

A well-known personality theorist argues that human beings develop in important ways from birth to death.[4] To be born is to begin the simultaneous process of growth and death; each day we live, we grow a little and we die a little. We constantly learn and constantly forget as we progress through life. We learn at different rates, learn different things from similar experiences, and are motivated by various stimuli to perform actions that differ from person to person. The same is true of forgetting. It is likely that many of these differences in learning and forgetting could be traced to differences in early childhood experiences.

But changes also continue into adulthood. As Gail Sheehy indicates in her book, *Passages*, there are "predictable crises of adult life."[5] She provides insight into the

"I miss the clatter of the typewriter keys, the constant ring of the bells and the grumbling as we erased errors!"

From *The Wall Street Journal*, with permission of Cartoon Features Syndicate.

developmental stages people pass through during their teenage years and beyond. Sheehy describes the teenage years as a time of pulling up roots. The "trying 20s" are a time of trying out different life scenarios and different partners with whom to make our lives. The "catch 30s" are a time to make, break, or deepen life commitments. The "forlorn 40s" are the years of reassessment, sexual panic, and opportunity for self-discovery. The "refreshed or resigned 50s" are the time to let go of old roles and find a renewal of purpose. Certainly Harvey in Home Computers is affected as he approaches his refreshed or resigned 50s—which shall it be? How is he different than he was when the company started and he was in the catch 30s? We explore these stages in greater detail in Chapters 5 and 6, as we work to understand the factors that motivate people.

The purpose of mentioning the stages of life and the importance of one's early years has been twofold. First, they will help you gain an understanding of yourself and how you might fit into an organization. Second, they will provide the basis for understanding the behavior of other people and should prove useful to you as a manager. We will return to these issues in Chapter 4 as we discuss personality and in Chapters 5 and 6 on motivation. For now, just let it sink in that **by understanding what people are like in the present, how they got there, and something about where they are headed, you are in a much better position to effectively work with and manage them**. Furthermore, the same analytical process can help us to understand ourselves and our potential in various situations.

Of course, we must not forget that people will continue to change throughout their careers. While the organization gets a used product in any new employee, the product is not a finished one in terms of organizational influence. Our analysis of people must continue into the future as they develop. For example, if you were a new employee, you would have to learn about the basic goals of the organization, the preferred means for attaining those goals, your responsibilities, and the accepted ways of behaving in your new organization. As you move from one position to another, and up the hierarchy, the organization will exert influence on you, causing you to change. How will you be different 10 years down the road? These issues will be explored in more detail both in Chapter 2 and in Chapter 4.

Interpersonal Relationships over Time

The second level of analysis in our model is interpersonal relations. As in the case of friendships, working relationships in organizations develop over time, may change for better or worse, and may end. Imagine yourself as a new employee going to work in one of the offices of a large business. You are introduced to your supervisor and to the people with whom you will work. To perform effectively, you will usually have to develop good working relations with these people.

But people manage (or lead) in different ways. By learning from other employees about their past experiences with this supervisor, you begin to learn what to expect from the manager. The combination of both of your personal histories and your own experience with the supervisor results in a relationship that may range from good to poor. From the supervisor's perspective, you will be analyzed and may be found to need a great deal of supervision in this new work situation. In time, however, the supervisor may decide that you are quite capable and then shift to a more general supervision. Various leadership theories allow us to analyze and understand the dynamics underlying the changes that will take place from day one to six months or several years later. But we must not forget that the past experiences of both you and the supervisor will interact in the present situation to determine the outcome of this relationship. We explore these interrelationships in detail in Chapters 7 and 8. For now it is important for you to understand that **the developmental aspects of leader-follower relationships interact with the dynamic properties of individuals.**

In addition to your relationship with the supervisor, you must develop working relationships and possibly social relationships with the other employees in your work unit. The work itself may dictate interactions between you and certain other people in the office. Interpersonal relations theories indicate that initial impressions also determine who you will come to know best, at least initially. People to whom you are attracted will become the focus of your interactions, and the more you interact with someone, the more likely you are to become friends. Sometimes, though, interactions can lead to the discovery that your initial attraction cannot be sustained and the relationship wanes. **Exchange theory** suggests that people continue a relationship for as long as the benefits equal or outweigh the costs of the relationship.[6]

Our experience tells us that change is the nature of interpersonal relationships. For example, people meet, become friends, one moves away, the friendship declines. Or, employees meet, learn to work together, become good co-workers; then something happens, and the relationship deteriorates, or one gets transferred or promoted. And we could think of countless other examples. Just look at what happened between Bill and Harvey at Home Computers. Their relationship changed because of changes in the company and probably because of changes in both Bill and Harvey, and Bill has moved on to other endeavors. Likewise, think about what happened to Bill's marriage. And as Box 1.2 suggests, maintaining these relationships can be a real source of stress in business. As a

---

Box 1.2
Business Stress, If Neglected, Can Be a Company's Undoing

Business is off sharply. The owner and founder of a small Massachusetts company is convinced he must cut back to survive. But that means firing members of "the family," employees who have been with the company from the beginning. He can't do it, so he calls in someone else to do the firing.

The stress problem for middle-aged owners is especially difficult because they are likely to be at the stage where they are reassessing their goals in life. "Often the problems of the organization have to do with the problems of the middle-aged manager" or owner, says Dr. Rosenthal, consultant to businesses.

The death of a parent or parents often occurs during this period. Children leave home. Today, while the man may be considering tapering off at work, his wife may be preparing to go back to work or start a career. Small-business owners must be aware that such changes occur during middle age and be prepared to deal with them, Dr. Rosenthal says. "He must keep his relationships with family well oiled and greased."

By Johnnie L. Roberts, *The Wall Street Journal,* December 14, 1982. Reprinted by permission of *The Wall Street Journal,* © Dow Jones & Company, Inc. 1982. All rights reserved.

manager, you must become adept at understanding and managing changing relationships. The key point is that **relationships take time to develop; they continue to change indefinitely; and they may end**. The interpersonal processes of leadership (discussed in Chapters 7 and 8), power and political relationships (discussed in Chapter 9), and communications (discussed in Chapter 10) must be viewed in this fashion if we are to understand how to effectively manage in organizations.

Work Teams and Their Development

The third level in our model is the work team or group of people who work together in organizational settings. What organization can operate without committees, task forces, work teams, and other groups of people? Yet people suggest that a camel is a horse made by committee —that groups cannot make decisions as efficiently as one person. The fact is that while **organizations depend very heavily upon groups of people, it is difficult to make a group operate effectively**. Fortunately, it is possible to have some very effective groups. And one key to understanding the operation of a work team is to appreciate and analyze the individuals who make up the team. As we have said, each person is unique and will bring unique elements to a group. The task of the group and its manager is to put the pieces of the puzzle together to form a complete picture. But there are exceptions to this puzzle analogy: (1) there is no guarantee that all the pieces will be present, (2) there is no guarantee that the pieces will fit together, and (3) the pieces continue to change through growth and development.

Another key, then, to understanding a group is to recognize that it—like individuals—will change over time. It is easy to see that groups add and lose people and must deal with people who have changed, and these changes make adjustments in the group necessary. But aside from these obvious changes, even an intact team evolves through different stages over time. Schutz has defined three stages through which groups evolve: inclusion, control, and affection.[7]

Inclusion is the initial process of determining who is really going to commit to the group; what skills, abilities, and other resources they bring to the group; and what their standards and motivation levels are. It is basically a time to get acquainted and to lay groundwork for later stages. The inclusion stage varies in length of time, and groups may later come back to it if they add or lose people. However, once these inclusion issues are basically settled, the control stage (which has already begun during inclusion) comes into focus.

The control stage involves the issues of who is going to lead the group — who is going to influence the direction of the team and with what style. Sometimes one person emerges as the leader, sometimes two or three people are in control, and sometimes influence is more or less equally shared by all team members. It can also happen that a group becomes stuck in the control stage when two or more people compete for primary influence and cannot resolve the issue.

Once the control issues are basically settled, however, the group enters the final stage of affection. This stage is basically a time of cohesion for the group. Members are clear on the commitment levels of other members, they know who has influence in the group, they have developed norms of operation, and they know what to expect from the group as a whole and from its individual members. Still, it takes continuing effort to maintain this cohesion. As we have said, changes in group membership can force the team back to earlier stages. And changes in the tasks assigned the group, in its relationship with other groups, or in its physical workspace can also take the group back to previous stages of evolution. In addition, unsuccessful groups may dissolve at any point in the three-stage process.

The key idea is that work teams that are successful over the long run are dynamic entities. They evolve over time and their evolution is influenced by many factors. In Chapters 11 and 12, we explore groups in detail and discuss research and theory development concerning these vital components in organizations.

The Dynamic Aspects of Organizations

The development of people, interpersonal relationships, and work teams occur in the context of the developmental nature of organizations as a whole. Thus the organizational context is the fourth level of analysis. We deal only with the tip of this iceberg in Chapter 13, for it would take an entire book to adequately cover the topic of organizations.

In the case of Home Computers, we saw that organizations are created; they grow and develop; and they may also decline and eventually fail. A number of writers have attempted to explain the development of organizations using a life-cycle metaphor. Lippitt and Schmidt defined three basic stages of organizational evolution: birth, growth, and maturity.[8] Greiner explained organizational development in terms of five stages, each involving a particular crisis:

1. Creativity, with the crisis of leadership.
2. Direction, with the crisis of autonomy.
3. Delegation, with the crisis of control.
4. Coordination, with the crisis of red tape.
5. Collaboration, with the crisis unspecified.[9]

More recently, Tansik, Chase, and Aquilano identified eight life-cycle phases of organizational evolution:

1. Birth of the system.
2. Design of the system.
3. Staffing the organization.
4. Startup of the organization.
5. Organization in steady state.
6. Improving the organization.
7. Revision of the organization.
8. Termination of the organization.[10]

However, this life cycle analogy is not completely satisfactory in understanding organizational evolution. Perhaps the most obvious shortcoming is, as stated before, that organizations may be born, grow, and decline. But instead of dying, they can be reborn (via a new product line, for example) and thus go back to an earlier stage of the process. Box 1.3 provides a good example of this type of revitalization, which happens quite often with organizations. Another problem is that the timing of the evolutionary steps is not at all predictable. Two organizations in the same industry may vary substantially in the length of time they remain in each stage of growth and development. Furthermore, some subdivisions of an organization may be growing and prospering, while others in the same organization are declining and experiencing significant problems. The four levels of analysis allow the possibility for different developmental rates at each level.

The point to learn from the life-cycle metaphor is that the past history of an organization has a major influence on its present state. **Past decisions of management and past events in the organization's history have a direct influence on present and future events and decisions in the organization's life.** For example, the past decision of Home Computers to manufacture small computers may limit the organization's ability to produce other products.

The commitment of human, financial, equipment, and time resources to the computer business may not leave the resources to go into, say, portable typewriters. Or a previous decision to locate on the East coast may impede Home Computers' development of markets on the West coast, at least until a certain size operation is achieved.

A developmental perspective to understanding organizations includes their historical context, as well as their natural evolutions. Certain aspects of organizations tend to evolve in predictable patterns. Technologies of organizations (that is, the methods of completing the organization's tasks) tend to evolve from a nonroutine and relatively unpredictable state to a routine and predictable state, as the bugs are worked out and systems are refined. The structure and procedures of organizations tend to evolve from loose and organic to rigid and bureaucratic. And people in organizations tend to evolve from unskilled to highly skilled in their jobs. **Overall, we suggest that organizations that survive over time generally evolve from uncertainty to a relative degree of certainty in accomplishing their objectives and tasks.**

While these developments may be generally predictable, effective managers pay attention to the details of the evolution. Some organizations may not evolve toward certainty and control of their situations, or their direction of evolution may reverse toward uncertainty. Thus, these organizations may become an addition to the statistics on business failures. Then too, changes in the environment may dictate that the organization remain less structured in order to meet the demands of a rapidly changing environment and still remain viable. Chrysler is a good example of a company that did not adapt well to a changing environment. They continued to make large cars when the public wanted high quality, small cars. The developmental perspective allows one to understand the forces operating in and around an organization and to determine what needs to be done either to rectify problems or to take advantage of opportunities. Knowing where an organization has been and having an appreciation for past decisions will help you as a manager to understand why the organization is where it is now, and where it may be going.

**The Changing
Environment**

We mentioned earlier that the developmental perspective allows us to incorporate the organization's history into our analysis. It also allows us to consider the organization's environment. As Figures 1.1 and 1.2 show, the environment of the organization is the final element in our model of organizations. While it is not a major focus of this book, we must recognize that it is there and that it plays a role in the application of individual, interpersonal, group, and organization theories and research that we will explore in this text.

To appreciate the influence of an organization's environment, we need only consider what has transpired in the U.S. industrial community since 1900. In 1900 the United States was basically an agrarian society only beginning to enter the age of industry. As we began to industrialize, people had to learn new skills and learn to live and work in cities. Industrial technology dictated that jobs be engineered for efficiency and designed to accommodate the lack of skills of the average worker. Scientific management (a method for breaking down jobs into simple tasks) led the way to an efficient and effective economy that saw the United States become a world leader.[11] As this environmental evolution continued, the standard of living increased and resulted in more highly educated and skilled workers. A series of studies conducted at the Hawthorne plant of the Western Electric Company in the late 1920s highlighted the need to seriously consider the impact of people on the job, as their skills began to catch up with the skill demands of the technologies employed in industry.[12]

In the 1950s, the advent of computers and other sophisticated technologies that grew out of World War II moved the United States into an era of tremendous growth and expanded influence. For a while it seemed that the sky really was the limit. But the 1960s brought serious unrest among people who were being left behind in this country and in other countries. The sky began to fall. Leaders were assassinated, and the United States could not seem to win a conflict in Southeast Asia. By the time the 1970s rolled around, we Americans were fighting among ourselves, being threatened by oil magnates in the Middle East, and dealing with numerous rules and regulations imposed by the Washington bureaucracy (for example, affirmative action and equal employment opportunity).[13]

Currently we find ourselves searching for solutions to these economic, political, and social ills. The White House and Congress search for ways to right our economic ship. Business and government search for methods of dealing with an economy that consists of international competitors, suppliers, and inflationary influences. At the same time, individuals try to cope with a world where they can no longer afford a house and where each year they lose ground economically.[14] The complexity and dynamism of the world has been multiplied many times since 1900, and many historical and current factors interact to create the management problems faced by organizations and individuals. By gaining an appreciation for the environmental history of our organizations, we will be better able to find solutions for today's problems.

This point is made vividly by a sign at the entrance to the Dachau, West Germany, concentration camp, which has been made a memorial to World War II by the West Germans. It reads: "Those who forget the past are condemned to repeat it." For managers, ignoring the past may make you attempt solutions that have already been tried and have failed. Furthermore, a knowledge of past trends, though not a perfect predictor of the future, may help you anticipate problems before they occur. In times of rapid change things may occur that upset the trend of events; but often several trends all predict the same future events and should not be ignored. For example, long before the oil shortages of the 1970s, people in oil companies were reporting a declining level of reserves in domestic oil, while the trend of oil consumption was clearly moving upward. No one seemed to take this seriously until the "surprising" oil shortage of 1973-74.

Chapter Highlights   The purpose of this book is to help you gain an understanding of the dynamics of behavior in organizations and learn how to effectively manage people in organizations. In the following chapters, we will explore the basic elements of organizational behavior (individuals, interpersonal relations, groups, and intergroup relations) from a developmental perspective. Everything we discuss will be viewed as in a state of flux. Nothing is static; even the theories we discuss will be viewed as dynamic rather than as the final answer. As a philosopher friend once told me, "The only good answer to a question is one that leads to the asking of another good question." **We must dig deeper and deeper in our understanding of concepts and theories; that is, we must search for greater understanding by constantly asking questions.**

As a student of organizational behavior and as a manager, you must **learn to learn**. If you only retain the theories as we presently know them, you will quickly become obsolete. For example, managers today who have not kept up with the explosive use of computers are truly behind in their organizations. We believe that **one key ingredient common to successful people in organizations is the ability to continue learning and adapting**. Your analytical skills need to be developed in school, and you need to learn to use the theories and research that do exist. However, you also need to keep questioning things over and over again in order to use a developmental perspective to understand and manage organizational behavior.

In this book, we will rely on the four levels of analysis of organizational behavior, overlaid with the developmental perspective. This system of analysis gives us a set of building blocks for understanding organizational behavior. First, you will gain an understanding of individuals in organizations, including their motivations, attitudes, and other key aspects, as well as their developmental properties. We will then use this information to develop your understanding of interpersonal relationships. In other words, if you are to understand leadership, power, and communications, you will need an understanding of what makes individuals operate as they do. We will build on your understanding of individuals and interpersonal relations as we explore group effectiveness issues. Finally, we will build on the first three levels to explore intergroup coordination and relationships. There will be a conscientious effort to integrate these four levels as we proceed through the book, since things in real organizations occur in a simultaneous, integrated, and developmental fashion.

By overlaying the developmental perspective on the four dissections, you will become aware of another integrating factor: namely, all four levels of analysis occur within a historical, developmental context. Awareness of the past, present, and future of organizational events will force us to integrate the four levels in our search for a realistic perspective on organizational behavior. For example, while we can discuss theories and research related to individuals, we cannot forget that their behavior takes place in an organizational and historical context. Organizations and people simply are not static entities, as the Home Computers case illustrates. To solve Harvey's problems, we must ask questions about how the organization, its people, and its subdivisions arrived at their present state. To ignore (1) the rapid growth of the company, (2) its evolution toward a more bureaucratic state, (3) the past history of conflict between sales and production, (4) the history of interpersonal relationships such as between Harvey and Bill, and (5) the growth and change in Harvey and his stage in life, means that we will not be able to adequately assess the present situation and determine what needs to be done to rectify the problems surfacing in Home Computers. For example, to determine that Harvey needs to devote more time to personnel issues may ignore a possible desire on his part to become less involved in the daily detail of Home Computers. In his 40s and after more than 10 years of making this company go, Harvey may really need a reorganization that frees him rather than a solution that ties him down. Likewise, the conflict between sales and production is quite likely more than a simple case of interdepartmental strife created by goal and priority differences. The rapid and continuing growth of the company suggests that some key people may have been moved up the ladder more quickly than was consistent with their ability and development. Thus, the solution to this conflict may rest in better selection of qualified people or training for present managers. Whatever the real solution for Harvey and Home Computers, a developmental and historical perspective will be more useful in the analysis process than a static look at things would be. Indeed, what would you do if you were Harvey?

The remaining chapters of this book provide much detailed information for enhancing your developmental, analytical skills. By the time you finish it, you should have gained a reasonably well-integrated, developmental understanding of behavior in organizations. You will also have become familiar with the language of a developmental perspective. Primarily this means that words take the -*ing* form, such as, ac*ting*, manag*ing*, lead*ing*, behav*ing*, mov*ing*, think*ing*. Everything you study will be in a state of be*ing* and becom*ing*, and your knowledge will be increas*ing* and form*ing* a solid beginn*ing* for understand*ing* and manag*ing* organizational behavior.

Review Questions

1. How would you define "organizations," "managing," and "organizational behavior"?

2. What are the five main elements of organizations, and how are they interrelated?

3. What does it mean to take a developmental perspective to understanding and managing organizational behavior? Why is this a useful perspective?

4. How does the analytical framework for the book integrate the levels of organizational analysis with the developmental perspective?

5. What are the developmental aspects of people in organizations?

6. "Relationships with others in an organization are dynamic and evolutionary in nature." What does this mean, and why is it important to appreciate this process?

7. Can you explain the developmental process as it applies to work groups?

8. Why are past decisions made by organizations important for a manager to understand and consider?

9. Can you explain the dynamic aspects of organizations and their environments?

10. What are the key developmental issues that relate to the current situation of Home Computers?

Notes

1. H. J. Leavitt, *Managerial Psychology* (Chicago: The University of Chicago Press, 1958).

2. J. R. Kimberly and M. J. Evanisko, "Organizational Technology, Structure, and Size." In *Organizational Behavior*, ed. S. Kerr (Columbus, Ohio: Grid, 1979), pp. 263–287.

3. B. L. White, *The First Three Years of Life* (New York: Avon Books, 1975).

4. E. Erikson, *Childhood and Society* (New York: W. W. Norton, 1950).

5. G. Sheehy, *Passages* (New York: E. P. Dutton, 1974).

6. J. W. Thibaut and H. H. Kelly, *The Social Psychology of Groups* (New York: John Wiley & Sons, 1959), pp. 9–30.

7. W. C. Schutz, "Interpersonal Underworld," *Harvard Business Review*, July-August, 1958, pp. 38–56.

8. G. L. Lippitt and W. H. Schmidt, "Crisis in a Developing Organization," *Harvard Business Review*, November–December, 1967, pp. 102–111.

9. L. E. Greiner, "Evolution and Revolution as Organizations Grow," *Harvard Business Review*, July–August,1972, pp. 37–46.

10. D. A. Tansik, R. B. Chase, and N. J. Aquilano. *Management: A Life Cycle Approach* (Homewood, Ill.: Richard D. Irwin, 1980).

11. F. Taylor, *Scientific Management* (New York: Harper & Row, 1947).

12. E. Mayo, *The Social Problems of an Industrial Civilization* (Boston, Mass.: Harvard University, Graduate School of Business, 1945).

13. C.A. Reich, *The Greening of America* (New York: Random House, 1970).

14. C. Lasch, *The Culture of Narcissism* (New York: W. W. Norton, 1979).

Resource Readings

Greiner, L. E. "Evolution and Revolution as Organizations Grow," *Harvard Business Review*, July-August, 1972, pp. 37–46.

Kimberly, J. R.; R. H. Miles; and Associates. *The Organizational Life Cycle: Issues in the Creation, Transformation, and Decline of Organizations*. San Francisco: Jossey-Bass, 1980.

Sarason, S. B. *The Creation of Settings and the Future Societies*. San Francisco: Jossey-Bass, 1972.

CHAPTER 2

Managing as a Changing Role

In Chapter 1 we defined **managing** as working with and through other people and groups of people to accomplish an organization's goals. Since you want to have a successful career as a manager, in this chapter we explore what is involved in a managerial career. The reason for dealing with the aspects of a career at this point in the book is to make the developmental perspective we defined in Chapter 1 more personal.The developmental perspective is a cornerstone of this book, and we want you to become aware of its impact on everything you will do as a manager. And since your career will occur over time, it makes a natural bridge between developmental ideas and you as a manager.

Stop for a moment now and think about the developmental perspective as it applies to your managerial career. Certainly, you can imagine many changes that you will encounter. The people and groups you manage will change; so will the organization or organizations in which you work. And of course, you will change too, as you progress in your working career. Let us begin our look at managing as a changing role by exploring what managers actually do.

Basic Managerial Skills

In performing a managerial role, to be effective you will need three basic types of skills: technical, human relations, and conceptual.[1] And as we shall see, the importance of these skills to you as a manager will change as you progress through the management hierarchy.

Technical skill is the ability to perform the specific kinds of activities required in a job. Included are the specific methods, procedures, and techniques that are a part of performing a job. For example, if the job is programming computers, the technical skills include knowledge of particular computer languages, the ability to use computer terminology, and an understanding of how computers operate. Katz suggests that technical skill is important at all levels of management, but it is most important to first-line managers, since they are so intimately involved with the producing of a product or providing of a service. In the Home Computers case, first-line supervisors in the two plants must rely heavily on their technical skill to get the work out. In the past, Harvey also needed a great deal of technical skill; but at his level in the organization now, he is much less dependent on his own technical skill, and more dependent on the technical skill of others.

Human relations skill is the ability to motivate, lead, and communicate with other people. A manager must be able to relate to people to get work done through them. As a manager, you cannot perform all the work for which you are responsible but must depend on others to complete the work. Thus, human relations skill is vital to your performance. Katz suggests that this skill is important for managers at all levels. Consider Harvey, for example. In the early stages of Home Computers, he had to manage production of the 16 employees through communicating, motivating, and leading. While this work demanded technical skill, it also required human relations skill. At present, Harvey still manages the upper-level management people and must get work done through them. Thus, his human relations skill is still important even though his technical skill is less important.

Finally, **conceptual skill is the ability to see the organization as a system of interacting parts and as a system interacting with its environment**. It is also the ability to diagnose and resolve a host of organizational problems. As Katz suggests, this is a top-management skill. It is not as essential at lower levels of management, but it is vital at the top. For example, Harvey, as president of Home Computers, must conceptualize the business, set priorities for the company, and analyze trends in the market. He must understand the interactions between sales and production if he is to eliminate the friction that currently exists. He must know what the competition is doing so that plans can be developed to maintain the company's growth pattern

To recap, managers need three very important skills. **All three skills are important at all levels of management. But at lower levels technical skill is the most important while at top levels conceptual skill is the most important. Human relations skill is important at all levels.** This pattern of skill emphasis (shown in Figure 2.1) suggests that to be successful in a managerial career, you will have to develop all three kinds of skills. And you must evolve

**Figure 2.1
Managerial Skill
Emphasis at Different
Management Levels**

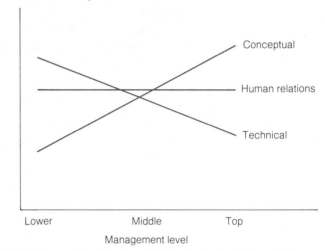

Amount of skill required

Conceptual

Human relations

Technical

Lower   Middle   Top

Management level

from an emphasis on technical skill early in your career to focus on conceptual skill later in your career, with constant attention to human relations skill. Because of its importance throughout your career, human relations skill is the primary focus both of this book and the field of organizational behavior.

What Managers Do

In thinking about the career of a manager, it is useful to consider what managers do in more specific terms. Research has suggested that first-level supervisors, who directly manage the work force, engage in literally hundreds of incidents each day, and few last more than two minutes.[2] These incidents consist primarily of giving orders, answering questions, dealing with problems, seeking information, listening to complaints, evaluating work, receiving instructions, granting permission, denying permission, and so forth almost without stop during the day. Because of this rapid pace, supervisors must be very current in the technical aspects of their subordinates' jobs. They must also be capable of handling a wide range of situations that involve human interactions. Supervisors often feel overwhelmed by paperwork and by meetings with other supervisors and with their bosses. The communication and information demands on them are great.[3]

As a person's career shifts to the middle levels of the hierarchy, the pace is no less swift. A typical middle manager may spend up to 80 percent of the day in verbal exchanges with subordinates, peers, and superiors—on the telephone, in face-to-face meetings, and in one-to-one exchanges.[4] Whereas the supervisor must carry out relatively specific activities within the unit of responsibility, the middle manager is responsible for developing specific action plans from the broad objectives laid out by top management. Another major activity category of middle managers, then, is the preparation of written reports—activities plans to be distributed to supervisors or reports to top management about the execution of those plans.

At top-management levels, the pattern of fragmented, interrupted, and brief activity persists. A study of chief executive officers determined that these managers engaged in over 50 activities each day, with approximately half lasting less than nine minutes.[5] Top managers spent 59 percent of the day in scheduled meetings, another 10 percent in unscheduled meetings, and 6 percent on the telephone. Desk work (reading reports and processing mail) accounted for 22 percent of the day; the remaining 3 percent was spent on tours of the workplace. In fact, this study suggests that top-level managers spend very little time in reflective thinking. The conceptual issues of policy, goal setting, and planning are certainly dealt with by these managers, but it does not appear that they do this work when they are alone. Rather the conceptual issues are dealt with in interpersonal settings—which explains why human relations skill is still important even at the top levels of management.

Now that we have seen a cross section of managers' activities at various levels in the organization, we need to view the pieces from a developmental and longitudinal perspective. We need to look at a managerial career as a changing role. How does one evolve through these various levels of management? How do the managerial skills evolve over a career? To do this, let us look at the career of an employee of Home Computers.

The Case of Louise of Home Computers

Louise is 45 years old and has had a very successful career working in the computer industry since her graduation from college 23 years ago. When Louise graduated from her computer science undergraduate program, she was immediately hired into one of the largest computer manufacturing companies in the country, indeed in the world. Having been raised in the South, she was excited to have the opportunity to move to New York as she began her career. She rented an apartment on the Upper East Side and took the subway to work her first day in September 1962.

Louise was fortunate to be given a challenging job in her initial assignment. She knew that many companies feel they should bring new employees along slowly, starting them on an easy project and then gradually adding more challenge and responsibility as the employees prove their ability. But Louise's first job was to work on the development of an accounts receivable package for one of the company's largest customers. Of course, she did not work on the project alone, and her supervisor was quite willing to help whenever Louise encountered problems. Louise worked on this project for six months in the corporate offices. Then she was asked to go to the customer's headquarters along with George Davis, an experienced programmer, to help install and debug the accounts receivable system.

Upon completing this initial assignment, Louise was given a series of challenging projects over the next few years. Louise's short-term goal was to become a project leader, so she could use her technical expertise in supervising others. In 1966 she achieved her goal. At this time, she was also asked to move to the Phoenix, Arizona, office where the demand for services was growing rapidly. Although she hated to leave New York, Louise saw this as a strategic move in her career; her next goal was to become a systems manager overseeing the accounts and projects of several customers. In Phoenix there was currently one systems manager, and the rapid growth suggested that the addition of another one was quite likely. While Louise was not sure what the company's plans were for her, she hoped to make the best of this opportunity.

In Phoenix, Louise found that her technical and human relations skills were constantly utilized. She had to assist new programmers, explain the clients' desires to the programmers, decide which programmer would work on which piece of the project, deal with programmer complaints and conflicts. It was a challenging assignment, but Louise enjoyed it very much. She was also very good at it.

While in Phoenix, Louise met a programmer named Steve, and they began dating. After several months of casual dates, it became apparent that there was something special about their relationship. They were married in April of 1969. In late 1970 they had their first child. Because Louise valued her career so much, she stayed out of work only eight weeks. Two years later their second child was born.

In that same year Steve was transferred back East to Washington, D.C., to become a systems manager. Louise had been a systems manager for a year already and found that she liked the shift in emphasis from the technical to the conceptual aspects of the work. The separation was difficult for Steve and Louise, as well as for their two children, but they decided it was the best for their respective careers. Nine months later Louise also had an opportunity to transfer back East to Baltimore. With Steve working in Washington, they were able to live together again. Now both their careers were taking off, with both operating at the middle level of management of the company.

In 1976, Louise learned that a colleague, Harvey Brown, and his cousin, Bill Adams, had quit the company to start their own home computer business. She was very interested in their venture and discussed it with Harvey at a party a few months later. Things were not going too well for Home Computers at that time, but Louise stayed interested. Steve suggested she forget it, since she had such a good career already, but she could not.

Both of their lives were extremely busy with work; and the demands of a six-year-old and a four-year-old were difficult to handle. Domestic life seemed boring; but Louise and Steve were committed to having successful careers and a successful family life. In 1979 Steve turned down a promotion which would have moved him back to corporate headquarters in New York, because he did not want to disrupt the family (both children were now in elementary school). Later that same year, Louise had an opportunity to go to work for Home Computers as Harvey and Bill saw the need for technically experienced sales managers.

Louise jumped at the chance, especially since she would not have to move, but could handle her work via travel. She became a regional sales manager for Home Computers in 1980. Her boss was Bill Adams. She found Bill a little difficult to work with, but the job was the most challenging of her career. Home Computers was so new and was growing so fast that Louise had many opportunities to draw upon her conceptual skills. Plans and decisions had to be developed for marketing and sales goals. She had to be aware of what the competition was doing. And because the company was so small, she knew the 15 people working for her very well. She liked interacting with them.

Because of her success as regional sales manager, Harvey promoted Louise to national sales vice president when Bill Adams left the company. In fact, it was Louise's idea to reorganize the sales division along product lines, rather than on geographic lines. Now Louise was really using her conceptual skill and no longer had much contact with the sales people.

Louise was very happy with the career decisions she had made and in the opportunities that had come her way. Her only real regrets revolved around her family life. Steve seemed jealous of her success, though he tried hard not to be. Louise also felt that she did not have enough time for her children. She really knew very little about their school life or extracurricular activities. She wondered what would happen in her family and in her career over the next few years.

Imagine yourself beginning a career now. What will it be like? What important decisions will you have to make? What can you learn by looking at Louise's career? Does the career viewpoint help you appreciate the importance of a developmental perspective to organizational behavior? In the remainder of this chapter, we will explore what we mean by a career as well as the stages of a career. We will also look at the key factors that influence the changing role of a manager.

Career Stages

We have now used the term **career** several times without defining it. Before we discuss the stages of a career, however, let us provide a definition. First of all, career does not imply either success or failure. Even if Louise had not moved up the corporate ladder so rapidly, we would still define her series of jobs as a career. In addition, her rapid movement might not be thought of as completely successful, as the end of the case suggests. A career consists not only of behaviors, but also of attitudes: How does Louise feel about her work life? **A career is a se-**

quence of work-related experiences and activities over a person's lifespan, and it includes the person's sequence of attitudes and behaviors in these work-related experiences.[6] Several authors have described various stages of a career. In the following pages we will discuss some of these. As we do, you will see how the developmental perspective applies to a managerial career.

The Career Stages of Super and Associates

Super and his associates long ago described four career stages and broke some of them down into substages.[7] They also closely tied their career stages to ages of people as show in Figure 2.2.

The first stage, the **exploration stage** (ages 15 to 24), was broken down into: (1) tentative—ages 15 to 17—where initial job choices are made and sampled in discussion, courses, and part-time work; (2) transition—ages 18 to 21—where the realities of abilities and motivation are given more weight as the person enters the job market or professional training; and (3) trial—ages 22 to 24—where the first regular job is found and tried out as a life work.

This trial substage continues into the **establishment stage** (ages 25 to 45). Here a person has found an appropriate field of work and is trying to make a place in that field. But the trial substage also continues—ages 25 to 30—in that a person may make several changes before finding a suitable field or realizing that a career will consist of a series of unrelated jobs. Stabilization—ages 31 to

**Figure 2.2
The Career Stages of
Super and Associates**

Stages	Substages	Ages
4. Decline stage	⌈ Retirement ⌊ Deceleration	(ages 71+) (ages 65–70)
3. Maintenance stage	⌈ None ⌊	(ages 46–64)
2. Establishment stage	⌈ Stabilization ⌊ Trial continued	(ages 31–45) (ages 25–30)
1. Exploration stage	⌈ Trial │ Transition ⌊ Tentative	(ages 22–24) (ages 18–21) (ages 15–17)

45—is the second substage of establishment, during which a person works hard to develop a secure place in the chosen field of work. As we shall shortly discuss, things may be a little different today than they were when Super did his work in 1957.

The **maintenance stage** (ages 46-64) was defined by Super as the time to hold on to one's place in the chosen field of work. It was seen as a time of little change; a continuation in already-established directions. Again, current practice suggests that this stage may be more volatile than Super thought. Many people now experience significant changes in their chosen field during midcareer and preretirement periods. Box 2.1 illustrates one such case, and you can probably think of others.

Finally, the **decline stage** (age 65 and up) is the period in a career when abilities begin to decline and work activities shift to coincide with this decline. The substage of deceleration—ages 65 to 70—occurs when the work pace

---

**Box 2.1
One Who Took
The Big Step**

T*he mother of five children, Mrs. Daley had worked at various secretarial and clerical jobs, so that both at home and at work, she had held "nurturing and mothering positions."*

When she decided to change careers, "I made some basic changes in myself," she says.

Building on her college degree and aptitude in music and her facility for math, she took accounting and data processing courses. She went from jobs in which she catered to the needs of others to a position in which, as a programmer analyst, she is in charge.

Mrs. Daley has her own checklist of what it takes to change careers:

√ *Be dissatisfied.*
√ *Decide you're going to change.*
√ *Find out how to go about it, the technique.*
√ *Find out what's selling.*
√ *Add up your pluses and minuses.*
√ *Get whatever training you need.*
√ *See what compromises you have to make. (Find out what's totally unacceptable, what's tolerable, what's desirable.)*

begins to slacken. People may shift to part-time jobs or to less active roles in their organizations. The substage of retirement—age 71 on—signals the ending of an occupation. Some people completely retire from work; others continue to gear down gradually. Still others find new challenges and continue working as hard as ever. For example, see Box 2.2 about the salesmen at Texas Refinery Corporation.

The AT&T Studies

A number of studies have attempted to analyze these career stages in field settings. One of particular interest was conducted in the late 1960s at American Telephone and Telegraph (AT&T).[8] A group of young managers was studied over a five-year period. During the first year of employment these managers expressed a great deal of concern about gaining recognition and establishing themselves in the organization. As we shall discuss later, these are **safety needs**; they relate to the question of motivation. By the fifth year of employment, though, this need for safety had significantly declined for these managers. In fact, it was the least important of the needs mea-

Box 2.2
Firm Recruits Older
People as Salesmen

Robert Stacey is one of Texas Refinery Corp.'s top salesmen. After joining the company last year, he earned $3,000 on his first sale, and ultimately was named "rookie of the year," with total commissions of $45,000.

The Elberta, Ala., salesman is so keen on peddling Texas Refinery's roof-protective coatings that he carries a pair of roofing shoes in his car, just in case he spots an opportunity to clamber onto a roof.

Mr. Stacey is 74 years old. He was a pharmacist in his first working life. "This is better than a lot of years I put behind the prescription counter," he says.

At Fort Worth-based Texas Refinery, Mr. Stacey is one of 20 salesmen over 70 who joined last year. A fifth of the firm's 3,000 or so salesmen are over 65, and one is 84. The company is one of the growing number of firms recruiting elderly workers.

By Maria T. Padilla, *The Wall Street Journal*, April 19, 1982. Reprinted by permission of *The Wall Street Journal*, © Dow Jones & Company, Inc. 1982. All rights reserved.

sured. It makes sense that gaining a feeling of establishment with the organization would be a high priority in the early years of employment. These initial years are clearly related to Super's establishment stage, and the trial substage.

During the same five-year period, the need for achievement and esteem in the job increased dramatically for these AT&T managers. By the fifth year they were concerned with moving upward and mastering the organization. This new stage was labeled the advancement stage, and it seems related to Super's stabilization substage of the establishment stage. During this time in one's career, promotion and achievement are the predominant goals. It is the time to be creative and to strive for advancement in the organization.

The Schein Career Model

One other career model is worthy of our attention, because it explicitly recognizes the connection between the career as it relates to the individual and the career as it relates to the organization's needs. In 1971 Edgar Schein of MIT proposed this model, which defines the opportunities for career growth in terms of three directions of possible movement within an organization.[9] In your career you will be able to move vertically, radially, and laterally (see Figure 2.3). **Vertical movement** is defined as moving up or down the hierarchy of the organization. **Radial movement** is defined as moving toward greater or lesser amount of influence in the organization: How central will you be to the decision making of the organization? How much influence will you have in the organization. Finally, **lateral movement** is defined as transferring horizontally to different functions, programs, or projects in the organization.

Schein argues that as you move in these three directions, you will change through a process called **socialization** (which we will explore in more detail in Chapter 4). You will develop new attitudes, new values, new competencies, new self-images, and new ways of conducting yourself in social settings. This socialization process will occur with peaks and valleys throughout your career; it even transcends movement from one organization to another. Schein suggests that the pressure for you to change

**Figure 2.3
Directions of Career
Movement**

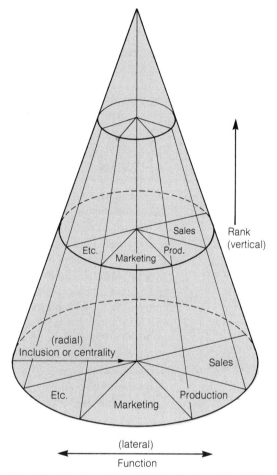

Source: Reproduced by special permission from *The Journal of Applied Behavioral Science,*
"The Individual, the Organization, and the Career: A Conceptual Scheme," by Edgar H.
Schein, volume 7, page 404, copyright 1971, NTL Institute.

will be most strong just before or just after you make a
move—whether that move is vertical, radial, or lateral.
Thus, **the organization exerts forces which will change
you throughout your career**. These pressures do, however,
tend to show a downward trend over one's career.

Schein also points out a reverse set of influences, namely
the influence the person has on the organization. This
process he calls **innovation**. Once you have learned your

role in a particular part of an organization, but before you look ahead to the next position in your career, you can exert the greatest influence to change the organization. This innovation process tends to have a general upward trend over the course of a career, though it probably drops off toward the very end. Schein's model reminds us of the directions you can move in an organization as you travel through the stages of your career.

Five Basic Career Stages

If we step back for a moment, we can see that **these career-stage models basically define five stages of a career: exploration, establishment, advancement, maintenance/influence, and decline** (see Figure 2.4). But it is important to note that these stages and ages are not fixed in concrete. They vary somewhat from person to person. For example, as we have already seen in Box 2.1, some people backtrack from the advancement stage to the exploration stage, as they change careers in midlife. Or some women have their children and then begin the exploration stage in their 40s or 50s. Still, the career-stage model in Figure 2.4 provides a general framework which can aid in developmentally understanding and managing people in organizations.

Let us briefly apply these career stages to the case of Louise. The **exploration** stage is where we search out

**Figure 2.4
Career Stages**

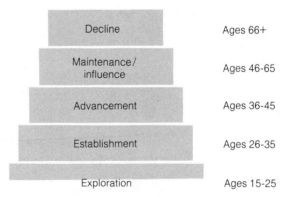

Decline	Ages 66+
Maintenance/influence	Ages 46-65
Advancement	Ages 36-45
Establishment	Ages 26-35
Exploration	Ages 15-25

the beginning of a career. In Louise's case we do not have much information about this stage, except to know that she studied computer science in college. We can speculate that her discussions, courses, and perhaps part-time work involved computer-related situations that influenced her decision to enter this field. The **establishment** stage is when we try to make a name in a chosen field. The case revealed that Louise received a challenging first assignment and that she worked hard on the project both in the corporate office and at the customer's headquarters. Because she was assigned a series of challenging projects after this first project, we can imagine that she began to feel established in her field. We are also told that she was looking for advancement at this time.

The **advancement** stage is when we can expect to move ahead rapidly, if indeed we ever will. The case shows that Louise moved rapidly along in the organizational socialization process. It appears that she moved radially as well as vertically in her transfer to Phoenix as a project manager. We must also point out something that we will discuss in detail later: The advancement stage often coincides with the family stage of settling down and having children, as it did for Louise. This interaction of career and family stages is not always easy to manage, especially in a two-career family.

The **maintenance/influence** stage is when we gain in stature and influence in our chosen field. As Louise entered this stage, she made the move to Home Computers. What did this do? First, it increased the effects of socialization on Louise. Home Computers was a small and growing company compared to her old company, and its expectations were quite different. Also, Louise was making a lateral move into sales. She had to learn to be more of a generalist in the small company and to sell hardware and software. But she had considerable experience, which placed her in the influence stage of her career. Up to this point she had shown very little concern for career maintenence; and she continued to desire advancement and influence. With her vertical move to national sales vice president (a position previously held by the cofounder of the company), she moved radially toward Harvey and the control of the company.

What will happen next to Louise we cannot say; but

we do know that her career can go any of several ways. If you were Louise, understanding how you got where you are would help you anticipate your next move. Should she stay at Home Computers? Does she have a real chance to become president of the company? What will happen in her personal life?

We now want to consider some specific factors of managing as a changing role. Our purpose here is to more fully acquaint you with the developmental aspects of a managerial career and to set the stage for our analysis of individuals in organizations.

Key Factors in the Changing Role of a Manager

There are three factors that will primarily influence you as you move through a career as a manager: your movement within organizations, new people you will encounter, and changes in the organizations themselves. We will discuss each of these factors below and how they create the developmental forces that will act upon your career in management.

Movement within Organizations

As Schein's career model and our earlier discussion of technical, human relations, and conceptual skills suggest, movement within an organization can significantly change your managerial role.

Lateral Moves

First of all, there are the lateral moves from one functional area to another. Louise experienced that in her move from programming at her old company to sales at Home Computers. It was also another type of lateral move; namely, from one organization to another. In the functional change from programming to sales, Louise moved from one culture to another. The two functions are different in terms of norms, goals, time frames, types of people, and so forth. To be successful Louise had to become socialized to the new situation quickly. Her move to Home Computers was also a change of cultures of a different order. Her old company was much larger than Home Computers. It was more formally organized, and her work more specialized. At Home Computers her technical, human relations, and conceptual skills were called upon.

Vertical Moves

As Louise moved upward in responsibility during her career at the two companies, she encountered new demands and was called on to develop different skills. She had to learn to rely less on technical skill and more on conceptual skill. She had to learn to see the bigger picture. But other aspects of vertical moves are also apparent in this case. Louise's husband, Steve, turned down a promotion—something that was seldom done in the past for fear that one such refusal would mean the end of upward vertical movement. That fear has subsided to some extent, as shown in Box 2.3.

The flip side of this is that some people who desire to get to the top of their organization do not make it. There are always fewer positions in top management than there are people who want them. Thus, some people do not achieve their career goals. This realization often occurs during the life stage where one expects to be climbing to the top. The difficult task then is to adjust career goals, to make a job or field change, or to substitute external goals for those in the organization. As we shall discuss in Chapters 5 and 6 on motivation, this transition can be trying; but it is essential to the continued motivation of the employee.

Radial Moves

Radial movement in a career is the most subtle and difficult to detect. It relates most directly to the attitudinal aspects of a career. As we shall see in the motivation chapters, everyone has a need for power and influence. Radial movement gets one closer to the seat of power and decision making in the organization. As this change occurs, there goes with it a shift in responsibility, both legal and moral. The coalition of people who make key decisions in an organization have the legitimate or legal right to obligate the organization by setting goals and policy and by making plans. They also are accountable for those decisions; that is, they are morally responsible to the organization's employees, stockholders, and cus-

A *chemical company official rejected a transfer from his beloved South. A canny electronics executive refused a promotion on the theory—correct as it turned out—that it would detour him from the surest road to the executive suite.*

These managers did what was once unthinkable—refused a promotion. And while employees aren't rejecting advancement in droves, particularly during this recession, they are doing it more than they used to. "There was a time when no one would consider saying no," says Betty Nelson, manager of employee relations for InterNorth Inc., a diversified energy company based in Omaha. That just isn't so anymore, she says, though she adds that "I won't say it never hurts them."

Resisting a promotion can brand an employee as disloyal or lacking in ambition, and reputations like that can scuttle promising careers. But personnel officers, consultants and career counselors say there can be good reasons to pass up a new job. Sometimes, refusing a position can save a worker from a dead-end job, protect him from a difficult boss or simply give him more time to enjoy life.

Concerns About Travel, Life Style

Take the chemical company executive. He passed up a $30,000 raise because it meant relocating at the company's Northeastern headquarters. "I love to play golf," he says. "I have a house on the golf course of the club that I belong to. It would be next to impossible to do that" at the home office.

tomers. These responsibilities demand that a manager have real wisdom—and they probably relate directly to to the increase in gray hair in higher level managers!

As a manager you must be prepared for these career moves. In addition, other forces will cause you to change.

New People You Encounter

As we have said, in your career you will meet many different people as you move vertically, radially, and laterally. If your career is to continue on a successful route, you must be able to draw on your human relations skill to work with and through these people. Let us look at the sources of some of the different types of people you will encounter.

Functional and Level Differences

As your career takes you into different functions within organizations, you encounter people with varying backgrounds, training, and expertise. For example, in programming, Louise encountered highly technical people who were very precise in their thinking, and who probably had little tolerance for others who could not understand their jargon. When she moved to sales at Home Computers, she met people with less technical training. They needed to be ambiguous at times, and liked to talk in more general terminology. These stereotypes of programmers and salespeople may not be totally accurate, but the point is that Louise had to recognize and deal with these differences to be successful. Likewise, as Louise moved up the corporate ladder, she first encountered people with a need to achieve and to have a challenging job. Further up the ladder she met people who wanted to influence the company. Could Louise operate in exactly the same way with these different types of people? Of course not.

New People from the Environment

As we said in Chapter 1, there has been a trend for several decades toward a more highly educated and skilled work force. Today, people a receive better education from their earliest years through formal education than they did in the 1940s or even in the 1960s. They also learn to expect more from a job and from life in general. For this reason, some employees feel the company owes them a job and good pay; they do not have to earn it. But this trend has also created employees who want a challenge and will not be satisfied with a boring job. This evolution may stimulate management to find ways to motivate these new employees, who want to have more contol over their careers.[10]

There are also other sources of different types of people entering the work force. Managers must be able to work with women, minorities, and dual-career-family members, if they are to be effective. Since the early 1970s, there has been a concerted effort to bring women and minorities into the work place. Affirmative action and equal employment opportunity efforts have been especially successful in blue collar and clerical jobs. Recent years have seen advances for women and minorities in the ranks of middle management and, to a lesser extent, in the executive suite. The changes brought on by these developments continue to occur. And these changes have far-reaching effects that will influence you as a manager. Just imagine having to deal with child-care problems or to grant paternity leave as part of your managerial responsibilities. These are very recent considerations for managers and their companies. They reflect the developmental aspects of dealing with people over your career.

We can also carry this issue one step further by considering the impact of dual-career families, where both husband and wife work full time. In such cases, child care and paternity leave issues are very important. And there are approximately 25 million dual-career families in the United States, with the number increasing rapidly.[11] With both wife and husband working—and working with a long-term outlook on jobs—a number of problems are encountered by managers. When job transfers or hirings are considered by the dual-career couple, both careers must be considered. Transferring one spouse means that the other spouse must likely relocate, too. And if a company wants to hire a person in a dual-career family, both people may have to be hired, or the company may have to help the spouse locate a suitable job. As a manager, you will have to become familiar with such issues and learn to deal with members of dual-career couples.

Of course, you too may be part of a dual-career couple. As such, you will no doubt face the relocation problem —which ultimately means the establishing of priorities. Just how important will your career be? What about for your spouse? The dual-career family must also face the issues of child care and household responsibilities. How are the children cared for while both parents work? Who stays home when a child is sick? Who does the laundry, the dishes, the vacuuming? Do you hire someone to do these things? A survey by the Catalyst Career and Family Center in 1980 revealed that wives and husbands agreed that allocation of time, finances, poor family communications, and conflicts over housework were the most troublesome problems for two-career couples.[12] The problems of the dual-career family will affect you in one way or another as you progress through your career. If you are to be succesful both in work and your personal life, you will have to manage the issues mentioned above. As we will discuss later, **the interacting aspects of career, family, and life stages are difficult to manage for the best of people**.

Changing Needs of People

Another source of "new" people is the changes that occur in people over their lifetime. As mentioned in Chapter 1, the evolution of life stages brings on changes in people as they progress from the trying 20s to the catch 30s to the forlorn 40s and beyond.. They change their goals; they change the perceptions of their capabilities; and they change their needs. For example, a 60-year-old person given a new and challenging job may not respond the same way a 30-year-old would. In the early years of a career (the establishment and advancement stages), people usually look for challenges and chances for advancement. They often overestimate their abilities and later, through experience become aware of this over-estimation. By midcareer and middle age (the maintenance/influence career stage), they have learned what they can accomplish. They may also be ready to move into the more conceptual and administrative aspects of their work. By the time they reach the decline career stage, they start to anticipate retirement (which is really a new career itself). Or as shown earlier in Box 2.2, they may actually explore and get into a totally new line of work after retiring from one job.

As a manager, how will you motivate these different people? How will you provide effective leadership for all of them? How will you manage your own evolution through the career, life, and family stages? These questions need to be answered for you to be a successful manager, both in your work and your personal life.

Changes in the Organization

The final key factor in the changing role of a manager is the change that occurs in the organizations for which the person works during a career. Is your company a high-growth company? Is it a company that is about to make a significant change in goals? Is it on the decline?

High Growth Companies

In the Home Computers case, it is apparent that the company has grown very rapidly. Certainly this growth is welcomed by managers in the establishment and advancement stages of their careers. The growth of the company opens up many challenging opportunities, and it allows rapid vertical movement in the organization. At first glance, this growth and expansion would seem to be all positive: Who would not want the chance for rapid advancement? The only real catch is that people may be promoted before they have gained the experience and knowledge necessary to succeed at the next higher level. The result can be disastrous for the manager, the employees, and the organization.

For a person to grow professionally as fast as some high-growth organizations require, it takes real dedication to the company. It means long hours of work and sacrifice both of one's self and for one's family. The career stages may come much faster than is compatible with the life and family stages. To be a successful manager, you must anticipate this development by determining if the company to which you belong is a rapid-growth company. If it is, are you prepared to grow rapidly with it?

Companies Changing Direction

If top management makes a significant change in a company's direction, it can have a far-reaching effect on the careers of company managers. Imagine, for example, that you work for Home Computers, which decides to acquire a small company that manufactures portable typewriters. You are asked to be a manager in this new division. Immediately, your technical expertise in computers loses some value; and you will have to develop expertise in typewriters. Are the employees that make typewriters motivated by the same things as those that make computers? The change could become either a real plus or a problem for your career, depending on how you handle this change in direction.

Now imagine the reverse situation: Home Computers

is purchased by another company. How will things be different under the new top management? What changes will be made in the operation of the company? Will you and your department have the same influence in decision making as before? Will it be more or less? Managers in many companies had to deal with these very issues during the recent recession (1981-82). Sometimes the results had significant impacts on the careers of managers in the acquired company. As the story in Box 2.4 about Sunbeam shows, the changes brought on by takeover can be devastating, especially if the result is the loss of your job.

Box 2.4
Employees' at
Acquired Firms Find
White Knights Often
Unfriendly

Late last year, Allegheny International Inc. came in as a white knight to acquire Sunbeam Corp., rescuing it from the clutches of an unwanted bidder.

But, to some Sunbeam employees, Allegheny itself has been none too friendly. The merger officially was approved by the two companies' shareholders on Dec. 29. D-Day was Feb. 19. On that day, many employees at Sunbeam's corporate office—from executives to middle managers to clerical workers—were bluntly, though politely, informed that the company no longer needed them.

Some are bitter. Many are disappointed. "I was declared 'redundant,'" a fired corporate vice president says sarcastically. A middle-level executive complains: "I didn't even get my day in court. That's what bothers me most. I was found guilty and executed without a trial."

Parting Gesture

Some executives left with "golden parachutes." During the takover battle, Sunbeam gave 21 executives termination contracts providing them with a year or two of salary, depending on their time with the company.

Other fired employees weren't so fortunate, though they did get severance pay. Executives received 12 weeks severance, managers and professionals received eight weeks and clerical workers received four weeks, with everyone receiving an additional week's pay for each full year of employment at Sunbeam.

By Lawrence Ingrassia, *The Wall Street Journal,* July 7, 1982. Reprinted by permission of *The Wall Street Journal,* © Dow Jones & Company, Inc. 1982. All rights reserved.

Declining Organizations

The story about Sunbeam also suggests another possibility—suppose the company you work for suffers a decline in business. The decline may only be temporary due to a normal business cycle or to circumstances in the economy. It could also be a sustained decline resulting in the eventual death of the organization. Every year thousands and thousands of companies go out of business. What effect does this have on the careers of the managers in those companies? Certainly, it may necessitate a relocation to find a new job. Problems could arise here because of a dual-career family or because of your age or other factors. It may be a real setback in the advancement of your career—or it could be the break that allows you to find a job that offers even better opportunities. While you may not be able to plan for this event, it is important to recognize that it can happen to anyone.

If the decline is temporary, it may only mean a slight delay in the desired career path of a manager. But for some managers, even a slight decline is unacceptable. If you find yourself in such a situation, it will be important to analyze the situation carefully. How long do you think the decline will last? Are there other opportunities you should explore at this time? What must you do to retain your position if layoffs are a possibility? In short, **many forces at the organizational level that are not controllable by you as a manager may have a big impact on your career as a manager**.

What Can You Do about Your Career?	Now that we have discussed the factors which affect the changing role of a manager, let us briefly conclude this chapter with a discussion of what you can do about your career. Simply **having an appreciation of the developmental aspects of career, life, and family stages can prepare you to better manage your career**. We have said that people are goal oriented and that they develop a perception of their abilities. Both of these are subject to change, as are the goals and operations of the companies for which we work. However, **when your goals/abilities and the goals/development plans of the organization**

are in agreement, a successful career is more likely. Such a convergence will encourage you to develop the skills and abilities needed for new jobs within the organization. It will also encourage the organization to invest in your career development. If, however, there is a lack of agreement between you and the organization, you will be dissatisfied—and so will the organization. In such an event, the best career move may be to look for work elsewhere.

With the developmental perspective, it is important to recognize the sources of our career orientations. It is also important to recognize that they may change over time. First of all, your goals and abilities are influenced by your childhood experiences. Social class is probably one of the primary factors that enters in here.[13] Children raised in a home where achievement is stressed will develop a different career orientation than those brought up in homes where other values are stressed.[14]

Another factor important in determining your career orientation is your previous organizational and job experiences. As we pointed out in Chapter 1, you are already a "used product." Your past experiences have given you feedback about your goals and abilities; and future experiences will continue to shape your perceptions. If you experience success, you will probably adjust your goals and perceptions of abilities upward. This can result in a reassessment of career aspirations and can begin a cycle of success—higher goals which when achieved lead to setting even higher goals. But it is also possible for another scenario to develop; continued success can breed a complacency that inhibits continued growth.[15]

Of course, if you experience failure, the result can be quite different. Such negative feedback can lead to a downward adjustment in career aspirations; and continued failure can begin to push you into a downward cycle. However, research has shown that initial failures can also lead to the exertion of greater effort to avoid repeated failure.[16] Thus, the scenario again has two main possibilities. And it is quite possible that your childhood experiences will determine your reaction to success and failure.

Other factors can also influence your career orientation both today and in the future. We have noted the impact that family stages can have on your career, and we have also mentioned the impact of life stages. Both factors will receive more attention in Chapters 3 and 4. For now, we would like to focus specifically on your career by having you complete the career-planning exercise at the end of the chapter. The steps outlined can be completed alone, but we encourage you to discuss the results with friends and/or relatives. And as you go through the exercise, think about the factors we have discussed that affect your career and its various stages. Then take a look at the chapter highlights and review questions which follow.

Chapter Highlights

The purpose of this chapter has been to make you think more personally about the developmental aspects of organizations. We want you to gain a true appreciation for this perspective before we proceed through the four levels of organizational behavior. To do this we have focused on managing as a changing role. More specifically, we have focused on the elements of a career—your career. You must realize that different skills are required as you progress through your managerial career. In particular, we discussed three types of skills. **Technical skill is important at lower levels of management but less important at upper levels. Conceptual skill is important at upper levels of management and less important at lower levels. Human relations skill is necessary at all levels.**

We also learned that a career can be broken down into various stages. Several breakdowns were explored and resulted in the definition of five career stages. The **exploration** stage is the period in our lives (ages 15-25) when we begin to choose our life's work. The **establishment** stage (ages 26-35) is the period of exploring various career paths and becoming comfortable in one field of endeavor (at least for the time being). The third stage, **advancement** (ages 36-45), is the time during which we determine how far we will go in our field of endeavor. At the end of this period people sometimes change fields, when they realize they will not be able to climb as high as they would like. The fourth stage is the **maintenance/influence** period (ages 46-65), and it is during this time that the real change from technical to conceptual skill utilization usually takes place. You will either reach a plateau at the beginning of this period or become a mentor for others. You can also exercise influence in the organization. The final career stage is **decline** (ages 66 and on). During this period you will begin to withdraw from your field of endeavor and may pick up another "career" in retirement. In fact, retirement may be a career all its own as people live longer.

Another important way to view your career is from the point of view of the organization. Schein's model explicitly recognizes three directions of career movement in an organization. You can move **vertically** up the organization ladder, **laterally** from one functional area to another, and **radially** toward the center of influence in the organization. **And as your career takes you vertically, laterally, and radially through one or more organizations, you will be changed as a result of the experiences you have. You will also have to manage and work in a context and with people that are different at each step of the way**. People in the different functions have unique orientations, goals, and norms of operation.

In addition, you will encounter changes in the work force. We discussed at some length the effects of increased numbers of women in the work force. A primary impact has been the rapid growth of dual-career couples. Such couples create special challenges for managers and organizations—and for the husband and wife, too. As you move into different family and career stages, you too may have to manage the stresses associated with a dual-career couple. You will certainly encounter the situation in one way or another.

The last two factors creating changes in your managerial career are changes in you and in the organizations where you work. Indeed, these are the fundamental developmental focuses in this book. As we discussed, **you will experience changes in your needs, goals and abilities as you traverse your career**. The organization (or organizations) for which you work will also change and create forces for change in your career. **The organization may grow rapidly, change directions, or decline, but regardless of the direction of movement your career will be affected**.

Throughout the chapter we have made reference to Louise and Home Computers. By understanding Louise's career stages, her movement through the two organizations, the different people she has encountered, her dual-career situation, plus the changes in Louise's needs and the changes in her organizations, we can better understand what is happening to Louise. By asking questions such as these of yourself, you will be better prepared to manage the career that unfolds before you.

We have now fully introduced the developmental perspective as it applies to the levels of organizational behavior and to your personal career as a manager. At this point we hope you have gained an appreciation for why the developmental perspective is so important in understanding and managing organizational behavior. As we begin to explore the individual level of organizational behavior in the next chapter, your understanding of this perspective will be most helpful to you.

Review Questions

1. Define the three basic skills of management: technical, human relations, and conceptual. How do these skills relate to levels of management?

2. What is the work of a manager like on a day-to-day basis? How does this work vary across different levels of management?

3. What is the definition of a career? How does this definition relate to a developmental view of work life?

4. What are the five stages of a career presented in this text? What typically happens during each career stage?

5. Schein defines three directions of career movement within organizations. What are the three and how are they defined?

6. How do Schein's directions of movement relate to various changes in the role of a manager?

7. As you move through your career, one factor creating changes for you will be the people you encounter. What are the three sources of "new" people who

will change your role as a manager? How might each source affect you?

8. How might the impact of belonging to a dual-career couple interact with the changing needs of a manager? What challenges would be encountered as the manager passed through various career stages?

9. What types of changes could occur in the organizations for which you work during your career and have an impact on your career? How would these affect your career?

10. How do the elements of career stages and the key factors in the changing role of a manager interact in the life of Louise at Home Computers? How does the developmental perspective help in understanding her situation?

Notes

1. R. Katz, "Skills of the Effective Administrator," *Harvard Business Review*, January-February, 1955, pp. 33–42.

2. R. H. Guest, "Of Time and the Foreman," *Personnel* 32 (May 1956), pp. 478–86.

3. L. R. Bittel and J. E. Ramsey, "The Limited Traditional World of Supervisors," *Harvard Business Review* 60 (July–August 1982), pp. 26–36.

4. L. Sayles, *Leadership: What Effective Managers Really Do . . . and How They Do It* (New York: McGraw-Hill, 1979); E. E. Lawler, L. W. Porter, and A. S. Tannenbaum, "Managers' Attitudes toward Interaction Episodes," *Journal of Applied Psychology* 52 (1968), pp. 432–39; and R. Stewart, *Managers and Their Jobs* (New York: Macmillan, Ltd., 1967).

5. H. Mintzberg, *The Nature of Managerial Work* (New York: Harper & Row, 1973).

6. D. T. Hall, *Careers in Organizations* (Glenview, Ill.: Scott, Foresman, 1976), p. 4.

7. D. Super, J. Crites, R. Hummel, H. Moser, P. Overstreet, and C. Warnath, *Vocational Development: A Framework for Research* (New-York: Teachers College Press, 1957), pp. 40–41.

8. D. T. Hall and K. Nougaim, "An Examination of Maslow's Need-Hierarchy in an Organizational Setting," *Organizational Behavior and Human Performance*, 3 (1968), pp. 12–35.

9. E. H. Schein, "The Individual, the Organization, and the Career:

A Conceptual Scheme," *Journal of Applied Behavioral Science*, vol. 7 (1971), pp. 401–426.

10. W. A. Randolph, B. Z. Posner, and M. S. Wortman, "A New Ethic for Work? The Worth Ethic," *Human Resource Management*, 14 (Fall 1975), pp. 15–20.

11. *Wall Street Journal*, January 21, 1982.

12. *Corporations and Two-Career Families: Directions for the Future* (New York: Catalyst Career and Family Center, 1981).

13. M. Carter, *Into Work* (New York: Penguin Books, 1966).

14. J. G. Goodale, "Effects of Personal Background and Training on Work Values of the Hard-Core Unemployed," *Journal of Applied Psychology* 57 (1973), pp. 1–9.

15. A. S. DeNisi, W. A. Randolph, and A. Blencoe, "Level and Source of Feedback as Determinants of Effectiveness," *Academy of Management Proceedings*, 1982, pp.175–79.

16. Ibid.

Resource Readings

Hall, D. T. *Careers in Organizations*. Glenview, Ill.: Scott, Foresman, 1976.

Jelinek, M. *Career Management for the Individual and the Organization*. New York: John Wiley & Sons, 1979.

Mintzberg, H. *The Nature of Managerial Work*. New York: Harper & Row, 1973.

Career-Planning Exercise

Purpose

To develop or reassess your career and life plans.

Introduction

This exercise will give you an opportunity to examine your own values and priorities for your life and to set career goals for yourself. It is helpful in an exercise like this to share the ideas you generate with other people in a small group setting because the feedback, support, and questions of others are helpful in clarifying your own values and goals.

However, you should always feel free to withhold any personal data from others if you would be uncomfortable in sharing it.

Procedure

Step 1. On a piece of notebook paper, write *WHO AM I* at the top. Then make 3 columns on the sheet. Label the first column *CAREER,* the second *AFFILIATIONS,* and the third *PERSONAL FULFILLMENT.* Write the numerals 1 to 5 in the the left margin.

In the first column, list 5 adjectives that describe you most accurately in regard to your *career.*

In the second column, list 5 adjectives that describe you most accurately in regard to your *personal affiliations.*

In the third column, list 5 adjectives that describe you most accurately in regard to your *personal fulfillment.*

Step 2. Take three more sheets of paper. Head them up as follows:

WHERE DO I WANT TO BE?—CAREER

WHERE DO I WANT TO BE?—AFFILIATIONS

WHERE DO I WANT TO BE—PERSONAL FULFILLMENT

On each sheet, write the numbers 1 to 3, leaving a blank in front of the numbers like this:

———1.

———2.

———3.

etc.

Fill in the first sheet as follows:

List 3 goals that describe your conception of ideal attainments in your *career.* Be as free as possible in selecting these goals. Summarize your career fantasies on this page. Example: I want to become president of my company.

Then fill in the second sheet:

What would be your conception of 3 ideal attainments in your *personal affiliations?* Be as free as possible in selecting these goals. Summarize your affiliation fantasies on this page. Example: I want to behave in such a way that my mother-in-law will be more accepting of me.

And then the third sheet:

What would be your conception of 3 ideal attainments with regard to your *personal fulfillment?* Be as free as possible in selecting these goals. Summarize your personal fulfillment fantasies on this page. Example: I want to learn to fly an airplane.

Go back to the first sheet and, in the blank in front of the numbers, assign a priority value to each of your *career* goals.

    a. Using the following four-point scale, write the appropriate value in the space provided in front of each goal.

        1—of little important
        2—of moderate importance
        3—of great importance
        4—of very great importance

    b. Assign a priority value to each of your *personal affiliation* goals (the second sheet). Using the four-point scale above, write the appropriate value in the space provided in front of each goal.

    c. Assign a priority value to each of your *personal fulfillment* goals (the third sheet). Using the four-point scale above, write the appropriate value in the space provided in front of each goal.

    d. Which of the three sheets (career, affiliations, personal fulfillment) has the most 4s? The most 1s? What does this tell you about the relative importance of these three aspects of your life?

Step 3. Take 1 more sheet of paper; head it up with *MY THREE GOALS.* From your three lists of goals in Step 2, select three that you want most to attain. Discuss these three in terms of the following questions:

    a. What are *my strengths and weaknesses* affecting my ability to achieve these goals?

b. What *obstacles* are to prevent me from achieving these goals?

c. Are these *goals realistic?* What will happen if I do not achieve these goals?

Adapted from: J. William Pfeiffer and John E. Jones, eds., *A Handbook of Structured Experiences for Human Relations Training,* vol. II, San Diego, Calif.: University Associates, Inc., 1974. Used with permission.

S E C T I O N 2

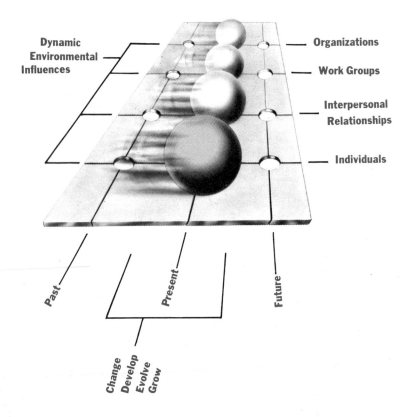

Dynamic
Environmental
Influences

Organizations

Work Groups

Interpersonal
Relationships

Individuals

Past

Present

Future

Change
Develop
Evolve
Grow

Individuals in Organizations

In this section of the book, we will take an in-depth look at the behavior of individuals in organizations. Over the next four chapters, we will deal with several important processes of individual behavior. These are highlighted with shading in the analytical framework we discussed in Chapter 1, repeated here for your reference.

Chapter 3 deals with the process of perception—how it is error prone and how it affects behavior and interactions—and with the related process of learning. We will explore how learning takes place over time, how forgetting occurs, and how learning and perception are interrelated. These discussions progress, in Chapter 4, to attitudes, and then to personality as the integration of learning, perception, and attitudes. With this information in hand, we then look at the interaction of the person and the organization, by focusing on the process of socialization. This process, in particular, highlights the developmental perspective of this book. We also look at stress as a reaction to one's situation and as an influence on personality.

The final two chapters in this section (Chapters 5 and 6) focus on the important issue of motivation. We will discuss such questions as: What motivates different people? How does motivation change over one's life? What can a manager do to increase the motivation of subordinates and peers?

Throughout these chapters it will be important for you

A Developmental Framework for Studying Organizations

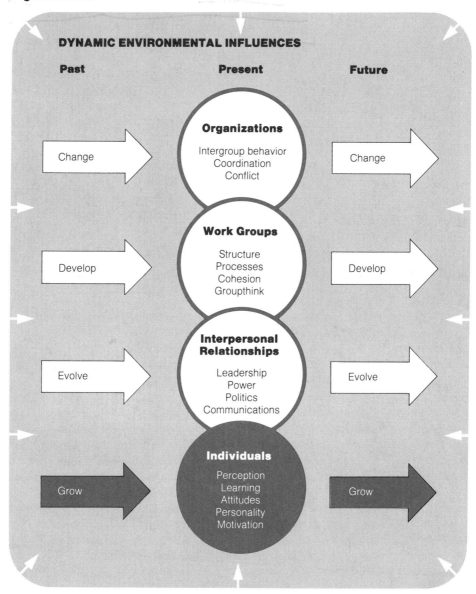

to do three things to obtain maximum benefit from the material presented. First, keep in mind that people are the basic building blocks of any organization. Second, remember that each person is unique and develops in important ways from birth to death. And third, think about yourself as you study this material; see what new things you may learn about yourself in organizational settings.

C H A P T E R   3

Understanding Perception and Learning as Dynamic Processes

As mentioned in Chapter 1 and shown in the figure at the beginning of this section, individuals are the basic building blocks of organization. They are where the work ultimately gets done. A manager needs to know a great deal about people to be effective.

Why You Need to Understand Individual Behavior

It is extremely important for you as a manager to understand the elements that make up individual behavior—perception, learning, attitudes, personality, socialization, stress, and motivation. These internal elements determine the behavior a person will exhibit as a result of external stimuli. For example, imagine a superior who tries to get a subordinate to do a certain task by yelling and pushing the subordinate around. Based upon perception, previous learning, personality, and so forth, the subordinate may perform the desired action or may turn around and punch the superior. Of course, different people respond differently to the same situation because of their unique personalities. Also, the **same** person may respond differently at different times due to stress or other dynamic factors. And people may respond differently at different points in their lives because of the evolution of personality. This developmental process is summarized in Figure 3.1.

Figure 3.1 The Elements of Individual Behavior from a Developmental Perspective

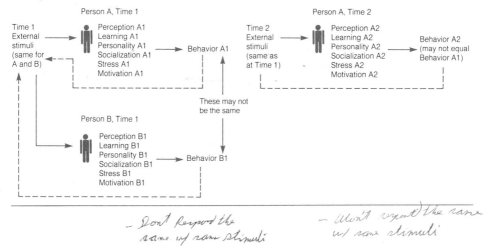

- Don't Respond the same w/ same stimuli

- Won't respond the same w/ same stimuli

In the figure, persons A and B are both exposed to the same external stimuli at Time 1. But because of their uniqueness (as represented by their individual and current—A1 and B1—perception, learning, attitudes, personality, socialization, stress, and motivation), their behaviors A1 and B1 may be different. Furthermore, person A (or B) may respond to the same external stimuli with different behavior (A2) at another point in time (Time 2). This is because the person has changed (as represented by the changed—A2—perception, learning, attitudes, and so forth). People are unique and dynamic beings, and **to be the most effective as a manager, you must be very familiar with the elements that make up the individuals you supervise: perception, learning, attitudes, personality, socialization, stress, and motivation**. This means being familiar with the theory that relates to each of these behavioral elements, as well as their interactions and developmental aspects. And it means being able to apply the theoretical concepts to the people you manage. To make this discussion more concrete, let us return to the case of Louise of Home Computers and her husband, Steve.

Louise of Home Computers (continued)

Louise's first job in 1962, long before joining Home Computers, was to work on the development of an accounts receivable system for one of the company's largest customers. She had just received her degree in computer science. Louise was fortunate to have attended an excellent school with some first-rate professors of computer science. She had developed a logical, analytical approach to learning and problem solving. Furthermore, she was fortunate to have had several women professors as role models in developing a self-concept of strength and confidence. Her attitude toward managerial problems and challenges was both optimistic and realistic. Louise was well prepared intellectually and psychologically to accept the challenges of her first job.

On the first day she met her boss, Sam Stewart, who had retired from the Navy with nearly 20 years' experience in computers and programming. Sam explained to Louise that she would be working on an important project for one of the company's largest customers. In fact, she and George Davis, an experienced programmer, would be co-leaders on the project. Their job was to work with the customer's representatives to determine exactly what they needed and then deliver it on time. They could call upon other programmers and resources within the company, as long as they kept Sam informed of their progress. Sam told her that he wanted progress reports every two weeks and that he wanted the job done right.

In addition to receiving these instructions from Sam on her first day, she met George Davis and began to get to know him. She also started to familiarize herself with the written description of the project. Soon she met the representatives from the customer company and learned more details about the project and the time schedule. In addition, she learned about the rest of her organization: how to get supplies, who she could trust and count on, where things and people were located, and so forth. And on top of this, she had to adjust to a new city and a new home.

Louise handled these varied and numerous stimuli very well. Her past training and life experiences had prepared her to deal selectively with her environment. She could distinguish the important facts and relationships from the unimportant ones. Also, she learned well from her first assignment and was asked to implement the system for the customer. She was then given a series of challenging projects.

In 1979 Steve, Louise's husband, turned down a promotion because he would have had to move to New York and disrupt his family life to do it. Instead, he chose to put his family before his career. Louise wondered what would have happened had the situation been reversed? Would she have chosen her career and the related stress on the family, or would she have made the same decision Steve did? Would the differences between Louise and Steve have resulted in a different decision for Louise? Well, one year later Louise jumped at the chance to go to work for Home Computers as a sales manager, even though Steve advised against it. The job change did not mean having to move, but it did mean more travel.

Currently, Louise is national sales vice president of Home Computers and is very happy in her career. However, she is now 45 years old and feels left out of her children's lives. She also feels Steve is jealous of her successes. She wonders what would happen now if Harvey stepped aside as president of Home Computers and offered her the job? If she accepted, her family might have to move, or she might have to commute to the headquarters outside New York City and stay over several nights each week. It would certainly be a step up the career ladder, and it might not involve moving to another location. But Louise is wondering whether she should accept if the possibility arises.

She is older now than when she came to Home Computers. She wonders about her career and how such a change would be received by her family. And what would Harvey think if she turned it down?

A number of aspects of the case are important for us to note. First, as Louise began her career she encountered a large number of stimuli from her environment. She received instructions from Sam; met people; learned a new city; and so forth. Could she pay equal attention to all of these stimuli? No.

Second, if Louise had been a different person, she might have felt threatened by Sam and the tough first assignment he gave her. She might also have perceived negative things about having to work with many men. For example, she could have felt inferior, or patronized, or sexually harassed. Someone with a high need to be liked, as opposed to Louise's high need to accomplish things, might have succumbed to such perceptions and been less effective on the job. And a person with less self-confidence than Louise might have felt overwhelmed by the challenging job.

Third, it is clear that Louise learned her jobs well and was very successful. However, as the case closes we see Louise pondering her next career move. She may have to move to a new location and take on additional responsibility. The question in her mind is whether her current family and life stages will result in these stimuli being perceived differently than similar ones she encountered when she first joined Home Computers. Will the present state of her learning, socialization, stress, and motivation result in accepting or rejecting the offer to become president of the company, should it arise? And what will be the reactions of her family and Harvey to her next career decision?

Let us now explore the process of perception in more detail. An understanding of this process will help us better understand Louise and the situations in her life. And it will also help you understand the situations you will face in your career.

The Process of Perception

In the preceding Home Computers excerpt, several aspects of the **perception** process are apparent, as we have noted. But just what is the perception process? Why is it so important in our lives? And why is it so error prone? For our purposes, perception **is the process by which people select, organize, interpret, and assign meaning to external phenomena.**[1] In other words, it is the process people use to make sense of the world around them.

Before we discuss a model of the perception process in detail, let us consider several reasons why the process is so important for you as a manager to understand. First, it is unlikely that any person's definition of reality will be exactly identical to an objective assessment of reality. For example, Louise's and Steve's perceptions of reality are influenced by their individual past experiences as well as by their sensory processes. Second, it is unlikely that two people's definition of reality will be exactly the same. The uniqueness of Louise's and Steve's pasts plus selection mechanisms determine that they will assign different meanings to the same situation. For another example, Box 3.1 makes this point by illustrating how different people respond to the issue of facing career plateaus. Third, individual perception directly influences the behavior exhibited in a given situation. **The bottom line is that people who must work together often see things differently, and this difference can create problems in their ability to work together effectively.** Furthermore, who is to say what the "objective reality" is? Both people in a situation may be wrong in the different meanings they assign to the same phenomena.

In order to understand perception, let us look at the model of the process in Figure 3.2. A glance at the model suggests its complexity as well as the potential for error and differences among people. And there is no way to avoid the perception process. It is physiologically impossible for us to jump from external phenomena to assignment of meaning. We must go through the senses, observation, and frame of reference filter before we get to assignment of meaning. Everything we see in the world around us is seen through this process. Let us walk through the model step by step; and as we do, think about all of

Box 3.1
More People Face Career Plateaus, A Relief for Some, Shock for Others

For some, it is a career crisis of major proportions, often resulting in agonizing soul-searching, marital troubles, drinking problems.

For others, it is a comfortable and relaxing time, when family and personal interests come before the job.

It is the plateau, that point in a career when further advancement looks unlikely or impossible. Popular conception holds that the career plateau is the menace of only middle-aged managers. But with the baby-boom generation reaching its 30s and 40s during a time of widespread unemployment and record numbers of business-school graduates, a career plateau can come to anybody in any profession at nearly any age.

"It's like aging," says the 50-year-old vice president of a pharmaceutical concern. "You hardly notice it until you wake up one morning and you've had the same job for five years and it isn't anywhere near where you planned to be by this time."

But some recent corporate studies show that a sizable number of executives and managers welcome a plateau as relief from the competition and pressure to keep moving ahead. An American Telephone & Telegraph Co. survey shows that after 20 years at the company, one-third of the managers deem advancement as "not important." And only 36% say they would give up more personal time for career success.

the potential points where errors may creep into the process. Also, think about the developmental nature of the process.

The Senses and External Phenomena

The first step in the model in Figure 3.2 (starting on the left side) is that multiple phenomena occur around us at all times. We saw this in the case of Louise. And at this very moment while you are reading this text, you are obviously seeing the words on the page; but what else is happening around you? You may hear a radio in the background, or someone talking to you, or a truck passing by your window. You may also smell coffee brew-

Figure 3.2 Model of the Perception Process

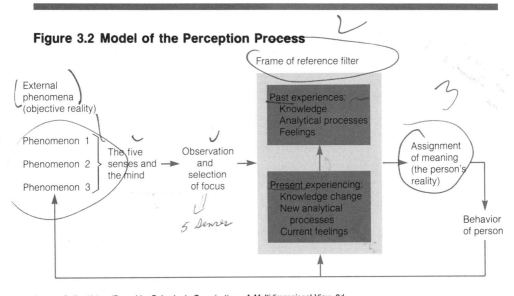

Source: Coffey/Athos/Raynolds, *Behavior in Organizations: A Multidimensional View*, 2d ed., © 1975, p. 68. Adapted by permission of Prentice-Hall, Englewood Cliffs, N.J.

ing, or taste the cup of coffee you are drinking as you try to stay awake to finish the chapter. You may also feel your chair getting very hard, or feel someone touching you on the shoulder to get your attention. Your mind may be on other things as well as on what you are reading. Perhaps you are thinking about your plans for the evening or about something that happened earlier in the day. The main point here is: which of these external phenomena will you choose to pay attention to? Which ones will you ignore?

Herein lies the first potential for variation from the "objective reality" and variation in the realities of two people. Perhaps you are highly motivated to absorb what is in this chapter. You therefore focus on the written page and ignore the external phenomena. Another person may be very concerned about an upcoming date and thus find that the words on these pages are not registering. What we are really talking about is the **selection mechanism** that is part of the perceptual process.

**Observation and
Selection of Focus**

What is it that makes two people observe the same phenomena but "see" different things? The most obvious reason is that the selection of focus step in the process is necessary, because there are more phenomena that bombard our senses than we can absorb. The characteristics of the perceived object, person, or problem, the characteristics of the situation, and the characteristics of the perceiver all affect the selection mechanism.

Characteristics of the Perceived

Physical properties of the perceived include size, intensity, contrast, and novelty. Dynamic properties include motion, repetition, and ordering.[2]

Size is an important physical property; larger objects, people, and problems tend to receive more attention. For example, the size of your office will influence people's perception of your importance in the organization. Or a request from a large customer may be perceived as more important than a request from a smaller one.

Intensity has to do with the brightness and loudness of a person or object. If your boss yells at you, she is more likely to get your attention than if she speaks in a whisper. Or suppose you are talking on the telephone at home and your baby starts to cry. If the crying is loud, you will probably put the phone down to go to the baby.

Contrast refers to the principle that objects that stand out against their background are more likely to be noticed. For example, material in this text that is printed in bold face color contrasts with the other and (we hope) receives greater attention from you.

Novelty (compared to familiarity) means that something is not as you would expect it. Such novel items or people tend to stand out and demand attention. Think about how often you pay attention to the shoes another person is wearing—probably not very often. Well, one time I was watching the "Tonight Show" with Johnny Carson. His guest was a rock singer who was dressed in a three-piece blue suit; but as the camera pulled back to give a full view, I realized the guest was wearing white tennis shoes. Now, that got my attention!

Motion is probably the most obvious dynamic property. Objects or people that are moving are more likely to get our attention than those standing still. A public speaker who stands like a statue behind the podium will not keep our attention as well as one who is more animated. And a problem in the work place that is becoming progressively worse is more likely to receive attention than one that may be severe but is static.

Repetition is another dynamic factor in the selection mechanism. The more often a stimulus is repeated, the more likely it is to receive attention. For example, suppose that you are reading this text and the telephone rings. If it rings only once, you might ignore it; but persistent ringing will invariably make you answer it. Likewise, work instructions that are repeated several times are more often heard than those given once. Of course, too much repetition can lead to boredom.

The final property of the perceived person or object that affects the selection mechanism is their **ordering**. Information that is entered early into the perception process will receive more weight than information entered later. Furthermore, early information tends to distort later data to make it more consistent with this early information. For example, in hiring interviews, recruiters often make their decisions in the first five minutes, even though they may not realize it; and the interview may go on for another half hour. However, information that is the last to be received can also have a great impact on perception, since there is no further information to weaken the impact of this last bit of data.

Overall, these physical and dynamic properties of the object, person, or problem being perceived are important determinants of which stimuli we will attend to in forming our perceptions. If our focus is on people as the perceived, we can expand some of these properties to include other aspects. For example, size can be broadened to include age, sex, race, and dress—in other words, physical appearance. Could the fact that Louise is a woman make a difference in the way she is perceived on the job? With regard to intensity, we immediately think about the verbal communications of people. Certainly, volume is one element; but so are tone of voice, accent, and choice of words. If you heard two people speaking, and one had an accent foreign to you, which person would more quickly attract your attention? As for tone, there are at least two ways for your boss to say, "Come into my office for a minute." One is loud and gruff and you know you are in trouble. Another is of moderate volume and said in a pleasant tone of voice. Finally, in combination with the verbal expression of people is nonverbal expression. If the verbal and nonverbal cues suggest different things, to which one do you pay attention? We will come back to these communications issues again in Chapter 10.

Characteristics of the Situation

Three elements of the situation make a difference in the phenomena that one selects to notice: the social context, the place of people within the organization (that is, their organizational roles), and the location of the perceptual incident.[3]

If the **social context** is, for example, one of stress and time pressure, the selection mechanism may focus on different things than it would in a more relaxed atmosphere. Under stress people often miss cues in the environment or imagine cues that are not present. The presence or absence of stress and time pressure is a dynamic variable; and over time people may learn to function well under stress. Of course, social context can consist of other factors, as well—for example, nature of the work, your relationship with others in the situation, and so forth.

Your **organizational role** can also influence the phenomena that you notice. If you are the superior in a two-person interaction, you will pay attention to different things than if you are the subordinate. As the superior you might focus on when a project will be completed and how the employee must work with little supervision. As the subordinate, you might focus on what is expected of you on the project and where you will obtain support to complete it on time.

A well-known study across functional units of an organization makes this point quite well.[4] Executives from different functional units were asked to analyze the facts about their company and to determine the major problem a new president should address. Sales executives saw sales problems as the greatest. Production executives saw production problems as the greatest. And industrial relations people saw human relations problems as the greatest.

They all had the same facts to study; their organizational roles made the difference.

Finally, the **location of an incident** can influence which phenomena we notice. Wrapping your arm around someone as you walk off the golf course may be interpreted differently than wrapping your arm around a co-worker in the office. Being on time is valued in the United States; it is rude in South America. People will notice different things about you if you are at a formal luncheon than if you are at the company picnic.

relative

Characteristics of the Perceiver

The last element in the selection mechanism is the individual perceiver. Basically, three aspects of the perceiver influence selection: learning, motivation, and personality.

From past experiences we **learn** to expect certain things to go together. For example, when we ask someone "how are you doing?" we expect them to respond, "Fine." But what if they do not? Do we still select to hear "Fine"? This learning serves us well in most cases—without it we would have to start from scratch each time we met someone new or encountered a new situation. It is the basis of attitudes which we formulate to help guide our behavior.

Our **motivation** also plays a role in the phenomena we select to notice. In a given situation involving a superior and a subordinate trying to solve a problem, a superior with a high need for power may attend to different cues from the subordinate than if the superior has a high need for affiliation. If you want to solve a problem, not just get credit for the selected solution, you are more likely to attend to all of the facts than just those that support your situation.

Finally, the **personality** of the perceiver will influence the selection mechanism. Your personality is the total you, involving emotional and cognitive elements. As we will discuss in detail in Chapter 4, some people collect information about their world based on feeling; others depend on thinking. "Feeling" people pay attention to their own and others' feelings; "thinking" people are analytical and focus on facts. Whichever personality type you are will influence your selection mechanism.

As you can see, the selection mechanism is an area where many differences among people can occur. For example, Steve and Louise may have perceived their promotion opportunities differently because of their differences in personality and motivation or because of differences in their two work situations and in what the promotions meant. The selection mechanism is also an area that is very dynamic. At present, you may select a different set of phenomena to focus on than at a previous time or in the future. You may even form different perceptions of the same phenomena on two different days. Perhaps this dynamism will yield a different perception for Louise on her second promotion than on her first. Furthermore, this is only the beginning of the perception process. The next step in our model in Figure 3.2 is the frame of reference filter.

The Frame of Reference Filter

Once our senses have selected particular phenomena, they are processed through our frame of reference (see Figure 3.2). This begins the assignment of meaning to the phenomena. Two aspects of our minds come into play at this point: the rational and analytical aspect, and the feeling and emotional aspect. In essence, the characteristics of the perceiver become predominant in the perception process. A look at the model reveals that this personal filter is composed of two parts: past experiences and present experiencing.

Past Experiences

The knowledge stored in your mind from previous experiences is a sounding board for the phenomena that have entered your system.[5] If you have been in similar situations before, your experience will help you in the present. As we said in Chapter 1, we are all "used products," based on our individual set of past experiences. Furthermore, experiences that occur in our lives during the first three years have a profound effect on our knowledge base.[6] By the age of four, we have developed intellectual abilities that will be used the rest of our lives. We have also developed a base level of trust that underlies our feelings about other people.

Our past experiences have also brought us into contact with various groups of people. Often it appears that all people who belong to a particular group exhibit similar properties. For example, all Southerners are slow moving and laid back; all Northerners are fast moving and curt. This stereotyping is useful in the filtering process, because it helps us draw conclusions more quickly; but as we shall see, it can also lead us to perception errors.

On the more emotional side, past experiences have been associated with particular feelings. When similar experiences are encountered, you will tend to rely upon past feelings to help interpret the phenomena. If, for example, you were once stopped for speeding, and you felt very anxious about the police officer giving you a ticket, the sight of a police officer stopping you again may bring on the same anxiety. But this time, the officer may be stopping you just to say that your rear tire is almost flat.

In short, these past experiences illustrate the developmental aspects of the perception process; the past makes a difference in how you interpret the present and think about the future. But the process is also developmental in that the present experiencing part of the filter allows new things to influence your perception. The present experiencing also modifies the past experiences part of the filter by providing new information.

Present Experiencing

As present phenomena enter your perception process, they bring in new knowledge, new analytical processes, and current feelings. This present experiencing also plays a part in the assignment of meaning to the phenomena entering your system. Perhaps new knowledge tells you that this slow-moving, laid-back Southerner is also very bright and very wealthy, and this alters the pure stereotypical image from your past experiences. If you meet someone from a different background, you may also encounter new ways of analyzing things or new ways of organizing ideas. Of course, encountering situations at different points in your life may encourage you to use different approaches for your analysis. For example, in the case of Louise, her analysis of the promotion to president would probably be different than her previous analysis of the job as national sales vice president. Her present experiencing will be different because of her different stage in life.

In fact, Louise's current feelings are probably different than they were when she joined Home Computers. Her expressed feelings about family have changed since the earlier job decision, and these current feelings will influence her assignment of meaning. As another example, why is it that a man sometimes meets a beautiful woman, feels very little emotional attraction, and simply becomes a friend. The man then meets another woman, feels a strong emotional tug, falls in love, and marries her. The different reactions to similar situations are heavily influenced by the man's current feelings.

The Assignment of Meaning and Behavior

The final step in perception formation (see Figure 3.2) is the assignment of meaning to the external phenomena that have been selected and then processed through the frame of reference filter. This final step is an interaction of characteristics of the perceived person or object, of the situation, and of the perceiver within a dynamic selection mechanism. It is also an interaction involving past experiences and present experiencing in the actual assignment of meaning. The resulting process is very dynamic and developmental. It should be clear that past events in your life will influence your perceptions and that present and anticipated future events will also have an impact. Take a look at *The Wall Street Journal* excerpt in Box 3.2 and see what perceptions you have about unmarried managers. How do your perceptions compare with those expressed in the excerpt? What past experiences help you draw your conclusions?

With your perception of reality now in hand, your behavior follows directly. Your behavior is consistent with your perceptions of the situation and the people involved. Of course, your behavior now becomes an objective phenomenon in the situation as the cycle in Figure 3.2 begins over again. In turn then, your behavior can influence the perceptions you form at a later date. Perhaps you perceive yourself as quite capable of completing a job; but your experience in the job is not good. This tells you that you really are not capable of doing this job,

Box 3.2
Unmarried Managers

Unmarried managers say their status can help—and hurt their careers.

Some executives feel they can get ahead faster in their corporations because they're single. "You can work late" without a spouse angry over "why you aren't coming home," says a New York magazine editor. Korn/Ferry, a recruiter, says many firms prefer to fill international executive spots with single people because of "inordinately" high travel needs. A Harris Corp. finance manager found it easy to move as a single.

But there are drawbacks for the unmarried manager. Some don't want to relocate but feel more pressure to do so than their married peers. And "many people in this company wouldn't hire" singles for management spots, says a divorced Zayre Corp. controller; she says they're older execs who fear distracting office romances.

One New York single executive recalls his transfer of a single woman to his department sparked rumors they were having an affair.

The Wall Street Journal, August 3, 1982. Reprinted by permission of *The Wall Street Journal*, © Dow Jones & Company, Inc. 1982. All rights reserved.

thus altering your original perception. This scenario clearly demonstrates the developmental aspect of the perceptual process. You constantly process new stimuli as they enter your perceptual system; and they alter your past experiences, as well as your behavior. Also, you may become more sophisticated in using your senses, selecting phenomena to attend to, and filtering things through your frame of reference. But you may also decline in your ability to form perceptions by falling into a number of perceptual errors.

Errors in Perception

The perception process we have just described is filled with possibilities for error. Certainly, you have seen some of these possibilities as we have discussed the model in Figure 3.2. In this section we will explore some of these perceptual errors, including stereotyping, halo or horn effect, selective perception, perceptual defense, projection, and the self-fulfilling prophecy) As we do so we will relate them to the various steps in the perception process.

Stereotyping

One of the most common perceptual errors is **stereotyping**. It is the process of (assigning attributes to people on the basis of a category to which they belong) In other words, the person is looked upon as a "type" instead of a person. Think about the perceptions that come to mind when we mention the following categories of people: police officer, business school dean, priest, real estate salesperson, top-level female manager, top-level male manager. Do the attributes you have imagined accurately describe any one person in these categories? No, but (we often use stereotypes, especially when meeting new people) And

Box 3.3
He Works, She Works
But What Different
Impressions They
Make

Have you ever found yourself up against the old double-standard at work? Then you know how annoying it can be and how alone you can feel. Supervisors and co-workers still judge us by old stereotypes that say women are emotional, disorganized, and inefficient. Here are some of the most glaring examples of the typical office double-standard.

The family picture is on HIS desk: Ah, a solid, responsible family man.	The family picture is on HER desk: Hmm, her family will come before her career.
HIS desk is cluttered: He's obviously a hard worker and a busy man.	HER desk is cluttered: She's obviously a disorganized scatterbrain.
HE'S talking with co-workers: He must be discussing the latest deal.	SHE'S talking with co-workers: She must be gossiping.
HE'S not at his desk: He must be at a meeting.	SHE'S not at her desk: She must be in the ladies' room.
HE'S not in the office: He's meeting customers.	SHE'S not in the office: She must be out shopping.

they are useful if we do not depend on them to much. Take a look at Box 3.3 to see if you agree with the stereotypes presented. The use of stereotypes grows primarily out of the knowledge part of our past experiences. They are often based on facts gathered in our past, but they are now being applied to new and different people who may not fit the mold.

A study of business students found that the sex of a manager influenced the perceptions of the effectiveness of the manager's style.[7] Using the same behavior descriptions but varying the sex of the manager, the study found that female managers were perceived as more effective when using an interpersonal style of leadership. Male managers were perceived as more effective when they emphasized task accomplishment.

HE'S having lunch with the boss: He's on his way up.	*SHE'S having lunch with the boss:* They must be having an affair.
The boss criticized HIM: He'll improve his performance.	*The boss criticized HER:* She'll be very upset.
HE got an unfair deal: Did he get angry?	*SHE got an unfair deal:* Did she cry?
HE'S getting married: He'll get more settled.	*SHE'S getting married:* She'll get pregnant and leave.
HE'S having a baby: He'll need a raise.	*SHE'S having a baby:* She'll cost the company money in maternity benefits.
HE'S going on a business trip: It's good for his career.	*SHE'S going on a business trip:* What does her husband say?
HE'S leaving for a better job: He recognizes a good opportunity.	*SHE'S leaving for a better job:* Women are undependable.

Source: From *Paths to Power* by Natasha Josefowitz, © 1980, Addison-Wesley, Reading, Massachusetts. Page 60. Reprinted with permission.

Halo or Horn Effects

The process by which we allow our perception of observed traits to influence our perception of other unobserved traits is called the **halo (or horn) effect.** If the observed traits are positive, we tend to apply a halo (positive) effect to other traits. If the observed traits are negative, we apply a horn (negative) effect. This application of the knowledge part of present experiencing is an efficient way to form an impression of someone, but generalizing from a limited set of information can also lead to errors. The process of **closure** is really what brings about the halo or horn error. We take the limited outline of the person and flesh it out into a total person. For example, if you make a good grade on your first test in this course and the professor assumes you are smart in all your classes, a leader in many situations, and a good tennis player, the professor may be making a halo-effect error. (But then again, maybe he or she is correct.)

Selective Perception

While **selective perception** is a necessary process, as we have discussed, it can also be a perceptual error. And it demonstrates the time dimension of the process. Once we have formed a perception of a person or a situation, we tend to select into our system only external phenomena that support our perception. Box 3.4 on Interior Secretary Watt is a good example of selective perception. Even when he tried to be conciliatory by reversing his position on off shore drilling, California's Governor Brown selected to focus on the things that Mr. Watt had not changed. By so doing, Mr. Brown was able to retain his negative perception of Mr. Watt.

Perceptual Defense

Another closely associated perceptual error is **perceptual defense.** Basically, perceptual defense takes the selected phenomena and alters them to be consistent with our existing perceptions. We do this in order to protect our ego that gets caught up in our perceptions of the world being right. Through the analytical processes part of our present experiencing, stimuli that really say one thing are distorted to mean something else. For example, a man who was competing with Louise for the job of national sales vice president might know that the best-qualified people are promoted in Home Computers; but

Box 3.4
Watt Softens His Line but Image as Extremist Cuts His Effectiveness
His Bid to Seem Conciliatory Only Inflames Foes, Who Include Some Republicans

During his first few months on the job, Interior Secretary James Watt was too busy discarding policies and staff left by the Carter administration to worry about his public image.

"I pledged to lock myself in my office," Mr. Watt recalls, "until I had brought about the policy changes" promised by President Reagan. Through touch management, intimate knowledge of the issues and rigid adherence to ideological principles, the Wyoming conservative hoped to defy critics and single-handedly open more federal lands for energy and mineral development.

Now that self-imposed exile is over. But the strategy has backfired, and Mr. Watt appears stymied in completing many of the changes close to his heart. "When I finally looked up from my work," the Interior chief confided in frustration to a group of newspaper editors last fall, "the hounds were in full cry (and) I was the prey."

Secretary Watt went out of his way to announce that federal offshore oil-and-gas leasing won't be permitted in four controversial Northern California basins. Apparently prompted by stiff opposition from state officials, environmental groups and local GOP leaders, Mr. Watt did an abrupt aboutface and acknowledged that the environmental risks are too great to allow drilling there. "We considered it quite a big step to appease critics," one department official recalls.

But it had just the opposite effect. Environmentalists and Gov. Jerry Brown immediately blasted the decision as a "hoax" and a "hollow concession" because Mr. Watt refused to rule out leasing of nine million additional acres along the central and Northern California coastline. Democratic Rep. Leon Panetta of California charged that the administration was "playing a shell game with the environment and economy" of unspoiled areas. Several Republican politicians fumed that the move reopened the entire issue during an election year.

this might be hard to swallow since Louise is a woman. Hence, the man might distort the facts and believe that Louise was promoted because Harvey wanted to look good from an affirmative action point of view or because of a special relationship between the two of them.

Projection

Another perceptual error is called **projection**. Past knowledge and feelings or current knowledge and feelings sometimes cause us to project onto other people, traits or feelings that are really our own. In other words, we often see others as reflections of ourselves without realizing it. In fact, projection often involves our believing something is true about the other person but not true about us. For example, we may not carry our share of the load in a group project, but we project that another group member is doing even less.

Self-Fulfilling Prophecy

The final perceptual error we will discuss is closely tied in with projection. It also points out the developmental aspects of perception. The **self-fulfilling prophecy** is the process by which our projection or perception of another person actually alters the external phenomena to become consistent with our perception. For example, suppose you are lazy on Friday afternoons, but you project this onto your subordinates. You therefore expect them to be lazy; and you treat them as if they do not want to work. As a result they do not work and therefore appear lazy. As another example, you go to see your professor after taking an exam to discuss a question you do not understand. What you really want is to learn something; you are not concerned with getting a few extra points. The professor, however, has just had a heated discussion with another student about the test and assumes you too will attack it. The professor thus responds to you in a defensive and counterattacking manner and proceeds to make you angry. You begin to fight back, and the professor's perception is confirmed. Here the past experience has influenced the present—and perhaps the future.

The entire perceptual process is one of continuous action and development. The past influences the present; the present influences the future. And behavior that is influenced by perception also influences subsequent perception. Furthermore, as we said earlier, there is no way to avoid the perceptual process and the tendency for the errors associated with it. But you may ask, "Is there any way to improve the perceptual process?"

**Overcoming
Perceptual Errors**

Is there anyone who can tell you what the "objective reality" is? No, but there are several ways to increase the probability that your perceptions approximate reality and are equal to the perceptions of others. First and foremost is to keep in mind the way the perceptual process works. By doing this, you will be aware of the tendency to make perceptual errors. And if you are aware of where errors can enter the process, you can do a better job of minimizing their effect. You will be more open to information which can correct your errors, as the perceptual process develops into the future. Second, communicate with others to compare perceptions and to gain additional information which will improve your perception accuracy. One of the best ways to determine if you have made a perceptual error is to compare your perception with those of several other people. Even though there is no way to know for sure if anyone has the correct perception, you can learn from this comparative process. If everyone agrees, there is a good chance you are correct. But if there is disagreement, communications can help you sort out the differences.

Third, focus on understanding other people's points of view; it may help you know when you are wrong.

"What did you expect a financial wizard to
look like?"

The key here is to understand the other person rather than try to convince him or her you are right. Fourth, be willing to change your perceptions when you encounter new information; it can help you overcome stereotypes, halo/horn effects, and perceptual defenses. Finally, view the world in dynamic terms. Recognize that while a current perception may be correct, phenomena may change to make it incorrect over time. Also, your own behavior can alter the phenomena which are the basis of your perceptions; so notice the impact of your own behavior.

Perception is a vital process in our organizational lives. It plays a key role in forming the basis of our behavior, since it is the vehicle for formulating our view of the world. Perception is also closely associated with the learning process, which is very important for you as a manager to understand. Let us now take a look at learning.

Learning—A Developmental Process

Next to perception, **learning is one of the most important individual processes that occurs in organizations.** Just as perception influences behavior, so does learning. Furthermore, learning and perception are themselves highly interrelated. The model of perception (Figure 3.2) shows how learning through past experiences influences current perceptions; but it also suggests how perception of external phenomena influences new learning. For our purposes, **learning is a relatively permanent change in an attitude or behavior that occurs as a result of repeated experience.**[8] In the following pages we will explore two basic approaches to learning: operant conditioning and cognitive learning.

Operant Conditioning

Operant conditioning is really an extension of classical conditioning, where a connection is made between a stimulus and a response.[9] For example, someone learning to type might be told by the instructor to hit the return key every time the bell rings indicating the end of a line. Eventually, the typist learns to associate the ringing of the bell with the hitting of the return key. Operant conditioning adds the dimension of **reinforcement** associated with the stimulus-response connection. For this reason it is often referred to as reinforcement theory. In the typing example, the typing instructor might say "Good!" when the typist hits the return key after hearing the bell ring, thus reinforcing the appropriate stimulus-response connection.

According to reinforcement theory, learning results from the consequences of previous behavior. When behavior is rewarded, we would expect it to be repeated and eventually learned. If no reward is forthcoming—or if punishment is administered after a behavior—we would expect the behavior not to be repeated. In a work setting, the use of reinforcements can cause the extinguishing of undesirable behavior and the learning of desirable behavior. From a managerial point of view, this type of learning is extremely important. There are several alternative methods of reinforcement. Suppose you have an employee who is absent too much. What can you do? Figure 3.3 illustrates four possible supervisory actions and labels the type of reinforcement applied. While any of the four could be applied, they will not be equally effective, as we shall see.

Figure 3.3
An Example of Reinforcement Theory on the Job

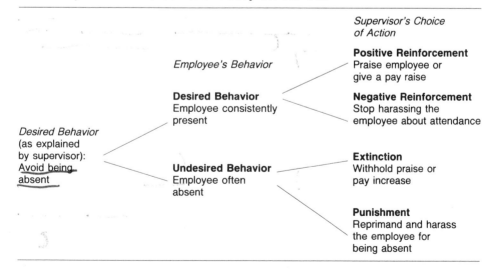

Positive Reinforcement

As the figure shows, **positive reinforcement** is the giving of a valued reward when the employee is consistently present. It is important for you to recognize several important factors about positive reinforcement. First, the employee must value the reward; thus perception plays an important role. If the employee in our example wants more responsibility and a bigger title, the praise and pay increase may not result in learning the desired behavior. Second, the reward must be clearly tied to the desired behavior. There must be little lapse of time between performing the desired behavior and receiving the reward. And the reward will have to be given numerous times for the desired behavior to become the employee's habit. Any manager who thinks that one word of praise for attendance on several consecutive days would correct a long-standing problem of absenteeism is in for a real shock. Time is a critical element in this process—both its length and the proximity of behavior and reward.

Negative Reinforcement

Another form of reinforcement is **negative reinforcement**. In the example, the employee is spared harassment when the desired behavior is performed. In other words, if the employee is absent he or she perhaps loses pay or is reprimanded by the supervisor—when the employee is present, the reprimand or loss of pay is removed. Something negative is taken away, thus reinforcing the desired behavior. The employee learns to avoid unpleasant penalties by doing what the supervisor desires. And the supervisor hopes that the desire to avoid these negative consequences will maintain the employee's behavior—being present every day.

Extinction

Extinction is really the reverse of positive reinforcement. Here the employee is told to be present and what reward to expect if he or she is consistently present. If the employee is absent, the desired reward is withheld until the appropriate behavior is performed. Thus, the undesired behavior of being absent is extinguished. Extinction and positive reinforcement can go together in eliminating undesired behavior and learning desired behavior.

Punishment

Finally, Figure 3.3 shows **punishment** as a way of molding behavior. If the employee is consistently absent, the supervisor (reprimands and harasses the employee.) The idea is that the employee will not be absent in order to avoid the supervisor's punishment. However, if the desired behavior is not just the opposite of the undesired behavior (as being present is of being absent), (punishment may only extinguish the undesired behavior without replacing it with the desired behavior.)

Application of reinforcement theory suggests that the most efficient combination of reinforcers involves extinction and positive reinforcement. Negative reinforcement does not appear to be as powerful as positive reinforcement, and punishment may only deal with half of the problem, as explained above. If you clearly tell employees what is desired and what reward will be given for performing the desired behavior, you can withhold the reward until the desired behavior is performed. This results in extinguishing the undesired behavior (extinction) while simultaneously helping the employee learn the desired behavior with rewards (positive reinforcement). Box 3.5 describes a real application of these ideas in altering behavior at Emery Air Freight. In reading this case, it is important to note that the feedback was self-administered, and that the praise was a simple pat on the back. And if good progress was not reported, there was no punishment—just no praise.

The case also suggests that it is (important to apply reinforcers very soon after the behavior.) In that way, there is (less chance of the employee linking the reinforcer to the wrong behavior.) Furthermore, we see that a particular reinforcer applied indefinitely may start to lose its effectiveness. This suggests that the topic of learning is more complex than a simple stimulus-response connection, as we shall see in the next section on cognitive learning.

Cognitive Learning

Learning involves the total personality, including both reinforcement-type learning and thought processes. The

Box 3.5
The Case of Emery Air
Freight

The program.   Perhaps the most widely known example of the application of behavior modification in industry is that of Emery Air Freight. Under the direction of Edward J. Feeney, Emery selected behavior modification as a simple answer to the persistent problems of inefficiency and low productivity. In an air freight firm, rapid processing of parcels is important to corporate profitability.

Emery Air Freight began with a performance audit which attempted to identify the kind of job behaviors which had the greatest impact on profit and the extent to which these behaviors were shown in the company. One area of special concern was the use of containers. Emery loses money if shipping containers are not fully loaded when shipped. Hence, one goal was to ensure that empty container space was minimized. Before the program was implemented, workers reported that they believed they were filling the containers about 90% of the time. However, the performance audit revealed that this was really so only about 45% of the time. In other words, over half of the containers were shipped unfilled.

The results.   Through the use of feedback (in the form of self-report checklists provided to each worker) and positive reinforcement (praise), the percentage of full containers rose swiftly from 45% to 95%. Cost reductions for the first year alone exceeded $500,000, and rose to $2 million during the first three years. In other words, when workers were given consistent feedback and kept informed of their performance, subsequent output increased rapidly. As a result of this initial success, similar programs were initiated at Emery, including the setting of performance standards for handling customer problems on the telephone and for accurately estimating the container sizes needed for shipment of lightweight packages. Again, positive results were claimed.

The aftermath.   While the use of praise as a reinforcer proved initially to be a successful and inexpensive reinforcer, its effects diminished over time as it became repetitious. As a result, Emery had to seek other reinforcers. These included invitations to business luncheons, formal recognition such as a public letter or a letter home, being given a more enjoyable task after completing a less desirable one, delegating responsibility and decision making, and allowing special time off from the job.

Source: Adapted, by permission of the publisher, from "Behavior Modification on the Bottom Line" by W. C. Hamner and E. P. Hamner, pp. 8–21, *Organizational Dynamics*, Spring 1976 © 1976 by AMACOM, a division of American Management Associations. All rights reserved.

cognitive model suggests that learning occurs by thinking about a situation and by synthesizing facts about it.[10] Such learning is very close to problem solving.

The Kolb Model

While there are numerous cognitive learning models, we will focus on a simple model that summarizes the important elements of learning as a problem-solving approach. David Kolb provides us with this model, which shows learning as a four-stage, cyclical process (see Figure 3.4).[11] Learning can begin with any of the four stages shown in the figure.

One stage in the Kolb model is the **concrete experience**. As we encounter new experiences, we begin the process of learning from those events (much like the process of perception). The experience may then be followed by **observation and reflection**. During this time, we try to make sense of what has happened. Of course, we can also observe and reflect on experiences of other people. This stage then leads into the **formation of abstract concepts and generalizations**. Here we try to compare our current experience to previous experiences, just like the process that occurs in perception. But the focus here is on the modification of those past experiences to take into account the new concrete experience. This stage can also involve the use of written material (for example, books) as a basis

**Figure 3.4
Kolb's Model
of Learning**

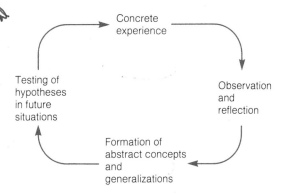

Source: Kolb, D. A., Rubin, Irwin M., and McIntyre, James M., *Organizational Psychology: An Experiential Approach to Organizational Behavior* 4th ed. (Englewood Cliffs, N.J.: Prentice-Hall, 1984), p. 37.

of comparison between theory and our experience. The next stage is the **testing of hypotheses in future situations**, which leads us back to new concrete experiences. Let us make this model more real through an example.

Suppose you go for a job interview and get turned down for the job (concrete experience). In thinking back over your interview you feel that you came on too strong and made too many demands (observation and reflection). So you conclude that to be successful in job interviews you should try to be less aggressive (generalization). On the next job interview you try out this idea (testing hypothesis) as the cycle continues with this new concrete experience.

Several aspects of this model are important to note. First, the model shows learning to be more than a stimulus-response process. Thinking and analysis occur during reflection and generalization, as well as in the testing of hypotheses. Second, the learning cycle is continuous. Previous learning influences current learning; and current learning influences future learning in a developmental process. While we have said that a great deal of base learning occurs before the age of four, important learning does continue throughout life. Certain motor-skill abilities are primarily developed in the earlier years of life; complex cognitive abilities develop during the teenage years. A sense of responsibility for others occurs later, as the individual matures.

In fact, forgetting can also be explained by this model of learning. Forgetting is caused not merely by the passage of time, but rather by the events that occur after the initial learning experience.[12] After the learning cycle is completed, an individual begins a new learning cycle. Perhaps the new learning invalidates the old learning or just consumes the person, thus not allowing practice of the previously learned behavior. If we expect a person not to forget something they have just learned, we as managers must allow them to continue to repeat it, so that forgetting does not occur. It also does not hurt to continue to reward desired behavior. As we discussed earlier, withholding a reward can cause extinction of behavior, which is much like forgetting.

The third point about Kolb's model is that since the learning process is cyclical, it is possible to begin new learning at any stage of the process) For example, one may read about a theory of golf before going out to experiment with a new grip. This means the person enters at the abstract conceptualization stage and then progresses to the testing hypothesis stage. (Where one starts and the direction learning takes depend on the individual's goals and needs as well as on previous learning and the stage that has been rewarded in the past.)

The three preceding points suggest the final point: (learning is a highly individualized process.) It is also a (process that is difficult for others to observe,) since it is an internal process. People have different styles of learning. Think about which of the four styles in Figure 3.5 best describes the way you learn.[13] When you have a feel for your learning style, you will find it interesting to compare with the styles of others. Also, think about how a manager might use this information in understanding and managing his or her subordinates, peers, and superiors. For example, (should a work team have people of similar learning styles, or would it be better to have a variety of styles?) With a very complicated problem to solve, what combination of styles would be most useful? How can you give different training to people with different learning styles?

In closing this chapter, let us repeat that(learning and perception are very important elements of individual behavior for a manager to understand.) Both processes occur continually, and both directly influence behavior. They also influence our abilities to deal with new situations, the formation of attitudes, and ultimately the development of personalities. We will discuss these important individual elements in the next chapter.

Chapter Highlights

This chapter has begun our analysis of individual behavior in organizations. We noted the extreme importance for you as a manager to understand individual behavior. **Primarily the individual interprets external stimuli before behavior follows; therefore the reaction we get from a**

**Figure 3.5
Kolb's Four Basic
Learning Styles**

An **orientation toward concrete experience** focuses on being involved in experiences and dealing with immediate human situations in a personal way. It emphasizes feeling as opposed to thinking, a concern with the uniqueness and complexity of present reality as opposed to theories and generalizations, an intuitive, "artistic" approach as opposed to the systematic, scientific approach to problems. People with a concrete experience orientation enjoy and are good at relating to others. They are often good intuitive decision makers and function well in unstructured situations. People with this orientation value relating to people, being involved in real situations, and having an open-minded approach to life.

An **orientation toward reflective observation** focuses on understanding the meaning of ideas and situations by carefully observing and impartially describing them. It emphasizes understanding as opposed to practical application; a concern with what is true or how things happen as opposed to what is practical; an emphasis on reflection as opposed to action. People with a reflective orientation enjoy thinking about the meaning of situations and ideas and are good at seeing their implications. They are good at looking at things from different perspectives and at appreciating different points of view. They like to rely on their own thoughts and feelings to form opinions. People with this orientation value patience, impartiality, and considered, thoughtful judgment.

An **orientation toward abstract conceptualization** focuses on using logic, ideas, and concepts. It emphasizes thinking as opposed to feeling; a concern with building general theories as opposed to intuitively understanding unique, specific areas; a scientific as opposed to an artistic approach to problems. A person with an abstract conceptual orientation enjoys and is good at systematic planning, manipulation of abstract symbols, and quantitative analysis. People with this orientation value precision, the rigor and discipline of analyzing ideas, and the aesthetic quality of a neat, conceptual system.

An **orientation toward active experimentation** focuses on actively influencing people and changing situations. It emphasizes practical applications as opposed to reflective understanding; a pragmatic concern with what works as opposed to what is absolute truth; an emphasis on doing as opposed to observing. People with an active experimentation orientation enjoy and are good at getting things accomplished. They are willing to take some risk to achieve their objectives. They also value having an impact and influence on the environment around them and like to see results.

Source: Kolb, D. A., Rubin, Irwin M., McIntyre, James. M., *Organizational Psychology: An Experiential Approach to Organizational Behavior* 4th ed. (Englewood Cliffs, NJ: Prentice-Hall, 1984).

subordinate may not be what we expect unless we have some idea of how our behavior toward the subordinate may be interpreted.

Next we explored the process of perception—the vehicle for assigning meaning to external phenomena around us. We pointed out that **there is no way to avoid the perception process and that it is an error-prone process**. Our senses are the initial means by which stimuli enter our individual system. We also select phenomena to focus on, since there are more phenomena out there than we can pay attention to at any point in time. This selection mechanism is influenced by characteristics of the perceived object, person, or problem, the situation, and the perceiver. We pointed out how this selection mechanism is developmental in nature. **It is heavily influenced by time, past experiences, and the behavior that follows perception and then becomes part of the external phenomena.**

The developmental aspects of perception become very clear in the next step in the process—the frame of reference filter. We use past experiences to try to make sense of current experiences. **Knowledge from past experiences, along with analytical processes and feelings formulated in the past are used to allow the past to help you interpret the present.** However, the present experiencing part of this filter allows new phenomena to alter the knowledge, analytical processes, and feelings which have been developed in the past. Hence, the frame of reference is constantly developing and providing new data to be used in assigning meaning to external phenomena.

The final step in the perception process is the assignment of meaning to the external phenomena. This assignment of meaning then relates directly to the individual's behavior. And the behavior is then part of the "objective reality" which will be processed through the perception mechanism for interpretation and influence on subsequent behavior. Thus, even in the short run, perception is a dynamic and developmental process.

We then pointed out a number of common perceptual errors: stereotyping, halo/horn effect, selective perception, perceptual defense, projection, and self fulfilling prophecy. The final points on perception dealt with ways of overcoming such errors. **The basic thrust of these ideas was to be open to new information and to modification** of perceptions, and to actively communicate with others while keeping in mind the perceptual process.

Finally, we discussed the related process of learning. We defined learning as a relatively permanent change in an attitude or behavior that occurs as a result of repeated experience. Our discussion focused first on operant conditioning, especially the reinforcement aspects of this learning model. We defined four forms of reinforcement available to you as a manager and illustrated them in Figure 3.3—namely, positive reinforcement, extinction, negative reinforcement, and punishment. The definition of learning suggests that change over time is a vital aspect of the learning process. And these reinforcers aid in this developmental process.

But there is more to learning than the simple stimulus-response connection of reinforcement theory with people. A person's mind plays a vital role in learning as the cognitive theories of learning point out. We explored the Kolb model of cognitive learning which involves four steps: concrete experience, observation and reflection, abstract conceptualization and generalization, and testing of hypotheses in new situations.

Throughout this discussion of perception and learning, we have tried to make it clear that these are developmental processes. Learning and perception are both continuing cycles of activity, with each new cycle altering us to varying degrees. Especially as we encounter new experiences, our perceptual processes are put to the test, and our frames of reference are altered for the future. As you continue through this book, we hope you will engage in exploration of yourself, allowing your perceptions to be altered and new learning to take place. To be an effective manager, you need to understand yourself both now and as you will change in the future. Without understanding and managing yourself, you cannot hope to successfully understand and manage others.

Review Questions

1. Why do we need to understand individual behavior in organizations?

2. What are the basic elements of individual behavior?

3. Why is the perception process so important for us to understand?

4. How would you describe the process of perception? What are the key elements of the process, and how are they ordered in time?

5. How do the characteristics of the perceived influence the selection mechanism? Which are physical properties and which are dynamic properties?

6. How do the characteristics of the situation and the perceiver influence the selection mechanism?

7. Focusing on the frame of reference part of the perception process, can you explain why perception is a developmental process? How is the frame of reference developmental?

8. How do errors creep into the perception process? How can one overcome these perception errors?

9. What is learning? Why is the process of learning so important for managers to understand?

10. Explain reinforcement theory and the four types of reinforcers. Which ones work best in which kinds of situations?

11. Explain Kolb's model of learning. How does it differ from the operant conditioning model of learning?

Notes

1. S. Asch,"Forming Impressions of Persons," *Journal of Abnormal and Social Psychology* 40 (1946), pp. 258–90; R. H. Forgus, *Perception* (New York: McGraw-Hill, 1966), pp. 1–6.

2. D. Krech, R. Crutchfield, and E. Balachey, *Individual and Society* (New York: McGraw-Hill,1962), pp. 20–34.

3. S. S. Zalkind and T. W. Costello, "Perception: Some Recent Research and Implications for Administration," *Administrative Science Quarterly*, 9 (1962), pp. 218–35.

4. D. C. Dearborn and H. A. Simon, "Selective Perception: A Note on Departmental Identification of Executives," *Sociometry* 21 (1958), pp. 140–44.

5. H. Helson, *Adaptation Level Theory* (New York: Harper & Row, 1964).

6. B. L. White, *The First Three Years of Life* (New York: Avon Books, 1975).

7. K. M. Bartol and D. A. Butterfield, "Sex Effects in Evaluating Leaders," *Journal of Applied Psychology*, 61 (1976), pp. 446–54.

8. G. A. Kimble and N. Garmezy, *Principles of General Psychology* (New York: Ronald Press, 1963).

9. B. F. Skinner, "Operant Behavior," *American Psychologist*, 18 (1963), pp. 503–15.

10. P. G. Zimbardo and F. L. Ruch, *Psychology and Life* (Glenview, Ill.: Scott, Foresman, 1975), pp. 109–11.

11. D. A. Kolb, I. M. Rubin, and J. M. McIntyre, *Organizational Psychology: An Experiential Approach*, 3d ed. (Englewood Cliffs, N.J.: Prentice-Hall, 1979), pp. 37–42.

12. M. Manis, *Cognitive Processes* (Monterey, Calif: Brooks/Cole Publishing, 1966), pp. 18–24.

13. A questionnaire to measure your learning style is available for purchase from McBer and Company in Boston, Massachusetts.

Resource Readings

Adams, J. S. *Learning and Memory*. Homewood, Ill.: Dorsey Press, 1976.

Forgus, R. H. *Perception*. New York: McGraw-Hill, 1966.

Klein, G. S. *Perception, Motives, and Personality*. New York: Alfred A. Knopf, 1970.

Zimbardo, P. G. and F. L. Ruch. *Psychology and Life*. Glenview, Ill.: Scott, Foresman, 1975.

C H A P T E R   4

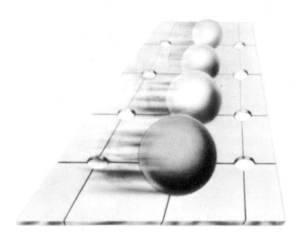

The Developmental Aspects of Attitudes and Personality

In Chapter 3, we looked at the processes of perception and learning as fundamental to the understanding of people as dynamic beings. In this chapter we will explore attitudes that people formulate as guides to their behavior. We will also discuss personality as a means of gaining an appreciation of the person as a whole. Personality will be our vehicle to integrate learning, perception, and attitudes. And as such, personality will prove important to you as a manager in understanding and managing people in organizations. Finally, we will look carefully at the interaction between the person and the organization, examining the socialization process and the effects of stress. In so doing, we will gain a better appreciation of how to manage these factors that influence ourselves and our employees. We will also prepare for the study of motivation in Chapters 5 and 6.

Attitude Formation

As a way to begin understanding personality, let us look at the formation of attitudes. First of all, attitudes, beliefs, and values are closely associated concepts. **Attitudes are opinions about things or people;** that is, they represent **our likes and dislikes. Beliefs are perceptions that a relationship exists between two things. And values are basic and pervasive standards by which we evaluate end-states of existence and modes of conduct.**[1] An example will help illustrate these points: We may **have a value** that says we should work hard at our job—the work ethic. We may believe that doing a good job at work will result in a promotion (belief). And we may experience a great deal of job satisfaction; that is, we like what we do (attitude).

From this example, you can see how closely values, beliefs, and attitudes are associated. Values and beliefs form the basis for our attitudes. But what may not be so apparent **is that values, beliefs, and attitudes are learned. Most behavioral scientists agree that we are not born with attitudes, beliefs, and values—we acquire them through life experiences.** In particular, many of our basic attitudes are formed during our early years of life. Research by Erik Erikson suggests that a basic life attitude of trust or mistrust occurs during infancy. If a child's basic needs are met in a loving manner, he or she will develop a sense of trust toward the world. In the reverse situation, a sense of mistrust develops. In early childhood (one to two years), the child also develops either a sense of autonomy or one of shame and doubt. Of course, personal development continues throughout life, but basic attitudes are strongly grounded in the early years.[3]

Later in this chapter we will explore Erikson's work in more detail. For now, let us see how attitudes are formulated and changed over time and how they affect behavior. In discussing perception and learning, we said that stereotypes are very important. Stereotypes are an example of attitudes and beliefs. And as you may recall from Chapter 3, stereotypes grow out of the past experiences part of our frame of reference. We develop stereotypes and other attitudes about a person or situation in three ways: (1) direct experience with the person or situation, (2) association with other similar persons or situations, and (3) learning from others about their association with the person or situation. These ways of formulating attitudes are styles of learning, according to the Kolb model of learning (discussed in Chapter 3). **Direct experience** is the concrete experience stage of learning. **Association** is similar to abstract conceptualization and generalization. And **learning from others** is like reflection and observation. Hence, we can see that attitudes are an extension of the learning and perception processes. Through the perception process, we learn about the world around us. We also formulate attitudes to help us interpret that world. Thus, attitudes both derive from and affect learning and perception. In addition, these individual aspects all affect a person's behavior. These points are summarized in Figure 4.1.

This linkage to behavior is what we as managers are concerned with—it is the behavior of our people that determines our paycheck, promotions, and so forth. By knowing how perception, learning, and attitudes affect behavior, you will be in a better position to be an effective manager. And by understanding how behavior affects attitudes, you will better understand the developmental processes that occur in your people. We can illustrate these

Figure 4.1
The Interrelationships of Perception, Learning and Attitudes and Their Impact on Behavior

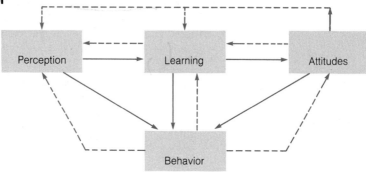

Note: Dashed lines indicate a recycling to begin the process again, as well as a feedback process.

points by discussing an extremely important attitude in the work place—job satisfaction.

Job Satisfaction

Job satisfaction (or dissatisfaction) is the set of attitudes we develop about our work. It reflects the fit between person and job, and has been considered very important by managers and researchers alike. Over the years, many studies have explored the relationship between job satisfaction and such variables as absenteeism, tardiness, turnover, physical and mental health, and productivity. For example, one review of these studies showed that dissatisfied workers are more likely to be absent or tardy. They are also more likely to quit a job.[4] A study of autoworkers found a positive relationship between job satisfaction and overall mental health.[5] Another study found work satisfaction to be the best predictor of longevity.[6] Thus, it is clear that the attitude of job satisfaction affects behavior on the job.

The relationship between job satisfaction and productivity has been elusive. One author has argued that there is no good reason for a direct relationship between these two variables; rather the perceived equity of rewards received alters the relationship between satisfaction and productivity.[7] But whether or not job satisfaction and performance are related, the point is that attitudes do have an effect on behavior.

It is also clear that an attitude (such as job satisfaction) is formed from a person's experiences on the job. In other words, job satisfaction is developed through our perceptual and learning processes. But **once formulated attitudes can be difficult to change.** As we discussed in Chapter 3, perceptual defenses can distort information which might lead to a change in attitudes. Box 4.1 provides an illustration of how this inertia of attitudes may hinder women in management.

As another example, a child's early trust and sense of autonomy tend to remain throughout life. And the job satisfaction experienced on one job will affect one's attitude toward a subsequent job. Thus, as the develop-

**Box 4.1
Series on Working
Women**

Women still climb the corporate ladder more slowly and for less money than men. Salary statistics tell part of the story: Only 0.8 percent of full-time working women earn $25,000, compared to 12 percent of such men.

A Harvard Business Review survey of 2,000 executives done 17 years ago tells another part—one most male managers are now reluctant to openly admit. Of those surveyed, 51 percent of the men believed women were "temperamentally unfit for management."

A LOUIS HARRIS POLL of corporate officials for Business Week magazine found that 41 percent of the executives surveyed felt it had been harder to promote women to high-level positions than they had thought it would be. The same percentage agreed that men don't like to take orders from women.

As a result, women tend to feel they have to try harder.

Connie Greaser found herself handling a multimillion dollar budget for the first time when she joined the Rand Corp. as the head of publications more than 10 years ago. She was the only woman in the boardroom: "I was afraid to ask for help. I thought I had to know all the answers myself.

"Women can't afford to make the mistakes men do. You're so visible, they remember whatever you do."

mental perspective would suggest, past formulation of attitudes influences current learning and perception, and hence behavior and new attitudes. Furthermore, recognition of the inertia of attitudes moves us one step closer to a discussion of personality. But first, let us drop in on Steve, the husband of Louise of Home Computers.

Steve, Louise, and Home Computers

Steve worked for the same large computer company that Louise did originally. Steve had received a degree in computer science at his state's major university. He came from a very strict family. His parents were always on him to do better work in school. And his professors in college figured Steve to be a bright student, but without much drive and ambition. His personal attitude and self-concept was one of self-doubt when it came to the big challenges in life. In fact, Louise proposed marriage to Steve rather than the reverse.

Steve's first job was as a programmer with very little responsibility. While on this job he completed a self-assessment questionnaire for the personnel office, which was standard practice in the company. As a way to identify talent and determine the proper channel of training and experience, the company gave each new employee a personality questionnaire. On this questionnaire, Steve was identified as an introvert, a thinking type, a sensing type, and a judging type. Louise, on the other hand was identified as an extrovert, a thinking type, an intuitive type, and a perceptive type.

The personnel department knew that Steve and Louise represented different personality types. But since the test results were not adequately explained to Louise and Steve, they did not think about them very long. Still, their personalities were different as a result of their unique past experiences.

Louise was the first child in her family, and she received a great deal of support and love in her early years. She was encouraged to experiment within clearly defined limits and her many successes were rewarded. In school she also encountered a great deal of success and gained a strong sense of identity. When she went to college it was a first-rate school several hundred miles from home.

In contrast, Steve was the second child. His older brother had a learning disability that required a great deal of his parents' attention. Steve received varying degrees of guidance. And he was sometimes made to feel guilty for his brother's disability. Steve learned to doubt himself and lack self-confidence. In school, he encountered numerous social and scholastic problems, though none were of a serious nature. Steve went to college at the State university in his hometown. Fortunately, the school had an excellent computer science program. Because he did well in his courses and seemed to gain in self-confidence, one of his professors recommended him for a job with a large computer company in nearby Phoenix.

Steve did a good job for the company, but he had trouble making friends at work. He had been working there for five years when Louise moved out from New York. The relationship between Steve and Louise was good for Steve. It began to change his attitude from one of distrust of people to one of trust. Steve gradually developed a capability both for achievement and for intimacy. After he and Louise were married and had two children, Steve was offered the chance for a better job in Washington, D.C. It was not without a great deal of thought and discussion that he accepted the transfer. His attitude toward himself had grown to be one of respect, and he had developed a desire to succeed in his career. During this same period, in his 20s and 30s, Steve also developed a sense of family and an attitude of wanting more than just a career.

On the other hand, Louise seemed to put her career before everything. She was very capable and jumped at chances to advance her career. Steve seemed to reflect more on his total life with his career only a part of it. But Louise is now having some doubts about where her life is headed. Is her personality gradually changing? Is Steve's? The work, family, and life stage forces operating now might result in a different score on the personality tests Steve and Louise took back in the early 60s.

Personality: The Total Person

We can use the concept of personality to better understand Louise and Steve as total people. As we have said, personality is a vehicle to integrate perception, learning, and attitudes and thus to understand the total person. **Personality is an individual's total awareness of self; it is an organizing force for the person's particular pattern of exhibited traits and behaviors.**[8] In essence, personality is the culmination to date of your experiences and genetic influences. As such, it is a dynamic construct which can be influenced by the organization through things like socialization and the stresses that you undergo. That is not to say, however, that personality is constantly flip-flopping from one type to another. The process of personality change is more evolutionary in nature. As with attitudes a certain level of inertia is present.

Aspects of Personality

At this point, it is important to explore several aspects of personality. **First, our personalities are based on the past and the present, since personality is largely determined through the processes of perception and learning. Second, personality is a result of growth and development.** Each of us is goal oriented and is striving to live up to our capabilities. **Third, although personality is dynamic, it is characterized by internal consistency in our behaviors.** That is, we attempt to engage in actions which are compatible with our other actions, and this consistency makes sense, given that personality is a total construct of the person.

In addition there are several factors that influence the evolution of personality: group experiences, group roles, situations, physical properties, and mental abilities. These factors are shown in Figure 4.2 and discussed below.

Physical properties and mental abilities are important determinants in that they reflect our capabilities. For example, if you are very intelligent, you may develop a different self concept of your achievement potential than someone who is less intelligent. But we know that mental abilities vary with age. They increase rapidly until about age 20; and they tend to continue increasing, though more gradually, as one's age increases.[9]

**Figure 4.2
Determinants of
Personality**

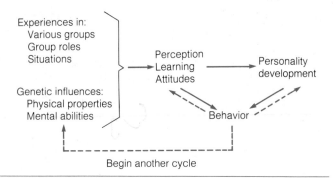

Of course, accidents and illness can cause rather dramatic changes in mental abilities (and thus in personality).

A second factor affecting the formation and evolution of personality is membership in various groups. As we are exposed to a new group situation, we go through a socialization process, that helps us fit into the group. And since we are members of different groups over time, our personalities are altered over time. Closely connected with group membership is the role we fill in each group. People fill different roles in different groups. For example, Louise and Steve fill different roles at work than they do at home. Both sets of roles, and the interaction between the roles and the people involved, help determine Louise's and Steve's personalities.

Finally, the situations to which we are exposed influence our personalities. We have already noted how the love and affection we receive during the first year of life heavily influence our basic trust of people. These situational influences continue throughout all of life. Probably one of the most dramatic examples of situational influences on personality occurs when we are placed in stressful situations. For example, the death of a loved one, getting married or divorced, the birth of a child, losing one's job, and so forth all are stressful situations that may result in changes in our personalities.

Development of Personality: Erikson's Eight Life Stages

As a way of further understanding how personalities develop over a lifetime, let us turn to Erikson's life stages. Erikson identified eight stages of life that characterize the unending development of a person.[10] He characterized each stage by a particular conflict that needs to be resolved successfully before one can move to the next stage. However, these eight stage are not totally separate; and the crises are never fully resolved. Thus, the movement is developmental. It can even involve regression to earlier stages when traumatic events occur. Let us briefly consider each of the eight stages.

Stage One: Infancy.   During the first year of life one resolves the basic crisis of **trust versus mistrust.** An infant who is cared for in a loving and affectionate way learns to trust other people. Lack of love and affection results in mistrust. While neither result is carved in stone, this first year makes a serious imprint on a child that influences events for the remainder of life.

Stage Two: Early Childhood.   In the second and third years of life a child begins to assert independence. If the child is allowed to control those aspects of life that the child can control a sense of **autonomy** will develop. If the child encounters constant disapproval or inconsistent rule setting, a sense of **self-doubt and shame** is likely to develop.

Stage Three: Play Age.   The four- and five-year-old seeks to discover just how much he or she can do. If the child is encouraged to experiment and to achieve reasonable goals, he or she will develop a sense of **initiative.** If the child is blocked and made to feel incapable, he or she will develop a sense of **guilt and lack of self-confidence.** As Erikson points out, these first three stages are the most important crises a child must successfully resolve. Without such resolution, the child will not be prepared to face the future problems of development. And adults who have never resolved these issues must be managed differently from those who have resolved them. You can imagine managing someone who lacks trust, autonomy, and initiative compared to someone who has these qualities. It would be quite different.

Stage Four: School Age.   From ages 6 to 12, a child learns many new skills and develops social abilities. If a child experiences real progress at a rate compatible with his or her abilities, the child will develop a sense of **industry.** The reverse situation results in a sense of **inferiority.**

Stage Five: Adolescence.   The crisis of the teenage years is to gain a sense of **identity** rather than to become **confused** about who you are. While undergoing rapid biological changes, the teenager is also trying to establish himself or herself as socially separate from the parents. The teenager, as you may recall from Chapter 2, is also beginning the exploration stage of a career. Many events unfold simultaneously during these years. The autonomy, initiative, and industry developed in earlier stages are very important in assisting the individual in successful resolution of this crisis and preparation for adulthood. From the facts presented in the case of Steve and Louise, we can imagine that Steve's sense of identity was not as clear and positive as Louise's as they entered adulthood.

Stage Six: Young Adulthood.   The young adult (20s and 30s) faces the crisis of **intimacy versus isolation.** The sense of identity developed during the teenage years allows the young adult to begin developing deep and lasting relationships. Simultaneously, though, the young adult is establishing himself or herself in a career and beginning advancement (as we discussed in Chapter 2). Thus, it is easy for one's achievement orientation to overshadow the need for people and intimate relationships—resulting in isolation. In our case, we saw how Steve learned intimacy from Louise and how Louise's ability for intimacy may be influenced by her career drives. Certainly, she faces a choice between the two.

Stage Seven: Adulthood.   During the 40s and 50s, adults face the crisis of **generativity versus self-absorption.** Self-absorbed persons never develop an ability to look beyond themselves. They may become absorbed in career advancement and maintenance; and they may never learn to have concern for future generations, the welfare of organizations to which they belong, or the welfare of society as a whole. Generative people see the world as much bigger than themselves. Productivity in work or child rearing or societal advancement become important to them. Through innovation and creativity, they begin to exert influence that benefits their organization. In the Home Computers case, it appears that Steve is developing this sense of generativity. The issue is still open for Louise.

Stage Eight: Later Life.   In the 60s and beyond, people who have followed a healthy development of personality in previous stages reach a level of **integrity,** while the alternative is **disgust with one's life.** The adult of integrity has gained a sense of wisdom and perspective that can truly help guide future generations. The career stage of influence and the innovative and creative influence on organizations to which the person belongs go along with the adult of integrity.

⟨The stages of life and the corresponding development of personality are intertwined with the stages of one's career and the stages of family life.⟩All of these influences help determine and alter our personalities.⟩Box 4.2 describes the changes in one woman's life that may have a bearing on her personality. Do you think Mrs. Kurtzig's personality is different now than before ASK Computer Systems, Inc.?

To gain a perspective on your personality in its current form, let us explore Jung's Personality Theory and its four dimensions. If you will take the time to seriously consider yourself in relation to each dimension, you will be able to learn some interesting things about yourself. Also, think about what your personality might suggest to someone managing you. What should they do to best use you as you are? Could you use this information to help with career decisions you will face?

Box 4.2
More Women Start up
Their Own Businesses,
with Major Successes

Los Altos, Calif.—When Sandra Kurtzig went into business for herself 10 years ago, she operated out of a room in her home and stashed all her business funds in a shoe box. If there was more money in the shoe box at the end of the month than the beginning, her company made a profit.

"I had no management experience," she recalls. "My long-range plans were figuring out where to go for lunch." Her business was simple enough.⟨ She developed computer software that let weekly newspapers keep track of their newspaper carriers.⟩

These days Mrs. Kurtzig has more complicated matters on her mind. Her little business, named ASK Computer Systems Inc., has grown to $22 million a year in sales, 200 employees, $2.3 million of profits and a reputation as one of the most successful computer software companies around. Sandra Kurtzig, founder and president, owns $66.9 million of ASK stock.

Success stories like this still happen, especially in the computer business and in places like here in the Silicon Valley.

By Earl C. Gottschalk Jr., *The Wall Street Journal*, May 17, 1983. Reprinted by permission of *The Wall Street Journal*, © Dow Jones & Company, Inc. 1983. All rights reserved.

Jung's Personality Theory

The theory of personality we will discuss is based upon the work of Carl Jung.[11] In the following pages, we will discuss the four basic dimensions of the model in more detail. However, let us first mention three basic assumptions made by Jung.

First, Jung asserted that our personalities are developmental in that they are influenced by our past and by our hopes for the future. Second, he viewed people optimistically in assuming that all people have the potential for growth and change. And third, Jung suggested that personality is the totality of a person's interacting subsystems. In particular, he discussed the conscious mind, the subconscious mind, emotional orientations, problem-solving styles, and general attitudes. Let us now discuss the last three subsystems since they can help you determine your personality along four dimensions.

Emotional Orientations

The two basic orientations of people are extroversion and introversion. While few people are purely one or the other, one orientation will tend to be dominant. Figure 4.3 indicates that **introverts are quiet people who like to work alone and stay to themselves. On the other hand, extroverts like action and interaction with people. They do not mind interruptions and they communicate freely.** Based on these definitions, are you an introvert or an extrovert? It is important to point out that neither orientation is "best." Each has its strengths and weaknesses. The point is to gain an understanding of yourself and to learn how understanding others can make you a better manager. For example, you can easily imagine how you might have to draw out an introverted person, while quieting down an extroverted employee.

Problem-Solving Styles

Jung identified two basic steps in problem solving: collecting information and making a decision. Collecting data for problem solving occurs along a continuum from **sensing to intuition.** Figure 4.4 gives details of these two extremes. Are you mainly a sensing or an intuitive type? As the figure indicates, **sensing types like to approach a problem in a step-by-step organized way. They work**

Figure 4.3
Extroverts versus Introverts: Characteristics of Each

Extroverts	Introverts
Like variety and action.	Like quiet for concentration.
Tend to be faster, dislike complicated procedures.	Tend to be careful with details, dislike sweeping statements.
Are often good at greeting people.	Have trouble remembering names and faces.
Are often impatient with long slow jobs.	Tend not to mind working on one project for a long time uninterruptedly.
Are interested in the results of their job, in getting it done and in how other people do it.	Are interested in the idea behind their job.
Often do not mind the interruption of answering the telephone.	Dislike telephone intrusions and interruptions.
Often act quickly, sometimes without thinking.	Like to think a lot before they act, sometimes without acting.
Like to have people around.	Work contentedly alone.
Usually communicate freely.	Have some problems communicating.

Source: Reproduced by special permission of the Publisher, Consulting Psychologists Press, Inc., Palo Alto, CA 94306, from *Introduction to Type* by Isabel Briggs Myers. Copyright 1980. Further reproduction is prohibited without the Publisher's consent.

Figure 4.4
Sensing Types versus Intuitive Types: Characteristics of Each

Sensing Types	Intuitive Types
Dislike new problems unless there are standard ways to solve them.	Like solving new problems.
Like an established way of doing things.	Dislike doing the same thing repeatedly.
Enjoy using skills already learned more than learning new ones.	Enjoy learning a new skill more than using it.
Work more steadily, with realistic idea of how long it will take.	Work in bursts of energy powered by enthusiasm, with slack periods in between.
Usually reach a conclusion step by step.	Reach a conclusion quickly.
Are patient with routine details.	Are impatient with routine details.
Are impatient when the details get complicated.	Are patient with complicated situations.
Are not often inspired, and rarely trust the inspiration when they are.	Follow their inspirations, good or bad.
Seldom make errors of fact.	Frequently make errors of fact.
Tend to be good at precise work.	Dislike taking time for precision.

Source: Reproduced by special permission of the Publisher, Consulting Psychologists Press, Inc., Palo Alto, CA 94306, from *Introduction to Type* by Isabel Briggs Myers. Copyright 1980. Further reproduction is prohibited without the Publisher's consent.

steadily and patiently with details. Intuitive types work in bursts and are impatient with details. However, they can be very patient with complicated situations.

Which type is best? Neither; the world needs both. Intuitives need sensing types to bring up facts, attend to details, and maintain a sense of realism. Sensing types need intuitives to bring up new possibilities, have enthusiasm, and tackle difficulties with zest. Which type would you want to prepare your income tax statement? What about to do a painting for your home?

In terms of making a decision, the continuum ranges from **thinking** to **feeling** types. Figure 4.5 describes **the thinking type as one who does not show a lot of emotion, who can put things into a logical order, and who can be firm and fair.** The feeling type is very aware of other people, dislikes telling people unpleasant things, and prefers harmony among people. Which type are you?

As with the sensing and intuitive types, the thinking and feeling types each have strengths and weaknesses. Feeling types need thinkers to analyze, organize, and help make the tough decisions. On the other hand, thinkers need feeling types to conciliate, sell, and be aware of

---

Figure 4.5
Thinking Types versus Feeling Types: Characteristics of Each

Thinking Types	Feeling Types
Do not show emotion readily and are often uncomfortable dealing with people's feelings.	Tend to be very aware of other people and their feelings.
May hurt people's feelings without knowing it.	Enjoy pleasing people, even in unimportant things.
Like analysis and putting things into logical order. Can get along without harmony.	Like harmony. Efficiency may be badly disturbed by office feuds.
Tend to decide impersonally, sometimes paying insufficient attention to people's wishes.	Often let decisions be influenced by their own or other people's personal likes and wishes.
Need to be treated fairly.	Need occasional praise.
Are able to reprimand people or fire them when necessary.	Dislike telling people unpleasant things.
Are more analytically oriented—respond more easily to people's thoughts.	Are more people-oriented—respond more easily to people's values.
Tend to be firm-minded.	Tend to be sympathetic.

how others might accept the decision. I recently saw a good example of how these types can complement each other. My father was having an operation by a very well-respected and competent surgeon. He had to do a very thorough analysis and make the tough decisions about the surgery (thinking type). But he was not very personable. To compensate, he had an assistant who met with our family to deal with our concerns and emotions (feeling type). They made a very good team.

The interaction of these two aspects of problem solving results in four problem-solving types. (1) The **sensing-feeling person** likes to collect data in an orderly way and make decisions that take into account the needs of people. They are very concerned with high quality decisions that people will accept and implement. (2) The **intuitive-feeling person** is equally concerned with the people side of decisions, but the focus is on new ideas which are often broad in scope and lacking in details. (3) **Sensation-thinkers** emphasize details and the quality of a decision; they are not as concerned with the people aspect of the organization as with a technically sound decision. And (4) **intuitive-thinking types** like to tackle new and innovative problems, but make decisions primarily on technical terms. They tend to be good planners but not so good at implementing.

While few people are any of these pure types, we all have dominant styles. You need to recognize the strengths and weaknesses of your dominant style and what you can do to compensate for your weaknesses (as in the example of the surgeon). What is your dominant problem-solving style? What are the dominant styles of people with whom you work?

General Attitudes

The last personality subsystem Jung identified was the general attitude toward work, namely **judging** or **perceptive. As Figure 4.6 shows, judging types like to follow a plan, to get things settled, and want only the essentials for their work. On the other hand, the perceptive type adapts well to change, wants to know all about a job, and may get overcommitted.** Which type are you?

The interaction of these four dimensions yields a dominant personality type for you—1 of 16 personality types.

Figure 4.6
Judging Types versus Perceptive Types: Characteristics of Each

Judging Types	*Perceptive Types*
Work best when they can plan their work and follow the plan.	Adapt well to changing situations.
Like to get things settled and finished.	Do not mind leaving things open for alterations.
May decide things too quickly.	May have trouble making decisions.
May dislike to interrupt the project they are on for a more urgent one.	May start too many projects and have difficulty in finishing them.
May not notice new things that need to be done.	May postpone unpleasant jobs.
Want only the essentials needed to begin their work.	Want to know all about a new job.
Tend to be satisfied once they reach a judgment on a thing, situation, or person.	Tend to be curious and welcome new light on a thing, situation, or person.

Source: Reproduced by special permission of the Publisher, Consulting Psychologists Press, Inc., Palo Alto, CA 94306, from *Introduction to Type* by Isabel Briggs Myers. Copyright 1980. Further reproduction is prohibited without the Publisher's consent.

Based on your assessments of each of the four dimensions shown in Figures 4.3–4.6, you can locate your personality type in Figure 4.7.

I = introvert	S = sensing
E = extrovert	N = intuitive
(from Figure 4.3)	(from Figure 4.4)

T = thinking	J = judging
F = feeling	P = perceptive
(from Figure 4.5)	(from Figure 4.6)

You should be able to select four of the eight letters to describe yourself; for example, ISTP or ENFJ. Then, in Figure 4.7 locate your four-letter combination to find your personality type and read the description.

It is important to recognize that each dimension of personality is a continuum, and the figures help identify only your dominant style. It is also important to recognize that this is a snapshot of your personality. Various factors in your life can cause evolution of your personality, and we will discuss some of these shortly. But first, let us see the personality types of Steve and Louise.

Figure 4.7 Sixteen Personality Types Based on Jung's Four Dimensions

	Sensing Types	
	With Thinking	*With Feeling*

ISTJ

Serious, quiet, earn success by concentration and thoroughness. Practical, orderly, matter-of-fact, logical, realistic and dependable. See to it that everything is well organized. Take responsibility. Make up their own minds as to what should be accomplished and work toward it steadily, regardless of protests or distractions.

Live their outer life more with thinking, inner more with sensing.

ISFJ

Quiet, friendly, responsible and conscientious. Work devotedly to meet their obligations and serve their friends and school. Thorough, painstaking, accurate. May need time to master technical subjects, as their interests are not often technical. Patient with detail and routine. Loyal, considerate, concerned with how other people feel.

Live their outer life more with feeling, inner more with sensing.

ISTP

Cool onlookers, quiet, reserved, observing and analyzing life with detached curiosity and unexpected flashes of original humor. Usually interested in impersonal principles, cause and effect, or how and why mechanical things work. Exert themselves no more than they think necessary, because any waste of energy would be inefficient.

Live their outer life more with sensing, inner more with thinking.

ISFP

Retiring, quietly friendly, sensitive, modest about their abilities. Shun disagreements, do not force their opinions or values on others. Usually do not care to lead but are often loyal followers. May be rather relaxed about assignments or getting things done, because they enjoy the present moment and do not want to spoil it by undue haste or exertion.

Live their outer life more with sensing, inner more with feeling.

ESTP

Matter-of-fact, do not worry or hurry, enjoy whatever comes along. Tend to like mechanical things and sports, with friends on the side. May be a bit blunt or insensitive. Can do math or science when they see the need. Dislike long explanations. Are best with real things that can be worked, handled, taken apart or put back together.

Live their outer life more with sensing, inner more with thinking.

ESFP

Outgoing, easygoing, accepting, friendly, fond of a good time. Like sports and making things. Know what's going on and join in eagerly. Find remembering facts easier than mastering theories. Are best in situations that need sound common sense and practical ability with people as well as with things.

Live their outer life more with sensing, inner more with feeling.

ESTJ

Practical realists, matter-of-fact, with a natural head for business or mechanics. Not interested in subjects they see no use for, but can apply themselves when necessary. Like to organize and run activities. Tend to run things well, especially if they remember to consider other people's feelings and points of view when making their decisions.

Live their outer life more with thinking, inner more with sensing.

ESFJ

Warm-hearted, talkative, popular, conscientious, born cooperators, active committee members. Always doing something nice for someone. Work best with plenty of encouragement and praise. Little interest in abstract thinking or technical subjects. Main interest is in things that directly and visibly affect people's lives.

Live their outer life more with feeling, inner more with sensing.

Introverts — Judging

Introverts — Perceptive

Extroverts — Perceptive

Extroverts — Judging

INTJ

Have original minds and great drive which they use only for their own purposes. In fields that appeal to them they have a fine power to organize a job and carry it through with or without help. Skeptical, critical, independent, determined, often stubborn. Must learn to yield less important points in order to win the most important.

Live their outer life more with thinking, inner more with intuition.

INTP

Quiet, reserved, brilliant in exams, especially in theoretical or scientific subjects. Logical to the point of hair-splitting. Interested mainly in ideas, with little liking for parties or small talk. Tend to have very sharply defined interests. Need to choose careers where some strong interest of theirs can be used and useful.

Live their outer life more with intuition, inner more with thinking.

ENTP

Quick, ingenious, good at many things. Stimulating company, alert and outspoken, argue for fun on either side of a question. Resourceful in solving new and challenging problems, but may neglect routine assignments. Turn to one new interest after another. Can always find logical reasons for whatever they want.

Live their outer life more with intuition, inner more with thinking.

ENTJ

Hearty, frank, able in studies, leaders in activities. Usually good in anything that requires reasoning and intelligent talk, such as public speaking. Are well-informed and keep adding to their fund of knowledge. May sometimes be more positive and confident than their experience in an area warrants.

Live their outer life more with thinking, inner more with intuition.

INFJ

Succeed by perseverance, originality and desire to do whatever is needed or wanted. Put their best efforts into their work. Quietly forceful, conscientious, concerned for others. Respected for their firm principles. Likely to be honored and followed for their clear convictions as to how best to serve the common good.

Live their outer life more with feeling, inner more with intuition.

INFP

Full of enthusiasms and loyalties, but seldom talk of these until they know you well. Care about learning, ideas, language, and independent projects of their own. Apt to be on yearbook staff, perhaps as editor. Tend to undertake too much, then somehow get it done. Friendly, but often too absorbed in what they are doing to be sociable or notice much.

Live their outer life more with intuition, inner more with feeling.

ENFP

Warmly enthusiastic, high-spirited, ingenious, imaginative. Able to do almost anything that interests them. Quick with a solution for any difficulty and ready to help anyone with a problem. Often rely on their ability to improvise instead of preparing in advance. Can always find compelling reasons for whatever they want.

Live their outer life more with intuition, inner more with feeling.

ENFJ

Responsive and responsible. Feel real concern for what others think and want, and try to handle things with due regard for other people's feelings. Can present a proposal or lead a group discussion with ease and tact. Sociable, popular, active in school affairs, but put time enough on their studies to do good work.

Live their outer life more with feeling, inner more with intuition.

Introverts   — Judging / Perceptive

Extroverts   — Perceptive / Judging

Steve and Louise (continued)

Steve's scores on the personality questionnaire indicated he was an introvert, a sensing type, a thinking type, and a judging type. Overall then, Steve was an ISTJ personality type. Steve was told he was serious, quiet, and earned success by concentration and thoroughness. He was the type to see that everything was well organized and to take responsibility (see further description in Figure 4.7).

Louise, on the other hand, was an extrovert, an intuitive type, a thinking type, and a perceptive type. Overall then, Louise was an ENTP personality type. She was told she was quick, ingenious, and good at many things. She was resourceful in solving new problems but might neglect routine assignments (see further description in Figure 4.7).

If you have not already done so, you should now make a general assessment of your personality type using Figure 4.7. Again, it is important to recognize that each personality type has its strengths and weaknesses. You will be a better manager if you know the pluses and minuses of your personality and learn to utilize your strengths and to compensate for your weaknesses. And by knowing the personality types of your subordinates, peers, and superiors, you will be in a better position to motivate and lead them, as we will discuss in later chapters.

Before we proceed to discuss some of the organizational factors that can change your personality, we need to make one point about the personality types you have just interpreted for yourself. Steve and Louise (and you, too) were subject to perceptual bias in their assessments. As we said in Chapter 3, the perception process is error prone; and this problem applies to self-perception as well as to perception of others. What we want you to appreciate is that the way you see yourself may not be the way others see you. And people will respond to you in terms of how they see you—not how you see yourself. To gain some insight into your bias, you might ask someone else to assess you on the four personality dimensions in Figures 4.3–4.6 and then compare the assessments. Such feedback and sharing is an excellent vehicle for gaining a better understanding of yourself.

The Johari Window

A simple vehicle for expanding this idea of learning about yourself is called the **Johari Window.**[2] It categorizes what we know about ourselves and what others know about us. As Figure 4.8 shows, there are two dimensions to the window: the horizontal dimension is you as perceived by yourself ("things known to self" and "things not known to self"). The vertical dimension is you as you are perceived by others ("things known to others" and "things not known to others").

Quadrant I is the **open area** of your life where things are known both to you and to others. This is the area in which you should generally operate to be effective in interpersonal relationships. The more you and others operate in the open area the more you understand each other. Hence, your own and others' perceptions will be more consistent; communications will be better; and it will be easier to work together. Furthermore, you will

Figure 4.8
The Johari Window

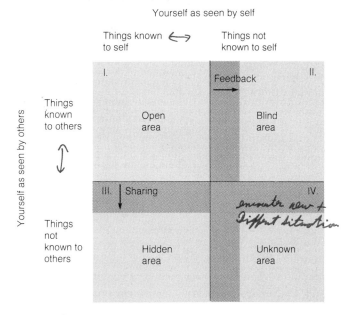

Source: *Group Processes* by Joseph Luft, by permission of Mayfield Publishing Company, Palo Alto, Calif. © 1984.

know yourself better if you operate in the open area. One key to effective management is to know yourself and your people, and operating in the open area means just that.

Quadrant II contains things unknown to you about yourself, but known to others around you. This is the **blind area** of your life. As the figure shows, feedback from others is the way to decrease this blind area and enlarge the open area. By being open to feedback and by asking for it, you can learn a great deal about yourself. If you operate in the blind area, you are more likely to unknowingly hurt other people and do things they do not like. You may be a poor manager and not even know it.

Quadrant III is the **hidden area** of your life where things are known to you but not to others. As the figure shows, sharing is the way to decrease this hidden area and enlarge the open area. Of course there will always be certain things you will want to keep to yourself, but we believe that minimizing these hidden things will make for better interpersonal relationships at work and in your personal life. It will also increase your likelihood of feedback, since people see that you desire to be open about who you are.

Finally, Quadrant IV is the **unknown area** of your life where things are not known to you or to others. By sharing and receiving feedback, you can reduce the unknown area, but the best way to reduce it is to encounter new and different situations. If you are then open to feedback and to sharing of yourself in these new situations, you can reduce the unknown area and enlarge the open area.

These steps of sharing and feedback will help ensure that your self-perception is a reasonably accurate measure of your personality, at least as it exists at this point in time. Now we will turn to two organizationally relevant sources of impact on your personality: socialization and stress.

Socialization as an Influence on Personality

The first organizational source of impact on personality is the socialization process that we briefly encountered in Chapters 1 and 2. Socialization is the process by which an individual is assimilated into and gains loyalty and

commitment to an organization. Through this process, one learns the goals of the organization, the preferred means to achieve those goals, one's responsibilities, and accepted ways of behaving in the organization. In addition, the person learns the organization's attitudes and values. Thus, it should be clear that socialization is a learning process as described in Chapter 3. And as the person becomes socialized in the organization, there is also a tendency to adopt the attitudes and values of the organization. Herein lies the potential impact of the organization on the personality of an individual.

Socialization from an Organizational Perspective

As a way of exploring the impact of socialization on personality, let us delve more deeply into this process of change. From the organization's point of view, there is a need to develop the commitment of its employees. Of course, there are many ways this socialization can occur. Some organizations have very formal and even severe socialization mechanisms. For example, the Marine Corps' approach is to tear down the person who enters basic training and build back the kind of person they want. Other organizations, such as Digital Equipment Corporation, use a more informal and drawn-out process. That is, gradual experience on the job reveals the company expectations to each new employee. Box 4.3 illustrates how IBM goes about the socialization process. Could this change you if you worked for IBM? Indeed, your personality could be affected as you attempted to achieve consistency between your attitudes and values and those of IBM.

Imagine yourself as a new employee in a large American business, for example—like Louise in her first job at the large computer company. As such, you will be exposed to various direct methods of socialization, such as orientation programs, employee handbooks, training programs, and assignments to particular work experiences. In addition, a number of informal mechanisms will be working simultaneously, such as the influence of your co-workers, supervisor, and subordinates. Socialization, then, is not a completely planned and controlled process. **Many factors dictate the amount of influence the socialization process has. Not the least of them is the individual's back-**

Box 4.3
Life at IBM: Rules and Discipline, Goals and Praise Shape IBMers' Taut World
Attitude and Loyalty Count; How a Promising Career Ran Afoul of Standards: Pressure Breeds Camaraderie

When Thomas J. Watson Sr. died in 1956, some might have thought the IBM spirit of the stiff white collar was destined to die with him. But indications are that the founder's legacy of decorum to International Business Machines Corp. still burns bright. Consider the way an IBM man on a witness stand in San Francisco the other day replied when questioned about an after-hours encounter with a competitor:

Q. "All of you were in the hot tub with the Qyx district manager?"

A. "The party adjourned to a hot tub, yes. Fully clothed, I might add."

That an IBMer invited to a California hot tub should fear that propriety demanded a swimsuit wouldn't surprise many people who have ever worked for the giant company. For, besides its great success with computers, IBM has a reputation in the corporate world for another standout trait: an almost proprietary concern with its employee's behavior, appearance and attitudes.

What this means to employees is a lot of rules. And these rules, from broad, unwritten ones calling for "tasteful" dress to specific ones setting salesmen's quotas, draw their force at IBM from another legacy of the founder: the value placed on loyalty. Mr. Watson believed that joining IBM was an act calling for absolute fidelity to the company in matters big and small.

Esprit de Corps

And just in case an IBM employee isn't a self-starter in the loyalty department, the company has a training regimen geared to instilling it. In brief, this consists of supervising new trainees closely, grading them, repeatedly setting new goals for them, and rewarding them amply for achievement. Suffused in work and pressure to perform, employees often develop a camaraderie, an esprit de corps.

What it all amounts to is a kind of IBM culture, a set of attitudes and approaches shared to a greater or lesser degree by IBMers everywhere. This culture, as gleaned from talks with former as well as current employees, is so pervasive that, as one nine-year (former) employee puts it, leaving the company "was like emigrating."

ground and existing personality. There are also stages associated with the process.

Stages of Socialization

Steers identifies three basic stages of socialization.[14] First is the **prearrival stage**. Individuals develop preconceived notions about an organization based on previous education, work experiences, and contacts with organization members. For example, you may already know that the company expects hard work and efficiency from its employees. You are thus already on your way to being socialized, assuming your perceptions are correct.

The second stage is the **encounter with the organization**. Your initial orientation, training, and experiences with other employees who exhibit the accepted attitudes in the organization all influence and change you.

The final stage is the **change of the person and acquisition of the new attitudes and values**. As you work in the company, you gradually learn what is expected and begin to develop a new personality that is consistent with the organization—assuming you stay a member for a sustained period of time. To truly become a member of the organization, you must be transformed, if only slightly and, usually, subtly. Otherwise, you or the organization may decide that it is better for you to move along.

It is also important to note that **the socialization process is not limited to the entry point in the organization. Rather, it is a continuous process throughout your career path**. Two reasons are primary for this continuation.

First, as we pointed out in Chapter 2, socialization occurs every time you make a move in the organization. As you move vertically up the organization's hierarchy, you encounter different norms, values, and attitudes. As at the entry stage, you must assimilate these new factors if you are to be successful; and the potential is there for an alteration in your personality. For example, at lower levels of the organization the norm may be to make decisions based on thinking, rational processes, and use of technical skill. At higher levels feeling, intuition, and conceptual skill may be more valued. You must make the same shift if you are to succeed. The same process will occur as you move laterally from one function to another and as you move radially toward greater or lesser influence in the organization.

The second reason that socialization continues throughout a career is that the organization itself may change. Economic conditions, competition, and technological advances, to name only a few reasons, can cause an organization to change its basic orientation. The resultant adaptation will bring new forces to bear on each organization member—forces which may alter their personalities.

Socialization from the Individual Perspective

There is, of course, another side to the issue of socialization. Each individual exerts influence on his own socialization. Obviously, people respond to situational and organizational forces for socialization based on their own perceptions of the forces and on unique past experiences. As we said in Chapter 1, people enter organizations as used products. They are a product of their past—and there have been many years of "past" before a person enters a full-time job. The works by Erikson and White emphasize the importance of the past in establishing one's personality.[14]

The influence that the person exerts on his or her own socialization is really an influence on the organization itself. Steers refers to **this process of the person trying to shape the organization to fit his or her own needs as individualization.**[15] Schein calls it innovation.[16] The point is that an individual's current personality exerts an influence on what his or her personality will be in the future. Also, people are proactive creatures, exerting influence on their surroundings, as well as being influenced by the surroundings.

The Schein Socialization Model

Schein identified three ways in which individuals respond to the socialization forces of the organization and thus exert influence on their own personalities.[17] Think about it for a moment. How would you exert influence on a new organization you had joined? Schein suggests that one approach is **rebellion**. You could attempt to fight the organization. The result might be dismissal, or change in the organization, or change in you (regardless of whether you win or lose). If you lose, you move closer to what the organization desires; if you win, your existing personality will probably be strengthened. A second alternative is creative individualism, where you accept the organization's values and attitudes that are pivotal, but reject the others. You use a combination of personal and organizational values in relating to the organization. For example, you may accept the value of responding to the customer as if the customer is always right, while rejecting the idea that you must come to the Christmas party every year. Usually this compromise works well unless the person or the organization is too rigid. Finally, you could simply conform to the organizational forces and exert very little influence on the organization.

Thus socialization is a process that exerts influence toward changing your personality. But previous socialization, learning, and attitude formation create forces that operate to maintain your personality as a consistent type. Finally, your perceptual process filters socialization forces in an attempt to maintain consistency between your surroundings and your self concept. The result depends on the strength of these forces, but one thing is clear: you can be sure that your personality will continue to develop and evolve over time.

Stress and Its Effects on Personality

Another organizationally relevant source of impact on one's personality is the stress encountered on the job and in personal life. **Stress is the set of physiological and psychological reactions of a person to characteristics of the environment which are perceived as a threat.** Stressful situations in our work and personal life can have various effects.

Stress Effects

When we encounter stressful situations, our stress reactions can take the form of **physiological changes.** And as we have already discussed, physiological changes can lead to changes in self-perception and ultimately the definition of one's personality. For example, someone who has a severe heart attack as a result of stress may have to start working at a lower level of effort on the job. He or she may have to learn to be less intuitive and more sensing (a personality shift). Recall that the intuitive type likes new challenges and bursts of enthusiastic work, while the sensing type works steadily using established skills. (Refer to Figure 4.4 for more detail on the differences.) Other physiological reactions have also been associated with stressful situations. Heart disease, as well as ulcers, mental illness, alcoholism, drug abuse, and depression are common stress reactions.

Psychological changes can also occur as a result of stress. Examples include: frustration, tension, and anxiety. However, stress reactions can also stimulate one to do a better job. These resulting feelings affect the behavior of an individual, and as we have discussed, behavior affects attitudes and ultimately personality. An example can help to illustrate this idea. If in the stressful situation of giving a report to the boss, a person's tension and anxiety result in an excellent performance, his or her self-confidence may be greatly increased. It is possible that this event could lead to a shift from introversion toward extroversion, at least around the boss. This also illustrates a very important point: namely, stress reactions can have positive outcomes. In fact, research has shown that a moderate amount of stress leads to higher performance than does a low level of stress.[18]

However, at high or prolonged levels of stress, performance is hindered, and the more negative physiological and psychological reactions are also present. Furthermore, stress can lead people to quit their jobs or to be absent or tardy a great deal. It can also lead to employee aggression and sabotage. Unfortunately, we live in a world filled with stress-producing factors.[19] Let us explore some of the major causes of stress as we think about how they can lead to shifts in our personality.

Some Causes of Stress

First of all, **occupations that require people to work under great time pressure or with little control over their jobs or under dangerous physical conditions or with major responsibilities for either people or money are high-stress occupations.** Examples include plant managers, production supervisors, inspectors on high-rise buildings, and air traffic controllers. Examples of low-stress jobs include crafts people, personnel employees, office clerks, and teachers in private schools. Thus, the occupation you choose will affect the level of stress you experience. In addition, the kind of stress you encounter may result in subtle and slow changes in your personality.

Another cause of stress is the degree of role ambiguity, role conflict and role overload you encounter in your job. **If the expectations for your job (which is what a role is) are unclear, conflicting, or too great to complete in the allotted time, you will experience stress.** It is not uncommon for people to be given a job with insufficient information about what the expectations are. On top of this ambiguity, you may receive conflicting signals about your role from different people. Your superior may expect you to work extra hours if necessary; but your family may expect you to be home at a particular time; and your peers may expect you not to be a rate-buster. There is some hint of role conflict in the case of Louise, in that she is being given the opportunity to excel in her work, but her family responsibilities seem to be giving her different signals. Her personality may be affected, and if you were her manager, it would help to know about these sources of stress. What would you do to reduce the stress for Louise; should you reduce it?

Finally, having too much to do must be the most common malady of our society. The manager may be faced with a budgetary problem, a worker morale problem, and an irate customer all at once (sounds like Excedrin headache number 25). The young college professor is faced with pressure to teach, conduct and publish meaningful research, serve on committees, and work with students all at the same time. With these role demands, there is a tendency for a person to feel incapable, resulting in a shift in personality, perhaps from intuitive type toward sensing type or from feeling type toward thinking type.

A related—and perhaps surprising—cause of stress is role underload. **A person with too little to do or work that is not really challenging may experience job stress.** And such stressful conditions can lead to low self-esteem, low satisfaction and increased physiological reactions.[20] Thus a fit between job demands and worker abilities results in lower stress than a situation where worker skills either do not measure up to or exceed the job demands. As a manager, you need to concentrate on producing the right amount of stress in your people, so that they are highly motivated to do a good job. And fit between job and person can be a critical factor in this regard. We will come back to this concept of fit in Chapter 6 on motivation.

Besides these job-related stress factors, there are many life-related ones as well. Certain events cause a great deal of stress: for example, the death of a spouse or close family member; marriage, divorce, or marital separation; jail term; major personal injury or illness; or loss of a job.[21] In addition, the natural evolution of life can result in stress. For example, when people move into their 40s, they often encounter what has been called the midlife crisis. They are no longer young; and they may look and feel older. They may sense their own mortality and feel that time will run out before they can accomplish their life goals. Stress reactions often result as they enter the adulthood crisis of generativity versus self-absorption.

Finally, there is also an influence exerted by the individual's existing personality. The past influences the present. A person who has developed an extroverted personality is likely to respond differently to a situation than someone with an introverted personality. For example, introvert Steve may experience greater stress than extrovert Louise in a social setting where they have to meet many new people. Depending on the level of stress Steve experiences, he may act more or less outgoing. And if he acts outgoing due to moderate stress, he may learn to be more extroverted. If he experiences high stress and withdraws, his introversion may be enhanced. To be an effective manager, it would help to be aware of how Steve is developing.

In summary let us say that there are many causes of stress in work and other life activities. **Your reaction to stressful situations is partly determined by your existing personality, and in turn, the level of stress experienced can affect your present behavior and ultimately your personality of the future.** Part of your challenge will be to manage stress situations so that you benefit from moderate levels of stress and alter your personality as desired. And you will have to help manage the stress felt by your people, if you are to get the most from them. Various techniques are available for managing stress, such as physical fitness, good health care, relaxation training, and support from friends and relatives. And these are becoming more and more common, as Box 4.4 illustrates. There are also particular techniques that you as a manager can use to help your employees, such as providing personal support, providing more job-related information, encouraging physical fitness in your employees, and providing training in interpersonal coping.[22]

Such positive approaches to stress management can lead to better performance, as we shall discuss in the Chapters 5 and 6. Furthermore, they can lead to positive improvement in the personalities of you and your employees. By "positive", we mean a better fit between the individual and the organization. So in closing this chapter, let us repeat that attitude formation is the result of learning and perception, and that personality is the concentration of all of these factors into the total person. But one's

Box 4.4
These Days Business Trips Often Include Sweating It Out Between Deals and Dinner

During the hours many businessmen are getting down to cocktails, William Elting takes a load off by lifting weights. At 5 p.m. he heads for the health club of the Hyatt Regency hotel where he is staying on a business trip to Dallas.

As vice president of the New York-based capital-markets group of Merrill Lynch, Pierce, Fenner & Smith Inc., Mr. Elting travels a lot. He finds the long meetings and social dining on business trips "absolutely stultifying" without regular exercise. "If you've been in a room all day long with the same people, it's not relaxing to leave that room and go to a cocktail lounge and talk to the same people for several more hours," he says.

Growing numbers of business and vacation travelers would rather sweat than swing after a busy day on the road. "It goes along with the whole fitness craze," says Anne Kiefhaber, a fitness consultant who works with government and business on health matters. "Some executives I know make reservations only with hotels that have exercise facilities."

Besides the physical benefits, Mr. Stephan says exercise also helps him erase the "frustrations and aggressions" of a trying day on the road. And Gayle Clement, a Baton Rouge, La., resident visiting Dallas on business, keeps up her running while traveling because it is "total escape, just like sleep," and "it's totally uncompetitive."

personality is dynamic—it results from dynamic processes (learning and perception). Personality is altered and formed through socialization and stress, while simultaneously influencing one's reaction to socialization and stressful situations.

Chapter Highlights

The purpose of this chapter has been to integrate the concepts of perception, learning, and attitudes through the concept of personality. First, we looked at the process of attitude formation as an extension of the processes of perception and learning. We learned that attitudes are opinions about things. Beliefs are closely related and represent our perceptions about relationships between two things. And values represent deep-seated standards by which we evaluate our world. **The past plays an important role in the development of attitudes, beliefs, and values. And in addition, our attitudes play an important role in our current perceptions and learnings**.

Next we briefly explored a very important attitude: job satisfaction. We discussed job satisfaction as an outgrowth of our experiences on the job. We mentioned that job satisfaction is related to absenteeism, turnover, tardiness, and physical and mental health.

Through the case example of Steve and Louise, we began to explore the integrating concept of personality. **Personality was defined as the culmination to date of a person's experiences and genetic influences**. We discussed how personality is determined by past experiences, growth, and development. Personality is dynamic, but it is characterized by internal consistency in our behaviors. We looked at several **factors that determine personality: physical properties, membership in various groups, the roles played in the groups, and exposure to various situations**.

We then discussed Erikson's eight stages of personality development. In so doing, we reemphasized the importance of the first few years (stages 1 and 2) of life in establishing a base and direction for your personality. We said that successful resolution of the crises of previous stages is essential to normal development at later stages.

During stages 3 to 5 you gained a sense of initiative, industry, and overall sense of identity. A positive identity is very important as you enter adulthood, because you must deal simultaneously with important career and perhaps family stages. At this time the issue of intimacy becomes paramount, but the development of personality does not stop here. Erikson suggests we still have the crises of generativity versus self-absorption and integrity versus disgust with life, while we simultaneously engage the development of a career and movement through family stages.

To provide some concreteness to the personality construct, we then explored Jung's personality theory. Jung's theory was explained via its four dimensions. **Emotional orientations were defined as extroversion or introversion. Problem-solving styles were defined along two dimensions: sensing or intuitive and thinking or feeling. Finally general attitudes were defined as judging or perceptive.** Your assessment of these four dimensions then identified you as 1 of 16 personality types, at least at present and as you see yourself.

To explain this last phrase, we then explored the Johari Window. We explained how you may see yourself as others see you (the open area); you may have blind spots; you may have hidden areas; and you may have things that are unknown both to you and to others. **We suggested that it is desirable to have a large open area, and we offered feedback and sharing as two ways to expand this area. In addition, we mentioned being open to new experiences as a third way to expand the open area.**

Next we turned to two aspects of organizational life that directly alter our personalities: socialization and stress. As we anticipate and encounter a new organization or new part of an organization (due to transfer or promotion), we encounter forces that try to shape us to better fit the new situation. **Through direct and indirect means, the organization acts to socialize us. At the same time we exert forces that influence our own socialization,** not the least of which is our previously developed personality. We try to make the situation fit us the way we are. Depending on the strength of these forces, our personalities are altered in various directions, but it is certain that they are altered in some direction to some extent.

Stress affects your personality through the physiological and psychological reactions to aspects of the environment which are perceived as threatening. Elation, depression, ulcers, heart disease, anxiety, tension, or frustration affect your behaviors and attitudes. And through learning and perception, these can also affect your personality. **But as with socialization, your existing personality will influence your reaction to stressful situations and thus the impact on your personality.** We said that stress is pervasive in our society, resulting from our jobs, from role ambiguity and role conflict, from role overload and underload, and from various events that occur naturally as a part of life (such as the death of a loved one).

Throughout this chapter, we have tried to make it clear that personality is the integration of the perception and learning processes, and attitude formation as well. As such, **personality is developed from previous experiences, and one's existing personality influences the next cycle through perception, learning, and attitude formation.** Socialization and stress are not the only forces that alter personality, but we feel that they are extremely important factors for you to understand in order to be an effective manager.

Review Questions

1. How are beliefs and attitudes related to each other, and to the process of learning?

2. Why is job satisfaction such an important attitude for you to understand?

3. What is personality, and what are the important aspects for you to understand?

4. Explain why personality is developmental in nature. What are the primary factors that influence the evolution of personality?

5. Why are the first three stages of Erikson's model of personality development so crucial to long term personality development? How do the crises of these three stages relate to the crises of the remaining stages?

6. Describe the subsystems of Jung's personality theory. Can you also explain the four dimensions of the theory?

7. What is the Johari Window and why is it a useful way to look at our own personalities?

8. Describe socialization from an organizational perspective and explain how it might influence one's personality.

9. How does a person's existing personality impact the socialization process and influence the individual's future personality?

10. Why does stress exert an influence on one's personality and what are the more prominent sources of stress in our lives?

Notes

1. D. J. Bem, *Beliefs, Attitudes, and Human Affairs* (Monterey, Calif.: Brooks/Cole Publishing, 1970), pp. 4–15.

2. E. H. Erikson, "Youth and the Life Cycle," *Children*, 7 (1960), pp. 43–49.

3. B. L. White, *The First Three Years of Life* (New York: Avon Books, 1975).

4. R. Mowday, S. Parker, and R. M. Steers, *Employee-Organization Linkages* (New York: Academic Press, 1982).

5. A. Kornhauser, *Mental Health of the Industrial Worker: A Detroit Study* (New York: John Wiley & Sons, 1965).

6. E. Palmore, "Predicting Longevity: A Follow-Up Controlling for Age," *The Gerontologist*, 9 (1969), pp. 247–50.

7. R. M. Steers, *Introduction to Organizational Behavior* (Glenview, Ill: Scott, Foresman, 1981), pp. 309–10.

8. F. Ruch, *Psychology and Life*, 6th ed. (Glenview, Ill.: Scott, Foresman, 1963), p. 353.

9. J.B. Miner and M.G. Miner, *Personnel and Industrial Relations*, 3d. ed. (New York: Macmillan, 1977), p. 72.

10. Erikson, "Youth and the Life Cycle."

11. C. G. Jung, *Collected Works*, ed. H. Read, M. Fordham, and G. Adler (eds.) (Princeton, N.J.: Princeton University Press, 1953).

12. J. Luft, *Group Processes* (Palo Alto, Calif.: National Press Books, 1970).

13. R. M. Steers, *Introduction to Organizational Behavior*, p. 324.

14. Erikson, "Youth and the Life Cycle," pp. 43–49; B. L. White, *The First Three Years of Life.*

15. Steers, *Introduction to Organizational Behavior*, p. 324.

16. E. H. Schein, "The Individual, the Organization and the Career: A Conceptual Scheme," *Journal of Applied Behavioral Science*, 7 (1971), pp. 401–26.

17. E. H. Schein, "Organizational Socialization and the Profession of Management," *Industrial Management Review*, 9 (1968), pp. 1–16.

18. J. E. McGrath, "Stress and Behavior in Organizations," in *Handbook of Industrial and Organizational Psychology*, ed. M. D. Dunnette (Skokie, Ill.: Rand McNally, 1976), pp. 1351–95.

19. McGrath, "Stress and Behavior," pp. 1351–95.

20. D. Katz and R. Kahn, *The Social Psychology of Organizations*, 2d ed. (New York: John Wiley & Sons, 1978).

21. L. O. Ruch and T. H. Holmes, "Scaling of Life Change: Comparison of Direct and Indirect Methods," *Journal of Psychosomatic Research*, 15 (1971), pp. 221–27.

22. J. E. Newman and T. H. Beehr, "Personal and Organizational Strategies for Handling Job Stress," *Personnel Psychology*, 32 (1979), pp. 1–38.

Resource Readings

Brief, A. P.; R. S. Schuler; and M. Van Sell. *Managing Job Stress*. Boston: Little, Brown, 1981.

Erikson, E. H. "Youth and the Life Cycle," *Children* 7 (1960) pp. 43–49.

Jung, C. G. *Collected Works*. Edited by H. Read, M. Fordham, and G. Adler. Princeton, N.J.: Princeton University Press, 1953.

Schein, E. H. "Organizational Socialization and the Profession of Management." *Industrial Management Review* 9 (1968), pp. 1–16.

CHAPTER 5

The Foundations for Understanding Motivation

Chapter Highlights
Review Questions
Notes
Resource Readings
Motivation Feedback Opinionnaire

In the last two chapters we looked at several important aspects of individual behavior. By gaining an understanding of the **perception** and **learning** processes, we were able to better understand the formation of **attitudes** and ultimately of one's **personality**. By considering **socialization** and **stress**, we could begin to appreciate the interaction between individuals and the organizations in which they work. In this chapter we will delve further into this interaction as we begin to explore the dynamic process of **motivation**. We will explore a number of theories of motivation that will lay the foundation for our developing in Chapter 6 an integrated model of the motivation process. By understanding these motivation theories and the integrated model, you as a manager will be in a better position to create a situation in which your employees are motivated to perform the actions necessary to accomplish organizational goals. In the process, you will also learn a great deal about your own motivation.

Motivation and Its Importance to a Manager

Motivation can be defined as that which energizes, directs, and sustains an individual to perform goal-directed actions. People are generally motivated to do something that will satisfy their needs. As a manager, your job is to see that your employees' actions are directed not only toward their own goals but also toward the goals of your unit and the organization. Thus, there are several reasons why motivation is an important topic for you to understand.

Why Study Motivation?

First of all, your employees are the vehicle for accomplishing the goals of your unit and organization. Thus, you must be sure that people are motivated to remain with you and dependably perform the tasks they were hired to do. In addition, you need creative and innovative employees who can complete their tasks in spite of unexpected interruptions.[1] Recall the old saying that performance on a job is 20 percent ability and 80 percent effort.

Motivation is the critical factor in mobilizing the efforts of your employees.

The second reason to study motivation is that organizations in the future will need to use more effectively all of their resources, including their human resources. With continuously tightening constraints from the economy, world competition, government controls, and consumer groups, organizations must draw heavily on their employees to increase productivity. As a manager, your knowledge of motivation can be extremely useful in achieving gains in the short- and long-run productivity of your organization. In the short run, you must use selection, placement, and rewards to ensure that there is a fit between employee needs and the demands of the job. In the long run, you must prepare employees (through training and on-the-job experience) to be future resources in new, different, or altered capacities. For example, who will replace you when you are promoted?

Third, motivation is important because it is a complex process that ultimately influences employee behavior. And often it is not easy to motivate people to do what you want them to do. Recall our discussions from Chapters 3 and 4 which explained how each person is unique— the used product idea. **Each employee brings to the work place a unique set of needs that has been determined by their past experiences. Therefore, two employees may be motivated very differently in the same situation, or in the same job, by the same reward.** It has often been said in union negotiations that we must treat all employees equally. But if we treat every employee the same—and if every employee is unique—are we not then treating people unequally? Some employees will be pleased with a nice pay raise; others might have preferred a promotion or more responsibility. Motivation occurs in a complicated process that influences the actions of each of your employees. It will pay you to understand this topic.

Fourth, motivation is important to understand because you must also be concerned with your own motivation. By knowing what motivates you to perform productively, you will be in a better position to maximize your work efforts and find jobs that are best for you. **For your work to be meaningful and to contribute to your overall satis-**

faction and health in life, you will need to understand how motivation works for you.

Problems Associated with Motivation

Another major reason for studying motivation is that it is linked to a number of organizational problems. For example, we often hear managers lament that workers do not put forth the kind of effort managers want. Managers are constantly concerned with **productivity** of their employees, and this concern seems to be growing in the face of foreign competition and increased constraints on profits. Many managers are searching for quick solutions, but the problem is more complex than that. Our exploration of the motivation process will help you analyze this problem of productivity.

Managers also frequently mention the problem of employee **dependability**. Often managers must deal with high levels of employee tardiness or absenteeism. These problems in dependability are very costly; they disrupt work schedules, lead to overstaffing, and reduce the organization's productivity. Steers has suggested that the costs associated with absenteeism in the United States—including salary, fringe benefits, temporary replacement, and profit loss—total over $26 billion annually, using 1977 costs.[2] With inflation, the costs today probably exceed $50 billion annually. As our study of motivation will reveal, a person basically makes a choice each day either to go to work or to do something else; to work hard or take it easy. Two factors that influence this decision—and which can be influenced by a manager—are the employee's satisfaction with the work and the various rewards associated with attendance—both related to motivation.

A third problem area associated with employee motivation is **turnover**, that is, employees quitting their jobs. As with absenteeism, turnover is rooted in the satisfaction that employees experience in the job. But quitting involves a longer decision process. The decision to quit involves the exploration of alternative jobs, the development of an intention to quit, and finally the act of quitting.[3] Absenteeism merely involves a choice between going to work today and doing something else for the day, with the intention of going to work the next day. As with absentee-ism and tardiness, the problem of turnover can be ana-lyzed from a motivation perspective using the motivation theories and model explored in this and the following chapters.

Besides the three problem areas mentioned above, low motivation can lead to a number of other problems: poor quality work, being present on the job physically but not mentally, lack of innovation and suggestions for im-provement, low employee morale, and many other unde-sirable outcomes. As a manager you will have to be con-cerned with increasing and maintaining the motivation of your employees. If it is relatively low, you will have to try to raise it, and if it is relatively high, you will have to work to maintain the high level of motivation. At the same time, you will also have to be concerned with your own motivation on the job and its potential for change over time.

Motivation as a Dynamic Process

Throughout the first four chapters we have noted changes that people undergo in the various stages of devel-opment of career, life, and family. We have seen that **people are likely to be motivated by different things at different points in their lives**. For example, a 22-year old may be looking for more money and greater challenge in a job; a 58-year old may be more concerned about retirement pension and maintaining a level of importance in the company. In fact, people vary from day to day in their motivation. Each of us has good and bad days—days when we are highly motivated to work and days when we have little desire to work.

Employee motivation can also be altered by changes in the job or the organization itself. Technological ad-vances in a job can take away or add interesting compo-nents to a job. Automation both eliminates and adds jobs, and in both cases jobs are changed. The question is: How is the motivation aspect of the job altered? As we will see, **the job itself is a very important factor in the motiva-tion process of employees**. For example, if a job is changed to include greater decision-making responsibility for the employee, the motivation potential of the job has been altered.

Organizational changes can also affect motivation—for example, growth, decline, or change in direction, as we discussed in Chapter 2. In a growing organization, there are many opportunities for advancement and increased responsibility that can influence the motivation of employees. As Box 5.1 illustrates, the reverse may be true in a

Box 5.1
Fear of Unemployment
Takes Emotional Toll
At White-Collar Levels

The human-resources manager at an ailing manufacturing company in Pittsburgh sits alone in an office at the end of a long corridor dotted by empty offices. "I still get here at 8 a.m. every day and put in nine, sometimes 10 hours, but more and more I'm asking myself why," he says.

Since February, nearly 20% of his co-workers have been laid off "and now all anyone can talk about is who's going to be next. It's depressing. You end up feeling that what you do doesn't matter, that it won't make a difference."

Similar feelings echo in corporate offices around the nation. In conference rooms and cubicles, managers ranging from first-line supervisors to vice presidents talk incessantly about the loss of job security and the stresses of keeping going in companies that are suffering production and people losses.

For those still employed, many who thought themselves immune to layoffs suddenly are facing uncertainty and must make do with less. Many are frightened—even ashamed—to discuss their situation, insisting on anonymity.

Manifestations of Grief

In fact, the retrenchment going on in corporations is affecting those who survive layoffs almost as much as those who are let go. The survivors go through the same traumas of thinking they may be fired and then, once they've been spared, often find themselves "overworked and overpressured," says James Lotz, a consultant at International Management Advisors Inc. in New York. "The leaves left on the tree are shaking," he says.

The search for new jobs goes on undercover. "People are terribly frightened that if they're seen looking, they'll be judged disloyal and fired," says Mr. Young, the executive recruiter. "One guy I had lunch with last week didn't want to be seen walking down the street with me."

declining organization. People operate with the fear that they may lose their jobs; their motivation to work and to search for alternative employment can be altered by the forces in this situation. By the same token, a change in company direction can influence the motivation of employees. Remember, **people are usually motivated to do something; the question is, what?** Later we will explore these dynamic aspects of motivation in more detail. But now let us discuss a number of theories of motivation that have been developed over the years.

An Introduction to Motivation Theories

As we said earlier, motivation operates through a complex process that ultimately influences the behavior of people in organizations. And because motivation is so complex, many theories have been advanced in an effort to explain it. We will explore a number of them in this chapter to form the foundation for our integrative model explained in Chapter 6.

The existing theories of motivation can be classified as either **content theories** or **process theories**. While it is not totally accurate, we can suggest that the content theories historically predate the process theories. There has been a progression from simple theories of motivation to more complex models as researchers have learned more about the motivation process. You are probably familiar with at least one of the content theories—Maslow's **need hierarchy theory**. Other content theories include Herzberg's **two-factor theory** and McClelland's **need for achievement, affiliation, and power theory**. More recently we have witnessed the development of Alderfer's **ERG (existence, relatedness, and growth) needs theory** as an extension of Maslow's theory. Also, we have seen the emergence of **social facilitation theory**, which suggests that people are influenced by the expectations of others around them. In summary, **content theories highlight the differences among people. Different people are motivated by different things.**[4]

The process theories which have been developed since about the mid 1960s include Vroom's **expectancy theory**, Adams' **equity theory**, and an application of Skinner's **operant conditioning** to motivation. Closely following the development of these models of motivation came Locke's **goal setting theory**. While the models differ in terms of the motivational mechanism which causes behavior, all four of **these process models define motivation as an individual choice process**.[5] They suggest that individuals rely on past and current information about their goals, expectations, and sense of fairness to choose their behaviors. People also rely on their expectations of the rewards or punishments associated with certain behaviors to make their choices.

Both content and process theories focus on the individual and certain characteristics about the individual (for example, needs and expectations) in explaining motivation. To some extent they also include other people who interact with the employee (such as, the supervisor and peers). In addition these theories focus on the reward and information systems of the organization. But one aspect of the motivational puzzle that seems to be slighted is the job that the person is performing. In the 1970s a job design theory of motivation was developed by Hackman and his associates at Yale University. This theory directly considers the motivating potential of the job. Thus we are provided with yet another aspect of the complex motivational process, and no doubt others will follow. Let us now look into each of these 10 theories in some detail.

Content Theories of Motivation

Content theories of motivation help us to understand the basic needs that people are motivated to satisfy by their actions. An unsatisfied need results in a driving force toward satisfaction of the need. A look at these theories as shown in Figure 5.1 reveals the types of needs that can motivate people.

Maslow's Need Hierarchy

The first content theory—and still the most popular one—was developed by Abraham Maslow in 1943.[6] No doubt you are familiar with this theory, so we will not spend much time explaining it. As Figure 5.1 shows, Maslow proposed that there is a hierarchy of needs ranging from physiological to self-actualization needs. **As long**

Figure 5.1 Major Content Theories of Motivation

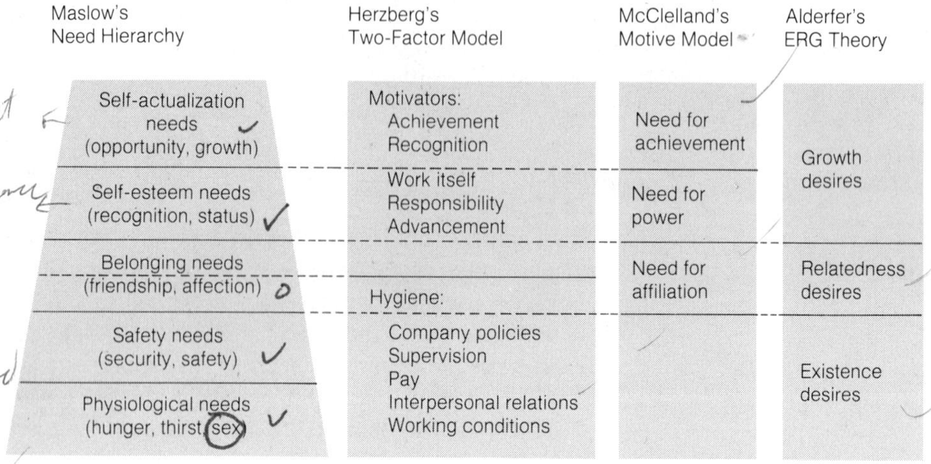

Maslow's Need Hierarchy	Herzberg's Two-Factor Model	McClelland's Motive Model	Alderfer's ERG Theory
Self-actualization needs (opportunity, growth)	Motivators: Achievement Recognition	Need for achievement	Growth desires
Self-esteem needs (recognition, status)	Work itself Responsibility Advancement	Need for power	
Belonging needs (friendship, affection)	Hygiene:	Need for affiliation	Relatedness desires
Safety needs (security, safety)	Company policies Supervision Pay		Existence desires
Physiological needs (hunger, thirst, sex)	Interpersonal relations Working conditions		

(handwritten margin notes: adult, adolescent, Child, life-time)

as a lower-level need is unsatisfied, an individual will choose actions designed to move toward satisfaction of that need. But once physiological needs are basically satisfied (and there is an expectation that they will remain satisfied), a person will turn to safety needs, and so on up the hierarchy.

Research on Maslow's hierarchy has resulted in several criticisms of the model, but none of the criticisms have been fatal. First, as we have suggested throughout this text, we would expect a person's needs to change over time. Certainly the needs of a young college graduate will differ from the veteran employee in an organization. And changes in a situation may result in changes in the importance of needs. For example: a recessionary economy with high unemployment may cause one to refocus from self-actualization needs to safety and physiological needs. Second, research suggests that more than one need may be operational at a time. People may work to satisfy their safety and self-esteem needs at the same time. But despite these criticisms, Maslow's theory has remained popular, because it is simple to understand and because individual needs appear to be critical to understanding individual behavior.[7] Take a few minutes now to complete and score the Motivation Feedback Opinionnaire at the end of the chapter. Be honest with yourself and see which of Maslow's needs are most important to you now.

Alderfer's ERG Theory

A more recently developed theory, Alderfer's ERG theory (shown on the far right in Figure 5.1) seems to address many of the criticisms of the Maslow hierarchy.[8] First of all, Alderfer reduces the five needs to three more general needs: existence, relatedness, and growth. Included under **existence needs** are hunger, thirst, shelter, pay, and working conditions—that is, the physiological and safety needs from Maslow. **Relatedness needs** include basically the same desires as Maslow's belongingness needs; namely friendship and affection from others. Finally, **growth needs** are the desires to be creative, to develop additional skills and abilities, and to feel a sense of status in an organization—that is, the self-esteem and self-actualization needs from Maslow.

Second, ERG theory suggests that the more the lower-level needs (for example, existence desires) have been satisfied, the greater is the drive to satisfy higher level needs like relatedness or growth. Thus, **the theory is not dependent upon full satisfaction of a lower-level need before moving on to a higher-level need**. It clearly allows for the simultaneous pursuit of both existence needs and relatedness needs, for example. Third, ERG theory builds in a frustration response as follows. An individual who has difficulty in satisfying a higher-level need (say growth), may focus more importance and effort on lower-level needs where there is a greater chance of satisfaction. Thus, this theory allows for movement both up and down the hierarchy. But **the primary proposition of need theory holds here as well; namely the less a need is satisfied, the more it will be desired.**

McClelland's Need Theory

Another content theory expresses the needs somewhat differently. The theory by David McClelland and his associates at Harvard defines needs for achievement, power, and affiliation.[9] **Need for achievement** is the desire to perform to high standards or to excel at your job. If you are a high need achiever, you like to set your own goals; you set goals that are neither too easy nor too difficult to achieve; and you like to receive immediate feedback on your work. Box 5.2 provides an interesting illustration of this need. The chirigami kokan is clearly

---

Box 5.2
It Isn't Easy to Work Alone in Japan—Ask A Chirigami Kokan
'Toilet-Paper Exchanger' Has Zero Prestige but Is Free of Bosses and Their Edicts

Tokyo—A small, weather-beaten truck inches along a street in a residential neighborhood, a public-address system on its roof. The voice of the driver, Tsuguo Suzuki, summons the populace.

"This is your familiar chirigami kokan," comes the voice from the loudspeaker. "If you have old newspapers, magazines, used cardboard or telephone directories you don't need, please let me know. I will come to your doorway to get them, and in return give you rolls of high-quality toilet paper."

Chirigami kokan—literally, "toilet-paper exchangers"—have become familiar sights and sounds on the streets of big Japanese cities. Toyko alone has more than 6,000 of them. Working alone, often driving old trucks rented by day, they scour the neighborhoods for wastepaper and sell it to junkyards that compress it for recycling. From the junkyards they pick up a supply of recycled tissue paper—to attract more wastepaper the next day.

Chirigami kokan exist because this island nation needs to conserve resources. There is a government-sponsored institution in Japan called the Paper Recycling Promotion Center, and it says the toilet-paper exchangers play a vital role in reducing wood-pulp imports.

But the job of chirigami kokan also serves another function in Japan: It offers a role for the individualist, for the lone wolf.

This is a nation where young people compete strenuously, from junior high to school to college, for a chance to go to work for a large corporation. Big companies offer higher pay, better benefits and, above all, the promise of lifetime employment. From these flows a fourth advantage—prestige. "It is for social status and respect as well as for the money" that Japanese strive to be part of a large corporate organization, says Hitoshi Hashimoto, a professor of social psychology at Tokyo's Waseda University.

Thus, in a nation of teamwork and team players, the chirigami kokan constitutes one answer to a question foreigners often ask about Japan: What happens to small entrepreneurs who go bankrupt and to those individualistic types who don't like working in big groups?

By Masayoshi Kanabayashi, *The Wall Street Journal*, February 12, 1982. Reprinted by permission of *The Wall Street Journal*, © Dow Jones & Company, Inc. 1982. All rights reserved.

working on his achievement need, as well as self-actualization, in a society that does not encourage individualism. The **need for power** is the desire to influence and control others. If you are high in need for power, you seek positions of leadership in groups; you freely give your opinion on matters; and you try to convince others to change their opinions. We should be quick to add that a high need for power is neither good nor bad. What you do with power determines whether it is good or bad. Thinking ahead a couple of chapters, we can note that leadership is defined as influencing the behavior of others; hence leadership and power are closely intertwined. A leader must have some base of power and utilize his or her need for power. Finally, **need for affiliation** is defined as the desire to develop close interpersonal relationships with others. If you are high in need for affiliation, you exhibit a real interest in the feelings of others; you like a great deal of interpersonal contact; and you look for support and/or approval from others.

As Figure 5.1 suggests, these three needs are not unlike the needs in Alderfer's and Maslow's models. Need for achievement is similar to self actualization and growth needs. Need for power is similar to self esteem needs and growth needs. And need for affiliation is similar to relatedness and belonging needs. In a manner similar to Alderfer, McClelland suggests that all three needs are operative at all times, but one or two of them will tend to dominate the individual at a point in time. Thus, you might have high needs for achievement and power and a low need for affiliation. And if so, you would have to be motivated differently than someone high in affiliation and power and low in achievement need. McClelland adds one other key point to our understanding of the needs aspect of motivation. He argues that **these needs are all learned, and this means that they reflect our pasts and can be altered via a continued learning process**.

Herzberg's Two-Factor Theory

One last content theory that has received a great deal of attention from managers must be explained. Herzberg defines a number of motivators and hygiene factors, as shown in Figure 5.1.[10] They relate to the basic needs defined by Maslow, McClelland, and Alderfer. **Motiva-**

tors relate to satisfaction of higher-level needs (self-actualization, self-esteem, and some belonging), while **hygiene** factors relate to lower-level needs (physiological, safety, and some belonging).

Herzberg argues that motivators are what lead to satisfaction on the job, while a lack of sufficient hygiene factors can lead to job dissatisfaction. Lack of motivators does not lead to dissatisfaction, and the presence of hygiene factors does not lead to satisfaction. This idea has been severely criticized in the research literature, primarily because of the way in which Herzberg collected his data.[11] He basically asked people to describe what made them feel good about their jobs and what made them feel bad about their jobs. The problem is that people have a tendency to attribute positive things to their own efforts and negative things to others. Hence the hygiene factors all relate to the company and the supervisor, while the motivators relate more to personal events.

In spite of this criticism, the two-factor theory continues to have broad appeal to managers. One reason is that managers see immediate applicability to real situations. Recognition, responsibility, and the other motivators give managers more concrete direction than saying that workers have unsatisfied self-esteem needs. This same practicality exists for the hygiene factors. Thus, for example, if some assembly-line workers are dissatisfied because of a lack of recognition (a motivator), putting more money into hygiene factors (pay, working conditions) will not alleviate the problem. If the managers want these workers to be more motivated, they must determine how to introduce more recognition into the job.

What we would suggest to make this theory more acceptable and useful is to talk in terms of employee potential that can be tapped via hygiene and motivating factors. Figure 5.2 depicts the explanation we would propose. Below a certain level of employee motivational potential which is average for all employees (say 30 percent of potential), the hygiene factors can produce improvement in the level of employee motivation. This would be true because supervision, working conditions and so forth may be inhibiting the employee's ability to do the job. **However, to tap the motivational potential of your outstanding employees and break through the 30 percent barrier, man-**

**Figure 5.2
An Adaptation of
Herzberg's
Motivational Model**

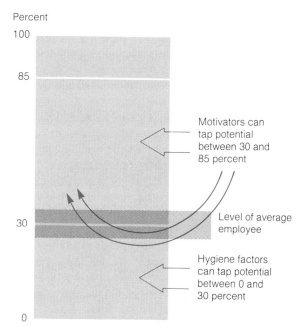

Percent

100

85

Motivators can
tap potential
between 30 and
85 percent

30

Level of average
employee

Hygiene factors
can tap potential
between 0 and
30 percent

0

Source: Adapted from F. Herzberg, B. Mausner, and B. Snyderman, *The Motivation to Work,* copyright © 1959 John Wiley & Sons, Inc.

agers must rely more heavily on the motivating factors. The area between 30 percent and 85 percent (a reasonable guess at the maximum achievable) is the challenge for managers. Not all employees will want the motivators in their jobs; some workers are happy with a lack of responsibility and the predictability of their job. But for those who want motivators, the hygiene factors are no substitute. Later, we will discuss Hackman's job design theory that draws heavily on Herzberg's model plus the differences in individuals.

**Social Facilitation
Theory**

While it is not strictly a content theory, **social facilitation** theory is related because it is connected to the belongingness needs. It suggests that our needs and goals are influenced by the expectations that our peers, superiors, and subordinates have for us.[12] As we go about our jobs, we come into contact with others in the organization on whom we depend and who depend on us. We develop expectations about the behaviors of these people, and they develop expectations about us. But what is most crucial is that these co-workers influence our sense of what is important. What goals do we value? What needs are important to us? For example, in one department in Home Computers there may be a great deal of discussion of salary and other money matters. As a result, if you worked in that department you might place greater importance on salary increments than if you were in a department where there was a great deal of discussion about advancement, recognition, and responsibility.

Another way to look at this theory is to think of your interactions with co-workers as a source of motivation for your actions. If your peers, for example, have set an informal norm of producing 10 computers per day, then you will be motivated to work up to, but not above that level. You learn some of your needs from the people who work around you. **Remember, the needs in the content theories are basically learned and are therefore subject to change over time**. Your co-workers are one source of influence on your needs. Let us now turn to the process theories of motivation.

Process Theories of Motivation

As we said earlier, there are several important process theories of motivation, each of which defines motivation as a choice process for individuals. Let us, in turn, discuss expectancy theory, operant conditioning, equity theory, and goal-setting theory.

Expectancy Theory

The first truly comprehensive explanation of expectancy theory was provided by Victor Vroom in the 1960s.[13] The basic premise of the theory is that people make choices about which of several behaviors to perform at a given point in time. Which behavior is chosen depends on which one they believe will lead to desired rewards. For example, you might choose between two behaviors concerning a report due by 5 p.m. today as follows: (1) Work on it over lunch to try to finish it on time, or (2) go ahead to lunch and then rush to finish it later. The question is, which behavior will lead to a good, timely report? And a good report is important because you believe it could lead to one of several possible rewards: (1) a bonus, (2) a promotion, or (3) an excellent performance review.

Expectancy theory suggests we look at this choice in three steps, as shown in Figure 5.3. The first step involves **expectancy**, hence the name of the theory. Essentially, **expectancy is your assessment of the probability that a particular level of effort will lead to a desired level of performance**. The question is: Can I do it; what is the probability I can? In the example, what is the probability that working over lunch will lead to a good and timely report; what about if you rush on it after going to lunch?

The second step involves **instrumentality, which is your assessment of the probability that the desired level of performance will lead to a desired reward**. The question is: Does performance lead to what I want? What is the probability it does? In the example, what is the probability

Figure 5.3 An Expectancy Theory Model

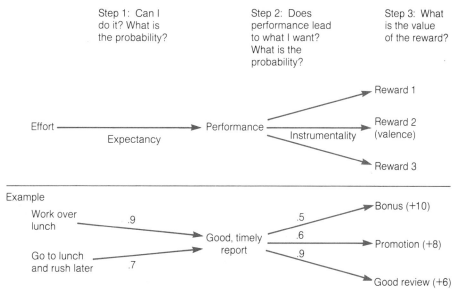

Source: Adapted from V. H. Vroom, *Work and Motivation,* copyright © 1964 John Wiley & Sons, Inc.

that a good, timely report will lead to a bonus, a promotion, and a good review?

The third step then assigns to each reward a **valence, which is the importance or value you place on each possible reward**. In the example, how important are a bonus, a promotion, and a good review? But the realistic value of the reward is really a function of the instrumentality between performance and reward. You might desire a bonus the most (valence of +10), a promotion next (valence of +8), and a good review least (valence of +6). But the probabilities of each, as associated with a good, timely report, may be .5, .6, and .9, respectively (as shown in Figure 5.3). Thus, the realistic values of the bonus, promotion and good review are +5, +4.8, and +5.4, respectively. These values are obtained by multiplying the valence times the instrumentality. Overall, the value of a good, timely report is the sum of these three realistic values—+15.2. The value could be much higher if the instrumentalities for a bonus and a promotion were higher.

To determine the motivational strength for the two behaviors, you multiply the expectancies that each will lead to the desired performance times the value of the report. Thus, work over lunch is rated .9 X 15.2 = +13.7, and go to lunch/rush later is rated .7 X 15.2 = +10.6. Clearly, the motivational strength related to working over lunch is stronger than going ahead to lunch. Of course, this relates only to getting the report done. It may be that the lunch has a higher motivational value because it is a romantic lunch that may result in engagement, which has a high value for you. The key point of the theory again is the process of choice.

A great deal of research has been conducted on the basic expectancy theory model, and it suggests that the model is probably more complete than the content theories.[14] One of the problems with the theory, though, is that it is a complex theory to test fully. And while the logic of the model is clear, we must wonder if people really go through the process of assigning values and probabilities for the multitude of actions performed each day. Still, the steps are useful for clarifying what managers can do to motivate people. For example, as a manager find out which rewards under your control have the highest valences for your employees. Then link these to the performance you desire. And if any expectancies are low, provide coaching, leadership, and training to raise them.

In keeping with the developmental theme of this book, it is clear that expectancy theory is a developmental theory. The valences, expectancies, and instrumentalities must come from past experience, and the step-by-step fashion of the model also introduces a time aspect. Indeed, we believe this model is quite useful; it will form the framework for integrating in Chapter 6 all of the various motivation theories discussed in this chapter.

Operant Conditioning

In Chapter 3 we looked at operant conditioning as a model of learning. Our discussion of it here as a process theory of motivation suggests the close link between learning and motivation. **Operant conditioning (or reinforcement theory) is a model for rewarding the kind of behavior you desire from your employees and not rewarding undesired behavior**. Thus, motivation is viewed specifically in terms of getting the employee to do what the organization wants. If the employee does what the organization wants and receives a valued reward, the employee's behavior should continue to fit the desires of the organization. An employee who does not do what the organization wants, will not receive the reward—or may instead receive punishment for the undesired behavior. Hence, the employee's behavior will probably change.

Application of this theory involves choices of the particular reward or punishment to be used and the frequency with which the reward is given. To be most effective in producing desired results, granting of the reward must be tied closely to the accomplishment of organizational goals. If you want a promotion and you work hard with good results, but the promotion goes to someone who is connected with the boss's family, the reinforcement model does not get the desired result of continued hard work. And the same result may come about if the wrong reward is given—for example a pay raise instead of a desired promotion. The bottom line is that for reinforcement theory to be most useful, **we must recognize that rewards only accomplish the desires of the organization when their receipt is tied to accomplishment of organizational goals and when the rewards are valued by the individuals receiving them**. Research has tended to favor use

"What makes you think you're not appreclated
here?"

From *The Wall Street Journal*, with permission of Cartoon Features Syndicate.

of rewards over punishment in achieving desired results.
There are times, though, where punishment can be very
effective.[15] For example, when college graduates fail to
repay their student loans, some U. S. attorneys have taken
away their cars. Usually this stops the delinquency and
payments resume—and the cars are returned. Thus punishment as a final approach can be useful when undesired
behavior must be stopped quickly.

Equity Theory

**Equity theory is a model of motivation which involves
comparison between employees.**[16] If, for example, you
perceive that the rewards from your job (pay, promotion,
etc.) relative to what you put into the job (effort, skills,
etc.) are equal to what other employees receive, you will
be satisfied and motivated to continue working as you
have been. In other words, you perceive equitable treatment of yourself and your co-workers. Of course, it is
also possible for you to perceive inequitable treatment.
You may feel that the ratio of your rewards to your
inputs is greater than the ratio for other employees; thus
you are being overrewarded. Or you may feel the ratio

Box 5.3
EPA's Drive to Loosen
Some Rules Angers
Firms That Have
Complied

For Bacardi Corp., the situation is hard to swallow. The world's largest rum producer fears it may be penalized for complying too readily with federal environmental laws.

Under pressure from the U.S. Environmental Protection Agency, the company has spent more than $10 million since 1979 to clean up water pollution from two distilleries in Puerto Rico. Bacardi built a sophisticated and unique treatment plant on the condition that the government would require the rest of the industry to meet equally stringent anti-pollution standards.

But now, as part of the Reagan administration's overall effort to ease regulation, the EPA is considering changes that would permit the company's major competitors, located in Puerto Rico and the Virgin Islands, to continue dumping large amounts of molasses residue into the Caribbean. Bacardi executives are discovering, much to their dismay, that some of the proposals would place them at a competitive disadvantage with smaller firms that steadfastly refused to invest in modern pollution-control equipment.

In an official filing with the EPA, Bacardi's attorneys warn the Reagan administration against trying to assign "extra environmental costs to whatever producer is currently more successful in the marketplace."

By Andy Pasztor, *The Wall Street Journal,* September 23, 1982. Reprinted by permission of *The Wall Street Journal,* © Dow Jones & Company, Inc. 1982. All rights reserved.

of your rewards to your inputs is less than the ratio for others; thus you are being underrewarded. In these latter two situations, your motivation will be altered by this information. And in turn, motivation may alter your effort and performance. Box 5.3 provides an excellent example of the theory involving the Environmental Protection Agency. Do you think Bacardi will be so agreeable next time?

The inequity situation of being **underrewarded** (like Bacardi) can result in several behaviors. You could decide to reduce your efforts so that the ratio of rewards to inputs would be reduced and become more comparable to the ratio for others. Another way to increase your ratio would be to ask for an increase in rewards (for example a pay raise). And since the key factor in this model is the perception of the individual, you could also distort the perception of your rewards and inputs, and the rewards and inputs of others to either increase your ratio or reduce the perceived ratio of others.

In the case of being **over rewarded**, the same perceptual distortion processes can result in lowering your ratio or raising the ratio of others. And you can also lower your ratio by reducing some of the subjective rewards that you receive or by increasing the effort you put into your job. It would seem that there are greater problems of motivation in the case of underreward than overreward. And in fact, research appears to lend stronger support to the underreward aspects of the theory.[17]

It is important to note that perception is such an important aspect of equity theory. **And since perception is influenced so heavily by developmental properties (as we discussed in Chapter 3), equity theory is also influenced by one's past and present experiencing of the situation.** Thus, equity theory is a developmental theory of motivation.

Locke's Goal-Setting Theory

As the final process theory, let us explore Locke's goal-setting theory.[18] Basically, **the goal-setting model of motivation asserts that we all have values and desires that determine the goals we set for ourselves. In turn these goals directly influence our behavior.** An individual's actions are directly influenced by both the individual and organizational goals that are desired. In particular, goal setting theory has revealed several findings that directly affect its use in organizational settings.

First, specific, clearly defined goals are more likely to result in increased performance. Second, up to a point, the more difficult a goal is, the more effort a person will put forth. However, if goals are set unreasonably high, the individual may become discouraged, though this possibility can be reduced if the person participates in the goal-setting. Third, participation in setting one's goals leads to greater satisfaction and may lead to increased performance. Likewise, research on the effects of feedback of performance results and peer competition for goal accomplishment suggests mixed impact on performance. Fourth, the extent to which employees accept the organizational goals has a direct influence on the effort they will expend. **If the organizational goals and the individual** goals are compatible, the person's actions will be directed toward organizational goals. If there is a lack of congruence between these two types of goals, the individual will tend to act to accomplish individually desired outcomes, unless there is extreme external pressure to accomplish organizational goals.

Job Design and Motivation

With your understanding of content theories that focus on individual needs and process theories that focus on individual choices, you have a great deal of information to aid you in motivating people. To some extent, these theories even take peers and supervisors into account. But they tend to ignore the job as a potential source of motivation, except for Herzberg's mention that the work itself is a motivator. This is understandable in that, historically, the design of a job has been viewed as a technical question. But over the years we have learned that the job a person performs, directly affects motivation.

History of Job Design Concerns

From the days of Frederick Taylor, scientific management encouraged the simplification and standardization of jobs in order to achieve the greatest efficiency.[19] This approach made a great deal of sense, given the abilities of the unskilled, uneducated work force of the early 1900s. Without simplified jobs, the demands of industrialized work far exceeded the skills of immigrant and poorly educated workers. The success of this approach resulted in a prosperous economy and an infatuation with technological efficiency which lingers today. It also resulted in a rapid improvement in the job skills of workers, as shown in Figure 5.4.

The Hawthorne studies of the 1930s were the first real indication that there was more to the job than the technical factors.[20] But it was not until the late 1940s that efforts were directed at the apparent convergence of job demands and job skills of the workers. In the 1950s we saw job rotation (moving people from one job to another during the day) and job enlargement (combining jobs of equal difficulty into one bigger job), but neither approach really changed jobs that much. All the while,

**Figure 5.4
A Comparison of Job
Demands and Worker
Skills and Desires
Since 1900**

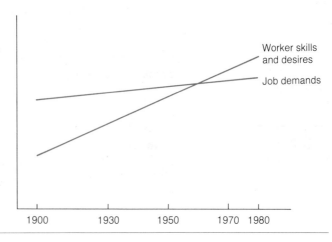

worker skills continued to increase and to surpass the demands of the job (see Figure 5.4). By the 1960s a real mismatch was developing between job demands and worker skills and desires. Worker skills had increased beyond what was needed on many jobs, and their desires for growth and opportunity on the job had increased even more. The result of this mismatch has been lower motivation, and the problem is widespread in the United States, as Box 5.4 illustrates.

**Hackman's Core
Dimensions Model**

In the late 1960s, Herzberg's model of motivation formed the basis of job enrichment as managers tried to build motivators into jobs. The intent was to expand jobs vertically by putting more managerial aspects into them and thus increasing the job demands and opportunities for growth and development in the job. And in the 1970s, Hackman and his associates at Yale added depth to job enrichment by identifying five core dimensions of jobs.[21] The five were skill variety, task identity, task significance, autonomy, and feedback. **Skill variety** is the extent to which the job involves doing different things and using different skills. **Task identity** is the extent to which the job involves performing a task from beginning to end (that is, a complete job). **Task significance** is the impor-

Box 5.4
An Oversupply of
College Graduates
Forces Some into
Lower-Level Jobs

In 1974, Anne Harbut went to Pennsylvania State University, at the age of 33, to earn a graduate degree because she wanted to run a social-services program. Today she is doing routine office work, and she is bitter.

"Basically, I shuffle a lot of papers across my desk, I fill out forms and interview people for low-level jobs," she complains. Unable to find a suitable post in her profession, she has worked since last summer as a personnel assistant at Philadelphia's Metropolitan Hospital.

"It's boring and at times it seems pointless," she says. "Once I had a job working on a construction gang in the Swiss Alps. It was more satisfying than this. At least we were accomplishing something. At the end of the day, we could see the road getting built."

Like Mrs. Harbut, large numbers of Americans are working at jobs for which their training has made them overqualified. They are the products of the nation's education binge over the last two decades, when colleges were churning out graduates at a far faster rate than the economy required. Government statistics show that while the proportion of college-educated members of the work force nearly doubled over that period, to 17.6% in 1979, there was more demand for service jobs than for general white-collar skills. This mismatch is exacerbated by the current recession.

The frustration of overqualified workers, some labor experts say, already is apparent. Robert Quinn, of the University of Michigan's Survey Research Center, found in a 1977 study that 36% of U.S. workers believe they have skills they are unable to use in their jobs. He says numerous studies have shown that overqualified workers have a high degree of job dissatisfaction. And, in turn, these studies link job dissatisfaction with high turnover and absenteeism.

By Robert S. Greenberger, *The Wall Street Journal*, February 25, 1982. Reprinted by permission of *The Wall Street Journal*, © Dow Jones & Company, Inc. 1982. All rights reserved.

tance of the job in the overall work of the plant or company. As shown in Figure 5.5, these three core dimensions result in the level of experienced meaningfulness by the employee performing the job. And these factors have virtually nothing to do with the employee's supervisor. Rather, they are dependent upon how the job is designed technologically. The next core dimension, **autonomy**, is the degree to which the job provides freedom and independence for the employee to make important decisions related to the performance of the job — for example, setting work schedules. As shown in Figure 5.5, autonomy affects the degree of responsibility experienced by the employee in doing the job. Finally, **feedback** is the degree to which carrying out the work activities results in the employees receiving direct information about how well they are doing. Such feedback directly affects the knowledge of actual results that the employee receives on a very timely basis.

This model thus suggests that the higher a job is in skill variety, task identity, and task significance, the higher it will be in meaningfulness. The greater the autonomy, the greater the experienced responsibility. And the greater the direct feedback from the job, the greater the knowledge of actual results — and without possible distortion as it passes through other people. In turn, Figure 5.5 shows that **the greater the meaningfulness, experienced**

Figure 5.5 The Job Characteristics Model of Work Motivation

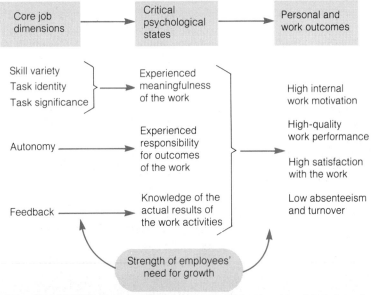

Source: Copyright 1975 by the Regents of the University of California. Adapted from J. R. Hackman, G. Oldham, R. Janson, and K. Purdy, "A New Strategy for Job Enrichment," *California Management Review,* vol. 17, no. 4, p. 62. By permission of the Regents.

responsibility, and knowledge of actual results, the greater will be internal work motivation, quality of work, and satisfaction with the work, and the lower will be absenteeism and turnover. However, there is one big qualifier to this statement: this relationship holds only for people who are high in what Hackman calls growth need strength. This concept refers to the desire the employee has for development of skills and abilities and for performing interesting and challenging work. If an employee does not have a high need for growth, increases in the core job dimensions will overwhelm the person and result in erratic performance, adjustment problems, and possible turnover and absenteeism.[22] The person with low growth need is best suited for a job which is low in the five core dimensions, whereas the high growth need person will be bored and unchallenged by a job low in the core dimensions. The message here is clear and it is one we have mentioned before. There must be a fit between the person and the job if desired outcomes are to result. And this applies both to cases where people are over and underqualified.

But how does one go about altering the core job dimensions? Figure 5.6 shows several ways to increase them.[23] By combining tasks into larger modules (basically job enlargement), both skill variety and task identity can be increased. Forming natural work units—that is, making the worker responsible for a more complete and identi-

**Figure 5.6
Principles for
Changing Jobs**

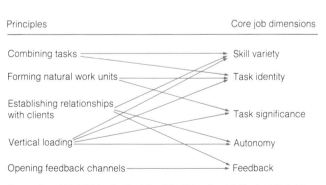

Principles   Core job dimensions

Combining tasks   Skill variety

Forming natural work units   Task identity

Establishing relationships
with clients   Task significance

Vertical loading   Autonomy

Opening feedback channels   Feedback

Source: Copyright 1975 by the Regents of the University of California. Adapted from J. R. Hackman, G. Oldham, R. Janson, and K. Purdy, "A New Strategy for Job Enrichment," *California Management Review*, vol. 17, no. 4, p. 62. By permission of the Regents.

fiable body of work (for example, sales of all products to a certain set of customers rather than sales of only one product)—leads to greater task identity and task significance. **Establishing client relationships**—that is, relationships with the users of the employee's work—increases skill variety, autonomy, and feedback. **Vertical loading**—that is, giving the employee greater discretion and decision making authority—leads to greater task identity, task significance, and autonomy. Finally, by **opening feedback channels** from the job itself, the employee can measure his or her own performance and thus receive better feedback. An analysis of a keypunch operator's job, as reported by Hackman will help to illustrate these ideas (see Box 5.5).

Box 5.5
Redesigning a
Keypunch Operator's
Job

T he problem.   Perhaps one of the clearest examples of the application of the Job Characteristics Model can be seen in one effort, to redesign the job of keypunch operators at Traveler's Insurance Company. Using the core job dimensions described in the model, the job of keypunch operator prior to enrichment can be described as follows:

> Skill variety. *None. Only a single skill was needed: the ability to accurately punch data on cards.*
>
> Task identity. *Little. Batches were assembled to provide an even work load, but not whole identifiable jobs.*
>
> Task significance. *Not apparent. While keypunching is a necessary step in providing service to company customers, the individual operators were isolated by an assignment clerk and a supervisor from any knowledge of what the operation meant to the receiving department, let alone to the ultimate consumer.*
>
> Autonomy. *Little. The operators had no freedom to arrange their daily tasks to meet schedules, to resolve problems with receiving departments, or even to correct information that was obviously wrong.*
>
> Feedback. *None. Once a batch was completed, the operators received no feedback on performance quality.*
>
> *Work redesign.   The investigators, using the Job Characteristic Model, made the following simple changes:*
>
> Natural work units. *Instead of randomly assigning batches of work, each operator was assigned continuing responsibility*

for certain accounts (particular departments or recurring jobs). All work for an account was given to the same operator.

Task combination. *Some planning and controlling functions were integrated with the main task of keypunching.*

Client relationships. *Each operator was given several channels of direct contact with clients. Operators, not assignment clerks, could now examine documents for legibility and autonomy. When a problem arises, the operator, not the supervisor, contacts the client.*

Feedback. *In addition to client feedback, the operators also receive feedback from the job itself. For example, all incorrect cards are returned to the operator for correction. Weekly computer printouts are provided listing error rates and productivity. These are sent directly to the operator, not the supervisor.*

Vertical loading. *Operators were given authority to correct obvious errors on their own. They could also set their own schedules and plan their daily work.*

Results.   As a result of the work redesign experiment, several desired outcomes emerged: (1) While the control group (where no changes were made) showed an increase in productivity of 8.1 percent during the trial period, the work redesign group showed an increase of 39.6 percent. (2) Prior to the study the experimental group had an error rate of 1.53 percent; following the intervention, the average error rate fell to 0.99 percent. (3) During the study period, absenteeism in the experimental group declined 24.1 percent, while it increased 29 percent in the control group. (4) While no attitude changes occurred in the control group, overall job satisfaction increased 16.5 percent in the experimental group after intervention. (5) Because of the improved operator proficiency, fewer controls were necessary, reducing supervisory needs. (6) Since the operators took over many of the mundane supervisory responsibilities, supervisors were now able to devote more time to developing feedback systems, setting up work modules, overseeing the enrichment effort, and planning. In short, supervisors were now able to manage instead of dealing with day-to-day problems.

Source: Copyright 1975 by the Regents of the University of California. Adapted from J. R. Hackman, G. Oldham, R. Janson, and K. Purdy, "A New Strategy for Job Enrichment," *California Management Review,* vol. 17, no. 4, p. 62. By permission of the Regents.

We now have 10 motivation theories to draw on as a manager. Let us look into some motivational problems at Home Computers to see if we can understand the situation and pose some solutions based on these theories.

Motivation at Home Computers

In the Home Computers plant in Dayton, Ohio, 330 employees work on the assembly of the EZ3 computer, which is designed for home use. The EZ3 was introduced in 1983, six years after the EZ2. In addition to the 330 assembly line employees, there are 75 clerical people in the plant, and 85 management employees in five hierarchical levels above the assembly line and clerical workers. Besides the plant manager, there are four department heads, a number of section heads, an even larger number of shift supervisors, and a large number of first line supervisors. But while 490 employees is a relatively large plant with a number of jobs and employee categories, it has not always been that way.

The Dayton plant was the first plant leased by Harvey and Bill back in 1977. At that time there were 16 employees in addition to Harvey and Bill. Everyone was on a first-name basis, and people generally worked on a computer from start to finish. There was a real feeling of involvement, challenge, and responsibility. In fact, the workers checked out each computer after assembling it to ensure that it worked—a self-administered quality-control system. Each employee worked on an hourly pay system with bonuses based on company profits at the end of each year. Hence, there was a great deal of incentive to do the best job possible in the shortest time possible.

From 1977 to 1980, sales increased dramatically (from 250 units to 3,000), and approximately 60 percent of these units were produced in Dayton, after the opening of the second plant in Denver, Colorado. With the number of computers produced in Dayton going from 250 to 1,800 in three years, a number of changes occurred in the plant. First, the number of employees working on production increased from 16 to 150. Second, the plant established a more structured hierarchy with line supervisors, shift supervisors, and several middle managers. The structure also involved the addition of approximately 30 clerical workers. And third, the plant operation went to two and then to three shifts to maximize use of plant and equipment. The fourth major change was the shift from a craft operation where each employee built an entire computer to an assembly-line operation where each employee worked with only part of the final product. For a while, the company did maintain the hourly pay plus bonuses. But it was so difficult for employees to feel any personal impact on profits that the fifth change was to go to a simple hourly pay scale. Fortunately, most of the original 16 employees (plus others who had joined Home Computers under the old pay plan) had either moved up into supervisory and managerial positions or had quit the company. Otherwise, there could have been some problems.

These changes toward a more structured organization, a more sophisticated technology for computer assembly, and a conservative pay plan have continued from 1980 until the present plant of 490 employees. Life on the Home Computers assembly line in Dayton is not exciting or challenging. As one employee recently said, "It takes more brains to change my kid's diaper than it does to do my job here." However, some of the employees seem to like the lack of responsibility in their job, and the predictability of the work. They get a steady paycheck and can go home at night and forget about Home Computers. However, some employees take advantage of the situation by being late or absent a great deal. In fact, productivity of computers has dropped in recent months, and part of this problem involves turnover and absenteeism of the work force.

Harvey has begun to explore the problems with his work force, with the help of a consultant. An attitude survey was administered to the employees in Dayton, and many of the managers were interviewed to delve into the problems. The attitude survey was designed to assess the need satisfaction of the employees. In general, the results indicated that the existence desires and lower-level needs were basically satisfied. The assembly-line employees seemed to be happy with their working conditions, their pay, and most company policies. There was some concern expressed about the constant changes in supervision due to growth and turnover and about the wide variety of people on the assembly line.

As for the higher-level needs, the assembly-line workers expressed very little satisfaction. In fact, the consultant pointed out that the concerns expressed about supervision and co-workers were probably unsatisfied belongingness needs. The workers felt very little sense of achievement in their work. They also felt little sense of responsibility and thought the work was boring and unchallenging. However, some of the workers reported liking their jobs as they were—they liked having very little responsibility and still receiving a good paycheck. As for the managers, some felt they had too much responsibility given their background; others felt they were not advancing fast enough. Some managers felt their work was too constraining and gave them no opportunity to exercise real control and decision making. Harvey interrupted the consultant during his report to say, "Things really seem to be messed up and very complicated as well. Some people seem to like what the others dislike. What am I going to do?" The consultant responded, "Yes, things are complicated, but let's not talk yet about what you are going to do. There's more data here to tell you about."

While the data suggested that employees were satisfied with their pay, they reported that they were not happy with the reward system of the company. Very little recognition was given for a job well done. And employees were often reprimanded only when a situation had really become severe; they were given no previous warning. But workers were really upset about the jobs they had. On the job-design part of the survey, employees rated their jobs low on meaningfulness, responsibility, and feedback. Many of the employees have associate degrees in computer science or computer experience from the military. But their jobs only allow them to do set, specific things. They felt quality would be better if they had more control over the production.

As for the managers, they too felt their jobs to be constraining, though some were overwhelmed by the managerial task. They felt that feedback was inadequate. But what really seemed to upset the managers was a lack of clear company goals. They felt that Home Computers was just being swept along by the tide with little direction. What this meant to the managers was constantly changing guidelines and responsibilities. Sometimes they were the last to know about a change—and if clear goals were established they felt there would not need to be as much change anyway.

Harvey is sitting there with the consultant mulling over these results and wondering what to do. Indeed, what needs to be done to correct a growing problem of motivation at Home Computers?

Applying the Theories to Home Computers

With the data supplied by the consultant's survey, we can now use the motivational theories to dig into the Home Computers situation. Let us see what the content theories suggest for our analysis.

Content Theories

The survey has revealed that most of the employees are satisfied with their lower-level needs. There is, however, a problem with their belonging needs and with the higher-level, growth-oriented needs. The employees seem to want more responsibility, more recognition for their work, and to feel a greater sense of achievement. So, what can be done? More information and clearer goals would seem to deal directly with the issues of concern to the employees. And a more orderly plan for employee development and career movement would also signal that the company is responding to the desires of the employees, while still focusing on company goals.

But we must not forget that the survey data suggested some of the employees liked the lack of responsibility in their jobs. How can we satisfy employees with such divergent needs? Ah, such is the life of a manager. Two choices seem possible. First, try to group employees together by the kinds of needs they are trying to satisfy. Second, drawing upon job design theory, try to match employees with their jobs: see that employees with high growth needs get the more motivating jobs and those with low growth needs get the less motivating ones. We can probably eliminate the first choice because we do not want to create pockets in the company of unmotivated employees. The second choice addresses the critical need for a match between worker and job. Essentially, the higher-need-level employees can be allowed to participate in the weekly meetings and can be expected to make better use of the information and goals that will be available to everyone. Of course, some people's needs may change depending on events that transpire; but the plans discussed above allow room for such change.

Process Theories

It seems that goals for the employees are not always clearly defined, and goal-setting theory would suggest that this is a problem source. But goals do not appear to be the only problem. The employees also do not know which rewards are associated with which good or poor performance, and reinforcement theory would suggest this is a problem. The old bonus system appears to have failed because control was taken away from the employees on the job. With clearer goals, a performance-linked reward system should be possible, hence clarifying the instrumentalities suggested by expectancy theory.

It is clear in the case that employees are making choices (for example, some are quitting), but the choices are not compatible with organizational goals. Equity theory would suggest that there are perceived inequities. Some of the managers welcome responsibilities, while others feel overwhelmed. Perhaps more training could help alleviate the problem. Likewise, some of the employees welcome the lack of responsibility in their jobs, while others want more responsibility. As we have suggested, this inequity could be handled by matching people and jobs. Indeed, the interaction of different personalities on the job can easily create feelings of inequity. And this fact also suggests the importance of social facilitation theory in our analysis. As the employees at Home Computers who are unhappy interact with other employees, their unhappiness can spread, and a morale problem can develop. A key factor for avoiding these problems brought on by different people is the job/person fit, so let us see what job design theory offers our analysis.

Job-Design Theory

The survey results suggest that the assembly-line workers feel their jobs lack meaningfulness, responsibility, and feedback. Job-design theory suggests that employees with a high need for growth will not be motivated in these jobs. High absenteeism and turnover and low satisfaction with the work—all problems presently experienced at Home Computers—are likely to result. The case does point out that the employees value higher-level needs. Thus, all the pieces seem to be in place to cause the problems experienced at Home Computers. Figure 5.6 suggests several principles which could be applied to improve the motivation of the work itself: (1) combining tasks, (2) forming natural work units, (3) establishing relationships with clients, (4) vertical loading, and (5) opening feedback channels. Not all of these may apply here, but Harvey and the consultant can consider several possibilities.

One option would be to have employees move along the assembly line with a computer so they can work on several steps in the assembly process. This combining of tasks should increase skill variety and task identity and result in more meaningful jobs. This approach should not create any severe training or staffing problems, since most of the tasks are simple. A second option would be to have all the workers for a particular section of the line (that is, those who do the same jobs) meet each week for an hour to discuss problems and suggestions for improvement on the line. In addition, two team representatives from each shift can meet to discuss any problems that cut across shift boundaries. Recommendations from these meetings can be forwarded to management for their consideration and written response. This establishment of relationships and vertical loading (that is, allowing decision making and problem solving) should increase the autonomy of the job. Finally, the employees on the line could conduct quality-control, keep a tally, and pass the word along the assembly line. This change should increase feedback. We have thus identified several promising changes that could make the employees' jobs more motivating and move them into the upper levels of their motivational potential (see Figure 5.2).

In summary, we can see how these 10 motivation theories are helpful in analyzing the Home Computers case. But the analysis still seems to fall short in a couple of ways. First, we have no way to integrate the use of the theories to assist our analysis. It is as though we are using a shotgun approach. Second, our analysis to this point tends to be rather static—yet we know that these motivational problems are grounded in a dynamic process. The problems did not come about overnight. In the next chapter we will try to address these two deficiencies through our integrative model of motivation.

Chapter Highlights

This chapter has begun our examination of motivation in work settings. First, we explored why motivation is important for managers to understand. **Motivation was defined as that which energizes, directs, and sustains an individual to perform goal-directed actions.** We pointed out that people are usually motivated to do something; your job as a manager is to see that their actions help the organization achieve its goals. We also pointed out the complexity of the motivation process by recalling the uniqueness of each individual, yourself included.

This point then led to consideration of some organizational problems which can be directly tied to motivation. These problems include low productivity, tardiness, absenteeism, turnover, poor-quality work, lack of mental presence on the job, lack of innovativeness, and low employee morale.

In concluding the introduction to this chapter, we briefly discussed how motivation is a dynamic process, mentioning first that **people are likely to be motivated by different things at different times in their lives.** And just as people change over time, so do their jobs and organizations. Organizations grow or decline and thus provide new or reduced opportunities for individuals to meet their needs and be motivated. And jobs can become more or less challenging and exciting due to technological and structural changes in the organization.

In the next section we discussed a number of content and process theories of motivation. **Content theories highlight the differences among people;** they include theories by Maslow, Herzberg, McClelland, and Alderfer. **Process theories focus on the choice process afforded individuals regarding their actions;** they include theories by Vroom, Adams, Skinner, and Locke. We also mentioned Hackman's theory of job design and social facilitation theory as two other important theories of motivation.

The Maslow hierarchy of needs was the starting point for tying together four content theories of motivation. Because of the developmental implications of the theory, we used it to relate Alderfer's ERG theory, Herzberg's two factor theory, and McClelland's motive model. These theories all suggest the importance of employees' needs; **the less a need is satisfied, the more it will be desired, and the more individual action will be directed toward satisfying that need.**

McClelland's motive (need) theory added another important element: **individual needs are learned.** This developmental aspect means that needs will change over time. It also means that different individuals will have unique needs (or at least strengths of needs), since they will each have unique backgrounds. Herzberg's theory added the important idea that **needs can, in a sense, become over-satisfied and thus fail to motivate behavior.** More of the same reward will not always motivate employees; sometimes you have to discover new rewards that will address new needs.

After a brief discussion of social facilitation theory—which helped us appreciate the impact of peers and superiors on our motivation—we discussed several process theories of motivation. First, we discussed Vroom's expectancy theory and stated that it will form the basis for our integrative model in Chapter 6. We discussed three steps in the expectancy model (expectancy, instrumentality, and valence). This step-by-step aspect of the model highlights the developmental nature of the model.

We then discussed operant conditioning (reinforcement theory) as a motivation theory. It helps us understand the interface between the organization and the individual. **One critical point to remember in applying this theory is that the reward must be perceived as important by the employee receiving it if it is to be an effective motivator.**

Equity theory was discussed to help us appreciate the way people compare their perceived inputs and outputs to those of other employees. **We must be aware that employees are influenced by what they perceive happens both to themselves and to others.**

The last process theory we discussed was Locke's goal-setting theory. Goals are an important element in motivation. **One of the challenges to you as a manager is to encourage employee actions which will help accomplish both organizational and individual goals.**

Next we turned to a discussion of job design as it relates to motivation. We learned that job design has been an important concern to managers since the early 1900s, but the primary focus has been on technical aspects of jobs rather than on full utilization of employee job skills. But since the 1970s, we have had a theory of job design which focuses on creating a job that is matched to the employee. **Giving an enriched job to a person who wants no challenge in the job is as bad as giving an unenriched job to a person who seeks a challenge.**

To help you better understand how to apply these various theories, we then looked into the motivational problems at Home Computers. Drawing upon all 10 motivation theories, a number of suggested solutions were developed. But in closing, we pointed out the need for a vehicle to integrate our use of these theories and to place them in a developmental framework.

Review Questions

1. How should motivation be defined to be useful to a manager?

2. Why is it important for a manager to understand motivation? How does a manager's job relate to motivation?

3. What are some key organizational problems that are related to motivation of employees?

4. Explain why motivation is a dynamic process. What work-setting factors create changes in employee motivation?

5. What is the primary distinction between content and process theories of motivation? What other motivation theories are important background for an understanding of motivation?

6. How can the theories of Maslow, Alderfer, Herzberg, and McClelland be tied together?

7. What unique contributions do the theories of Maslow, Alderfer, Herzberg, and McClelland provide for our understanding of motivation?

8. What is the importance of social facilitation theory to our understanding of motivation?

9. How do operant conditioning and equity theory tie together to provide useful information for our understanding of motivation?

10. Goal-setting theory developed by Locke is helpful in our understanding of which aspects of motivation? What challenge for management grows out of this theory?

11. Detail the development of job design theory and how it has led to both a current dilemma and a new theory of job design (Hackman's model).

12. Describe the important elements and relationships in Hackman's model of job design. Where do individual differences enter into the model?

Notes

1. D. Katz and R. Kahn, *The Social Psychology of Organizations*, 2d cd. (New York: John Wiley & Sons, 1978).

2. R. M. Steers, *Introduction to Organizational Behavior* (Glenview, Ill.: Scott, Foresman, 1981), p. 328.

3. W. H. Mobley, "Intermediate Linkages in the Relationship between Job Satisfaction and Employee Turnover," *Journal of Applied Psychology*, 62 (1977), pp. 237–40.

4. T. R. Mitchell, "Motivation: New Directions for Theory, Research, and Practice," *Academy of Management Review*, 7 (1982), pp. 80–88.

5. Ibid.

6. A. Maslow, "A Theory of Human Motivation," *Psychological Review*, 80 (1943), pp. 370–96.

7. G. R. Salancik and J. Pfeffer, "An Examination of Need-Satisfaction Models of Job Attitudes," *Administrative Science Quarterly*, 22 (1977), pp. 427–56.

8. C. P. Alderfer, *Existence, Relatedness, and Growth* (New York: Free Press, 1972).

9. D. C. McClelland, "Power Is the Great Motivator," *Harvard Business Review*, 54 (1976), pp. 100–10.

10. F. Herzberg, B. Mausner, and B. Snyderman. *The Motivation to Work* (New York: John Wiley & Sons, 1959).

11. S. Kerr, A. Harlan, and R. Stogdill, "Preference for Motivator and Hygiene Factors in a Hypothetical Interview Situation," *Personnel Psychology*, 25 (1974), pp. 109–24.

12. G. R. Ferris, T. A. Beehr, and D. C. Gilmore, "Social Facilitation: A Review and Alternative Conceptual Model," *Academy of Management Review*, 3 (1978), pp. 338–47.

13. V. H. Vroom, *Work and Motivation* (New York: John Wiley & Sons, 1964).

14. T. R. Mitchell, "Expectancy Models of Job Satisfaction, Occupational Preference, and Effort: A Theoretical, Methodological, and Empirical Appraisal," *Psychological Bulletin*, 81 (1974), pp. 1096–112.

15. D. J. Cherrington, H. J. Reitz, and W. E. Scott, "Effects of Contingent and Non-Contingent Rewards on the Relationship between Satisfaction and Performance," *Journal of Applied Psychology*, 56 (1971), pp. 531–36; W. C. Hamner, "Reinforcement Theory and Contingency Management in Organizational Settings." In H. L. Tosi and W. C. Hamner, *Organizational Behavior and Management: A Contingency Approach* (New York: John Wiley & Sons, 1974), pp. 86–112.

16. J. S. Adams, "Injustice in Social Exchange." In *Advances in Experimental Social Psychology*, vol. 2, ed. L. Berkowitz (New York: Academic Press, 1965).

17. R. T. Mowday, "Equity Theory Predictions of Behavior in Organizations." In R. M. Steers and L. W. Porter, eds., *Motivation and Work Behavior*, 2d ed. (New York: McGraw-Hill, 1979)

18. E. A. Locke, "Toward a Theory of Task Performance and Incentive," *Organizational Behavior and Human Performance*, vol. 3 (1968), pp. 157–89.

19. F. W. Taylor, *The Principles of Scientific Management* (New York: Harper & Row, 1911).

20. F. Roethlisberger and W. J. Dickson, *Management and the Worker* (Cambridge, Mass.: Harvard University Press, 1939).

21. J. R. Hackman, G. Oldham, R. Janson, and K. Purdy, "A New Strategy for Job Enrichment," *California Management Review*, 27 (1975), pp. 57–71.

22. Ibid.

23. Ibid.

Resource Readings

Adams, J. S. "Injustice in Social Exchange." In *Advances in Experimental Social Psychology* 2. ed. L. Berkowitz. New York: Academic Press, 1965.

Alderfer, C. P. *Existence, Relatedness, and Growth*. New York: Free Press, 1972.

Hackman, J. R. "Work Design." In *Improving Life at Work*. ed. J. R. Hackman and J. L. Suttle. Glenview, Ill.: Scott, Foresman, 1976, pp. 96–162.

Hamner, W. C. "Reinforcement Theory." In *Organizational Behavior and Management: A Contingency Approach*. ed. H. T. Tosi and W. C. Hamner. New York: John Wiley & Sons, 1977, pp. 93–112.

Herzberg, F., B. Mausner, and B. Snyderman. *The Motivation to Work*. New York: John Wiley & Sons, 1959.

Locke, E. A. "The Nature and Causes of Job Satisfaction." In *Handbook of Industrial and Organizational Psychology*. ed. M. D. Dunnette. Skokie, Ill.: Rand McNally, 1976.

Maslow, A. H. *Motivation and Personality*. New York: Harper & Row, 1954.

McClelland, D. A. *Assessing Human Motivation*. New York: General Learning Press, 1971.

Vroom, V. H. *Work and Motivation*. New York: John Wiley & Sons, 1964.

MOTIVATION FEEDBACK OPINIONNAIRE
Part 1

Directions

The following statements have seven possible responses.

Strongly Agree	Agree	Slightly Agree	Don't Know	Slightly Disagree	Disagree	Strongly Disagree
+3	+2	+1	0	−1	−2	−3

Please mark one of the seven responses by circling the number that corresponds to the response that fits your opinion. For example: if you "Strongly Agree," circle the number "+3."

Complete every item. You have about 10 minutes to do so.

1. Special wage increases should be given to employees who do their jobs very well.   +3 +2 +1   0 −1 −2 −3
2. Better job descriptions would be helpful so that employees will know exactly what is expected of them.   +3 +2 +1   0 −1 −2 −3
3. Employees need to be reminded that their jobs are dependent on the company's ability to compete effectively.   +3 +2 +1   0 −1 −2 −3
4. A supervisor should give a good deal of attention to the physical working conditions of his employers.   +3 +2 +1   0 −1 −2 −3
5. The supervisor ought to work hard to develop a friendly working atmosphere among his people.   +3 +2 +1   0 −1 −2 −3
6. Individual recognition for above-standard performance means a lot to employees.   +3 +2 +1   0 −1 −2 −3
7. Indifferent supervision can often bruise feelings.   +3 +2 +1   0 −1 −2 −3
8. Employees want to feel that their real skills and capacities are put to use on their jobs.   +3 +2 +1   0 −1 −2 −3
9. The company retirement benefits and stock programs are important factors in keeping employees on their jobs.   +3 +2 +1   0 −1 −2 −3
10. Almost every job can be made more stimulating and challenging.   +3 +2 +1   0 −1 −2 −3
11. Many employees want to give their best in everything they do.   +3 +2 +1   0 −1 −2 −3
12. Management could show more interest in the employees by sponsoring social events after-hours.   +3 +2 +1   0 −1 −2 −3
13. Pride in one's work is actually an important reward.   +3 +2 +1   0 −1 −2 −3
14. Employees want to be able to think of themselves as "the best" at their own jobs.   +3 +2 +1   0 −1 −2 −3
15. The quality of the relationships in the informal work group is quite important.   +3 +2 +1   0 −1 −2 −3
16. Individual incentive bonuses would improve the performance of employees.   +3 +2 +1   0 −1 −2 −3
17. Visibility with upper management is important to employees.   +3 +2 +1   0 −1 −2 −3
18. Employees generally like to schedule their own work and to make job-related decisions with a minimum of supervision.   +3 +2 +1   0 −1 −2 −3
19. Job security is important to employees.   +3 +2 +1   0 −1 −2 −3
20. Having good equipment to work with is important to employees.   +3 +2 +1   0 −1 −2 −3

Opinionnaire (*continued*)

Part II

Scoring

1. Transfer the numbers you circled in Part I to the appropriate places in the chart below:

Statement Number	Score	Statement Number	Score
10	2	2	2
11	2	3	1
13	2	9	-2
18	1	19	2
········		········	
Total	7	Total	3
(Self-Actualization Needs)		(Safety Needs)	

Statement Number	Score	Statement Number	Score
6	1	1	3
8	3	4	1
14	2	16	2
17	1	20	1
········		········	
Total	7	Total	7
(Esteem Needs)		(Basic Needs)	

Statement Number	Score
5	2
7	3
12	2
15	1
········	
Total	8
(Belonging Needs)	

Opinionnaire (*concluded*)

2. Record your total scores in the chart below by marking an "X" in each row next to the number of your total score for that area of needs motivation.

	−12	−10	−8	−6	−4	−2	0	+2	+4	+6	+8	+10	+12
Self-Actualization										X			
Esteem										X	X		
Belonging											X		
Safety									X				
Basic										X			

Low	High
Use	Use

Once you have completed this chart, you can see the relative strength of your use of each of these areas of needs motivation. There is, of course, no "right" answer. What is right for you is what matches the actual needs of your employees and that, of course, is specific to each situation and each individual. In general, however, the "experts" tell us that today's employees are best motivated by efforts in the areas of Belonging and Esteem.

Source: Reprinted from: John E. Jones and J. William Pfeiffer, Eds., *The 1973 Annual Handbook for Group Facilitators*. (San Diego, Calif.: University Associates, Inc., 1973). Used with permission.

CHAPTER 6

An Integrative Approach to Motivation

In Chapter 5 we discussed 10 different theories of motivation. In exploring both content and process theories, as well as social facilitation and job design theories, we provided you with a great deal of information for analyzing motivational problems. And we applied these theories to the Home Computers case. In this chapter we go one step further in making these theories useful to you by providing an integrative model of motivation. With the 10 theories as background, an integrative model should make it easier to fully analyze motivational problems in organizations.

An Integrative Model of Motivation

Our integrative model of motivation is based on the expectancy theory we discussed in Chapter 5.[1] This theory provides a strong basis for our model because it is both process oriented and has developmental features, as we discussed in the last chapter. By modifying the model somewhat and expanding it in certain areas, we can develop a very useful integrative framework for understanding motivation in organizations. The model is shown in Figure 6.1. It describes the motivational process that unfolds in determining an individual's motivational level. Ovals 1, 2, 3a, 4, and 5 represent the five basic steps in the process. The model also shows the interaction between an individual and the desired outcomes of the organization (oval 3b and 3c). Let us go through the model to learn how it works.

Imagine that you have an unsatisfied need for greater recognition in your work (oval 1). In oval 2 you consider alternative actions which you think will lead to satisfaction of that need (oval 5). You might consider: (1) increasing your contacts with the boss so he or she knows who you are, (2) working harder on the job to increase your productivity, or (3) attending training courses to demonstrate your interest in advancement. At this point your choice will be influenced by the reward you believe will lead to satisfaction of your esteem need (ovals 4 and 5). Let us say that you feel it will take a promotion to satisfy your esteem need. Furthermore, you believe that in your organization a promotion will follow high productivity

Figure 6.1 An Integrative Model of the Motivational Process

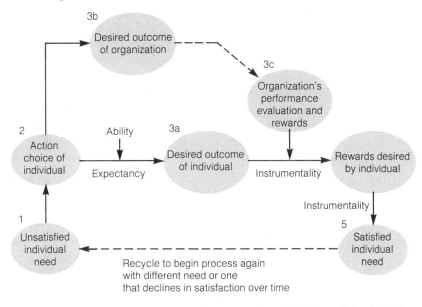

Source: Adapted from Vroom's Expectancy Theory, in V. H. Vroom, *Work and Motivation*, copyright © 1964 John Wiley & Sons, Inc.

in your present job; that is, high productivity has the highest instrumentality value. This opinion is developed from your experiences in the organization. Thus, high productivity becomes your desired outcome (oval 3a). And of your three action choices, working harder is the choice you believe will lead to higher productivity (oval 2); that is, it has the highest expectancy value.

The Amount of Motivation

The actual amount of your motivation (according to expectancy theory) depends on several factors shown in the model. First is the **expectancy** that your hard work (oval 2) will lead to the desired outcome of high productivity (oval 3a). If you feel that you are capable and that the outcome of your job is primarily determined by your efforts alone, your expectancy will be high. But if you doubt your capabilities and know that your performance is heavily determined by others, your expectancy may be quite low. The fit between you and the job is a critical aspect of this analysis. What type of job do you hold, and how capable are you in the job? The next factor is the **instrumentality** that the desired outcome of high productivity (oval 3a) will actually lead to a promotion (oval 4). **Instrumentality is thus the link between desired outcome and rewards desired. It is very important in the model because it links the motivation of an individual to actions of the organization.** If you believe that high productivity in your organization almost always leads to a promotion, your instrumentality for high productivity will be quite high. But if you believe that luck, who you know, and other factors sometimes determine promotions, your instrumentality for high productivity may be lower.

Valence is the actual value or importance you place on the promotion; that is, on your desired reward (oval 4). If it is very important, your valence will be quite high. If it is only moderately important, the valence will be lower. In actual practice, the valence is really based on another instrumentality link—rewards desired to satisfied need (ovals 4 and 5). In other words, if you feel that a promotion will be very important in satisfying your need for recognition, the valence of the promotion will be high. If you are not so sure about this link, the valence of the promotion will be lower. **The need to be satisfied carries its own valence that affects the valence of the rewards desired.**

For you to be highly motivated to work harder in your job, the expectancy between action and desired outcome (ovals 2 and 3a) must be high; the instrumentality between desired outcome and desired rewards (ovals 3a and 4) must be high; and the valence of the reward must be high. And as we have explained, this means that the instrumentality between reward and satisfied need (ovals 4 and 5) must be high. Furthermore, the need for recognition, which is to be satisfied, must be very important to you. **If the expectancy or instrumentality connections are weak, or if the valence of the reward and the satisfied need are low, your motivation will be low.** The reason is that the process is multiplicative in nature. It is like a chain whose strength is determined by its weakest link. For example, if you are unsure if the high productivity will lead to a promotion (low instrumentality between ovals 3a and 4), your motivation to work hard will tend to be lower, regardless of the valence and expectancy.

Thus far in our explanation, it should be clear how both expectancy theory and the content theories relate to our integrative model. Expectancy theory is the basis for the model, and the content theories elaborate the types of needs that people act to satisfy. Herzberg's two-factor theory helps us understand the link between rewards and satisfied need (ovals 4 and 5). The reason is that all of the hygiene and motivating factors relate to actions and aspects of the work—that is, the rewards desired by a person (oval 4). The other content theories relate directly to the needs in ovals 1 and 5. Furthermore, we have acknowledged how social facilitation and job design theories tie into the instrumentality and expectancy aspects of the model. And meaningfulness, responsibility, and feedback, as spelled out in the job design theory, are rewards that people may desire in addition to financial rewards. Both skill variety and autonomy also relate to the action choices by expanding the range of choices and the control a person has over the choices.

The Dynamic Nature of the Model

The explanation of our model, however, is still not complete. We have not yet dealt with the dynamic nature of the process. Let us explore this aspect of the model by tracing what happens as you begin to work harder and try to satisfy your need for recognition. Whether your hard work pays off in increased productivity depends heavily on your ability. **Performance is a function of both motivation and ability**. Thus you may work very hard but still not be very effective if you lack the abilities needed for certain aspects of your job. If you do fail to achieve the desired outcome, you will learn something about yourself that will affect your motivation in the future. For example, you could decide that you will never get a promotion in this company and become motivated to look for another job.

At this point we must also consider your action as it relates to the desired outcomes of the organization (oval 3b). Obviously, your superior and co-workers will be evaluating your hard work. And your superior will evaluate your performance in light of organizational goals. The ideal situation is when your actions achieve both your desired outcome (oval 3a) as well as the desired outcome of the organization (oval 3b). **In fact, it would be simply fantastic to work in an organization where your every action enhanced both your goals and the organization goals simultaneously; and this matching might be viewed as a task for managers in organizations.** Questions such as, Do you know what the organization expects of you?, and Does the organization tie rewards to its goals? are important as we consider the interaction of ovals 2, 3a, and 3b in our model. Perhaps you work hard and increase productivity—but because of lack of clear organizational goals, you increase productivity in the wrong areas. Or perhaps in your hard work you ignore certain organizational norms that are considered equally important as performance goals. These events all come together in the instrumentality between the high productivity and the desired reward (promotion) that the company controls (ovals 3a, 3c, and 4). This also marks the point at which goal-setting and reinforcement theories fit into our model. Providing desired rewards for behavior the organization desires should increase the likelihood those behaviors will be repeated. And if the reward does not come, motivation to continue the behavior desired by the organization will decrease.

Let us assume that your hard work has led to better performance, but you do not get the desired promotion. Instead, you receive a nice pay increase. What went wrong? Have you misread the desired outcomes of the organization? Has the organization misread your goals? Another piece of information helps complete the puzzle. You find out that the promotion you wanted went to someone else, who just happens to be connected to the boss's family, and plays golf with the boss on weekends. You have misread the real criteria for promotion and feel cheated. Alternatively, someone else receives the promotion, but the boss explains why you were passed over this time and that the pay raise is meant to tell you that you are doing a good job. Keep up the good work and the next promotion is yours. Obviously, your future motivation will be influenced quite differently in these two situations, and equity theory helps us understand this aspect of the model. The rewards you value and the actions you believe will lead to those rewards are clearly influenced by what happens to you in comparison to others in the organization.

But let us assume that you receive the promotion you wanted. Everything has worked out for you as desired. Is your need for recognition satisfied? What is the actual link between promotion and need satisfaction (ovals 4 and 5)? Perhaps you find that the feeling of recognition is not as great as you thought it would be. Thus your need is still unsatisfied; your cycle must begin again. Or perhaps the need for recognition is now satisfied—but you find the new job to be too constraining. You are actually less free than you were in the old job. Thus, your need for achievement or greater challenge may rise and become the focus of your motivational energies.

From this description it should be clear why we say motivation is a complex process. It involves many pieces, much like a huge puzzle. And it should be clear that the process is dynamic. The model involves sequential steps that occur in a cyclical process over time. And many of the pieces of the model require a look at the past in order to make the current assessment of those pieces—for example, instrumentality, expectancy, and needs all grow out of a time context. They do not just appear at a given moment. Change and evolution can enter the process at almost any point. As we consider an example for applying the model, think about these dynamic properties; we will return to them later.

Box 6.1 presents the situation faced by recent graduates of MBA programs. As the article suggests, the situation is rather bleak and has resulted in a reconsideration of the appropriate actions. Since the action to obtain an MBA (oval 2 in our model) and the achievement of the desired outcome of the MBA degree (oval 3a) have not resulted in the desired reward of a good job (oval 4), the instrumentality between ovals 3a and 4 has been reduced. Therefore, people like Rachel Russo are led to question past decisions, as suggested in the quote from Tom Keffer. And in Rachel's case, she has just about decided to look for a job as a secretary. That is, she is about to change her desired reward (oval 4). But how motivated will she be in that position? A related situation is presented by Bill Schwochow's choice to slack off on

Box 6.1
New MBAs Are
Scrambling for Jobs
as Recession Brings
Drop in Hiring

Rachel Russo graduated last June from Northwestern University's J. L. Kellogg Graduate School of Management, one of the best business schools in the country. Today, she can't find a job.

She spends 10 to 20 hours a week writing letters, telephoning and interviewing at companies—so far without success. "In terms of getting a job," she says, "graduate school was a waste of time."

If she doesn't soon find a job in her field—personnel management—Mrs. Russo may try to be secretary. But that, too, poses problems. "How many people want a secretary who has more education than they have?" she asks.

"There's no question there are fewer opportunities," says Karen K. Stauffacher, director of placement at the University of Wisconsin's Business School in Madison. She advises students to take advantage of personal connections at companies and to be flexible in considering salary, locations and jobs. The school's alumni placement file has grown to 250 names from 75 in the past year; the list of job openings has shrunk to two pages from 10.

"A lot of people gave up good jobs to get an MBA here," says Tom Keffer, editor of the Wharton Journal. "A lot feel they've wasted their time."

Letting Schoolwork Slide

The tight job market means many students will have to work harder wooing employers. "I'll be honest with you: I'm letting my work slide to prepare for these interviews," says Bill Schwochow, a 23-year-old University of Wisconsin student who has been searching since December. Before interviews, he spends one to two hours reading annual reports and business publications to bone up on companies. So far he hasn't had any success. "I try to avoid taking (rejection letters) personally," he says.

Over the long term, the MBA markets should improve as the post World War II baby boom population thins. After reaching a peak of about 59,000 business graduates in the 1984–1985 academic year, the number should decline to less than 55,000 by 1989, according to the National Center for Education Statistics.

Comments Albert P. Hegyi, president of the Association of MBA Executives Inc., a professional group: "You're going to see some excellent opportunities at the end of the decade."

schoolwork in order to work harder to find a job. In his case, he has decided that the appropriate action (oval 2) for getting a job (oval 3a) is not more schoolwork but rather more job searching. Of course, this decision will affect his motivation in the classroom; it may not satisfy the organizational goals as represented by the teacher (oval 3b). So again we have an example of how the choice process of our motivational model works and how it is affected by outcomes and rewards further on in the process. This example points out the potential for changes in action choices, as well as changes in the other components of the model. Let us now turn to a more systematic discussion of the dynamic and developmental aspects of the model, before applying it to the Home Computers case.

Changes in Motivation over Time

As we have suggested in describing our model of motivation in Figure 6.1, many factors can change over time and thus affect the motivation of employees. The primary factor in the developmental nature of motivation is change that occurs in employees over time. However, we will also discuss changes in the organization and the job that can interact with the employees to create changes in motivation.

Changes in People

We made the point in Chapters 3 and 4 that people are unique as a function of their background. Therefore, **as a manager you must deal with a multitude of motivational issues if you manage a number of people.** In addition, the fact that these employees may represent different life and family stages as well as career stages means their motivational needs will differ. And on top of this variation, the motivational needs of people will change over time. Maslow saw his hierarchy of needs operating over a person's lifetime. He saw the various needs that motivate people being different for a young person than for an older one.[2] More recently, research by Sheehy, based upon Levinson's work, has outlined life phases and key events that occur during each life phase (see Figure 6.2).[3] As

Figure 6.2
Adult Life Phases As Adapted from Sheehy and Levinson

Age	Key Events	Basic Issues
Late teens/ early twenties	Striking out on your own; college, job, military service. Early thoughts on a career and family life. Possibly marriage.	Achieving independence from your family. Search for identity. Determining what one should do in life.
Late twenties/ thirties	Change in occupation. Return to school. Marriage or possibly divorce. Family activities and children are important. Important job promotion.	What is life really about? What do I want in life? Achieving a sense of stability. Self doubts and awareness of getting older.
Forties	Realization that life goals may not be achieved. Change of career. Death of parents.	Real awareness of aging of your body. Stagnation in life, career, family. Who am I, really?
Fifties	Reaching your highest career level. Substituting new goals for your life.	Feeling of satisfaction with life versus self doubt. Development of a sense of wisdom.
Sixties and beyond	Retirement. Health problems. Aging.	What to do? Death of others and self. Need to belong. Importance of family and friends.

Source: G. Sheehy, *Passages* (New York: E. P. Dutton, 1976), and D. Levinson, *The Seasons of a Man's Life* (New York: Alfred A. Knopf).

we take a look at these, you will be able to see how motivation might vary across life phases.

We must hasten to point out that the following paragraphs are general statements about people. The stages we will discuss below can vary a great deal from person to person. In fact, the key events may even occur at different life points for different people. So the point of presenting these life stages and the motivation implications is to provide a general framework, which must be modified based on each individual's background. As our case in Chapter 4 illustrated, Steve probably needed more in terms of belongingness than did Louise. Thus, the best way to motivate these two people would have to vary, even though they were in the same life stage.

Sheehy points out that the late teens and early 20s are a time of trying to locate oneself in a peer group apart from the home and family. It is also the time of trying out an occupation. The questions being asked are: Who am I? and What do I want to do? What is really occurring at this time is the combination of the exploration stage of a person's career (as discussed in Chapter 2) with the adolescence personality stage (as discussed in Chapter 4). The person at this stage is searching for both a career and an identity. Sheehy describes two primary alternative scenarios. In one the teen/20s person looks for a ready-made form to fit into. In the other, the individual jumps from one personal encounter and one job to another. As a manager you must know what basic needs motivate them. **The teen/20s person typically seeks a sense of belonging; friendships and co-worker relationships are important**. Thus, to be effective, a manager will try to provide this opportunity and will also provide feedback directed toward the person's search for identity. In other words, feedback that tells the person how he or she is doing on the job.

The next life stage is during the late 20s and 30s. In this period, a settling process takes place for most people. There may be a job change. One may go back to school. Marriages usually occur in this period, and children may enter the picture. Essentially, this stage is an interaction of the young adult personality stage and the career stage of establishment (as discussed in Chapters 4 and 2, respectively). It is a time of asking: What do I want out of life? Will I be able to achieve my life goals? For many people this is a time of growing stress, for one is passing into true adulthood. The birth of children begins a process that draws one away from work, while work is attracting the employee to see what he or she can accomplish. **The result for the 20s/30s employee is likely to be an unusual combination of needs for security and income with needs to succeed and progress in an occupation**. For the blue-collar worker, the need for progression may be replaced by a need to be recognized for one's accomplishments and abilities. In either event, to be effective a manager should probably define opportunities to utilize the talents of a 20s/30s employee, while recognizing the family demands he or she is experiencing at this time. This recognition can come simply from an interest in the employee's personal life, without prying where the manager is not wanted. Again, however, analysis of each employee involved will determine which behaviors of the manager will more likely motivate them.

During the next life phase, the 40s, people begin to realize whether or not their life ambitions will be achieved. And because of the process of aging and bodily decline, people experience what is known as the midlife crisis. Basically, people realize that they are getting older and that time for achieving their ambitions is limited. These same issues continue into the next life phase, the 50s, and set the stage for the critical issues of the adulthood personality stage (as discussed in Chapter 4). People must come to grips with whether they are basically satisfied with their life or whether they sense failure. This life stage interacts with the career stage of maintenance/influence (discussed in Chapter 2).

If the 40s/50s person senses possible failure or a plateau of ambitions, security needs will be predominant, along with needs to belong. The manager may then want to provide support for this person—and perhaps some counselling as to how to handle this plateau or decline. This kind of employee can be expected to be very loyal to the company, but his or her performance will depend heavily on the support the manager and co-workers provide. **On the other hand, if the 40s/50s person feels successful with life, he or she will want to remain involved and productive in the company**. Thus the manager should probably try to utilize the expertise and wisdom of this older employee. And if the person is capable, the manager should provide a number of ways to involve this person in the company.

As people move into the life stage of the 60s, they definitely begin to experience a sense of the end of their working life. There is a tendency to review past accomplishments and to view their job in perspective with other important aspects of life, such as family and friends. Obviously, the career stage of decline (Chapter 2) and the later-life personality stage interact to yield either a sense of integrity or disgust in these older workers. To get the most out of them, the manager must endeavor to make them feel important, so they gain a sense of integrity. **Self-esteem and belonging needs tend to be predominant in the older employee, and the manager must provide**

ways for these needs to be met if this person is to be motivated.

An exploration of these changes in people should point out that jobs must change for a person to remain motivated over a career. And as people become better educated and gain more experience, they demand more from their jobs. Can jobs keep up with the rate of change in people? Do the changes in jobs affect the motivation of the people in the jobs? Let us look for answers to these questions as we look at the changes that occur in jobs.

Changes in the Job

Changes that occur in a job will definitely affect the motivation of people in the job. Pick up almost any popular business magazine and you will read about technological advances that are vastly changing jobs. Machinists' jobs that in the past involved manual expertise now require an ability to interact with a computer. Secretaries now use word-processing equipment rather than electric typewriters. Robots perform many of the jobs that workers previously performed in the manufacture of automobiles. And we could go on and on—the point is that these changes affect the motivation of employees. Sometimes, automation takes away the meaningfulness, challenge, and responsibility of a job. For some people this makes the job much less interesting. In addition, technological advances may make the skills of a worker obsolete. This can result in frustration and eventual lack of motivation for the employee. As Box 6.2 suggests, the need to deal with changes in technology is a growing problem. And as a future manager, you will be right in the middle of this revolution. **The key point to remember is that technological advances must be viewed in terms of their impact upon the employee and the job**. Otherwise, you wind up with some difficult motivational problems. Couple this with the changes that occur in workers, the differences in workers, and the changes that occur in organizations, and you have a challenging problem to manage.

Changes in the Organization

At the macro level of the organization, we can also anticipate changes that will affect the motivation of employees. As mentioned earlier, growing organizations pro-

**Box 6.2
Automation: Few Jobs
Or New Jobs?**

A period of explosive technological change lies ahead, producing changes in the nature of work that will be as massive as the Industrial Revolution, and telescoped into an even shorter period of time, according to experts in government, business and universities. But there is no consensus among the experts on whether this newest, strongest wave of automation will produce more new jobs than it eliminates.

In one vision of the future, technology sets the stage for even greater growth in a healthy economy, solves the problems of the long-range slowdown in work-force growth, minimizes dirty and tedious work and creates enough jobs for those who need them. In this vision, former textile, steel and auto workers build robots and Prontows, and displaced government workers, printers and grocery clerks enter the world of information processing.

But there is another, much more pessimistic scenario. In the second, a growing group of increasingly bitter, jobless young people find themselves without the skills to do the jobs created by technology and forced to compete with illegal immigrants and refugees for the few unskilled·jobs available.

Skilled machinists look befuddled at the computer consoles of new equipment that eliminates their jobs. Working at home, with no one monitoring wages and hours, poorly paid workers are trapped in the "electronic cottage," turning out reams of documents at word-processing terminals.

Meanwhile, in some other country, factories hum with the activity of non-U.S. workers producing the machines of the new technology.

vide many opportunities for people to take on responsibilities and challenges. In fact, the changes may come so fast that they are almost overwhelming. Often this can result in poor communications, unclear directions, and managers expecting more than subordinates can deliver. Also, it can allow people to move into positions for which they are not yet qualified. And this can create problems for both the individual and the organization. Of course, some people thrive in this rapid-growth environment; it allows their talents a chance to be used. Others may be left behind. At Home Computers, we can imagine that

Louise would thrive in this situation, but Steve might have some problems.

Of course, all organizations do not grow rapidly; some may even decline. And with decline, there are usually shrinking opportunities for employee growth and development. In fact, some employees will be confronted with a loss of job. Others will operate out of fear of losing their jobs. The effect on people and their motivation can be severe, as shown in Box 6.3. Just imagine what Mr. Labas' motivation will be like when he finds another job.

Another source of organizational change is a change

Box 6.3
Middle-Aged Officials
Find New Group Hit by
Slump: Themselves

Comfortable in their careers, ensconced in their suburban enclaves, some even counting down toward retirement, middle-aged managers are getting the jolt of their lives.

What once was rare is growing commonplace: Middle managers in their 40s and 50s are being forced out.

Too young to retire but too old to start anew easily, nearly all of them travel through a valley of soul-searching, depression and anxiety. The initial shock can be as devastating as a death in the family. One Ohio manager at a capital-goods company, let go in his late 50s, was so traumatized he saw almost no one and did practically nothing for three months.

Unlike younger employees, older workers generally find the psychological blow of dismissal much worse than the financial worries. Mr. Labas, a 52-year-old former consumer-finance regional supervisor for Leucadia National Corp., played strictly by the rules of what once was the corporate game—giving loyalty to get security.

"The part that bothers me is that you give your best effort over 26 years. I could count the number of days I missed on one hand and have fingers left over," the balding father of four says, slowly shaking his head. "I was a dedicated company man, but they (the corporation) just didn't give a damn about the people."

That feeling of betrayal turns up commonly among older employees, job counselors say. "They've given most of their lives to the company and then are rejected by it." "They're more committed to the system" than younger workers tend to be.

By Margaret Yao, *The Wall Street Journal,* September 1, 1982. Reprinted by permission of *The Wall Street Journal,* © Dow Jones & Company, Inc. 1982. All rights reserved.

in company direction. Perhaps top management decides to bring out a different product line, go into different markets, switch from a production to a marketing orientation, or make other strategic changes. Each of these changes could create a different situation for the employees. Such redirection could raise or lower the status of a particular department. For example: in the switch from production to marketing orientation, the status of marketing may increase; the status of production may decline. Certainly, it is not hard to imagine how this might affect the motivation of people in the two departments. In addition, such changes might mean relocation of some employees both geographically and from one work group to another. This change will have an effect on the affiliation needs of the employees that cannot be ignored.

The 1984 breakup of the old AT&T is a good example of this situation. Brought on by the courts, the breakup resulted in eight new directions for the company—one for each regional phone company and one for the parent company. Employees in all of the companies were confused about their new roles, their security, and their work relationships. Motivation was clearly affected, at least temporarily.

The key point to remember is that change at the organizational level can result in changes in the need satisfaction and rewards of employees, as well as in the action choices afforded them. Now that we have explored the dynamic aspects of our motivational model and thus gained a more complete understanding of the model, let us try to apply it to the Home Computers case from Chapter 5.

Analyzing Motivation in Work Settings

Figure 6.1 provides a useful model for understanding the motivation of people in a work setting. The model makes clear several key elements in the motivational process: individual needs, feedback of information, desired rewards, the impact of supervisors and peers, and organizational goals. And as we have noted, the job itself is also important. To make the best use of these elements in analyzing actual work settings, it is helpful to think of them as constituting a puzzle. **For motivation to be maximized, each of these elements must be "fit" together with**

all of the other elements into a congruent whole, as suggested by **Figure 6.3**.

**The Concept of
Congruence**

In order for an individual to be truly motivated and
effective, there must be a high degree of congruence (or
fit) between the person and the work itself, between the
person and other people at work, between the person
and the reward system, and between the person and the
information system. Likewise, there must be a high degree
of fit between the other people and the work itself, between
the other people and the information system, and between
the other people and the reward system — and so forth
for the other three elements in Figure 6.3. **In essence
we can determine the degree of fit that exists between
these various elements by asking a series of questions**.
To illustrate this point, let us apply the idea and the
model in Figure 6.1 to the Home Computers case from
Chapter 5 (you may first want to reread the case).

**Figure 6.3
Motivation as a
Process of "Fit"**

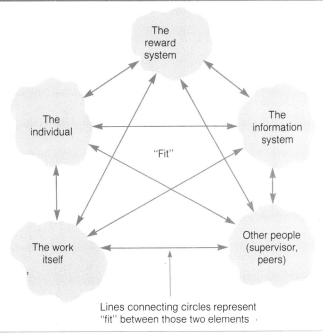

Application to Home Computers

Obviously, there are some motivational problems at Home Computers. Absenteeism and turnover (including managerial turnover) are high, and productivity is down. Let us try to understand why by looking at the changes that have developed in the company over the years.

What has happened to the work itself? The involving, challenging and responsible craft work of the late 1970s—where each employee assembled an entire computer—has been replaced by assembly-line work that is not exciting, challenging, or responsible. Each person does only a part of the assembly job, and quality is checked by someone else. In addition, having shift operations means that employees are affected by the work performed by other people they seldom see. There is probably a sense of a loss of control in the job. As we discussed in Chapter 5, job design theory suggests several ways in which the jobs might be altered to better meet the needs of the employees.

What has happened to the information system? Home Computers has become more bureaucratic, with five hierarchical levels replacing the original team approach. Obviously, this is necessary when a plant grows from 16 to 490 employees. But with this more complex organization, feedback becomes much more difficult. People can begin to feel left out. The informal information system of the early company has been replaced by a more structured system that invariably results in distorted information, and a lack of information for some people. On the survey, both employees and managers reported they felt left out on key information. This was especially apparent on the feedback questions. Perhaps a return to self-assessment of quality would be sufficient to improve the information system. But the managers also seem to want a clearer picture of the overall company goals and strategy. Even their own unit goals are sometimes not well defined. Perhaps Harvey should lay out some plans and goals for the future. Once these are shared with the middle managers, a dialogue could allow for sharing reactions and receiving additional details. This clarification exercise should enable the managers to guide employee actions to achieve both organizational and individual goals (ovals 3a and 3b in Figure 6.1).

What has happened to the reward system? The only information we have on this element is that the bonus system has been dropped. The impact of this change would be to decrease the sense of involvement and responsibility of the typical employee. And this is consistent with the changes in the jobs, both of which are demotivating. The previous section supplies a suggestion for this question, as well. With better-defined goals, it should be possible for managers and employees alike to assess performance. A financial reward could be tied to goals achieved, much like the old bonus system. Or the reward might need to be a promotion, or something else; the managers could determine what would be appropriate. Clearer goals for a particular job and unit, plus the suggested job changes should make it possible to establish a reward system that can motivate desired performance.

What has happened to supervisors and peers in the organization? First, there is a sizable degree of managerial turnover—probably a result of some of the factors mentioned previously (such as decreased responsibility). This means that employees must constantly adjust to new supervisors, who may lack supervision experience. Indeed, in a rapidly growing company like Home Computers, it is not unusual for people to be promoted too quickly into positions for which they are not prepared. For example, a good computer technician may not make a good manager. The problem here seems to be that the workers are rarely praised, but often reprimanded for mistakes by their new, inexperienced supervisors. The data from the survey suggest that some of the managers feel overwhelmed by the job. Perhaps more training on how to manage could help alleviate this problem. And clear goals could also help provide a sense of direction and control. Second, the rapid growth has probably meant the hiring of people with more widely divergent values and needs. Some of the workers seem bored with their jobs. Others like the lack of responsibility. Since these people must interact on the job, there is the possibility of motivation being reduced even further for the high potential people. Quite likely, clearer goals, better information, and more task interaction will improve these interrelationship problems.

What has happened to the employees at Home Computers? Here we encounter the difficulty of knowing what is going on inside people's heads, but we do have some evidence. In the earlier days, the company probably attracted people who wanted to be involved, challenged, and responsible. Why else would someone go to work for a brand-new company that might not be around tomorrow? Hence, these people probably liked the opportunity to make a complete computer, earn bonuses, receive informal and timely information, and work with others who also wanted challenge and responsibility. As the situation changed, some of these people have moved on. Others moved up in the growing organizational structure. Some of those who moved up have probably encountered a situation they could not handle very well—and some of them moved on. Others who moved up found increasing constraints as Home Computers attempted to get a grasp on its rapid growth.

At the worker level, some employees who have been around for several years have probably grown to want more responsibility, but less is being given. And some of the newer employees do not want much responsibility. This more heterogeneous mixture creates obstacles to finding satisfaction of people's needs. Things that please some people upset others—and the job of management is made more difficult.

Hence, it should be clear that an analysis of motivation in an organization is a very complex task. Many elements and interactions are involved, and all aspects are subject to change. Our analysis has (we hope) made clear the need for using a developmental perspective in understanding motivation in organizations. The past history of Home Computers and each of the elements in Figures 6.1 and 6.3, plus the 10 theories from Chapter 5 have been extremely important in our analysis. We hope that the integrative model and idea of fit have been helpful in your understanding of the motivational problems at Home Computers. Certainly, they have allowed us to generate a substantial list of suggested changes for the company. In the final section of this chapter, we review some motivation problems with new solutions that are being tried in industry today.

New Approaches to Motivation

In recent years, a number of approaches based on various theories of motivation have been tried in industry. In this section we briefly summarize several of the more promising applications. As we discuss them, think about how they relate to our integrative model of motivation.

Job-Oriented Approaches

One approach—which we have already discussed to some extent—is the redesign of work itself. Beginning with the suggestion of Herzberg, job enrichment has become a popular way to increase the job's ability to satisfy higher-level needs of the employees.[4] Two industrial applications have gained widespread attention; they have also introduced other names for the approach, such as **industrial democracy**, **job redesign**, and **sociotechnical job design**.

The Gaines Pet Food Plant in Topeka, Kansas, built a plant in 1968 which would aid in developing meaningful and challenging jobs.[5] The plant was designed around self-governing work teams. They determined their own hiring and firing policies, scheduled their own workers, and made other major decisions which affected their work. All employees in the plant were classified in a single job classification, and the work teams were provided information formerly available only to management. The results have been outstanding. Costs are down; quality is up; absenteeism and turnover are down; and employee attitudes are good. A number of changes have had to be made, however, due primarily to concerns expressed by the former middle managers, many of whose jobs were eliminated. Still, the company hails the experiment as a success and is using the idea in other settings.

The other widely noted experiment in job redesign was at the Volvo plant in Sweden.[6] This particular effort was truly sociotechnical in nature. Both the people aspects of the jobs and the technical way of making cars were changed. A new carrier was designed to transport an entire car around the plant to various work teams responsible for major parts of the assembly. There is no assembly line. Each work team has control over its work pace, inspections of work, and scheduling of its workers. The team members must meet to resolve any problems they encounter. The results of this experiment have been dramatic. Turnover has been reduced, and worker attitudes are greatly improved. Quality of the cars did seem to suffer at first, but many of those problems now appear to be solved.

The other major change occurring in jobs is **automation**. More and more, simple and boring jobs are being eliminated through automation. The Japanese, for example, have revolutionized automobile manufacturing by designing robots to make the many thousands of spot welds needed to make a car. Their machinists now must be computer operators, as well as technicians. The result seems to be more exciting jobs for the workers who are retrained. But whether automation results in a net loss or gain in jobs remains a point of controversy. Certainly, it can mean relocation and retraining of many workers. The result could be quite positive for employees, since companies would have to take a greater interest in their development over their entire careers. And such employer commitment is likely to result in greater commitment on the part of employees.

It is clear that these changes in jobs affect the **work itself** component of our motivation model. And they directly address the employee needs related to achievement, responsibility, and satisfaction with the work.

Context-Oriented Approaches

A number of new motivation ideas relate to the context in which employees work. Their design is consistent with the organizational aspects of our model of motivation. In particular, these approaches affect goals and rewards of employees.

One approach, **management by objectives (MBO)** involves a more concerted effort to define and clarify employee goals.[7] Really an application of goal-setting theory, MBO has been widely used since the mid 1960s. Sometimes objectives are set jointly by the employee and the manager; sometimes the manager merely lays out the objectives. The basic idea is that if employees know clearly what their goals are, they will work to achieve them. Furthermore, specific and difficult goals inspire the greatest effort from individuals.[8] Coupled with the goal setting is the promise of rewards for accomplishing the goals. This is consistent with the connection in our model between desired organization outcomes and rewards desired by the person (see Figure 6.1, ovals 3a and 4). Goal-setting depends heavily on self-control of the individual and on an individual need to have responsibility. Often the goal is specified—but the means to accomplish it must be determined by the employee.

Another application that alters the situation is called **behavior modification**.[9] In many ways, behavior modification is similar to goal setting, but there are some significant differences. The primary difference is that behavior modification focuses specifically on behaviors of the employee and consequences that follow behavior. If the employee performs the desired behavior, a reward is given. If the employee does not perform the desired behavior, the reward is withheld, or in some cases a punishment is administered. As you recall, we discussed reinforcement theory as a theory of motivation earlier in Chapter 5. Behavior modification is merely an application of that theory. As with goal-setting, the choice of reward is critical to the success of the program. Rewards must satisfy needs of the employees if the program is to succeed. The case of Emery Air Freight discussed in Chapter 3 is a good example of the application of this approach. The company (through behavior-modification principles) motivated and helped workers learn to use bulk cargo containers instead of small containers for shipping packages. The result was a tremendous savings for the company and satisfaction of some of the workers' important needs.

One other approach to motivation involves **ownership of the business by the workers**. The basic idea is to appeal to the entrepreneurial spirit of the workers. In our terminology, ownership gives the workers responsibility, advancement, and opportunity for achievement—not to mention the chance to make more money if the company succeeds. Naturally, the risk is also higher. But having so many people committed to making the company work has to be a secure feeling.

Individually-Oriented Approaches

Some of the newer approaches to motivation are designed to directly satisfy the needs of the employees, without changing the basic structure of either the job or the organization. One of the most straightforward approaches is modifying the work week. Basically, two forms seem promising. One is called the **4/40 work week**: employees work ten hours a day for four days each week and have a three-day weekend. The other is **flexitime**.[10] It designates a core time each day when everyone must be present at work—say 9:30 AM to 4 PM. Starting time is anytime from 7:30 AM to 9:30 AM; quitting time can range from 4 PM to 6 PM. Everyone is expected to work the normal eight hours a day. Obviously a good record-keeping procedure is necessary, though experience with flexitime has shown little abuse of the system.

Another individually-oriented approach is **job sharing**, where two people split a 40-hour-a-week job between them. Each works half time, but the complete job gets done. Typically, the two employees do not receive full fringe benefits (unless they contribute a larger portion of their salaries). But they do have more free time to pursue other interests. On the other side of the coin, companies often get more than 40 hours a week from the two people, but coordination of effort can create some inefficiencies.

Another approach that seems to be gaining steam now is the **quality-of-work-life (QWL) approach** of giving workers a voice in plant decisions.[11] In some applications, this approach has resulted in far-reaching changes in the management of plants (for example, the Topeka, Kansas, pet food plant discussed earlier). But in many applications, the workers' decisions are limited in scope. One example is **quality circles**, where workers meet regularly to discuss production problems and recommend solutions. On technical grounds, this approach makes sense, because of the workers' intimate involvement with production processes and because of the level of education of typical workers as compared to their job demands (recall Figure 5.4). The workers work with the production problems every day; thus it makes sense that they would have ideas that management might overlook. It also makes sense in terms of the satisfaction of the workers' higher-level needs. Their needs for power and esteem, as well as growth, can be tapped through the QWL approach to worker motivation. They can begin to feel more a part of the organization and can have more pride in solutions that they themselves develop.

Finally, a number of companies are experimenting with **health enrichment programs**. The idea has grown out of the increased interest in health by people in general. More and more people are jogging and joining health spas (probably to address their self-esteem and self-actualization needs). And some companies are providing these opportunities at work in hopes of gaining commitment and attracting and keeping better-quality employees. As the Wall Street Journal excerpt in Box 6.4 suggests, it is too early to determine the bottom-line impact of such programs, but they are clearly gaining in popularity.

Persistent Problems

In spite of the many theories of motivation, the years of study, and the new approaches just discussed, problems persist in motivating our workers and managers. Probably the most serious is the inability to deal effectively with individual differences of the employees. Any solution applied to a group of employees is bound to satisfy some workers, but not others. As we have said many times in this text, each employee is unique. A second problem relates to the systems nature of the motivational process.

Box 6.4
A Special News Report on People and Their Jobs in Offices, Fields and Factories

Fitness pays off: Employee exercise programs boost health and morale.

Corporate physical fitness programs grow more elaborate and widespread; most also seem immune to recession cuts because of their perceived benefits. Shaklee offers workers an indoor track, weight-lifting equipment, bicycles and even workout clothes. It says the effort cuts absenteeism, smoking and excess weight. Fluor executives report fewer back and stress problems because of its fitness center.

PepsiCo, whose program includes swimming and golf facilities, finds "fewer visits to our medical department" and help in recruiting "top-notch people." Xerox, too, puts a big emphasis on physical-fitness programs, but an official concedes, "it's difficult to measure the (programs') bottom line."

As we discussed in these last two chapters, many elements affect motivation (the work, the person, rewards, information, other people—see Figure 6.3), and their effects are interactive. A solution such as goal setting must consider the work and the person, as well as the reward, if it is to be successful. For example: if the work dictates a great deal of dependence on other people, the goals may have to be geared toward the group rather than the individual.

In addition to these two primary problems, we can identify several other persistent ones. First, technological constraints may negate control by the workers. Second, the cost-versus-benefits ratio of the motivational approaches is often difficult to measure. This is especially disconcerting when the costs are high. Third, management often wants quick solutions and is not willing to properly diagnose a given situation. As we saw at Home Computers, motivational problems can be quite involved; they can result from a series of developments over time. Any solution may take time to yield results, and things may get worse before they get better. Finally, managers, workers, and unions may resist change fearing that things will actually get worse. For example, unions have often viewed QWL experiments as management attempts to get more work for the same pay.

In short, many problems remain for you as a manager to grapple with. We hope the theories and the analytical model provided in the last two chapters will be useful tools in this endeavor.

Chapter Highlights

This chapter completes our study of individual behavior. In it we built upon the 10 motivation theories from Chapter 5 to provide an integrative model of motivation. This model is based primarily on Vroom's expectancy theory, but draws from the other motivation theories as well. Our model is an attempt to tie together the several content and process theories along with social facilitation and job design theories. Our goal has been to provide a model that will help you better use the many theories of motivation found in the literature. **The model focuses** on individual needs and action choices, as well as outcomes and rewards desired by an individual. In addition, it focuses on outcomes desired by the organization, as well as the organization's evaluation of an individual's performance and the forthcoming rewards.

The amount of motivation for various actions an individual, such as yourself, may choose depends on several factors, according to the model. Most basic is the importance to you of the unsatisfied need. Other factors include the probability that the rewards given by the organization will help satisfy your need, and the probability that your desired outcome will lead to your desired reward. There is also a probability associated with whether your chosen action will lead to your desired outcome. Finally, the links in the model are like links in a chain. If one link is weak, the resulting motivation will be low. **So as a manager, you must be concerned with all of the links in the motivation model as they relate to your subordinates.**

In completing the description of our model, we stressed its dynamic nature. Depending on what happens as you progress through the model, your need is either satisfied, not satisfied, or perhaps only partially satisfied. This result will influence your future action choices, because it may alter the instrumentalities or expectancy factors in the model, or may even alter the valence of the need. In discussing this aspect of the model, we explored several scenarios to illustrate this important point.

In the next section of the chapter we explored the three major actors in the motivation puzzle (people, jobs, and organizations) in terms of how changes in these elements influence the motivation of employees. First, we looked at changes in people. You as a manager must manage people at different life, family, and career stages; therefore each person presents a particular challenge. Employees in their teens and 20s will have different needs from those in their late 20s and 30s. Likewise, employees in their 40s and 50s will have different needs from their younger colleagues. The same is true for employees in their 60s. **As we discussed, a manager needs to recognize the different needs of different people (where age is only one influential factor) and try to provide rewards and actions that help satisfy those needs.** This means that continuing analysis of your employees will be necessary in order to stay current with their needs.

Second, we explored how changes in a job can create changes in the motivation of employees. **Changes in jobs thus must be viewed in terms of their impact on motivation,** if the maximum benefits from the changes are to be achieved.

Third we considered how changes in the organization can create changes in employees' motivation. **As organizations grow, decline, or simply change production or marketing strategies, employee motivation is affected.** Rewards may be altered, as may action choices and needs to be satisfied.

In the next section we provided a framework for analyzing motivation in work settings. Basically, we suggested that for motivation to be greatest, there must be a high degree of fit between the individual, the work, the reward system, the information system, and other people in the work setting. A series of questions was applied to the Home Computers case to help us analyze the motivational problems that exist there.

In the final section of the chapter, we briefly mentioned several new approaches to motivation that are being tried in industry today. We explained how they relate to our model of motivation. First, we discussed two job-oriented changes: redesign of work and automation of menial jobs. Second, we mentioned three context-oriented approaches: management by objectives, behavior modification, and employee ownership. Last, we mentioned several individually oriented approaches: modified work week, flexitime, job sharing, quality-of-work-life plans, quality circles, and health enrichment programs.

Finally, we discussed several persistent motivation problems in organizations: dealing with individual differences, the systems nature of the problem, technological constraints, costs of programs versus benefits, quick solution attempts, and resistance to change by employees, managers, and unions. In spite of the persistent problems, we believe that the model provided in this chapter plus the theories in Chapter 5 can equip you as a manager to better deal with motivation in organizations. We hope that you will agree as you attempt to apply these ideas.

Review Questions

1. Explain the integrative model of motivation that is presented in this chapter. What are its important elements? How is the amount of motivation determined? How is the model dynamic?

2. Explain why motivation is developmental in nature. What changes in people lead to developmental influences on motivation? What changes in the job or the organization create developmental influences?

3. Explain the concept of "fit" as we have applied it to the analysis of motivation in work settings. What are the elements in this framework for analysis?

4. Describe the new approaches to motivation that were mentioned in this chapter.

Notes

1. V. H. Vroom, *Work and Motivation* (New York: John Wiley & Sons, 1964).

2. A. H. Maslow, *Motivation and Personality* (New York: Harper & Row, 1954).

3. G. Sheehy, *Passages: Predictable Crises of Adult Life* (New York: E. P. Dutton, 1976); D. Levinson, *The Seasons of a Man's Life* (New York: Alfred A. Knopf, 1978).

4. F. Herzberg, B. Mausner, and B. Snyderman, *The Motivation to Work* (New York: John Wiley & Sons, 1959).

5. E. M. Glaser, *Productivity Gains through Worklife Improvements* (New York: Harcourt Brace Jovanovich, 1976).

6. P. G. Gyllenhammar, *People at Work* (Reading, Mass.: Addison-Wesley Publishing, 1977).

7. G. S. Odiorne, *Management by Objectives* (New York: Pitman, 1965).

8. E. A. Locke, "Toward a Theory of Task Motivation and Incentives," *Organizational Behavior and Human Performance*, 3 (1968), pp. 157–89.

9. W. C. Hamner and E. P. Hamner, "Behavior Modification on the Bottom Line," *Organizational Dynamics* (1976), pp. 2–21.

10. P. Dickson, *The Future of the Workplace* (NewYork: Wybright and Talley, 1975).

11. L. E. Davis and A. B. Cherns, eds., *The Quality of Working Life*, vol. 2 (New York: Free Press, 1975).

Resource Readings

Katz, D. and Kahn, R., *The Social Psychology of Organizations.* 2d ed. New York: John Wiley & Sons, 1978.

Levinson, D. *The Seasons of a Man's Life.* New York: Alfred A. Knopf, 1978.

Sheehy, G. *Passages: Predictable Crises of Adult Life.* New York: E. P. Dutton, 1974.

Tichy, N. M. "Problem Cycles in Organizations and the Management of Change," in *The Organizational Life Cycle.* ed. J. R. Kimberly and R. H. Miles. San Francisco: Jossey-Bass, 1980.

Walton, R. E. "Establishing and Maintaining High Commitment Work Systems," in *The Organizational Life Cycle.* ed. J. R. Kimberly and R. H. Miles. San Francisco: Jossey-Bass, 1980.

S E C T I O N   3

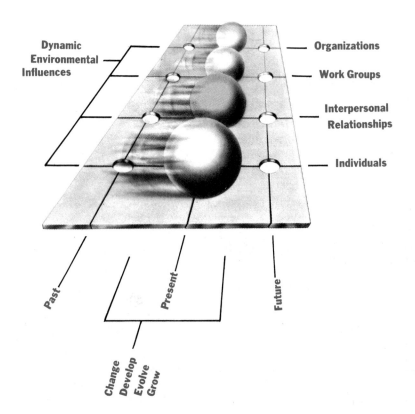

Interpersonal Relations in Organizations

Now that we have completed our analysis of individuals, we will begin to explore interpersonal relations in organizations. We will look at the interaction patterns of people and how these interactions can be managed. Chapters 7 and 8 deal with leadership processes and their developmental and contingency aspects in organizations. By discussing the factors that are critical for effective leadership, you will learn more about yourself as a leader and how to enhance your leadership abilities.

In Chapter 9 we will explore power and politics in organizations as vehicles for exerting leadership. You will learn how to determine your own and others' sources of power. And you will learn how to use power to help you lead more effectively. In the final chapter in this section (Chapter 10), we will look into communications in organizations. Some managers have referred to communications as the life blood of an organization. We will learn how communications play a vital role in leadership, politics, and motivation.

Throughout these chapters, you should keep in mind the material we covered in Section II of the book—Individuals in Organizations. Also, recall from Chapter 1 the model of organizations that is guiding our analysis of organizational behavior. We repeat it here for your reference, with the interpersonal relations part of the

A Developmental Framework for Studying Organizations

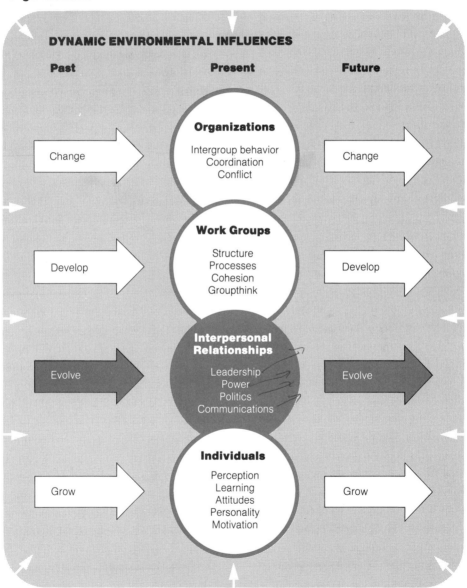

framework highlighted. Remember that people are the basic building block of any organization. In this section of the book we focus on the next level in the building block process—the interactions of individuals.

C H A P T E R   7

Leadership in Organizations

Just as each person is unique, the interactions between any two people or between any leader and a group of people are unique. Also, each interaction has a beginning, continues into the future, and may have an end. As we saw in Chapter 1, change is the nature of relationships in organizations. As we move into a discussion of leadership, think about your past and present relationships in work situations, and in the school situation where you are now. This chapter will help you better understand the leadership interactions you have with others in these settings.

Why You Need to Understand Interpersonal Relations

To be an effective manager, you need to understand the critical aspects of interpersonal interactions. **The very essence of managerial work is to do things through other people**. If you cannot effectively interact with others, you will never become a truly effective manager. Your interactions with your subordinates help determine their motivation to do a job, help provide them with the knowledge to do a good job, and help resolve problems that may arise. In addition, your interactions with other managers on your level help determine the effectiveness of your work unit, help resolve conflicts between work units, and help ensure a smoothly running organization. Also, your interactions with superiors influence your future career with the company, help provide critical information up the organizational hierarchy, and help resolve problems that may affect both your work unit and the organization as a whole.

To be an effective manager over time, you must become familiar with factors that affect interpersonal relationships in organizations. You must know how to apply the theories that relate to leadership, power, politics, and communications in organizations. And you must learn to appreciate the developmental aspects of interpersonal relationships. Can you learn when to apply the appropriate theoretical ideas? And can you make adjustments as the interpersonal situation changes over time? Let us turn now to a discussion of leadership and why it is important to you as a manager.

The Importance of Leadership to a Manager

Leadership is the process of influencing the behavior of other people or groups of people toward the achievement of organizational goals.[1] There are two important aspects of this definition. First, leadership involves two or more people, but the designation of appointed leader is not mentioned in the definition. Indeed, there is a distinction between being the **leader** and exerting **leadership**. While an appointed leader can and should exert leadership, he or she may or may not be the true leader of a group of people. Any member of the group can influence the behavior of the members of the group and thus be a leader. The appointed leader draws upon different sources of power from a leader who emerges from the group, and we will discuss these in Chapter 9. But we can all think of situations where people followed someone other than the appointed leader. The point is that **leadership is more than being the appointed manager; it has to do with who other people are following.**

The second aspect of leadership that is important in organizational settings is: managers exert leadership within a context. There are the followers; there are the peers; there are people higher in the organization than the manager; and there are the organizational goals and constraints on behavior. Leaders receive their authority to lead from each of these sources. And in turn, each of the factors acts to determine the appropriate behavior of the leader if he or she is to have others follow effectively.

Why Study Leadership?

As the definition and comments above imply, there are several reasons why you should study leadership. Let us explore them.

First, as a manager you must be able to influence the behavior of your subordinates. Once you cross the line from worker to supervisor or manager, you become dependent on other people to get work done. As a manager you acquire certain legitimate forms of influence to use to get the work done (for example, pay increases, promotions, and disciplinary actions). But to be a truly effective manager, your leadership must be willingly accepted by your subordinates.[2] This means that you will have to rely upon other, more personal, sources of influence (for example, your expertise, your charisma, and your ability to relate to people).

The second reason to study leadership is that it is so closely connected to the motivation of your subordinates and others you try to influence. And as we saw in Chapter 5, the growing need for more complete use of human resources means you will have to depend on your ability to motivate people. In turn, your ability to motivate will depend upon your ability to exert appropriate leadership.

Third, we must study leadership because it is a process that you can learn to use in organizations. It is probably true that some people are just born leaders—or at least their early development results in traits and abilities that make them natural leaders. But it is also true that most of us can improve as leaders if we study the process of leadership and work to apply the principles that have been determined through research. Leadership is, however, a complex process to master. It involves **your abilities and traits** as the manager, the **abilities and motivation of your subordinates**, and the **relationships** between you and your subordinates. Furthermore, it involves the **nature of the task**, especially as it relates to the abilities and experience of you and your subordinates. It also involves the kind of **situation** in which you must lead: is there time pressure? is there ambiguity? are there enough resources? Finally, leadership involves the **context** in which you must lead. As a manager, you are still a subordinate to someone higher in the organizational hierarchy. And you are a peer to other managers on your level. This context both constrains your leadership and provides opportunities to exert it sideways, upward, and downward in the organization. Box 7.1 provides an interesting example of these context factors at work, as they relate to women managers. And in addition to there being many factors that determine your situation, the factors are themselves constantly changing. Thus, you must lead in a complex and **dynamic** situation.[3]

Leadership as a Dynamic Process

As with other topics we have covered in the first six chapters of this book, leadership also has developmental aspects. **This means that effective managers cannot use the same style of leadership with all people, in all situa-**

Box 7.1
Female Bosses Say
Biggest Barriers Are
Insecurity and 'Being a
Woman'

T*hey are senior executives at large U.S. companies with average salaries of about $92,000. Their titles range from corporate secretary to president and chief executive officer, and while most are single, those who are married say they are both the main breadwinner and the main homemaker.*

They attribute their successes to ambition, drive and a willingness to take risks, and they blame their failures on a male world and their lack of confidence in it. They were more often the first-born or only child in their families and favored their fathers.

This is part of a picture that emerges from a study of executive women recently completed by Korn/Ferry International, an executive search firm, and the University of California, Los Angeles, Graduate School of Management.

Work-Place Problems

Asked whether "barriers to women have fallen at the senior management level," 63% of the women say no. And 70% say women don't receive equal pay for comparable jobs. Female executives most frequently mention "being a woman" as their major career obstacle, citing "the old-boy network," "insecure men," and the attitude that they're "too good looking to take seriously . . . will run off and get married" as work-place problems.

In comments on her questionnaire, a vice president of corporate finance says her biggest career obstacle has been her appearance. "I didn't look or sound the part—5' 3½, female, with a Southern accent," she says. A vice president and director of manpower development complains of "lack of acceptance based on competence . . . the unwillingness of people to give me the toughest assignments." And a regional vice president says her biggest barrier to success has been her "tendency" to unconsciously intimidate male superiors."

tions, and without change over time. For example, managing a 49-year-old experienced machine operator would call for a different leadership approach than managing a 23-year-old inexperienced machine operator. But even more important, you would have to alter your leadership style as the 23-year-old grew in experience and maturity over the various life stages we discussed in Chapter 6.

And let us not forget that you have developed into the kind of leader you are now as a result of your past experiences. And you will change and develop different abilities, perceptions, and motivations as time passes. These changes may also result in changes in your leadership. Furthermore, your superiors and peers may develop different expectations for you as a manager that will influence the appropriate leadership approach for you to use. For example, as you move through career stages (as discussed in Chapter 2) you may be given added responsibilities. This may mean that you must delegate some of your past responsibilities to others if you are to continue to be successful.

Changes in the tasks and technology for your unit in the organization can also create the need for changing your approach to leadership. Suppose that you manage a clerical department that has depended heavily on calculators and typewriters, and on outside computer services for certain aspects of the work. Now top management decides that your people will all have computer terminals at their work stations. The terminals will allow direct access to the main computer and to the files stored there. It will also allow word processing functions to be performed and will eliminate the need for typewriters in the unit. Under these new conditions, you may have to provide more directive leadership than you have in the past—at least during the transition period. And some of the workers may be resistant to the changes, while others welcome the new challenges. Your leadership may have to vary from person to person.

And this point suggests another factor that is developmental in leadership: the group of people you manage will change over time. If they stay together over a long period, they will develop as a group (a topic we will discuss in Chapters 11 and 12). But more likely people will be leaving and joining the work group. And these changes can influence the group's ability and motivation—which again exerts a force for change on your leadership.

Another developmental aspect of leadership is that you will probably move up the corporate ladder. And as we saw in Chapter 2, management at different levels requires different skills. As you move up, the need for technical skills declines; the need for <u>conceptual skills increases;</u> and the need for human relations skills remains about the same during the ascent. As one moves up the hierarchy, the manager's job tends to become broader and more ambiguous. Furthermore, the subordinates become both more capable and more motivated, as a general rule. Your leadership must adjust to these conditions if you are to continue to be successful.

Finally, changes in the organization and its environment can create the need for changes in your leadership approach. In a tight economy or a declining organization, the reins may need to be held tighter. You may have to manage people who are fearful of losing their jobs. In a rapidly growing industry or organization, you may be constantly challenged by subordinates who want to move up the ladder. Your responsibilities may increase faster than you can handle—and this may dictate that you train subordinates to handle increasingly greater delegated responsibilities.

An Introduction to Theories of Leadership

Now that we have discussed what leadership is and why we need to study it, let us explore the leadership theories that have been developed over the years. Unfortunately, there is no definitive single theory. Rather, the evolution of leadership research has resulted in the development of many theories—and each one can claim at least some empirical support. Thus, we should view these theories not as competitors but rather as pieces of the leadership puzzle.[4]

The Evolution of Leadership Theories

Serious study of leadership only dates back about 75 years. It began with efforts to identify a set of traits common to all good leaders. Traits that were studied fell primarily into six categories: (1) physical characteristics, (2) social background, (3) intelligence and ability, (4) personality characteristics, (5) task-related characteristics, and (6) social characteristics.[5] While it might have made life simpler, research has not been able to distinguish a meaningful relationship between these traits and leader effectiveness. But the point here is not that traits are totally irrelevant in predicting leader abilities. Rather it is that **traits alone cannot predict leader ability and performance**.

The growing dissatisfaction with trait theories in the 1940s resulted in the emergence of the behavioral theories of the 1950s. These theories focused on what the leader **does** and began the search for a "best style of leadership." Early attempts to categorize leader behavior identified two extremes on a continuum: (1) authoritarian leadership, and (2) democratic leadership.[6]

Another approach to behavioral leadership theory, developed at Ohio State University, identified two basic dimensions of leadership that remain with us to this day: (1) initiating structure, and (2) consideration.[7] A great deal of effort went into the study of these two dimensions. Many researchers proposed that a leader must exhibit behavior high in both dimensions to be effective.

In fact, a training program based on this research, but developed elsewhere, was designed to teach people this high initiating structure/high consideration style of leadership.[8] The program was known as the Managerial Grid and this style was called the Team Leader. Literally thousands and thousands of managers have completed the program since it was started in the 1960s.

But as more and more studies were conducted, effective managers were found with the other combinations of initiating structure and consideration.[9] Researchers began to realize that the **best leadership style is contingent on the situation and may need to vary over time**.

Since the 1960s, several contingency theories of leadership have been developed. The three most widely known were developed by Fiedler, Hersey and Blanchard, and House. These three contingency theories all try to define **situational** characteristics which determine how favorable the situation is for the leader. Then—depending on the situation—the leader can select the most effective style of leadership.

In the remainder of this chapter, we will review all six of these leadership theories in more detail. In Chapter 8 we will tie them together in an integrative model of leadership. But before proceeding, let us define what we mean by an effective leadership style for a manager. **Effective leadership results in the efficient accomplishment of the task assigned to the work group and in the development of the capabilities of the people in the work unit so that long-run performance is also good**. It is more than just getting the job done. Effectiveness also includes the idea that people do the job because they want to do it.[10] They may do it out of a sense of loyalty, obligation, or duty, but they do it because they want to do it.

Trait Theories of Leadership

While researchers have noted many problems with trait theories of leadership, we cannot totally dismiss them. A recent book by John Kotter titled *The General Managers* supports the idea that traits do tell us something about a manager's leadership abilities.[11] Many motivational, interpersonal, temperamental, and cognitive factors are important in distinguishing effective and ineffective managers. In fact, one researcher has suggested 16 traits for successful senior managers—see Box 7.2. But we believe that **traits are primarily useful in determining whether a leader can exhibit the appropriate style of leadership**. Traits are an indicator of the fit between the manager and the leadership style appropriate for a given situation. For example: if a situation calls for a leader to delegate, a highly motivated, temperamental, power-seeking leader may have difficulty delegating.

And as Kotter points out, we must take a long-term view of the manager if we are to understand his/her personal characteristics. **The traits and personalities that people exhibit are developed over an entire lifetime**. Childhood experiences, family, and early career experiences all interact to determine who a person is (discussed in Chapters 3 and 4). So, to understand ourselves and others as managers, we need to know something about who we and the others are. By knowing something about the manager's traits, we may gain a clue to the behavior to expect in a given situation. But as we have stressed, traits do not tell us enough about effective leadership. We must look further at behavioral and contingency theories to gain a more complete understanding of the process.

**Box 7.2
Why Are Some
Managers Top
Performers? A
Researcher Picks Out
16 Characteristics**

*S*enior managers require 16 defined characteristics to work at the top of their form. "The corporate culture is much more complex and requires more skills than sports, arts or science cultures," says Mr. Garfield. [*Charles Garfield is a consultant who has studied peak performers in many organizations.*]

The Six Characteristics

Good business managers at any level have the same six characteristics that mark top performers in other fields, he notes, These people transcend previous performance, avoid getting too comfortable in their jobs, enjoy the art of their work, vividly rehearse coming events in their minds, don't hold trials to place blame for mistakes, and examine the worst consequences of an action before taking the risk.

At the level of general manager of, say, sales, research or advertising, four more traits and skills come into play. Top performers at this level always have time for planning and didn't merely swing from crisis to crisis like monkeys caught in a forest fire. "Lower-performing managers would tend to get wrapped up in anything that looked like a crisis," says Mr. Garfield. "High performers were able to sift through and sort out the real crises."

They also were adept at selling their ideas, and sought responsibility instead of artfully dodging it, like bureaucrats. They bore rejection and loss well. Finally, they were inclined to champion new ideas and projects rather than letting them die untried.

The Ability to Act

In the upper reaches of management, the additional characteristic most apparent was an ability to reject perfectionism and act. "Many others were paralyzed by perfectionism," says Mr. Garfield. "They felt that if they tried it out and it didn't work, they'd be in trouble."

The best senior managers usually didn't have nicknames like Genghis Khan or Bloody Mary, either. They created a balance between autonomy and direction, setting goals for subordinates but not dictating how those goals were to be met. They were good team-builders too, limiting the number of staffers involved in projects to avoid "bureaucratic neutralization."

The most effective senior managers sought quality rather than just quantity in their work, and saw clearly that the training and development of other managers and employees was a vital function. "To them, it's more than just a nice thing to do to give people management training," adds Mr. Garfield.

Behavioral Theories of Leadership

The behavioral theories of leadership of the 1950s provide useful descriptive categories of leadership styles. Indeed, they are the basic styles we will use in our integrative model in Chapter 8. Let us consider the two most popular behavioral theories.

Autocratic-Democratic Continuum

One behavioral theory of leadership developed in the 1950s labeled behavior along a continuum from autocratic to democratic.[12] Figure 7.1 shows the continuum and identifies the sources of authority. **The autocratic leader makes decisions and announces them to the subordinates.** He or she relies heavily on power inherent in the manager's position to get people to carry out the decision and can utilize punishment for those who do not carry out the decision. On the other hand, **the democratic leader permits subordinates to function within limits defined by the manager; the leader shares the decision-making responsibility**. He or she relies less on power from the posi-

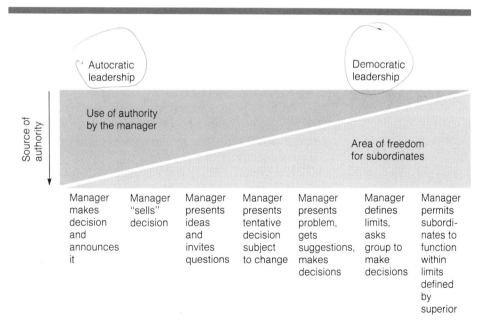

tion of manager and more on powers of persuasion. As the continuum in Figure 7.1 indicates, there are many types of leadership between these two extremes. The use of authority by the manager and freedom allowed the subordinates vary along the continuum to create the different leadership styles.

For example, suppose Louise of Home Computers decided that a progress report should be given to her each Monday morning by her project teams. She could choose to be autocratic and announce the decision to begin the reports next week. And she could specify the frequency and format of the reports. Programmers who complied would receive praise and a good rating on their performance review. Those who failed to comply would be reprimanded and perhaps rated lower on their review. In other words, as an autocratic leader, Louise would use the power of her position to demand compliance from the programmers. If, on the other hand, Louise chose to be democratic, she would share the decision-making responsibility with the programmers—she would allow them to operate more freely, within certain limits. Louise would depend less on the power of her position as manager and more on her powers of expertise, experience, and persuasion. She might sit down with the programmers and explain the need for update reports and then lead a discussion on ways to provide them on a timely basis. The reports are needed—and that parameter has been set—but the programmers can have a say in their format and frequency. Louise is still responsible for the decision that is made. But the programmers who must implement it have input into the decision.

Under the autocratic approach, Louise will probably get the reports as she wants them, but we can wonder about the long-run effectiveness of this approach. Performance may remain good while long-run resentment is building. And this resentment could eventually lead to less productive programmers or even the loss of good programmers. This point emphasizes the developmental aspect of leadership. Under the democratic approach, Louise will probably still get the reports—though the format and frequency may not be as she prefers. And if the programmers do not have the information, expertise, and desire to make a responsible decision, Louise will be asking for trouble. Still, the programmers will probably appreciate the chance to have had a say in the decision—and it may improve working relationships between Louise and the programmers.

The problem with this autocratic-democratic continuum theory is that leadership is viewed as a one-dimensional concept. Subsequent research has discovered at least two dimensions (initiating structure and consideration). Furthermore, this model does not really guide a manager in choosing a leadership style along the continuum—it just describes the behavior. Tannenbaum and Schmidt do indicate that you should analyze: (1) forces in yourself as the manager, (2) forces in your subordinates, and (3) forces in the situation. For example, what are your values? How secure do you feel? How much confidence do you have in your subordinates? Are your subordinates self-motivated? What are the norms of your organization? How much time pressure do you face? Unfortunately, they do not provide much guidance on how to use the answers to these questions to choose along the continuum. Still, their ideas were a forerunner to the contingency theories of the 1960s.

The Ohio State Model

The other most popular behavioral leadership theory from the 1950s was developed at Ohio State University.[13] It defined two dimensions for describing leader behavior. **Initiating structure** was defined as the degree to which the leader organized and defined the task for the subordinates. **Consideration** was defined as the degree to which the leader developed a trusting and supportive relationship with the subordinates. By combining these two dimensions, there are four possible combinations of initiating structure and consideration that define four styles of leadership, as shown in Figure 7.2. Since the 1950s, these four leadership styles have been the most commonly used by both researchers and practicing managers. You may be interested in learning which of the four is most descriptive of your leadership. A copy of the Leader Behavior Description Questionnaire (LBDQ) and scoring instructions are included at the end of this chapter for your use. Take a few minutes now to complete it, score it, and plot your scores on the grid provided. If you

**Figure 7.2
Ohio State Leadership
Dimensions**

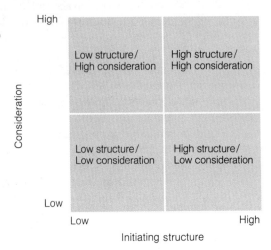

High

Low structure/
High consideration

High structure/
High consideration

Consideration

Low structure/
Low consideration

High structure/
Low consideration

Low

Low   High

Initiating structure

J. K. Hemphill, *Leader Behavior Description* (Columbus, Ohio: Ohio State University Press, 1950).

do not have much leadership experience, try to imagine how you would respond to each statement in the questionnaire.

Regardless of where your score comes out, it should be viewed as your perception of yourself. And since **we know that leadership is situational in nature, your general style may not always describe what you would do in a given situation**. Nevertheless, if you scored high in structure and low in consideration, you tend to be directive in your leadership. High scores in both dimensions means you tend to be both directive and people oriented. A high score in consideration and a low score in structure means you are a participative leader. And finally, if you scored low in both dimensions, you are either a delegator or rather laissez-faire.

Unfortunately, we do not know from the LBDQ if you are an effective leader. As we said before, early research on the model suggested that effective managers exhibit both high initiating structure and high consideration. But we know now that the best leadership style is contingent on the situation. Thus, what we can say is that your style would be effective in some managerial situations, but not all. We can begin to give you some insight about which situations by looking at the contingency theories of the 1960s.

Contingency Theories of Leadership

Fiedler's Theory

One of the most widely researched contingency theories of leadership was developed by Fred Fiedler.[14] The central idea of this model is: the effectiveness of a work group in accomplishing its immediate task depends on the favorableness of the situation in combination with a leadership characteristic Fiedler calls "least preferred co-worker score." Let us briefly define the three situational characteristics Fiedler specifies. **Leader-member relations** relates to the degree of confidence, trust, and respect that subordinates feel for the manager. **Task structure** is the degree to which the group's task is clearly specified. This includes the clarity of goals, the number of ways to accomplish them, and the ease of evaluating goal accomplishment. For example, an assembly-line worker's job would be more structured than that of a researcher in a laboratory. The final situational factor, **position power**, is the amount of power inherent in the leader's position in the organization. To what extent does the leader have the power to influence the behavior of subordinates?

These three factors, according to Fiedler, determine the overall favorableness of the situation and suggest the appropriate style of leadership. However, Fiedler's definition of different leadership approaches is really based on an aspect of the leader's need structure—he calls it the "least preferred co-worker (LPC) score." The LPC instrument asks people to assess the co-worker with whom they would least like to work. A copy of the LPC is included at the end of the chapter. Take a minute now to fill it out and score your LPC.

A **low LPC score** means that you are basically ready to reject those co-workers with whom you would least like to work. This is basically an **attitude** that you have; but we can infer that your behavior would tend to be task oriented, much like the person high in Initiating Structure. On the other hand, a **high LPC score** means that you perceive even your worst co-worker in a relatively positive light. The behavioral approximation of this attitude is one of working toward successful interpersonal relationships, much like the person who scores high in Consideration. Compare your scores on the LPC with the LBDQ which you completed earlier; there will probably be a consistency between the scores. But if there is not, do not be alarmed. It is probably the fault of the instruments and not your fault. Remember, the LBDQ was designed to describe behavior, while the LPC was designed to assess attitude.

Combining the three situational factors and the LPC score, Figure 7.3 indicates in which situations low LPC leaders and high LPC leaders will be most effective, according to Fiedler. Situation categories 1 through 3 define a favorable situation, and the low LPC (high initiating structure) leader will be the most effective. The same low LPC leader will be most effective in situation category 8, which is a very unfavorable situation. For the middle

Figure 7.3   Fiedler's Contingency Model of Leadership

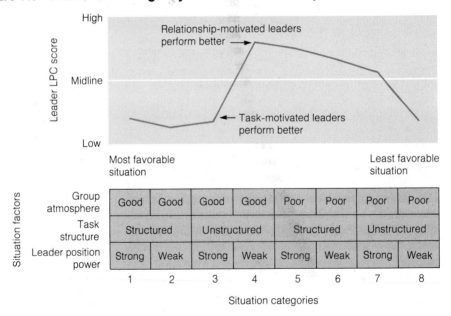

Adapted From Fiedler, F. *A Theory of Leadership Effectiveness* New York: McGraw-Hill, 1967.

categories 4 through 7, the situation is moderately favorable, and the best leader will be the high LPC (high consideration) leader.

Fiedler's leadership theory is quite useful to us in understanding the contingency aspects of leadership. It provides three important situational factors, and the relationship between LPC score and a work group's productivity has repeatedly been supported with research. Still, there are several concerns about the theory.[15] Fiedler contends that it is easier to alter the situation than to change the leader's LPC score, since it is a fundamental aspect of the person. It may be more accurate to say that both are somewhat difficult to change. Second, the theory assumes that a leader who exhibits initiating structure cannot at the same time exhibit consideration. But the Ohio State studies have clearly shown this to be an oversimplification. Third, the definition of effectiveness used in the theory is restricted to "getting the group's task done in an efficient manner." It ignores future implications about the development of subordinates' abilities, and the potential for developing resentment among them. Fourth, the subordinate's impact on the situation is minimized. Task structure, for example, is a relative term: a highly trained programmer might view as relatively structured a task that an inexperienced programmer would see as very unstructured. Furthermore, as the inexperienced programmer gains experience, the same task might seem more and more structured over time. Finally, the leader can interact with the situational variables to change them over time—and the model does not seem to account for this possibility. For example, a friendly leader is likely to improve leader-subordinate relations, while an aloof leader is likely to make them worse. Still, the theory has much to offer for our understanding of leadership.

The Hersey-Blanchard Theory

Unlike Fiedler's theory, the Hersey-Blanchard theory has not been widely researched, but it has been widely used in industry for manager training.[16] And it is based on the four leadership styles from the widely-researched Ohio State model. The theory explicitly focuses on the fit between situation and subordinates by defining the situation in terms of the "maturity" of the subordinates.

But maturity is defined in a unique way as: (1) the capacity of subordinates to set high but attainable goals (need for achievement); (2) the willingness and ability of subordinates to take responsibility for their work; and (3) the task-relevant education and experience of the subordinates. **Basically, maturity is the subordinates' ability and desire to do the job.**

By determining the subordinates' maturity level, a manager can choose the appropriate leadership style, using Figure 7.4. As you can see, the maturity continuum (which reads from right to left for increasing maturity) and a developmental curve are simply added to the four leadership styles from the Ohio State model. The model is used in the following manner. If analysis shows the subordinates' maturity to be low, you can draw a vertical line up from the point on the maturity curve to where

**Figure 7.4
The Hersey-Blanchard
Leadership Model**

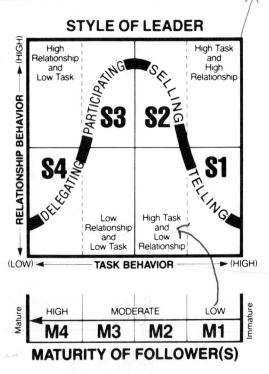

Source: P. Hersey and K. Blanchard, *Management of Organizational Behavior* 4th ed. (Englewood Cliffs, N.J.: Prentice-Hall, 1982), p. 152.

it intersects the developmental curve to determine the appropriate leadership style. Hence, the developmental curve indicates the leadership style needed for high performance, given a particular level of subordinates' maturity. For example, **low subordinate maturity needs high task/ low relationship leadership**.

As we consider followers of increasing maturity, leaders must first reduce their task orientation and increase their relationship orientation, as we move along the developmental curve from right to left. However, past the midpoint of maturity, both task and relationship orientations need to decrease. For example, moderately high mature followers (M3) need low task/high relationship leadership.

As a way of further explaining this theory, let us share with you several questions from a questionnaire based on the Hersey-Blanchard model, as modified by Blanchard, and called the Leader Behavior Analysis.[17] We will first share the four questions so you can decide which of the four alternative actions (a, b, c, or d) you would choose for the given situation. Then we will indicate the scoring for each question and explain the rationale. This procedure should allow some interesting discussion among your colleagues in class, so circle the choice you think you would use.

1. The interdepartment task force which you manage has been working hard to complete its division-wide report. One of your task force members has been late for the last five meetings. He has offered no excuses or apologies. Furthermore, he is way behind in completing the cost figures on his department. It is imperative that he present these figures to the task force within the next three days.
   a. Tell him exactly what you expect and closely supervise his work on this report.
   b. Discuss with him why he has been late, and support his efforts to complete the task.
   c. Emphasize when the cost figures are due and support his efforts.
   d. Assume he will be prepared to present the cost figures to the task force.
2. In the past, you have had a great deal of trouble with

one of the people you supervise. She has been lackadaisical, and only your constant prodding has brought about task completion. However, you recently have noticed a change. Her performance has improved and you have had to remind her of meeting deadlines less and less. She has even initiated several suggestions for improving her performance.

a. Continue to direct and closely supervise her efforts.

b. Continue to supervise her work, but listen to her suggestions and incorporate those that seem reasonable.

c. Incorporate her suggestions and support her ideas.

d. Let her take responsibility for her own work.

3. Because of budget restrictions imposed on your department, it is necessary to consolidate. You have asked a highly experienced member of your department to take charge of the consolidation. This person has worked in all areas of your department. In the past, she has usually been eager to help. While you feel she has the ability to perform this assignment, she seems indifferent to the importance of the task.

a. Take charge of the consolidation but make sure you hear her suggestions.

b. Assign the project to her and let her determine how to accomplish it.

c. Discuss the situation with her. Encourage her to accept the assignment in light of her skills and experience.

d. Take charge of the consolidation and indicate to her precisely what to do. Supervise her work closely.

4. Your staff has asked you to consider a change in their work schedule. In the past, you have encouraged and supported their suggestions. In this case, your staff is well aware of the need for change and is ready to suggest and try an alternative schedule. Members are very competent and work well together as a group.

a. Allow staff involvement in developing the new schedule and support the suggestions of group members.

b. Design and implement the new schedule yourself, but incorporate staff recommendations.

   c. Allow the staff to formulate and implement the new schedule on its own.

   d. Design the new schedule yourself and closely direct its implementation.

The following table indicates how each of the four choices would be labeled, in terms of leadership style, and also indicates which styles would be the most and least effective for the particular situation:

Question	Telling	Selling	Partici- pating	Dele- gating
1	a^B	c	b	d^W
2	a	b^B	c	d^W
3	d^W	a	c^B	b
4	d^W	b	a	c^B

Note: W indicates worst choice.
     B indicates best choice.

Let us explore the rationale for the best and worst choices above. For Question 1, the individual clearly is not motivated to do the work, and may lack the ability to do it alone. Thus, we have a low maturity (M1) situation, and Figure 7.4 indicates a Telling style would be the best choice. Delegating would obviously be the worst.

For Question 2, the employee seems to be improving in performance and motivation, whereas in the past you had to use a Telling style. It appears she is moving into a moderately low maturity (M2), and Figure 7.4 suggests a Selling style is most effective. On the other hand, to leave the person alone (Delegating) would be too much, too soon—hence the worst.

For Question 3, you have assigned the task to someone who clearly has the ability to perform the task, but seems to lack the motivation. Hence, it appears we have a moderately high maturity (M3), and Figure 7.4 suggests a Participating style is most effective. On the other hand, Telling would apply too much task orientation and be the worst—it would undercut the person's confidence.

Finally, for Question 4, you are dealing with a very competent and motivated group who are aware of the need for change—a high maturity (M4). Figure 7.4 suggests the best style is Delegating, while Telling would be the worst. It undercuts their ability and is not a good use of your time, as the manager.

The four questions thus allow you the chance to practice identifying the four different leadership styles, as applied to real situations. They also allow you to see how the theory can be used to help you analyze real world situations.

The primary strengths of the Hersey-Blanchard theory revolve around its explicit inclusion of subordinates, its developmental focus, and its expanded definition of effectiveness. By focusing on the subordinate and the fit with the task, we are forced to recognize that a manager must simultaneously lead more than one subordinate. Thus you may have to lead both mature and immature subordinates and will need to vary your leadership style slightly from person to person. Likewise, people may be mature in one task and immature in another one. Thus, you may have to vary your style from task to task.

This model also recognizes that situations may change (develop) over time. In fact, it is quite probable that a group of subordinates will move toward maturity over time as they gain experience with the task. For one thing, time on the job will increase task-relevant experience, if nothing else (unless there is a great deal of turnover of personnel). The leader's style thus must change over time to maintain effectiveness. And if the group reaches high maturity, you should delegate things to them (low task/ low relationship leadership).

But wait a minute. You may be wondering what a manager does with his or her time when they get to the point of delegating. It is all too easy to forget that leadership in organizations involves more than just managing the tasks of the work group. It also involves managing the relationships with other work groups and with higher-level managers in the organization. Furthermore, it should involve developing your subordinates' abilities and motivation. The Hersey-Blanchard theory takes this broader definition of effectiveness. This is one of the major differences from Fiedler's model, which focuses on getting the job done as quickly as possible.

In fact, this difference in definition leads to a very different choice of effective leadership style in the favorable (or high maturity) situation. Fiedler's time-efficiency orientation leads him to select the high initiating structure leader (see Figure 7.3). In the favorable situation, Hersey-Blanchard's focus on developing subordinates leads them to select delegation (low structure/low consideration). However, there are some similarities between the models. In the unfavorable (low maturity) situation, both theories suggest a high structure/low consideration leadership style as best. And in the moderately favorable (moderate maturity) situations, both suggest high consideration styles of leadership. And both models use task structure as one aspect of the situation. We will use the strengths of both theories in developing our integrative model of leadership in Chapter 8. The Hersey-Blanchard theory will be central to it.

The biggest concerns about the Hersey-Blanchard model revolve around the limited research that has specifically addressed it. Furthermore, it assumes that a manager can learn to adapt his or her style to each situation in rapid succession. Such changes may not be that easy. Much research on people would suggest that it is not easy to change something as fundamental as one's leadership style from moment to moment.[18] But then, many situations change in evolutionary rather than dramatic ways—and this developmental change may be more in line with what Hersey and Blanchard mean. And we cannot forget that thousands of managers have learned to use this model of leadership and have found it helpful.

House's Theory

House's path-goal leadership theory is closely related to the expectancy model of motivation we discussed in Chapter 5.[19] The basic idea of the model is that a manager's job is to increase the motivation of workers by "increasing personal payoffs to subordinates for work-goal attainment, and making the path to these payoffs easier to travel by clarifying it, reducing roadblocks and pitfalls, and increasing the opportunities for personal satisfaction in route" (1971: p. 322). This model thus ties together leadership and motivation aspects of management: **what a manager does in terms of leadership affects the subordinate's motivation**. And increased worker motivation should lead to both increased performance and satisfaction.

Path-goal theory explains how a manager can choose from among four leadership styles by analyzing characteristics about both the subordinates and the task. The four leadership styles can be defined as follows:

Directive leadership is the clarifying of paths to the goals for the subordinates. It is similar to the high initiating structure/low consideration style.

Supportive leadership is the giving of support and consideration for subordinates. It is similar to the low structure/high consideration style.

Participative leadership is characterized by sharing information and consulting with subordinates in making group decisions. It is similar to the high structure/high consideration style of leadership.

Achievement-oriented leadership is characterized by setting high goals for the subordinates, seeking improved performance and showing confidence that the subordinates will perform well. It is similar to the low structure/low consideration (delegation) style.

As to the **subordinates**, the model defines three employee characteristics that help define the situation and relate to the most effective leadership style: (1) ability, (2) locus of control, and (3) need structure. **The greater an employee's ability to perform the task, the less he/she will want directive leadership**. As in the Hersey-Blanchard model, the high ability employee will prefer achievement-oriented leadership (delegation). Locus of control is similar to the "willingness to take responsibility" idea of Hersey-Blanchard, and the prediction from path-goal is consistent with their ideas. **The more an employee desires control in a situation, the less he/she will be satisfied with directive leadership**. Rather, this worker will desire participative or achievement-oriented leadership. Finally, need structure refers to Maslow's hierarchy of needs. The question is: Does the employee desire high- or low-level needs? **The more an employee desires high-level needs, the less he/she will want directive leadership**. More specifically, people who desire safety and security needs will respond positively to directive leadership. Those who desire belongingness will respond positively to supportive leadership. And those desiring self-esteem and self-actualization will respond positively to participative and achievement-oriented leadership.

Finally, as to the **task**, House refers to the degree of task structure in a manner similar to both Fiedler and Hersey-Blanchard. Like the others, path-goal theory suggests that **employees working on an unstructured task will want directive leadership.** In these unstructured task situations, the manager's job must be to initiate structure, clarify goals, and define expectancies for the subordinates. When the manager can do this, he/she reduces worker uncertainty, and this leads to increased motivation and performance. **If the task is more structured, supportive and participative leadership styles will be more effective.** This prediction is consistent with the Hersey-Blanchard model.

To date the biggest drawback with path-goal theory is that it has not been fully researched. Rather, relationships between particular subordinate or task characteristics and particular leadership styles have been explored independently. This creates a problem for a manager who must operate where all three subordinate characteristics and task structure are simultaneously present. For example, if ability is high, locus of control is medium, need structure is low, and task structure is medium, path-goal theory is not too helpful. High ability suggests using achievement-oriented leadership; but concern for lower-level needs suggests using directive leadership. Rather than being a complete theory of leadership, path-goal seems to be a set of independent propositions. Unlike Fiedler's theory, path-goal theory does not specify leadership styles for all possible combinations of the situational characteristics.

A second problem is that the outcome variable in the model is employee satisfaction/motivation, rather than performance. It is not difficult to imagine situations where employees are satisfied but where productivity is low. Furthermore, path-goal theory implicitly assumes that employee satisfaction leads to higher performance, but research has indicated that it may be that high performance leads to satisfaction.[20] In the long run, it may be that both variables influence each other in a developmental manner. For example: high performance leads to

satisfaction which leads to motivation to yield high performance.

Despite these criticisms of path-goal theory, it is still
useful, since it helps integrate leadership and motivation.
It is also consistent with the other two contingency theories in several important areas. Most importantly, when
subordinates must deal with an unstructured task, they
appreciate and respond well to directive leadership. But
as their ability develops, they respond better to participative leadership and finally to delegation.

By understanding these trait, behavioral, and contingency theories of leadership, you have a great deal of
information you can apply to leadership in organizations.
Unfortunately, no single theory seems adequate in a practical and analytical sense. We need a way to integrate
the 6 leadership theories from this chapter, so we can
capitalize on the strengths of each one. But this chapter
has gone on long enough now. Rather than try your patience, let us save our integrative model and an application
to the Home Computers case for Chapter 8.

Chapter Highlights

We began this chapter by outlining the topics to be
covered in this section of the book on interpersonal behavior in organizations: leadership, power, politics, and communications. We noted the importance of interpersonal
behavior to you as a manager. **Your interactions with
subordinates, peers and superiors determine your effectiveness as a manager**.

We then turned to a discussion of the importance of
leadership to a manager. **Leadership was defined as the
process of influencing the behavior of other people or
groups of people toward the achievement of organizational goals**. Leadership thus takes into account both the
interpersonal nature and the situational aspects of the
process.

Next we mentioned five reasons why it is important
for you as a manager to understand the leadership process.
First, as a manager you must be able to influence the
behavior of other people. Second, leadership is closely
connected to the motivation of your subordinates. Third,

you can learn to use the process of leadership to make you a more effective manager. Fourth, leadership is a complex process and requires study if you are to understand it. And fifth, you need to learn how the context in which you operate influences and constrains your leadership style choice.

We then explained the developmental aspects of leadership. **As people (yourself included) and situations change over time, you must change your leadership style to remain effective**. You and your subordinates develop as we discussed in Chapters 3 through 6; and the tasks and technology of your people can also change over time. You may also have people leave or join your group of subordinates, and this can necessitate changes in your leadership. And we hope you will move from one setting to another as you move up the organizational hierarchy in your career. Finally, changes in the overall organization to which you belong and its environment may create the need for you to alter your leadership style.

The next section of this chapter introduced a number of leadership theories by reviewing how they have evolved over the past 75 years. We then began to delve into the theories in more detail.

First we looked at trait theories, which tell us something about a leader's abilities. And more important, **traits are useful in determining whether a leader can exhibit the style called for by the situation**. Traits are also developed over an entire lifetime; they therefore help emphasize the importance of viewing leadership developmentally. But traits alone do not tell us enough about leadership.

So we next turned to a discussion of the behavioral theories of leadership, which were developed in the 1950s. These theories provide descriptive categories for leadership behavior. We first explored the autocratic-democratic continuum. **Autocratic leadership is the style in which the leader makes all the decisions and announces them**. On the other hand, **democratic leadership is the style in which the leader allows the subordinates to become involved in the decision-making process**.

We then explored another popular behavioral theory developed at Ohio State University. This model identifies two dimensions of leadership behavior which have been important for over 30 years: initiating structure and consideration. Next, we turned to the contingency theories of the 1960s to learn more about the situational aspects of leadership.

The first contingency theory we discussed is the most researched of all, namely Fiedler's model. We explored how **leader-member relations, task structure and position power of the leader help determine how favorable the situation is for the leader.** In turn, the favorableness of the situation determines whether a high or low LPC leader will be effective. And **Fiedler defined LPC as the attitude one has toward the "least preferred co-worker."**

In reflecting on this theory, we mentioned several concerns. The theory assumes leaders cannot change their LPC score very easily. It assumes that consideration and initiating structure cannot be exhibited simultaneously. It defines effectiveness only in terms of "getting the job done in an efficient manner." It minimizes the impact of subordinates in a given situation. And it does not allow for developmental changes in the situational variables. Still, we found Fiedler's theory would be useful in developing our integrative model in Chapter 8.

Next we discussed the contingency theory developed by Hersey and Blanchard. This theory adds a subordinate maturity dimension to the Ohio State grid to define how favorable the situation is for the leader. We pointed out that **maturity is basically the ability and desire of the subordinates to do the job.** The higher the subordinates' need for achievement, willingness to take responsibility, and task-relevant education and experience, the higher their maturity and the more favorable the situation for the leader.

The primary strengths of this model are its explicit inclusion of the subordinates as they relate to the task at hand, its developmental focus, and its expanded definition of effectiveness. The concerns about the Hersey-Blanchard theory revolve around a lack of rigorous research on the model and the assumption that leaders can easily change their style from moment to moment.

The final contingency theory discussed was House's path-goal theory. We pointed out that this theory is useful for linking leadership and motivation. **What a manager does in terms of leadership affects the subordinate's motivation.** Path-goal theory is based on three employee characteristics: ability, desire for control, and the level of needs desired, plus the degree of task structure. Limited research has supported relationships between these situational factors and the four leadership styles defined for the theory: directive, supportive, participative, and achievement oriented. We believe the linkage of leadership and motivation this theory provides makes it useful to us.

We closed the chapter by suggesting the need for a way to integrate these six leadership theories to help us better use them in organizational settings, and we noted that the development of such an integrative framework will be our task in Chapter 8.

Review Questions

1. What is leadership? How is exerting leadership different from being the appointed leader?

2. Why is it important for you as a manager to know about leadership and be able to apply it to managerial situations?

3. What factors suggest that your leadership will have to vary from situation to situation and from time to time?

4. Why is it important to define effectiveness as more than just getting the job done as efficiently as possible?

5. Why is it important to include trait theories as a basis for understanding leadership?

6. What are the trade-offs one makes between autocratic and democratic leadership styles?

7. What is the biggest weakness of the Ohio State model of leadership? Why do you think this theory has been so popular for over 30 years?

8. Can you define the three situational factors in Fiedler's model of leadership and explain how they determine the best leader (based on LPC score) for a given situation? What are the biggest weaknesses of Fiedler's model of leadership?

9. Can you explain how Hersey-Blanchard define maturity of subordinates and how maturity determines the best leadership style for a given situation? What are the primary strengths and weaknesses of the Hersey-Blanchard model of leadership?

10. What are the fundamental differences between Fiedler's and Hersey-Blanchard's theories of leadership? How are they similar?

11. Can you explain the relationships between the three employee characteristics and task structure and the four leadership styles defined in path-goal theory? How does path-goal theory link leadership to motivation? What are the biggest weaknesses of this theory?

Notes

1. B. Bass, *Stogdill's Handbook of Leadership* (New York: Free Press, 1981).

2. C. Barnard, *The Functions of the Executive* (Cambridge, Mass.: Harvard University Press, 1938); and more recently reemphasized by T. Kochan, S. Schmidt, and T. DeCotiis, "Superior-Subordinate Relations: Leadership and Headship," *Human Relations*, vol. 28 (1975), pp. 279–94.

3. K. Weick, "Middle Range Theories of Social Systems," *Behavioral Science*, 19 (1974), pp. 357–67.

4. A. G. Jago, "Leadership: Perspectives in Theory and Research," *Management Science* 28 (March 1982), pp. 315–36.

5. Bass, *Stogdill's Handbook*.

6. R. Tannenbaum and W. H. Schmidt, "How to Choose a Leadership Pattern," *Harvard Business Review*, 36 (1958), pp. 95–102.

7. J. K. Hemphill, *Leader Behavior Description* (Columbus, Ohio: Ohio State University Press, 1950).

8. R. R. Blake and J. Mouton, *The Managerial Grid* (Houston: Gulf Publishing, 1964), and *The New Managerial Grid* (Houston: Gulf Publishing, 1978).

9. A. Korman, "Consideration, Initiating Structure, and Organizational Criteria: A Review," *Personnel Psychology* 19 (1966), pp. 345–62; and S. Kerr and C. Schriescheim, "Consideration, Initiating Structure and Organizational Criteria: An Update of Korman's 1966 Review," *Personnel Psychology* 27 (1974), pp. 555–68.

10. B. Bass, *Leadership, Psychology and Organizational Behavior* (New York: Harper & Row, 1960).

11. J. P. Kotter, *The General Managers* (New York: Free Press, 1982).

12. Tannenbaum and Schmidt, "How to Choose a Leadership Pattern."

13. Hemphill, *Leader Behavior Description*.

14. F. Fiedler, *A Theory of Leadership Effectiveness* (New York: McGraw-Hill, 1967).

15. C. Schriescheim and S. Kerr, "Theories and Measurement of Leadership: A Critical Appraisal of Current and Future Directions," in *Leadership: The Cutting Edge*, J. Hunt and L. Larson, eds. (Carbondale, Ill.: Southern Illinois University Press, 1977), pp. 22–27.

16. P. Hersey and K. H. Blanchard, *Management of Organizational Behavior: Utilizing Human Resources*, 4th ed. (Englewood Cliffs, N.J.: Prentice-Hall, 1982).

17. The complete Leader Behavior Analysis questionnaire (20 questions) and scoring instructions are available from Blanchard Training and Development, Inc., Escondido, CA. 92025.

18. F. Fiedler, "Engineer the Job to Fit the Manager," *Harvard Business Review* 51 (1965), pp. 115–22.

19. R. House, "A Path-Goal Theory of Leadership," *Administrative Science Quarterly* 16 (1971), pp. 321–38

20. D. P. Schwab and L. L. Cummings, "Theories of Performance and Satisfaction," *Industrial Relations* 9 (1970), pp. 408–30.

Resource Readings

Bass, B. *Stogdill's Handbook of Leadership*. New York: Free Press, 1981.

Fiedler, F. *A Theory of Leadership Effectiveness*. New York: McGraw-Hill, 1967.

Hemphill, J. K. *Leader Behavior Description*. Columbus, Ohio: Ohio State University Press, 1950.

Hersey, P. and Blanchard, K. H. *Management of Organizational Behavior: Utilizing Human Resources*, 4th ed. Englewood Cliffs, N.J.: Prentice-Hall, 1982.

House, R. "A Path-Goal Theory of Leadership," *Administrative Science Quarterly* 16 (1971), pp. 321–38.

Kotter, J. P. *The General Managers*. New York: Free Press, 1982.

Tannenbaum, R. and W. H. Schmidt, "How to Choose a Leadership Pattern," *Harvard Business Review* 36 (March–April) 1958, pp. 95–102.

Ohio State Questionnaire on Leader Behavior (LBDQ)

Put a check in the column that describes you.

	always	often	occasionally	seldom	never
1. I make my attitudes clear to the group	✓				
3. I try out my new ideas with my group	✓				
5. I rule with an iron hand			✓		
7. I speak in a manner not to be questioned			✓		
9. I criticize poor work				✓	
11. I assign subordinates to particular tasks		✓			
13. I schedule the work	✓	✓			
15. I maintain definite standards of performance		✓			
17. I emphasize the meeting of deadlines				✓	
19. I encourage the use of uniform procedures				✓	
21. I make sure that my part in the organization is understood		✓			
23. I ask that subordinates follow standard rules and regulations				✓	
25. I let subordinates know what is expected of them	✓				
27. I see to it that subordinates are working up to capacity			✓		
29. I see to it that the work of subordinates is coordinated		✓			
Total	3	4	2	6	0

Consid.

	always	often	occasionally	seldom	never
2. I do personal favors for subordinates					✓
4. I do little things to make it pleasant to be a member of the group			✓		
6. I am easy to understand		✓			
8. I find time to listen to subordinates	✓				
10. I mix with subordinates rather than keeping to myself			✓		
12. I look out for the personal welfare of individuals in my group			✓		
14. I explain my actions to subordinates		✓			
16. I consult subordinates before action		✓			
18. I back up subordinates in their action		✓			
20. I treat all subordinates as equals		✓			
22. I am willing to make changes	✓				
24. I am friendly and approachable		✓			
26. I make subordinates feel at ease when talking with them		✓			
28. I put suggestions made by my group into action			✓		
30. I get group approval in important matters before acting	✓				
Total	3	5	5	1	1

Questionnaire *(continued)*

Directions for Scoring LBDQ

Total checks in each column of the previous page and enter in square below each column. The columns on the left hand represent the Initiating Structure values. The right hand columns represent Consideration values. Record the column totals in the Initiating Structure and Consideration boxes below. Multiply each of these totals by the weighting factors indicated. Add these for a grand total representing the Initiating Structure value and Consideration value.

Initiating Structure   Consideration

Initiating Structure		Consideration	
Always	3 × 4 = 12	Always	× 4 = 12
Often	4 × 3 = 12	Often	× 3 = 15
Occasionally	2 × 2 = 4	Occasionally	× 2 = 10
Seldom	6 × 1 = 6	Seldom	× 1 = 1
Never	0 × 0 =	Never	× 0 = 0
	Total 34		Total 38

Locating Yourself on the Ohio Model

Directions: In order to locate yourself in one of the four quadrants of the Ohio State Model below examine your score for *Initiating Structure*. If this score is 40 or above you would be considered high on that dimension; if it is below 40 you would be considered low on that dimension. For *Consideration*. If this score is 40 or above you would be considered high on that dimension; if it is below 40 you would be considered low on that dimension. In which quadrant does your score place you?

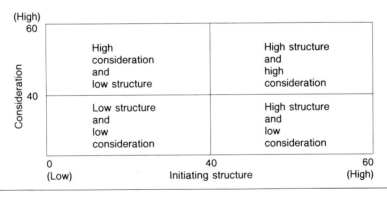

(High)
60

| High consideration and low structure | High structure and high consideration |
| Low structure and low consideration | High structure and low consideration |

40

0
(Low)

40
Initiating structure

60
(High)

Consideration

Fiedler's Least-Preferred Co-Worker Scale (LPC)

Think of a person *with whom you have had difficulty working*. It does not have to be a person you really dislike, just someone you *must* work with and with whom working is difficult. Describe the person on each of the scales below by circling the number between each pair of adjectives that best describes that person. Then transfer the numbers to the spaces at the right and total them.

Pleasant	:__:__:__:__:__:__:__:	Unpleasant	_____
	8 7 6 5 4 3 2 1		
Friendly	:__:__:__:__:__:__:__:	Unfriendly	_____
	8 7 6 5 4 3 2 1		
Rejecting	:__:__:__:__:__:__:__:	Accepting	_____
	1 2 3 4 5 6 7 8		
Tense	:__:__:__:__:__:__:__:	Relaxed	_____
	1 2 3 4 5 6 7 8		
Distant	:__:__:__:__:__:__:__:	Close	_____
	1 2 3 4 5 6 7 8		
Cold	:__:__:__:__:__:__:__:	Warm	_____
	1 2 3 4 5 6 7 8		
Supportive	:__:__:__:__:__:__:__:	Hostile	_____
	8 7 6 5 4 3 2 1		
Boring	:__:__:__:__:__:__:__:	Interesting	_____
	1 2 3 4 5 6 7 8		
Quarrelsome	:__:__:__:__:__:__:__:	Harmonious	_____
	1 2 3 4 5 6 7 8		
Gloomy	:__:__:__:__:__:__:__:	Cheerful	_____
	1 2 3 4 5 6 7 8		
Open	:__:__:__:__:__:__:__:	Guarded	_____
	8 7 6 5 4 3 2 1		
Backbiting	:__:__:__:__:__:__:__:	Loyal	_____
	1 2 3 4 5 6 7 8		
Untrustworthy	:__:__:__:__:__:__:__:	Trustworthy	_____
	1 2 3 4 5 6 7 8		
Considerate	:__:__:__:__:__:__:__:	Inconsiderate	_____
	8 7 6 5 4 3 2 1		
Nasty	:__:__:__:__:__:__:__:	Nice	_____
	1 2 3 4 5 6 7 8		
Agreeable	:__:__:__:__:__:__:__:	Disagreeable	_____
	8 7 6 5 4 3 2 1		
Insincere	:__:__:__:__:__:__:__:	Sincere	_____
	1 2 3 4 5 6 7 8		
Kind	:__:__:__:__:__:__:__:	Unkind	_____
	8 7 6 5 4 3 2 1		

Total _____

There are two different leadership styles which are measured by the Least Preferred Co-worker scale?

1. *Relationship-motivated* (High LPC—score of 64 and above). These leaders seem to be most concerned with maintaining good interpersonal relations and accomplishing the task through these personal relationships. Sometimes the high LPC leader becomes so concerned with relating to group members that it interferes with completion of the assignment or mission. In relaxed and well-controlled situations, this type of leader tends to impress the boss.

2. *Task-motivated* (Low LPC—score of 57 or below). These leaders place primary emphasis on task performance. Low LPC leaders work best from guidelines and specific directions and if these are lacking, the low LPC will make the organization and creation of these guidelines the first priority. However, under relaxed and well-controlled situations when the organization is running smoothly, the task-motivated leader takes time to attend to the moral of group members.

C H A P T E R   8

An Integrative Approach to Leadership

In Chapter 7, we reviewed six different theories of leadership, each of which helps us to better understand leadership in organizations. However, to be most effective as a manager, you need to draw on all of them. To help you do this more effectively, we will develop, in this chapter, an integrative framework of leadership.

This integrative model will be useful in analyzing situations to determine which of four leadership styles to use, and whether that style can be used by a particular manager in a given context. Also, the model emphasizes the need to view leadership as a developmental process. After developing the model, we will apply it to the Home Computers case to see how it works. And we will close the chapter by considering several implications of the model.

An Integrative Model of Leadership

All six theories discussed in Chapter 7 contribute to the analytical model we will develop. They suggest that we must analyze leader, subordinates, task, and situation if we are to determine the leadership style that will be most appropriate in a given situation. We will develop the integrative model in two steps: (1) picking the leadership style most appropriate for the task/subordinate fit, and (2) adjusting that choice based on leader and context characteristics. It will become clear very quickly that the Hersey-Blanchard leadership theory forms the basis of our model; we then add to it from the other theories to yield a more complete model. Their model is chosen as the basis primarily because of its developmental orientation and because it is easy to grasp. The basics of our integrative model (related to step 1 above) are shown in Figure 8.1.

The basic style choices are shown in the two-dimensional diagram, where initiating structure and consideration are the two dimensions. As noted above, these two dimensions became popular in the 1950s and have remained with us. Indeed, they seem to capture the two most critical elements of the manager's job: the task to be done and the people who must do it. Our model includes the four basic leadership styles:

1. High structure/low consideration (cell 1, which we call directing).

2. High structure/high consideration (cell 2, which we call coaching).
3. Low structure/high consideration (cell 3,which we call supporting).
4. Low structure/low consideration (cell 4, which we call delegating).

Now the question is: how to know when to use which style and how to move along the developmental curve in Figure 8.1 as the situation changes over time.

To determine the appropriate leadership style for a given situation, we draw heavily on the contingency theories developed in the 1960s. The developmental curve in the model and the ability and motivation continuum are an adaptation of Hersey and Blanchard's leadership model. If we can determine where a group of subordinates

Figure 8.1 A Framework for Analyzing Leadership Situations

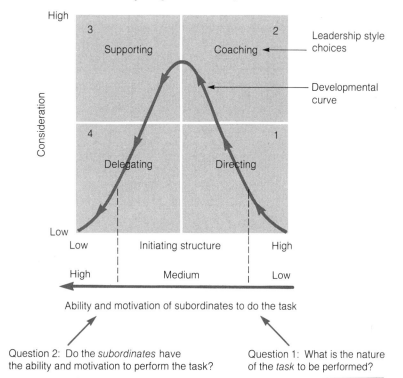

lies on the ability and motivation scale, we can then choose the right style of leadership. We do this by asking two questions.

Task Characteristics

The first question is: what is the nature of the task to be performed? (lower right-hand corner of Figure 8.1).[1] All three of the contingency theories (Fiedler, Hersey-Blanchard, and House) consider the degree of task structure as an important situational variable. Fiedler and House explicitly state that we need to know the degree to which subordinates' jobs are clearly defined. Hersey-Blanchard look at the fit between task structure and employee capability. Hence, to answer the first question, we need to analyze the task characteristics of structure, variability, and intrinsic motivation. Is the task clearly specified in terms of goals, the means to the goals, and the manner of evaluating goal accomplishment? Is the task highly variable in what must be done from day to day, and is it difficult to predict these variations? Also, is the task intrinsically motivating, that is, challenging and meaningful? Recall the job design model in Chapter 6. By looking at these task characteristics, we can get a feel for how difficult and how routine the job is. And if we consider the past and present of these characteristics, we can tell whether the job is becoming more or less difficult.

Subordinate Characteristics

Coupled with this analysis of the task, we must analyze the subordinate characteristics. Thus, **the second question is: do the subordinates have the ability and motivation to perform the task**? (lower left-hand corner of Figure 8.1).[2] Both the Hersey-Blanchard and House theories suggest that we must determine if subordinates are motivated toward higher-level needs (such as achievement); the more they are, the more a leader needs to emphasize consideration instead of initiating structure. House's path-goal theory also suggests the need to assess the employee's desire for control, while Hersey and Blanchard suggest we assess the employees' ability (experience and education). Several subquestions can be asked to get a handle on the subordinate characteristics, as related to the job. Do the employees have the ability to take responsibility for the task? Are they willing to take responsibility for it? Do they have education and experience that is relevant to the task? Do they have a high need for achievement (as defined in Chapter 6)? Are the employees interested in higher-order needs (such as self-actualization and self-esteem) or in lower-order needs (such as safety and physiological needs)? And finally, do the employees want control over their daily job activities? Each of these questions must be answered in terms of the task to be performed. **It is the current match between employees and task that really dictates whether the ability and motivation of the subordinates to perform the task is high, medium, or low**. And if we consider the past and present of these characteristics, our analysis will reveal trends about this match. Is it becoming better or worse?

Our analysis thus far will reveal where the subordinates are along the ability and motivation scale in Figure 8.1. If the employees are unable and unmotivated to do the job, they will be at the low end of the scale (to the right). The more able and motivated they are, the closer they will be to the high end (to the left). And ability is the key to pushing them toward the high end of the scale. Unable but motivated employees will rate lower than able but unmotivated employees. Once we locate the employees' position on the scale, we can draw a vertical line from that point on the continuum up to the developmental curve in the diagram to determine what style of leadership is appropriate for the given task/employee combination. For example, if the ability and motivation are low, the dashed line in Figure 8.1 indicates that high structure and low consideration, or directing leadership is the best choice. On the other hand, if the ability and motivation are high, the dashed line in the figure indicates that low structure and low consideration, that is, delegating leadership is the best choice.

Up to this point, our integrative model is similar to the Hersey-Blanchard leadership theory. We have used House's and Fiedler's theories to make the considerations of the task more explicit, and we have formulated two questions to ask. We have also drawn upon House's path-goal theory to help you more fully understand how to assess the subordinates' ability and motivation to do the task.

After you think through the two questions about task and subordinates as they apply to your situation, you are able to determine the best leadership style to help a particular set of subordinates do the given task effectively. But we do not know if the leader can actually pull off this style of leadership. In addition, we cannot tell what kind of influence the surrounding environment will have on the manager's ability to use the desired leadership style. Figure 8.2 adds these two considerations to our model—at the top of the figure as questions 3 and 4. The answers to them may necessitate an adjustment to the leadership style chosen from the first two questions.

Leader Characteristics

Thus, **the third question to ask is: what characteristics of the leader might influence his/her ability to use the chosen leadership style**? (upper left-hand corner of Figure 8.2).[3] Fiedler suggests that poor leader-member relations will generally call for a leadership style high in consideration. The trait theories suggest that a leader's experience and knowledge, power needs, and personal bases of power may be important in determining a leader's effectiveness. Thus, as a manager you must analyze your relations with your employees. Are they good or not so good? Do you have the bases of power and influence needed to exercise the desired leadership style? Do you have the experience and knowledge? And what are your power needs?

If you have a high need for power, you may tend to exert structure when it is not needed. And if you have a high need for affiliation, you may tend to show consideration when it is not desirable. Box 8.1 illustrates how strongly personality can influence the leader's style of leadership. Your personality and needs will influence your perception of a situation (as we discussed in Chapter 3). In turn, your perception will influence your analysis of the situation and push you toward one leadership style or another. Then too, your experience and knowledge may allow you to be more directive (that is, high in structure). But if you lack experience, it may be difficult for you to be directive, even if the situation calls for it.

Figure 8.2 An Expanded Framework for Analyzing Leadership Situations

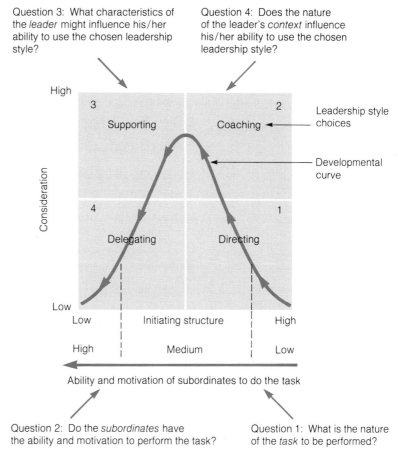

Question 3: What characteristics of the *leader* might influence his/her ability to use the chosen leadership style?

Question 4: Does the nature of the leader's *context* influence his/her ability to use the chosen leadership style?

Leadership style choices

Developmental curve

Consideration

High

3 Supporting

2 Coaching

4 Delegating

1 Directing

Low

	Low	Initiating structure	High
	High	Medium	Low

Ability and motivation of subordinates to do the task

Question 2: Do the *subordinates* have the ability and motivation to perform the task?

Question 1: What is the nature of the *task* to be performed?

As for relations with subordinates and bases of power, high charismatic or expertise power and good relations with subordinates may enable you to be directive when it is needed. If however, your relations with the employees are not very good, high relationship behavior may actually lead to improved relations. On the other hand, poor relations may necessitate directive leadership for short-run effectiveness. Finally, if your expert power is low, you may have to depend more on relationship-oriented leadership than the model in Figure 8.1 would indicate. Again,

**Box 8.1
Reagan's Management
by Delegation Begins
to Concern
Supporters**

Washington—*After Richard Nixon attended Anwar Sadat's funeral last fall, he flew on to Saudi Arabia for some official-sounding talks with its leaders. Reagan administration officials were irked. The White House, they said, hadn't known of Mr. Nixon's side trip and surely wouldn't have approved of it.*

But a day or so later, the aides' annoyance turned to mild embarrassment. It turned out Mr. Nixon had indeed told someone at the White House of his plans—and that someone hadn't both-ered to pass the word to Ronald Reagan's top aides.

The someone Mr. Nixon told was none other than Ronald Reagan.

The incident was small, but it says a lot about Mr. Reagan and his style of managing his awesome job. Presidential aides and Reagan watchers almost universally describe him as a man-ager of great personal security and charm, someone who can and does make tough decisions but who gives his staff great leeway and responsibility. Yet many also detect a certain presidential passivity, an inability to identify problems before they become acute and a slowness at recognizing the implications of issues. As the Reagan administration enters its second and perhaps most critical year, these perceived shortcomings are of increasing con-cern even among the President's friends—to say nothing of his critics.

White House aides often liken their boss's management style to that of a corporate chairman of the board. If that is so, though, Mr. Reagan's model clearly isn't a hard-charging detail man like, say, Chrysler Corp.'s Lee Iacocca. The President sees his job as "keeping his eye fixed on the very basic goals and principles of the administration."

"His strengths and weaknesses as a manager are almost inter-twined," suggests Helene von Damm, Mr. Reagan's former per-sonal secretary and now a White House personnel official. "His style is to tell people what he wants done and then leave it to them to do it." This approach, she says, encourages a certain type of person to be creative, "to go out and not want to let him down." But, she says, other types of people can't deal with the latitude—or else interpret Mr. Reagan's general approach as a license to pursue their own objectives rather than his.

By Rich Jaroslovsky, *The Wall Street Journal,* February 22, 1983. Reprinted by permission of *The Wall Street Journal,* © Dow Jones & Company, Inc. 1983. All rights reserved.

the key point in adding leader characteristics to our model is that the best style of leadership as defined by the task/subordinate fit may have to be altered due to characteristics of the leader. For example, if being relationship oriented is not your best style, it may be better to go ahead with high structure and try to adapt your style over time. Or perhaps the employees can adapt to your style and still yield good results.

Context Characteristics

Now let us look at how context characteristics can alter our analysis from Figure 8.1. **The fourth question is: does the nature of the leader's context influence his/her ability to use the chosen leadership style?** (upper right-hand corner of Figure 8.2).[4] Fiedler's theory points out the need to consider the power the leader derives from the position. And the autocratic-democratic continuum indicates that a leader must have position power in order to exercise initiating structure styles of leadership. Thus, how much power do you have because you are the manager (that is, position power)? Can you fire someone? Can you give someone a pay raise? If your position power is low, you may have to depend more on personal power bases, such as the admiration of your employees or your expertise. And this is likely to result in more relationship-oriented leader behavior than the model in Figure 8.1 might suggest. Of course, a great deal of position power would allow you to exercise directive leadership when it is suggested by the model.

The other context variables relate to the climate of your position as manager. What was the leadership style of the previous manager in your position? What is the leadership style of people around you in the organization (that is, your peers and superiors)? And what are the norms of the organization? If previous leaders in your position and other leaders in the organization are directive leaders, you may be better off to move gradually toward coaching leadership rather than adopt it at once—even if the subordinate/task fit suggests the coaching style. This idea is consistent with the Hersey-Blanchard model. since they indicate it is not appropriate to radically change the leadership style used with a group of employees.

And there are many pressures in an organization to

conform to certain expectations and adhere to norms of behavior. Managers who ignore these pressures usually encounter difficulty in their careers. Box 8.2 illustrates how expectations of people around a leader can exert constraining forces on his/her behavior. Of course, your situation may not be as extreme as the one described by Mr. Henderson. But norms and tradition will be important factors influencing your choice of an effective leadership style. These context variables clearly stress the importance of viewing leadership as a developmental process. **The situation into which you walk as a leader will always have a past and a future. You must read the developmental process of the context if you are to be an effective leader**.

Now that we have fully described our integrative model of leadership, let us consider the following situation involving Louise of Home Computers, since we already know quite a lot about her from earlier chapters. We will then apply our model to the case.

**Box 8.2
Firm Teaches Third
World Managers**

Management skills taught by U.S. business schools often don't apply in the developing world. Robert Youker, who teaches at Economic Development Institute, a training center run by the World Bank in Washington, says sophisticated techniques often are "totally unrealistic."

Verne E. Henderson, a management psychologist and protestant minister who teaches MEI's course in ethics, cites the case of an African student who worked for a bank. The student had been assigned to help open the first bank office in his home village. The first loan applicant was the village elder, whose tribal authority was unquestioned but whose credit rating wasn't. The elder couldn't meet the bank's lending guidelines; the student turned him down.

When the student went home that evening, Mr. Henderson says, his family was "up in arms." The student agonized over the issue of violating either his bank's guidelines or his tribe's traditions. Mr. Henderson says he advises students to resolve such questions by stating goals and consequences of actions. In this case, he says, granting the loan would have been both ethical and pragmatic, because without the elder's support, the branch would fail.

The Wall Street Journal, February 3, 1983. Reprinted by permission of *The Wall Street Journal*, © Dow Jones & Company, Inc. 1983. All rights reserved.

Leadership and Louise of Home Computers

As Louise took over the project manager's job in Phoenix, she realized that she had stepped across a significant boundary. She was now management, where before she had just been a systems analyst. In her old position she had relied heavily on establishing good relationships with other programmers whose services she needed on her projects. But now as a manager, she had other legitimate sources of power to use. As she contemplated this new position, she recalled her first boss, Sam Stewart, and how he had given very clear direction—but a great deal of discretion—in how she did her work. She had liked that approach; and she wondered if it would work for her in Phoenix.

Many of the programmers in her office were very new in their jobs. Some of them seemed quite capable; others appeared to need a great deal of guidance. The Phoenix office was growing quite rapidly, and many of the customers were engineering companies with extremely technical problems to be solved. Louise found the Phoenix office in a state of real disunity. The new programmers, while they had good credentials, did not know what to do. The more experienced programmers jumped from one project to another to try to put out fires as they arose. It appeared that the rapid growth of the office had led to the signing of many contracts, without determining how the work could be done.

While Louise was not the systems manager for the entire office, she had several projects under her responsibility, and she decided to try to get those projects in good shape. She also decided to work with the systems manager, John Wood, to see if she could help correct the overall office problems. But she knew she would first have to develop some credibility with John, so she focused her energies on the projects directly under her.

She analyzed the situation in the following manner. The job facing her and her programmers was somewhat ambiguous in that the technical problems of the customers were difficult. Furthermore, the quantity of work was very great. Fortunately the work was very challenging—in fact, too challenging for her new, inexperienced programmers. They wanted to perform well, because they saw this job as a great opportunity. But they were in over their heads. The history of the company suggested that Louise was expected to produce, no matter what it took. Indeed, Louise was in a tough situation, and her boss, John, was so inundated that he could not help her very much.

Fortunately, Louise had a great deal of self-confidence. In addition, she was alert and outspoken and enjoyed solving problems by applying logic. Her experience suggested that her group would have to cut back on the number of new projects and focus on the ones they had, or they would be in danger of putting out a bad product. She knew that in the long run this would cause more problems than cutting back production. John was not too sure about this solution, but when Louise was so adamant, he consented to her wishes.

Louise proceeded to establish priorities among the existing projects and to refuse new projects for the time being. She then organized the programmers by mixing experienced and inexperienced programmers on each project. Each project was given specific instructions on how to proceed and strict deadlines to meet. But once these parameters were established, she appointed a project leader to carry out the plans. Then each week she would meet with all project teams to discuss problems and progress toward the deadlines. The previous project manager had constantly been on the backs of the programmers and was always showing them how he would do the job.

The programmers responded well to this delegation of responsibility. They became very involved in turning out a good product in a reasonable time. In fact, after about 18 months, it became apparent that Louise's group was not only turning out excellent products, but they were beginning to turn them out faster. Many new clients wanted Louise to handle their projects, and many programmers in the office wanted to work in her group.

Louise began to have a great deal of influence with the other project managers in the office, as well as with John Wood, her boss. Her ability to handle the rapid growth situation and get the most out of her subordinates made other managers want to listen to her. In fact, many of her peers began to come to her for advice, instead of John. Fortunately, her unit had clear direction and her staff had developed to the point that she did not have to devote all of her time to the unit. She saw this as her opportunity to begin directly influencing John and the entire Phoenix office. But she wondered if the same approach that had been so successful with her programmers would also work for the entire office.

By analyzing the situation much as she had done when she first came to Phoenix, Louise determined that she would have to focus more on her relationship with John than on the pure task of reorganizing the office. For one thing, she did not have the authority to tell John what to do. Furthermore, John was a very capable manager. Then too, the company protocol suggested that one should respect the chain of command at all times. Louise adjusted to the new situation; and soon everyone knew that she was the one responsible for making the Phoenix office one of the best in the company. In 1971 Louise was rewarded with the systems manager's job at Phoenix, when John was promoted to a larger, more established office on the West Coast.

Applying Our Integrative Model to Louise's Situation

Let us now apply our integrative model in Figure 8.2 to the Home Computers case by asking the four questions in the figure. First, what is the nature of the task to be performed? As a project manager, Louise faced a situation that was not well structured and was constantly changing. The projects were ambiguous, overwhelming, yet very challenging and meaningful. The programmers had a rather difficult task, thus pointing toward a need for an initiating structure leadership style. But what about their abilities and motivation?

The second question in our model addresses this issue: do the subordinates have the ability and motivation to perform the task? The programmers appear to be motivated—the experienced programmers jumped from project to project to do the best they could to keep things on track. They were willing to take responsibility and had a high need for achievement. They also had a high desire for control over their work. These clues also suggest that they were capable within reasonable limits. In other words, they appeared to have the skills to be excellent programmers—but the situation was so unstructured they could not apply them effectively. As for the new programmers, they had good credentials and (by inference) reasonable abilities, but they were unclear about what to do.

So, what was the level of ability and motivation of the programmers to handle the task? The programmers did not appear to lack ability and motivation—rather their jobs were so unstructured that they did not know what to do. They were willing but not able due to the lack of clear direction; thus the ability/motivation appeared to be medium-low. The lack of task structure was overriding the capabilities of the employees. They wanted to perform well, but the unstructured task made them unable to do so. From the model in Figure 8.2, it appears that the appropriate leadership style was high on both structure and consideration (that is, coaching leadership). And this is what Louise did: she restricted the number of projects to be handled and set priorities for each project. She also gave specific guidelines for each project. On the consideration side, she mixed the experienced and new programmers and met with each project team weekly to discuss progress. Otherwise, she left things up to the project leader. As the case reports, Louise and her programmers performed very well, indeed.

The case also illustrates another aspect of the model. By providing the overall structure to the task, Louise created a better fit between the task and the programmers; this moved their ability and motivation from medium-low toward medium-high, by providing the needed structure. This movement then created the need for her to move into cell 3 of the model and decrease her initiating structure dimension as applied on a daily basis (a supporting style). And as the case mentions, she actually moved into cell 4 (delegating) within 18 months, as the programmers moved into high ability/motivation. This developmental process is consistent with the Hersey-Blanchard model, which indicates that such development is both natural and a goal of an effective leader.

Thus far the model in Figure 8.2 suggests that the best leadership style initially for Louise was high in both structure and consideration. But we also need to factor in the leader and context characteristics. The third question in the model is: which characteristics might influence the leader's ability to use the chosen leadership style? We know that Louise has a great deal of self-confidence, and she is also alert and outspoken. Material on Louise from Chapter 4 indicates she has a lot of knowledge and expert personal power. These factors suggest that Louise will be comfortable with an initiating structure leadership style. If Louise had not had experience and self-confidence, she might have found it difficult to stand up to John Wood and to initiate the structure of reducing the number of projects. On the other hand, since Louise is new in the position, she has no working relationship with the employees in Phoenix; thus the leader-member relations exert a force toward a consideration leadership style.

In short, Louise is well suited to the style of leadership suggested by the model—she would appear to have the ability and personal characteristics to exercise the coaching style of leadership. But it is not difficult to imagine a person who might lack the knowledge and self-confidence to get the job done. It also appears that Louise can be flexible, since she gradually moved to a supporting style and then to a delegating style.

Our final question from Figure 8.2 is: does the nature of the context influence the leader's ability to use the chosen leadership style? It would appear that the necessary position power is present for Louise to set priorities and control the situation faced by her programmers. Thus, she can follow through with the initiating structure needed in Phoenix. And what we know about her boss, John Wood, suggests that Louise has flexibility in her position. John is not so demanding about the situation as to dictate a style to Louise.

Finally, we are told that the previous project manager was constantly on the programmers' backs and forever showing them how to do their jobs. Thus, Louise stepped into a situation where her predecessor had been almost all structure and very little consideration. But he structured the details of the jobs rather than the larger picture which Louise attacked. The previous leader's style probably made it easy for Louise to change the situation, since the programmers did not like his style. By structuring the overall situation and then allowing freedom and showing consideration for the programmers, Louise was moving in a direction the able and motivated programmers desired. But the past history suggests that it was wise to move initially no further along the developmental curve than the coaching style of leadership.

Thus in this case we can see how the two leader and context questions do not contradict the basic model; rather they provide added support for the choice from the basic model. And, more important, it is easy to imagine how the leader and context characteristics could, in some cases, alter the choice of leadership style. **By analyzing not only the subordinates and the task, but also the leader and the context, we are able to gain a realistic perspective on the leadership style which will work in a given situation.**

Implications of the Model

With our integrative model now fully described and applied to Louise, we can note several important implications of the model. First, the developmental curve in the model highlights the changing nature of both task and subordinate characteristics. **By analyzing the past history of the task and the subordinates' ability and motivation, a manager gains an idea of how to handle the present situation. But the analysis must continue into the future, since both task and subordinates may undergo change.** And it has been argued that one of the manager's jobs is to move the subordinates along the ability and motivation continuum by moving leadership along the developmental curve from right to left.[5] Indeed, normal forces usually create a right-to-left evolution along the curve. Over time, the ability of subordinates will tend to increase through experience, and the complexity of the task will tend to decrease.

The second implication follows from the first. Past performance of the subordinates will influence the appropriate leadership style choice for the manager. And future performance of subordinates will influence adjustments in leadership style. Yes, **subordinate behavior affects leadership style just as leadership style affects subordinate behavior, as should be clear if one takes a developmental view of the situation.**[6] Louise chose a style that got positive results. She then shifted her style along the developmental curve. But suppose the high structure/high consideration style had failed to work. She would then have had to shift to either high structure/low consideration or low structure/high consideration.

The new style she would have chosen leads to the third implication from the model. Would she attribute the continued poor performance to problems with the task? Or to problems with the subordinates' ability? Or to problems with their motivation? Obviously, her attribution would affect her choice of appropriate leadership style.[7] And we can imagine that different leaders might interpret the same phenomena differently—just as Louise might interpret them differently at different times in her career. Indeed, the development of the leader is an important aspect of our model.

The fourth implication is that a manager must lead a number of people in performing a number of tasks. **Since** each subordinate and each task may differ slightly, the manager will need to vary his/her leadership style from task to task and from person to person.[8] Indeed, Louise might well have varied her leadership style between the experienced and new programmers. The implication here is important: it suggests the need to analyze not only the group of subordinates but also each subordinate individually.

The final implication is apparent from the case. When Louise created structure for the programmers by limiting the number of projects and setting priorities among them, she reduced the need for daily structuring of programmer activities. These rules and procedures, plus the mixing of new with experienced programmers, actually serve as substitutes for leadership.[9] The task-relevant experience and education already in our model are other substitutes for leadership. The key point is that **if employee motivation and ability are high, and if the task is structured, leader behavior can be minimized**. In the model, this situation would put us in cell 4 where delegating is the appropriate leadership style.

Our hope is that you now have a better understanding of leadership and how the six theories from Chapter 7 tie together to provide a useful framework. If you work with our integrative model, you will be able to better analyze leadership situations. And through experience, you can also learn to implement the leadership style appropriate for given situations.

Chapter Highlights

In this chapter, we have developed an integrative model of leadership which will be useful to you in analyzing situations to determine the appropriate leadership style. We used the six leadership theories from Chapter 7 to develop our integrative model of leadership. The model includes four styles of leadership: directing, coaching, supporting, and delegating. By drawing from the Hersey-Blanchard, Fiedler, and House models **we ask two questions about task and subordinate characteristics to determine the ability and motivation of subordinates to handle the task at the present time**. To apply the model you would first analyze the task structure and variability and its intrinsic motivation. To determine the fit between task and employees, you would then analyze the subordinates' ability and willingness to take responsibility, their task-relevant education/experience, their need for achievement, their present need structure, and their desire for control. From this analysis you could determine where on the ability and motivation continuum in Figure 8.2 to place your employees. And by drawing a vertical line up to intersect the developmental curve, you could select the appropriate style of leadership for the situation.

Next the model calls for an analysis of leader and context characteristics (using two more questions) to see if the chosen style can be implemented. **The leader characteristics of relations with subordinates, experience/knowledge, power needs, and personal power bases will influence the leader's analysis of the situation.** In addition, **the context characteristics of the position power of the leader, the style of previous people in the leader's position, the style of other leaders around the manager, and organizational norms of operation will act to constrain the leadership choices available to the manager.** These additional aspects can influence the choice of appropriate leadership style for a given situation.

We then applied the model to the Home Computers case, after which we discussed several of its implications. First, the model emphasizes the developmental aspects of the leadership process. Second, it allows for the fact that subordinate behavior can affect leader behavior, as well as the reverse. Third, leader characteristics influence the analysis that he/she makes of the situation. Fourth, managers must vary their leadership style from subordinate to subordinate and from task to task. And fifth, the leader's behavior influences the context in which he/she must operate.

Our goal in this chapter has been to draw on a number of leadership theories in developing an integrative model of the leadership process. We have tried to provide a model that will be useful to you in analyzing situations to determine the appropriate leadership style to use. What remains is for you to become proficient in its use and experienced in putting into practice the leadership styles appropriate for the situations you encounter.

Review Questions

1. What are the four basic leadership styles in our integrative model? What are the basic factors which determine the appropriate leadership style for a given situation?

2. Explain how the basic integrative model presented in this chapter can be used to analyze a given situation and determine the best leadership style for that situation.

3. How might leader characteristics and context characteristics cause you to alter the leadership style chosen in the basic integrative model (Figure 8.1)? Is it appropriate to consider altering the basic choice based on leader and context variables?

4. Can you explain the expanded model of leadership in Figure 8.2 as it relates to the leadership theories from Chapter 7? Speculate on the next generation of leadership theories that will help us better understand the process of leadership.

5. What are the important implications of the integrative model of leadership?

Notes

1. The task characteristics and the resulting questions are based on Fiedler, *A Theory of Leadership Effectiveness* (New York: McGraw-Hill, 1967); House, "A Path-Goal Theory of Leadership" *Administrative Science Quarterly* 16 (1971), pp. 321–38; and J. R. Hackman, G. Oldham, R. Janson, and K. Purdy, "A New Strategy for Job Enrichment," *California Management Review*, 27 (1975), pp. 57–71.

2. The subordinate characteristics and the resulting questions are based on Hersey and Blanchard, *Management of Organizational Behavior: Utilizing Human Resources*, 4th ed. (Englewood Cliffs, N.J.: Prentice-Hall, 1982), and House, "A Path-Goal Theory."

3. This section draws on the work of several researchers: Fiedler, *A Theory of Leadership*; D. C. McClelland, "Power Is the Great Motivator," *Harvard Business Review*, 54 (1976), pp. 100–110; V. H. Vroom, "Can Leaders Learn to Lead?," *Organizational Dynamics*, 4 (1976), pp. 17–28.

4. This section draws on several researchers: Fiedler, *A Theory of Leadership*; B. J. Calder, "An Attribution Theory of Leadership," in *New Directions in Organizational Behavior*, ed. B. M. Staw and G. R.

Salancik (Chicago: St. Clair Press, 1977), pp. 179–204; J. Pfeffer, "The Ambiguity of Leadership," *Academy of Management Review*, 2 (1977), pp.104–12.

5. Hersey and Blanchard, *Management of Organizational Behavior*.

6. G. F. Farris, "Organizational Factors and Individual Performance: A Longitudinal Study," *Journal of Applied Psychology* 53 (1969), pp. 87–92; C. N. Greene, "A Longitudinal Investigation of Modifications to a Situation Model of Leadership Effectiveness," *Academy of Management Proceedings* (1979), pp. 54–8.

7. W. A. Knowlton and T. Mitchell, "Effects of Causal Attributions on a Supervisor's Evaluation of Subordinate Performance," *Journal of Applied Psychology* 65 (1980), pp. 459–66.

8. G. Graen, "Role-Making Processes in Organizations," in *Handbook of Industrial and Organizational Psychology*, ed. M. D. Dunnette (Skokie, Ill.: Rand-McNally, 1976).

9. S. Kerr and J. M. Jermier, "Substitutes for Leadership: Their Meaning and Measurement," *Organizational Behavior and Human Performance* 19 (1978), pp. 370–87.

Resource Readings

Graen, G. "Role-Making Processes in Organizations." in *Handbook of Industrial and Organizational Psychology*. ed. M. D. Dunnette. Skokie, Ill.: Rand-McNally, 1976.

Kerr, S. and J. M. Jermier. "Substitutes for Leadership: Their Meaning and Measurement." *Organizational Behavior and Human Performance* 19 (1978) pp. 370–87.

Pfeffer, J. "The Ambiguity of Leadership." *Academy of Management Review* 2 (1977) pp. 104–12.

Vroom, V. H. "Can Leaders Learn to Lead?" *Organizational Dynamics* 4 (1976) pp. 17–28.

CHAPTER 9

Power and Politics in Organizational Behavior

In the last two chapters we explored a number of leadership theories and developed an analytical, integrative model of leadership. In so doing, we were giving you a tool to use in determining which of the four leadership styles is the most appropriate for a given situation. But as we pointed out in those chapters, leadership is more than simply knowing which style to use. It is being able to use that appropriate style. And it is even more than using the appropriate style. [Influencing the behavior of others—which is how we defined leadership—involves using power that is available to you and understanding and using organizational politics for the good of the organization.]

The Need for Power and Politics in Organizations

Now, some of you may not like the idea of using power and politics to influence the behavior of others. But, it is a fact of life in organizations—and both power and politics can be used for good purposes as well as bad. In Chapter 5 we said that to be a leader, you must have a base of power. And in Chapter 8, we explored how power bases can affect the choice of leadership style in a situation. Yes, **power is essential to a leader**. But this does not mean that you have to carry a big club. There are other power sources, which we will explore in this chapter. As Kotter found in his research, successful general managers want power and are not afraid of it. They use it to achieve the goals desired by the organization.

In addition to power, political behaviors are a natural part of every organization. As a young marketing analyst just out of college, I discovered that favoritism, little white lies, going outside the chain of command, and other political behaviors were rampant in the large oil company for which I worked. Being naive about organizations, I was shocked at these behaviors. My engineering training had taught me that rational and logical decision making was the norm in successful organizations and for effective managers. Thus, one of the reasons I left business was to find a less political world, such as I thought existed in universities. Well, again I was shocked to find political behaviors the norm in both my graduate university and the universities for which I have worked since graduation. From these experiences, I learned that politics is a part of every organization. As the cartoon which is shown below suggests, more than logic is needed to succeed as a manager. Indeed, politics is a part of our human existence—in families, in churches, in clubs, wherever people operate collectively. But I also learned something else. **Politics is not always bad. It is simply a tool which people can use for the good of the organization or for personal gain.** In this chapter we will explore both the positive and negative aspects of politics in organizations.

Thus, our starting point is that power and politics in organizations are as natural and necessary as leadership. Indeed, they complement leadership behaviors. **Managers cannot lead without developing bases of power to call upon.** And while leadership is usually viewed as the behavior that is expected in achieving organizational goals, organizations do not always work according to plan. **Political behaviors can be used to deal with the flaws in an organization and to help ensure the achievement of organizational goals.** In this chapter, we will learn where power comes from in organizations and how to develop and use your bases of power. We will also learn what political behaviors are designed to achieve, and why people engage in organizational politics. In so doing, you will be learning how to become an effective manager in

organizations which are powerful and political, as well as rational.

Power and Its Sources

Mention the word **power**—and almost everyone has some image of what it means. Many of us think of someone negative. We think of a Hitler, an Al Capone, a boss who belittled us, or a teacher who embarrassed us in front of the class. But we could also think of a Gandhi, a President Kennedy who made others feel powerful, a boss we really respected, or a teacher who was challenging and stimulating. **Power is neither good nor evil. It is simply the capacity to influence other people's behaviors.**[2] As Kanter elaborates, power is the ability "to mobilize resources, to get and use whatever is needed for the goals a person is attempting to meet."[3] And it is possible to use our power as a manager to give power to our subordinates—that is, to make them feel influential in the organization.

The situation at Chrysler described in Box 9.1 points out the importance of "swift and decisive management action in troubled times." Can a manager take such action without a base of power? No! Indeed, this article also illustrates the political aspects of using power to influence behavior, as Chrysler did with the banks. In Chapter 7, we defined leadership as "the process of influencing the behavior of other people or groups of people toward the achievement of organizational goals." Since "power is the capacity to influence other people's behavior," it is thus necessary to the process of leadership. **Power essentially provides the resource which is the basis for leadership.** But where does one get this resource called power? In other words, what sources are available for gaining power in organizations.

Personal Sources of Power

The two most commonly recognized personal sources of power are **referent** and **expert**.[4] **Referent power** comes from the admiration, respect, and identification that one person feels for another. As a manager, you might have a reputation, personal attractiveness, or charisma that makes your subordinates want

Box 9.1
Chrysler Typifies the
Hard Times of the
Industrial Giants

To understand the fall of American industrial might, you need look no further than Chrysler Corp.

Chrysler in 1979 was nearly driven to insolvency by mismanagement, stiff competition, inefficient plants, high labor costs and a relentlessly volatile economic climate. Even today, the brink remains uncomfortably close.

Their experiences dramatize, among other things, the importance of swift and decisive management action in troubled times.

Iacocca's High Marks

Bankers and suppliers give Chrysler management, particularly Mr. Iacocca, high marks for aggressive and consistent leadership. He was visible and forceful, whether testifying in Congress or jabbing a finger at the American public in his television commercials. "There was a conscious strategy to put Iacocca out front, to say to the world, 'Everything's all right, Jack, come to the dealership,'" says a source familiar with Chrysler.

Chrysler had resorted to some desperate measures. At a press conference, it threatened to close a plant in Belvidere, Ill., if a bank near there didn't agree to the rescue plan. Company officials said that bankruptcy was just days away unless the bank fell in line. When a horde of angry workers thereupon lined up to close their accounts, the bank caved in.

Chrysler lobbied hard for the federal loan guarantees, shuttling dealers into Washington to talk to their congressmen. Before the government intervened by guaranteeing up to $1.5 billion in loans, current and former Chrysler officials insist, bankers were prepared to pull the plug. "The bankers were dragged into it by the government, kicking and screaming," a former company official says.

By Hal Lancaster and Sue Shellenbarger, *The Wall Street Journal,* January 28, 1983. Reprinted by permission of *The Wall Street Journal,* © Dow Jones & Company, Inc. 1983. All rights reserved.

to be like you. Thus, as these subordinates try to copy your behavior they give you a great deal of power to influence their behavior. But how can you develop this kind of power? Unfortunately, while referent power is based to some extent on accomplishments in the job, it is also a matter of style that may be difficult to pinpoint. For example, John Kennedy as President in the early

1960s was not responsible for passage of nearly the number of pieces of legislation as his successor, Lyndon Johnson. But Kennedy was more revered and admired, because he had that "something" which other people want to imitate. He exuded a great deal of confidence that many people admired and respected.

Expert power comes from a person's abilities, skills, and talents. As a manager, you will have expert power if you can exhibit competence in performing certain aspects of the job. Perhaps you are especially good at analyzing and evaluating situations. As this becomes known to others with whom you work, you will gain power to influence their behavior in this particular area. **Expert power is normally very limited in range, in contrast to referent power which is wide in scope.** For example, a master machinist may have a great deal of expert power in the use of certain equipment in a plant. New workers and even inexperienced supervisors may yield to the advice of this expert craftsman. However, if the company switches to computer-guided machinery, which does not require the machinist's expertise, the expert power once held is now greatly reduced.

Both referent and expert power are developed over time, and they can also decline over time. Before your subordinates recognize your expert power, you must show that you have more expertise than others that they work with—and it must be expertise in an area that they value. For example, for a machinist to be an expert in English literature would probably not be important to workers at the plant. With referent power, the same developmental process takes place. People learn to admire you because of what you do on your current job. Or, your reputation may precede you on a new job.

Once it is established, referent power is more difficult to reduce than expert power. The two most likely ways to lose referent power are for you to do something to tarnish your attractiveness or reputation, or for someone more attractive and with more charisma to come along. On the other hand, expert power can easily be lost if you teach others about your area of expertise. For example, if a manager tells subordinates all he or she knows about a particular issue, the expert power is reduced.

Perhaps this is one reason why managers never tell all to their subordinates. Of course, this same action could increase the manager's referent power—the employees might admire a manager who uses this more participative style of leadership.

Position Sources of Power

French and Raven also identified three sources of power which are more attributable to the manager's position than to the person.[5]

Reward power is based on a person's ability to reward other people for desired behavior. If, as a manager, you have some control over pay, promotions, time off, praise, and so forth, your subordinates will be inclined to do what you want, in order to receive these rewards. However, it is important to note that **the reward must be valued by the subordinate if it is to influence behavior**. We made this point in Chapter 3 in discussing reinforcement theory as applied to learning. And we also discussed using rewards as a way to motivate people in Chapters 5 and 6. Because rewards are useful in changing people's behavior (that is, learning), reward power may be most useful with new employees or with employees who are asked to learn something new in their work. A best-selling book, *The One Minute Manager* emphasizes the use of praise rather than reprimand in helping employees become more effective performers, especially when they need to learn things they do not already know.[6] In other words, if the employee's abilities need to be improved, you must motivate the person to learn new behaviors. Reward power can be used very effectively in these cases.

The counterpart to reward power is **coercive power**. It is power based on a person's ability to punish other people for not doing what the person wants. To stop undesired behavior, a manager can use punishment in the form of reprimands, reduced pay, demotion, undesirable work assignments, firing, and so forth. **But the punishment must be viewed negatively by the subordinate if it is to have the desired effect.** For example, you might reprimand an employee only to find the employee thankful for receiving attention that was lacking in the past. And the undesired behavior may thus continue.

As you may recall, in Chapter 3, we discussed punishment as it relates to learning and in Chapters 5 and 6 as it relates to motivation. As pointed out in Chapter 3, punishment has the disadvantage of working only to eliminate undesirable behavior. The employee still has to learn to do what is desired. Of course, it is possible that if employees already know what to do, the threat of coercive power may make them perform as desired. Or as *The One Minute Manager* suggests, a reprimand is appropriate when dealing with one of your better employees who has let you down. **The key is to use the reprimand on the employee's behavior and couple it with praise of the employee as a valuable asset to the organization.**

The final source of power proposed by French and Raven was **legitimate power**. It is based on the perception that a person has the right to influence behavior because of his or her position in the organizational hierarchy. This power base also includes the perception that subordinates are obligated to obey the manager. Clearly, legitimate power is based on the position of the manager, in relation to the position held by the subordinate. For example, it is generally recognized that an Army drill sergeant has the right to tell trainees what to do and that the trainees have an obligation to obey the drill sergeant.

Since legitimate power is based on your position in an organization relative to others around you, it has a developmental aspect. As you move up the ranks of the organization, you will gain in legitimate power. A general has more legitimate power than a major, who has more legitimate power than a lieutenant. Conversely, your legitimate power can be reduced if you are assigned to a position that is perceived to have less influence and status within the organization. For example, if you move from the engineering department in a highly technical organization to the personnel department, your legitimate power may be reduced.

Another aspect of legitimate power is the area of responsibility within which you have the right to make decisions. As long as you remain within the perceived zone of your legitimate power, you can use this source of power to influence the behavior of employees. If you move outside of this zone, however, your power will drop off rapidly. For example, you may have the legitimate power to get employees to work overtime, but you may not have the power to make them use the company product in their personal lives. Some people who work for Chrysler drive Fords.

Much has been written about how the range of influence of managers over their employees has declined over the last several decades. In the early 1900s, before the days of union influence, the limits to managerial legitimate power were very few. But as unions gained in strength, they reduced this power by giving the employees a strong voice to counter unreasonable managerial requests. And during the 1960s a cultural revolution brought into question many of the rights that had previously been assumed by managers. Today employees feel that they have certain rights which limit the legitimate power of managers. A number of changes in the work place have reduced the legitimate power of lower-level managers and supervisors. Computers have taken away part of their job. A worth ethic has developed to replace the old work ethic. Employees feel they have worth beyond their jobs and thus feel obligated to follow only those orders which relate directly to their jobs and which demonstrate respect for them as people. However, we might add that the recession of the 1980s tended to increase the perceived legitimate power of managers, because employees were more concerned about job security than they had been during the 1960s and 1970s. These events should make it clear that legitimate power is susceptible to change, both increasing and decreasing. It is also influenced by societal events and by movement through the hierarchy.

In a moment we would like to take a look at Home Computers to see power in operation. But first, take a few minutes to complete the power questionnaire at the end of this chapter to find out which sources of power appeal more to you. There is no one best answer, so be honest with yourself. By answering and scoring this questionnaire you will gain insight into yourself in terms of these five power sources. You will determine which ones you like to rely on and which ones you may be ignoring.

The Home Computers Case—Rob and Tom

Both Rob and Tom have worked as production engineers for Home Computers since joining the company in 1979 in the Dayton, Ohio plant. They both graduated from Ohio State University in engineering in 1979 and immediately joined Home Computers. Up until 1982 their careers were remarkably similar. Starting out as first-line supervisors on the production line for the EZ2 computer, both Rob and Tom demonstrated an ability to get the job done. Furthermore, they both learned a great deal about the internal workings of the computer and about the history of Home Computers.

But there are some differences in the way they each operate and how they are perceived. Rob is always praising his employees for their good work. Furthermore, he does what he can to get raises for his people at every opportunity. His people seem to have a great deal of respect and admiration for Rob. They also put out a good effort and typically beat their quota in both quantity and quality. On the other hand, Tom comes down hard on his people when they make a mistake and is seldom seen giving a pat on the back for a job well done. It is as though a good job is what is expected, and you do not reward people for doing only what is expected. You reward them for doing something above and beyond the call of duty. Tom's people do what he says partly out of fear and partly because of their respect for the company. The result is a good product, but sometimes Tom has problems in terms of quality, especially when he has to be away from the floor for some reason.

In 1982 Rob was promoted, based on his outstanding record as a supervisor, to the job of section head. As section head he was responsible for the work of several first-line supervisors, including Tom, and that was awkward. Rob and Tom were good friends, but their relationship was now altered by their status difference within the company. As section head, Rob continued to operate much as he had as a supervisor, relying on his technical expertise and the respect he had gained in the company, and giving praise. As often happens, Rob found that his promotion gave him more control over rewards and punishments in the organization. Furthermore, it seemed that his employees showed even greater respect for him than they had previously.

Tom, however, was disappointed about not receiving the promotion himself. He decided to show the company that he was really better suited for the job than Rob was. He knew that as a section head Rob would be dependent on the first-line supervisors for information important for the decisions he would have to make. Tom also knew that Rob's connections with the other supervisors might be weakened due to the normal distance between supervisors and section heads. Tom thus began to withhold certain information from Rob and to make comments to the other supervisors about how Rob was not representing their best interests. And indeed this was true, since Rob did not have all of the information he needed to make the best decisions. In fact, Tom would sometimes introduce the "new" information at important supervisors' meetings. And he was always sure to talk about helping the company achieve its goals, as he introduced this information. Rob was often caught off guard.

After awhile, Rob began to feel as though he were out to sea in a boat without a paddle. Many activities in his section occurred without his involvement, and his weakened position with the supervisors also served to weaken his position with superiors. It was clear to Rob's superiors that he had talent and was generally liked by his people, but he was not getting the job done. Both the quality and quantity of computers produced by his people were declining. It was not long before the decision was made to move Rob into the personnel department for a new experience and to promote Tom into the section head position. Tom quickly held a supervisors' meeting to ensure them he wanted their ideas and suggestions—he would be a different leader from Rob.

After a year in these positions, Rob has again demonstrated his ability to get a job done. Tom is also doing a good job, though he does not appear to be popular with his people.

The Power Sources in Action

It is not enough to merely have a strong power base; **power must be used if it is to influence the behavior of others.** If we stop to analyze this case, we can identify the sources of power used by Rob and Tom. Both Rob and Tom appear to have expert power in the job of first-line supervisor. They know what to do, and they get it done. They understand both the product and the company. Since they both have the same position, they have the same amount of legitimate, reward, and coercive power, because these depend on the position more than the person. However, the extent to which they rely on these three sources of power does vary. Tom relies more on coercive power, whereas Rob relies more on reward power. In using these different power bases, Rob and Tom are using the legitimate power they have to act in a supervisory role. Rob appears to have more referent power than Tom, and this may be because of greater reliance on reward power, as opposed to coercive power. Indeed, the interactions among these five sources of power must also be considered.

Interactions among the Power Sources

As you use your power bases, it is typical to find that the way you use one power base influences the other power sources. For example, Rob's use of reward power seems to enhance his referent power. But Tom's use of coercive power seems to reduce his referent power. However, if Rob had rewarded desired behavior and punished undesired behavior, his expert power would have increased. He would have demonstrated his ability to specify desired behaviors and to distinguish between desired and undesired behaviors.

We also saw how Rob's promotion, which increased his legitimate power, initially increased his referent power. Increases in legitimate power can also result in an increase in expert power if people assume that promotions are based upon good performance on the job. For example, the best salesperson in a territory gets promoted to sales manager, thus increasing the perception that this person has expertise as a sales manager. Finally, referent power can cause an increase in all other sources of power. If you are admired and respected as a manager, people are more likely to assume you are an expert and that you effectively use both rewards and punishments. But there are also some other important aspects of power that can be learned from the Home Computers case.

Organizational Sources of Power

In addition to legitimate, reward, coercive, expert, and referent power, the case illustrates several other important sources of power. First, Tom used **information power** to create problems for Rob and gain his goal of a promotion. Information power is based on a person's access to information or knowledge that is of value to others.[9] In any managerial job, information is important for coping with the uncertainty that exists. Those people who through their knowledge and information can help ensure a smooth flow of work in an organization are perceived as more powerful because of the uncertainty they control.] It is clear that, once he was promoted, Rob's lack of information diminished his ability to manage the production of high-quality computers. He could not cope with the uncertainty in the job, and his power was thus reduced.

Tom also used **connection power**, which is based on a person's links with important and influential people in the organization.[10] His connections with the other supervisors allowed him to discredit some of the legitimate and referent power Rob had. Connection power can also be used to gain influence over another person because of that person's desire to gain favor from someone with whom you are connected. In his book, *The General Managers*, Kotter talks about network building, which is very similar to developing connection power.[11] As a manager, you need to build a network of people to help carry out your agendas and plans.

One final source of power is **resource power**, which is best defined as "the person who controls the gold makes the rules." To the extent that you, as a manager, control vital employees, money, equipment, supplies, raw materials, customers, and so forth, you will have influence over the behavior of others. For example, if Rob as section head had been the key contact with a particular supplier of a critical part for the computers, his centrality in the access to this resource would have greatly increased his power. If, on the other hand, he held no such critical position (as was apparently the case), he would not have any great degree of resource power. Another aspect of this resource power is the degree to which it is easy to replace the resource provided by a manager. If it is easy to substitute for the resource or to get it from other managers, then you resource power will be diminished. In fact, some managers go to great lengths to ensure that there is something unique about their contribution to the organization just so they have greater resource power. For example, it is not hard to imagine that Tom tried to develop information that was both critical and unique to him in order to strengthen his position relative to Rob's position.

Some Other Important Aspects of Power

Another aspect of power that is evident from the Home Computers case is that it is dynamic. When Rob was promoted, his legitimate power increased, but his expertise as a manager was not as great as his expertise as a supervisor. Recall from Chapter 2 that as you move up the organizational hierarchy, there is a decreasing need for technical skill and an increasing need for conceptual and administrative skill. Thus, after the promotion, Rob's expert power was based on a different area—managerial expertise. His managerial expertise was apparently lower than his technical expertise, and this created problems for Rob.

As a manager you will have to be aware of the development and erosion of power bases over time. A popular book titled *Power: How to Get It, How to Use It* details the two sides of this coin of developing and keeping power.[12] Some ways of doing this are:

1. Try to put yourself in a position to deal with critical issues affecting the organization.
2. Try to gain control over resources that are valued by others.
3. Demonstrate your ability to deal effectively with organizational problems.
4. Try to gain a position in the organization which is central to the work flow.
5. Make sure you develop some unique aspects to your contribution to the organization.
6. Demonstrate behaviors that will be admired and respected by others.
7. Be sure that you are successful when you use your power bases.[13]

Successful Use of Power

As we have said, it is not enough merely to have power. You must use it and use it well. And to use power successfully, you will have to do a number of things right.

First, you must recognize the power sources that are available to you and develop them for your use. In so doing, you will need to use the power you have to help develop other power bases. For example, you may be able to use your expert power in a position to gain a

promotion which will give you greater legitimate and referent power. Second, if a situation is uncertain and
marked by scarce resources, you can expect that resource
power will be used. These situations will be appropriate
times to use the power you have—unless you perceive
others to have greater power. In that case, you may decide
to save your power for another situation where you have
a greater chance of influence. Third, you must recognize
that there are costs to using power. You may lose the
issue at hand, you may lose some of your power, or you
may create long-term negative effects if you use power
inappropriately. Fourth, successful managers constantly
work to develop additional power sources and to shore
up the ones they have. Over a range of situations, you
will probably have occasion to use many sources of power.

"SORRY YOU CAN'T COME ANY CLOSER, BUT THAT'S
THE WAY MY POWER CONSULTANT WANTS IT."

© Sidney Harris

Therefore, you need as many sources of power available as possible, and you must know when to use each one. For example, note how Secretary of State Shultz in Box 9.2 uses expert and referent power, while staying within the limits of his legitimate power.

Fortunately, a specific connection between power bases and leadership styles has been made by Hersey and Blanchard.[14] They suggest that if you are managing people who are low in ability and motivation, you will have to rely more on coercive power in order to achieve compliance (see Figure 9.1). This coercive power will be helpful in using a high task/low relationship style of leadership. As shown in Figure 9.1, for subordinates who are in a medium-low level of ability and motivation, first connec-

---

Box 9.2
The State of State: Shultz's Logical Style Wins Him High Marks at Home and Overseas

As debate in the meeting developed, Mr. Shultz quietly pulled out a piece of paper and began jotting down a list of specific agricultural trade issues each side mentioned. Finally, he spoke up and proposed a solution: Rather than debate trade philosophy, both sides should examine the list of detailed complaints to see whether they could find practical solutions. His suggestion evolved into an agreement to undertake an intensive joint study of agricultural exports. The two sides emerged and announced that they had averted a full-blown trade war.

That incident typifies the Shultz style: cool, methodical, logical. Some would call it uninspiring. But the style is making Mr. Shultz a success, in the eyes of most U.S. and foreign officials, after five months in office. It has enabled him not only to ease serious squabbles with the European allies but also to pilot through administration councils big foreign-policy initiatives like the Middle East peace plan. And his mastery at piecing together a consensus and mediating disputes has prompted the White House to pull him into domestic budget deliberations.

Reporters accompanying the secretary on his European trip suggest that that he appears more animated and sure-footed when discussing domestic economic matters than when talking about foreign policy. Still, Mr. Shultz's restrained style makes it unlikely he will throw his weight around on domestic issues. Aides predict he will avoid the risk of antagonizing people who could hurt him on his own foreign-policy turf.

**Figure 9.1
Power Bases and
Leadership Styles**

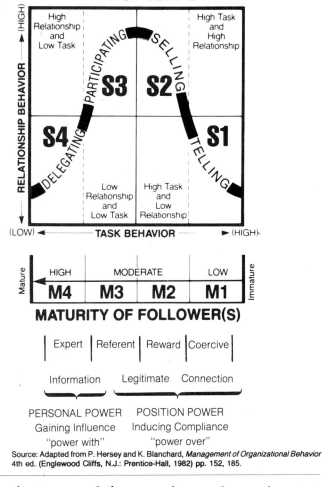

STYLE OF LEADER

Source: Adapted from P. Hersey and K. Blanchard, *Management of Organizational Behavior*
4th ed. (Englewood Cliffs, N.J.: Prentice-Hall, 1982) pp. 152, 185.

tion power and then reward power become important means of influence. Your connection with powerful others is important to these subordinates because they are becoming interested in better performance. And your use of rewards can encourage them to continue to improve their performance.

And as Figure 9.1 shows, legitimate power is important in this middle range of subordinate ability and motivation. Unless your employees believe you have the right to be the decision maker, it is unlikely they will respect your desires as you begin to move from the position types of power to the personal types. For indeed, at the medium-high level of ability and motivation, Hersey and Blanchard suggest that referent power is the appropriate source to draw on. In using a high relationship/low task style of leadership, you are, to some extent, giving up the use of your position as a means of influence. Therefore, people must respect you if you are to have influence as a supporting leader.

Finally, for employees of high ability and motivation, your power base must be one of information and expertise. Without these, your subordinates will be doubtful of the goals and problems you delegate to them. By using the appropriate power base you can have more confidence in achieving the desired results as a manager—but you must be aware of several possible reactions to your use of power.

Possible Reactions to Power

Before we end this section on power, let us briefly consider the potential outcomes of using power. There are basically four responses when power is used to influence an individual's behavior: compliance, identification, internalization, and alienation.[15]

Compliance (or **calculative behavior** as Etzioni calls it) is based on a subordinate's response to your use of rewards and punishments. The employee tries to engage in behavior that will maximize the receipt of rewards and minimize the receipt of punishments. For example, if you ask people to work overtime to finish a project, they may do it because they expect extra pay or recognition from you or because they fear the consequences if they say no. They are complying with your request because of the sanctions you control, not necessarily because they agree with what you want them to do.

A second response is **identification**. Your subordinates may follow your request because of admiration or respect for you as a manager. They hope that carrying out your request will result in further improvement in your relationship. Employees may also feel that you would work late to finish a project, and they are therefore willing to do the same because of a desire to be like you. It is clear that referent power is strongly at work in this case.

Internalization is the third response, and it is based on a congruence between your request and the subordinates' values and priorities. Thus, Etzioni calls this response "moral." When you ask someone to work late, your subordinate sees this as needed, and feels a responsibility to get the project done right and on time. The employee does not think about receiving a reward or about your relationship. The allegiance is to the project. Even if you had not made the request, the employee might have stayed late if he or she knew the deadline might be missed. Most likely, this response would be coupled with your use of expert and information power, and it is also consistent with a delegating type of leadership.

The final response is one that you hope to avoid in using power. It is **alienation** of the other person. Especially with the use of coercive power, you must be careful to avoid alienating your subordinates. If you frequently demand that people work late and threaten them if they do not, you will be likely to destroy relationships and build up alienation. In the long run, you will have to pay the price for such alienation by losing good people, failing to get good work, or other undesirable outcomes.

Figure 9.2 summarizes our discussion up to this point. Eight sources of power are shown along with the four possible reactions to the use of power. It should be clear that you would want to avoid the alienation response. Instead you would like to see the internalization response so you can do more delegating and thus be freed for other activities. But compliance and identification can also be useful responses as you move people along the developmental curve in the leadership model in Figure 9.1. The key is to have all of the power sources available and to use each one at the right time.

Political Behaviors

When we consider power and its use in organizations, we need to think about political behaviors, as well. Politics in organizations is an important element in using your power sources. And like power, politics can also be used to help accomplish organizational goals or to achieve personal goals at the expense of the organization. **Political behaviors are as common in organizations as are leadership behaviors.**

You probably have your own definition of organiza-

Figure 9.2 Power, Its Sources and Possible Reactions

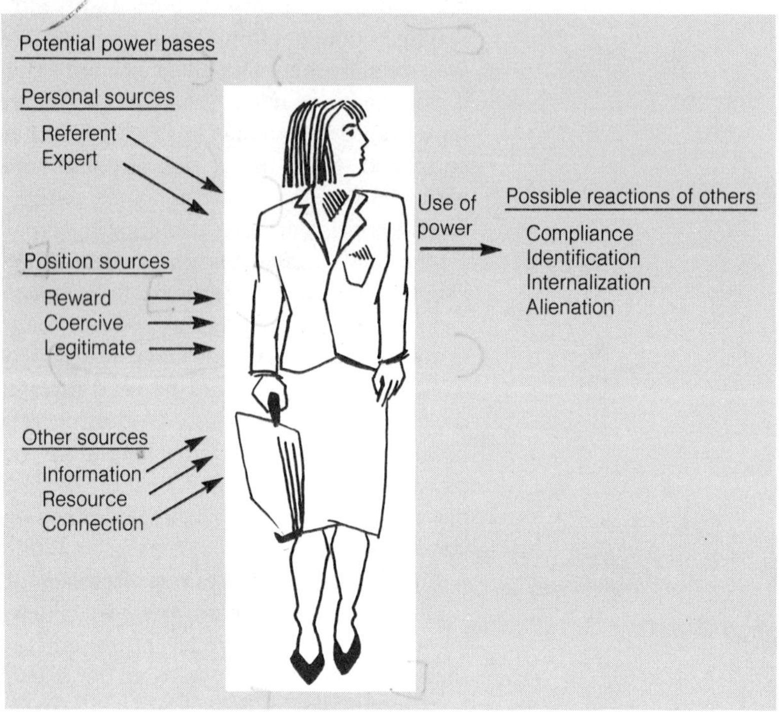

Potential power bases

Personal sources
  Referent
  Expert

Position sources
  Reward
  Coercive
  Legitimate

Other sources
  Information
  Resource
  Connection

Use of power

Possible reactions of others
  Compliance
  Identification
  Internalization
  Alienation

tional politics. Some people define politics as "ways to get ahead in an organization."[16] Others define it more broadly as a "dynamic process of influence that produces organizationally relevant outcomes beyond the simple performance of job tasks."[17] In this text, we will use the definition that organizational politics is **the management of influence to obtain ends not sanctioned by the organization or to obtain sanctioned ends through non-sanctioned influence means.**[18] As with leadership, political behaviors involve using the power bases one has. Let us explore these political behaviors in more detail.

Defining Political Behaviors

Our broad definition of organizational politics points out the possibility that politics can be used for or against the organization and its members. Furthermore, this definition emphasizes that we need to consider both **ends** and **means** (that is, goals and behaviors) as critical factors in organizational politics. Consideration of both ends and means helps us determine when politics are positive or negative, as we shall see. And Figure 9.3 depicts the four cells that follow from combining the two dimensions of ends and means.

In Figure 9.3, both cells 1 and 3 lead to functional behavior as far as the organization is concerned. Cell 1 describes the behavior that is expected in an organization. The ends and the means are both sanctioned by the organization. This type of influence characterizes the leadership behaviors we discussed in the last two chapters.

Cell 3 describes means (behaviors) that are not sanctioned by the organization, but they are geared toward organizationally sanctioned ends. For example, perhaps as a manager you need some critical information from one of the salespeople in the field. The sanctioned means are to go through channels up to your boss, then across

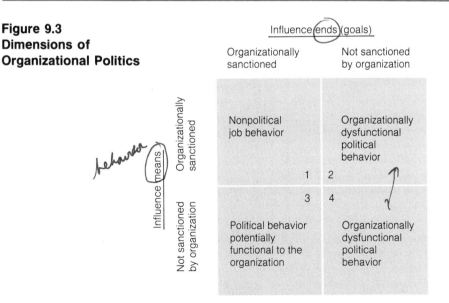

**Figure 9.3
Dimensions of
Organizational Politics**

Influence ends (goals)

		Organizationally sanctioned	Not sanctioned by organization
Influence means	Organizationally sanctioned	Nonpolitical job behavior 1	Organizationally dysfunctional political behavior 2
	Not sanctioned by organization	3 Political behavior potentially functional to the organization	4 Organizationally dysfunctional political behavior

Source: B. T. Mayes and R. W. Allen, "Toward a Definition of Organizational Politics," *Academy of Management Review*, Volume 2 (1977) p. 675.

to the sales manager, and then down to the salesperson from whom you need information. Then the information reverses this path back to you. You know that this will take several days at best, and you need the information by tomorrow for an analysis you are completing. So what do you do? You pick up the telephone and call the salesperson. In so doing, you intrude on the salesperson's time without approval from his or her boss. So while your goal is proper, your behavior might be questioned by some. Your behavior is clearly political, but we can call this kind of behavior "positive politics."

Cells 2 and 4 in Figure 9.3 both depict behaviors that are geared toward goals which are not sanctioned by the organization. Perhaps in this case you are more concerned about how you will appear in the situation than about accomplishing the organization's goals. At Home Computers, we could classify Tom's behavior as political and falling into one of these two cells. His goal was to achieve the position that Rob got—even if it meant discrediting Rob and hurting the organization in the process. But was he in cell 2 or cell 4?

Cell 2 portrays behavior that is sanctioned by the organization, even though the goals are not sanctioned. On the other hand, cell 4 portrays both behavior and goals which are dysfunctional to the organization. It would appear, then, that Tom's behavior fell in cell 4. He withheld important information from Rob and tried to discredit him with the other supervisors. As a result, the organization suffered in terms of both quality and quantity, even though Tom got his promotion.

Using our definition of organizational politics, we can proceed to look at some typical political behaviors, why people engage in politics, and what types of people are most likely to be political in organizations. But first, turn to the end of this chapter and complete and score the Political Orientation Questionnaire. As with the power questionnaire, there are no right or wrong answers, so just be honest with yourself and see how political you might be.

Typical Political Behaviors

What are the most typical political behaviors used by managers? In a study conducted in 1979, managers at several levels were asked about typical political behaviors in their organizations.[19] The ones mentioned most often were:

1. Attacking or blaming others.
2. Selective use of information.
3. Image building.
4. Developing a base of support.
5. Praising others.
6. Coalitions with strong allies.
7. Creating obligations for others.

The first one, **attacking or blaming others**, should be fairly clear. This is one way that coercive and information power can be used. Blaming another person for a problem puts them on the defensive from the start. And often this tactic is used with a third party, when the person being blamed is not present. Thus, the opportunity for the accused to present a defense is greatly hampered. The third party, who is probably influential in the organization has formed an opinion before even speaking to the person who was blamed.

The **selective use of information** means that you control what information is in the hands of others and when it reaches them. Clearly, this behavior uses information power and others become dependent upon you as you use information in this manner. By timing the release of information and the choice of information, you can obviously distort the perception that others will form from the information. For example, some of the information Tom withheld from Rob in the Home Computers case might have been brought up at a meeting between Rob and the production managers just as Rob was about to make a decision that could have been altered by this information. By introducing the information at this time, Tom made Rob look unprepared, while he appeared to have helped the department avoid a serious mistake. He thus earned respect from his peers at the expense of Rob—a form of negative politics.

Image building is the process of appearing to always do the right thing at the right time. It relies on referent power while also enhancing referent power. For example, you may be out for personal gain, even at the expense of the organization, but you constantly cite organizational goals as the reason for your behaviors. You may also be very careful to know and adhere to the norms of the organization and to the preferences of your boss. Thus, you appear to be doing things for the good of the organization, while you are upgrading your image.

Establishing a base of support is the process of gathering people and resources to back you up in times of critical decisions. By doing favors for others, feeding superiors critical information, and building relationships with key people, you develop a network of people you can count on. As Kotter has noted in his book, network building is a primary means for implementing the goals you wish to accomplish.[20] By building your reputation in the eyes of others, making them feel obligated to you, making others feel dependent on you, and encouraging others to identify with you by praising them, you can develop a network that will support your efforts. Indeed, this base of support builds your connection and resource bases of power.

Praising others is one means of building a relationship with other people. By complimenting them on behaviors you like, they are more likely to repeat those behaviors (as we have discussed in both Chapters 3 and 5). Furthermore, you develop the kind of referent power that is desired by political actors. People do the things you want because they like and admire you. We should add that praising others can be negative politics when you do it to benefit yourself and simply build up your referent power. But it can also be positive politics if you use it to complement limited financial rewards and thus help accomplish organizational goals.

Forming coalitions with powerful people in the organization is primarily a means for increasing your connection and legitimate power. By doing things for powerful people in the organization, you can become a part of the coalition whose members do things to help each other. And this association with powerful people will make others perceive you as more powerful. It will appear that what you want to do is what the coalition wants to do, and you are less likely to encounter resistance in achieving your goals and agendas. This too is part of the network process described by Kotter.[21] Of course, you can form

"scratch by Boch"

coalitions to help achieve organizational goals (positive politics) or simply to advance your career (negative politics).

The final tactic to discuss is creating obligations from others. When you do a favor for someone, you build up a credit or an IOU that you can call in at a later date. Thus, you may get someone to support one of your ideas by supporting one of his or hers. Obviously, you will have to keep tabs on the balance of credits and debits in your political account to avoid using your credits foolishly. You must weigh each situation to determine if it warrants the calling in of an IOU. This behavior is a way of building connection and coercive power for a manager.

There is, however, another set of more subtle political actions which Pfeffer has identified and which we will briefly discuss.[22] They include the political use of language, ceremonies, symbols, and settings. In legitimizing and justifying decisions and various organizational behaviors, people can use language that draws on the sanctioned goals and means of the organization even when pursuing more personal goals and when using means that are not sanctioned by the organization. For example, when Tom planted ideas about Rob in the heads of his peers, he used the language of the organization and talked up the good of the organization while trying to get himself promoted. Furthermore, upon being promoted he used the promotional ceremony to mobilize support and quiet any opposition that might have developed. Indeed, he assured the supervisors that he would be soliciting their ideas to avoid the misinformed decisions that Rob had made. In other words, he used the ceremony to try to completely alter the situation which he had created before his promotion.

As one way to achieve this change, Tom set up a symbolic meeting for the purpose of letting his people give him ideas and information. Besides serving the real meaning of information sharing, this meeting was a symbol that Tom intended to do things differently from his predecessor. Certainly, symbols are an important aspect of the legitimate power that goes with various positions in an organization. People can use their titles, their reserved parking spots, the size of their budgets, and other such

Bull Shit

symbols to achieve their desired goals. Finally, closely related to symbols are the **settings** in which people operate. The size, location, and arrangement of a physical setting are all important aspects of the political behaviors that occur in organizations. Where do you meet with subordinates—in your office or theirs? By meeting in your office, you have the advantage of home turf, which can be used to help you get what you want. Likewise, if, at a meeting, you sit at the head of a table or near the head person, you can gain a political advantage. Indeed, these subtle issues are quite important to successful political actors in organizations. You would do well to learn as much as you can about them if you want to be a successful manager.

Certainly, these few political behaviors are not the only ones you will see in organizations. They are intended only to illustrate some of the more common ones. Look at Box 9.3 (a continuation of the article in Box 9.2) to see what political behaviors Secretary of State Shultz uses. Notice his development of a base of support, his praise of others, and his use of coalitions with the President.

Why People Engage in Politics

With this understanding of typical political behaviors, we can discuss why people engage in these actions.[23] It is not simply because of personal ambition. The primary reason people engage in organizational politics is that there are always at least two sets of goals for employees to pursue: individual goals and organizational goals. As people pursue their own goals, they also pursue their perceptions of the organizational goals which affect them on their job. And since political actions involve both goals and behaviors, people who agree on the same goals may still want to use different means to achieve them. In the Home Computers case, even before Rob's promotion, he and Tom went about achieving the same goals using very different means and power bases.

At another level, individual goals relate to an individual's career. People typically work not only to do well in their present jobs, but they also do things which will lead to the achievement of their career goals. In fact, this career influence was apparently at the heart of Tom's

Box 9.3
He Shepherds the
Peace Plan, Eases
Spats with Europe and
Aids in Budget Talks

When Mr. Shultz became secretary of state, he wanted to make a bold move. He wanted to end President Reagan's sanctions against companies supplying gear for the Siberian-European gas pipeline. But before moving, he spent weeks holding private discussions with other cabinet members to line up support for his idea of substituting for the sanctions a broader, but vaguer, allied agreement to limit trade with Russia.

He met with the president to win him over. Finally, when time came for an administration meeting to consider Mr. Shultz's plan, it was anticlimactic. "People had said it would last all day and there would be blood all over the floor," one State Department official recalls. "But it lasted 35 minutes, and in the end it was unanimous." Mr. Shultz got the green light to pursue his plan.

He used similar tactics in pushing the plan for Palestinian self-government. "There are two ways to accomplish things," says special trade representative William Brock. "You can roll over people, or you can bring them in. He chooses the latter whenever humanly possible."

To smooth the road for his initiatives, Mr. Shultz also works assiduously at winning friends inside the administration. During one top-level discussion of a messy disagreement with Western Europe over steel imports, Mr. Shultz interrupted to lavish praise on Commerce Secretary Malcolm Baldrige, who was the point man in talks with Europe on the issue. "We all owe you a debt of gratitude, Mac," Mr. Shultz said. He asserted that without Mr. Baldrige's deft work, the split with Europe would have been even worse.

"It was shrewd. Shultz could be sure that for the next 10 or so cabinet meetings, he'd have at least one ally."

political behaviors to get himself appointed as a section head. Of course, such behaviors may not always be as obvious as Tom's. People often push for a goal which will benefit the organization, but there is a clear slant to favor their own career goals.

A third reason people engage in politics is their affiliations with different segments of the organization. When an organization is divided into departments and divisions, each unit develops its own goals, norms, priorities, and time frameworks) As the people in the departments interact, they operate with these different backgrounds. Often the politics of these interactions become quite obvious when it is time to allocate money or other scarce resources to the various departments. Each department's goals become its primary focus, while organizational goals fall behind.) For example, as a department head you might have a need to hire an additional employee. But other department heads have the same need, and there will not be enough new-hires to go around. As you start to make your case for the new employee, you downplay other departments' needs, exaggerate your needs, and engage in other political behaviors to get the person. Your departmental goal is your primary focus, whether or not you really need another person as badly as other departments may.

The final reason people engage in politics is simply: There are limits to the amount of information, number of criteria, and points of view that we can handle. It is impossible for decisions and behaviors to be totally rational, and this leaves the door open for nonrational and political behaviors. In the example of working with people in other departments, you as the manager, will probably have your hands and mind full just running your own department and dealing with other departments with which you must routinely interact. To understand all departments in the organization plus the overall picture in detail may be next to impossible. Hence, your political behavior may be your only choice if you are to achieve the organizationally sanctioned goals for your department. You cannot always know the best course of action for the organization in advance. Managers with different responsibilities often see the situation differently. **You must accept that political behaviors are inevitable and work to ensure that they have positive rather than negative results for the organization and yourself.**

There are two conditions that actually determine how prevalent politics will be in an organization. First, how important are the issues over which there is conflict? If an issue is not important to you as a manager, you might be better off to save your political resources for the more important issues. Second, what is the distribution of power? If you have very little power relative to the other parties involved in the situation, you may be foolish to try to use political behaviors to win. You are probably safer to use political behaviors when you have equal or greater power, although they may be useful for balancing power when you have only slightly less power. But when you use political behaviors, you must recognize the ethical responsibility that goes with them. While organizational goals are usually the desired end, along with satisfaction of personal goals, one must have respect for justice (fair play) and for the rights of others. Otherwise, you can easily fall into political behaviors that have long-term negative effects on both the organization and yourself.

Personal Characteristics and Politics

Some people are more willing to engage in organizational politics than are others (recall your Political Orientation score). And research has identified several characteristics which seem to be related to using politics. **Political activities are greater for people who are: (1) high in the need for power, (2) high in Machiavellianism, (3) internal in their locus of control, and (4) willing to take risks.** Let us explore each one in turn.

First, people who are high in need for power are more likely to use political behaviors than people low in need for power. As we noted in Chapter 5, a high need for power seems to be related with success in organizations, at least in terms of progression up the hierarchy.[24] And political behaviors are more prevalent at higher levels of organizations.[25] Thus, a high need for power seems compatible with the situation where politics are most common—high up in the organization.

A second personal characteristic of political actors is Machiavellianism which is the tendency to use deceit in interpersonal relations. People with Machiavellian views of the world see guile and deceit as natural ways of influencing other people. They tend to be manipulators of others, and they are very good at using power in interpersonal relations. In addition, Machiavellian individuals seldom trust others to a great degree. In short, it is easy to imagine them pursuing goals that are not sanctioned by the organization and using means that also are not sanctioned.

A third characteristic of political actors is that they

believe that events that happen to them are largely under their control. That is, they have a high internal locus of control.[27] People with an external locus of control believe that powerful others, chance or luck determine what happens to them and thus tend to be passive people in organizations. But since internals assume that they can make a difference, they are likely to also recognize that political actions are necessary in some situations.

A fourth characteristic associated with political behaviors is a person's willingness to take risks. Since political behaviors almost always have some risk associated with them, people who are **risk seekers** are more likely to engage in politics than are **risk avoiders**.[28] When you pursue goals that are not sanctioned by the organization or use means that are not approved by the organization, you are obviously taking a risk, even if you successfully achieve your goal.

By understanding these personal characteristics you will be in a better position to recognize political behaviors when they occur. Such recognition may allow you to counter negative politics and to appreciate the need for positive politics. Understanding these factors may also help you to appreciate your tendencies toward political behaviors.

In summary, we can say that political behaviors in organizations are inevitable, and they are not always bad. As a manager, you need to recognize the situations where the use of politics is likely, as described earlier, and be able to determine if political behavior would be desirable for you at that time. **As with leadership style, it is important to understand that politics must be adjusted to fit the situation.** Do not take the risk of politics if the situation is not favorable to you. But be willing to use political behaviors to help both the organization and yourself achieve desired goals. And remember the ethical responsibility that goes with the use of political behaviors.

Chapter Highlights

In this chapter we have complemented the material on leadership by focusing on the use of power and politics in organizations. While you may not like the idea of using these means to influence the behavior of others, **both**

power and politics are facts of life in organizations. Furthermore, they can be used for good as well as bad purposes. Managers cannot lead without power. And politics are necessary for dealing with the flaws in organizations and to help you achieve organizational and personal goals.

We defined power as the capacity to influence other people's behavior. Two personal sources of power are available to you as a manager. **Referent power** is based on respect. **Expert power** is based on ability. Both referent and expert power are developed over time and can decline over time. People must learn to admire you and to know your abilities before these sources of power become meaningful. Likewise, if you do something that people do not respect, you can lose your referent power. And if you teach others about your expertise, you may lose your expert power.

Three sources of position power were then discussed. **Reward power** is based on giving desired rewards. **Coercive power** is based on giving punishment. **Legitimate power** is based on your rights as a manager. Since these sources of power vary by position in the organization, they too have a developmental aspect. As you move up the hierarchy, you will usually gain in legitimate, reward, and coercive power. However, societal influences have tended to decrease position sources of power over the past few decades.

Next we looked into the situation at Home Computers involving two production engineers, Rob and Tom. We saw how the five sources of power interact with one another. We also saw that merely having a source of power does not mean much unless it is used. The case also suggested that there are other sources of power: **information, resource, and connection.**

To successfully use power, you must recognize your power sources, recognize situations where power will be used, understand the costs of using power, and continuously work to both to develop new sources of power and to maintain existing ones. To close out this section, we discussed how the various sources of power can be related to the leadership model developed in the previous two chapters. We also mentioned four possible reactions that other people may have to your use of power: **compliance, identification, internalization, and alienation.**

With this understanding of power, we then focused

on political behaviors that put power to work. **We defined political behaviors as unsanctioned means that achieve organizational goals or sanctioned means that achieve personal goals at the expense of the organization.** This led to definitions of two dimensions of politics (ends and means) and a four cell grid. Behaviors involving organizationally sanctioned ends and means are defined as "nonpolitical job behavior". If the ends are sanctioned by the organization, but the means are not, we have "political behavior that is potentially functional to the organization." If the ends are not sanctioned but the means are, we have "organizationally dysfunctional political behavior." And finally, if both ends and means are not sanctioned, we also have "organizationally dysfunctional political behavior."

We then discussed several common political behaviors:

1. Attacking or blaming others.
2. Selective use of information.
3. Image building.
4. developing a base of support.
5. Praising others.
6. Developing coalitions with strong allies.
7. Creating obligation for others, that is, IOU's.

In addition, we briefly discussed a subtle set of political behaviors involving language, ceremonies, symbols, and settings.

We then discussed why people engage in politics in organizations. The primary reason is that **people are always pursuing two sets of goals: individual goals and organizational goals, and these two sets may not always be compatible.** Closely related is the fact that people are working not only to succeed at their present jobs, but also to succeed in a career. A third reason is that people represent different parts of an organization, each with its own goals, norms, priorities, and time frameworks. Fourth, people engage in political behaviors because there are limits to the amount of information, number of criteria, and points of view they can handle—decisions cannot be totally rational.

The final section of this chapter mentioned four characteristics that are associated with a tendency for people to be political. **People will tend to be more political the** higher their need for power, the more Machiavellian they are, the more their locus of control is internal, and the more they are willing to take risks.

Thus, we can conclude this chapter by saying that **the use of power and politics in organizations is essential for you to be a successful manager**. By understanding and developing your sources of power, you will be in a better position to influence others toward the goals of the organization and to satisfy your personal goals.

Review Questions

1. Why is it so necessary for you as a manager to understand the use of power and politics in organizations?

2. What is power, and why is it neither good nor bad?

3. Define the two sources of personal power and explain why they are personal, as opposed to positional, in nature.

4. Define reward, coercive, and legitimate power and explain the importance of the value of the reward or punishment to the person you wish to influence. Also, why do we say these sources of power are positional, rather than personal?

5. Explain the importance of information, resources, and connections as sources of power.

6. Why do we say that power is developmental in nature? Be specific with regard to the various sources of power.

7. Of the four reactions to the use of power, what determines the reaction you will get in a given situation? In other words, how can you be successful in using power in an organization?

8. Using the four categories of political behaviors defined in this chapter, can you explain why organizational politics are present in all organizations?

9. When are people most likely to engage in political behaviors in an organization?

10. Can you explain how people in organizations use the most common political behaviors, as described in this chapter, to achieve the goals that they desire?

11. Give a profile of a person who is most likely to engage in political behaviors?

Notes

1. J. P. Kotter, *The General Managers* (New York: Free Press, 1982).

2. G. R. Salancik and J. Pfeffer, "Who Gets Power—And How They Hold on to It: A Strategic-Contingency Model of Power," *Organizational Dynamics* 3 (1977), pp. 3–21.

3. R. M. Kanter, *Men and Women of the Corporation* (New York: Basic Books, 1977), p.166.

4. J. R. P. French and B. Raven, "The Bases of Social Power," *Studies in Social Power*, ed. D. Cartwright (Ann Arbor: University of Michigan Institute for Social Research, 1959), pp. 150–67.

5. French and Raven, "The Bases of Social Power."

6. K. Blanchard and S. Johnson, *The One Minute Manager* (New York: Wm. A. Morrow Co., Inc., Publishers, 1982).

7. C. A. Reich, *The Greening of America* (New York: Random House, 1970).

8. B. Z. Posner, W. A. Randolph, and M. . Wortman, "A New Ethic for Work? The Worth Ethic," *Human Resource Management* 14 (1975), pp. 15–20.

9. B. H. Raven and W. Kruglanski, "Conflict and Power," in *The Structure of Conflict*, ed. P. G. Swingle (New York: Academic Press, 1975), pp. 177–219.

10. P. Hersey and M. Goldsmith, as noted in P. Hersey and K. Blanchard, *The Management of Organizational Behavior* 4th ed. (Englewood Cliffs, N.J.: Prentice Hall, 1982), p.178.

11. J. Kotter, *The General Managers*.

12. M. Korda, *Power: How to Get It, How to Use It* (New York: Random House, 1975).

13. M. W. McCall, Jr., "Power, Authority, and Influence," in *Organizational Behavior*, ed. S. Kerr (Columbus, Ohio: Grid, 1979), pp. 185–206.

14. Hersey and Blanchard, *Management of Organizational Behavior*.

15. These four responses are drawn from H. C. Kelman, "Compliance, Identification, and Internalization: Three Processes of Attitude Change," *Journal of Conflict Resolution* 2 (1958), pp. 51–60, and A. Etzioni, *A Comparative Analysis of Complex Organizations* (New York: Free Press, 1961).

16. M. Wallace and A. Szilagyi, *Managing Behavior in Organizations* (Glenview, Ill.: Scott, Foresman, 1982), p.181.

17. B. T. Mayes, and R. W. Allen, "Toward a Definition of Organizational Politics," *Academy of Management Review* 2 (1977), pp. 672–78.

18. Ibid, p. 675.

19. R. W. Allen, D. L. Madison, L. W. Porter, P. A. Renwick, and B. T. Mayes, "Organizational Politics: Tactics and Characteristics of Its Actors," *California Management Review* 22 (1979), pp. 77–83.

20. J. P. Kotter, *The General Managers* pp. 67–75.

21. Ibid.

22. J. Pfeffer, *Power in Organizations* (Marshfield, Mass.: Pitman Publishing, 1981), pp. 211–29.

23. This section is based primarily on R. H. Miles, *Macro Organizational Behavior* (Glenview, Ill.: Scott, Foresman, 1980), pp. 154–61; and Pfeffer, *Power in Organizations*, ch. 3.

24. D. C. McClelland and D. H. Burnham, "Power Is the Great Motivator," *Harvard Business Review* 54 (1976), pp. 100–10.

25. J. Gandz and V. V. Murray, "The Experience of Work Place Politics," *Academy of Management Journal* 23 (1980), pp. 237–51.

26. G. R. Gemmill and W. J. Heisler, "Machiavellianism as a Factor in Managerial Job Strain, Job Satisfaction, and Upward Mobility," *Academy of Management Journal* 15 (1972), pp. 48–58.

27. L. W. Porter, R. W. Allen, and L. L. Angle, "The Politics of Upward Influence in Organizations," *Research in Organizational Behavior* 3 (1981), pp. 109–49.

28. Ibid.

Resource Readings

Kanter, R. M. *Men and Women of the Corporation*. New York: Basic Books, 1977.

Korda, M. *Power: How to Get It, How to Use It*. New York: Random House, 1975.

Kotter, J. P. *The General Managers*. New York: Free Press, 1982.

Pfeffer, J. *Power in Organizations*. Marshfield, Mass.: Pitman Publishing, Inc., 1981.

Salancik, G. R., and J. Pfeffer. "Who Gets Power—And How They Hold on to It: A Strategic-Contingency Model of Power." *Organizational Dynamics* 3 (1977) pp. 3–21.

Power Questionnaire

In this questionnaire, we are interested in some of the ways in which you would try to relate to people on the job and why others might do what you suggest or request.

Please indicate the degree to which each statement below describes how you would act in a work setting. Do this by writing the appropriate number (based on the scale below) in the blank to the far left of each statement. Make your assessments as objectively and factually as you can. There are no right or wrong answers.

The scale for your use is as follows:

Very Little Extent	1 2 3 4 5 6 7	Very Great Extent

The questions are: "To what extent would you":

__2__ 1. Try to make your subordinates feel uncomfortable when they've made an error or broken a rule?

__5__ 2. Expect them to do what you suggest because you're the boss?

__5__ 3. Try to warrant your subordinates' trust and respect?

__4__ 4. Try to know a great deal about how to do their jobs?

__4__ 5. Try to influence (determine) how much money (or pay increases) they receive?

__4__ 6. Serve as a source of information/advice on job-related issues?

__3__ 7. Pull "rank" in asking people to do some task?

__3__ 8. Believe that, as your subordinate, they have a duty to follow your requests?

__1__ 9. Criticize people and/or their work?

__5__ 10. Try to behave in ways your subordinates would like to copy?

__3__ 11. Try to have a say (or have control) over how much of a pay increase or promotion they might receive?

__6__ 12. Try to demonstrate behaviors or characteristics others admire?

__6__ 13. Use your position (or authority) to get them to do some tasks?

Power Questionnaire *(concluded)*

_/___14. Reprimand people for making a mistake?

_5___15. Try to act in a manner that your subordinates admire and aspire to be like?

_6___16. Try to demonstrate behaviors that your subordinates really respect?

_6___17. Have knowledge that is important to your subordinates in performing their job?

Source: W. A. Randolph, B. Z. Posner, G. N. Powell, and D. A. Butterfield, "Operationalizing French and Raven's Bases of Power: Empirical Assessment in Field and Laboratory Settings," Paper presented at Southern Management Association Meeting, November 1983.

Power Questionnaire Scoring Key

In the appropriate spaces below, record your answers from the previous questions. Then add your total in each column to find out how much you would like to use each of the five power bases (referent, expert, reward, coercive, legitimate). A higher score means you would like to use this power base more. In parentheses are the mean scores for a sample of 250 middle managers from a variety of industries. You can use these as a basis for comparison.

Referent		Expert		Reward	
3.	5	4.	4	5.	4
10.	5	6.	4	11.	3
12.	6	17.	6	Total	7
15.	5	Total	14	÷ 2	3.5
16.	6	÷ 3	4.7		(5.92)
Total	27		(4.90)		
÷ 5	5.5				
	(4.75)				

Coercive		Legitimate	
1.	2	2.	5
9.	1	7.	3
14.	1	8.	3
Total	4	13.	6
÷ 3	1.3	Total	17
	(2.68)	÷ 4	4.25
			(3.74)

**Political
Orientation
Questionnaire**

Directions: Answer each question Mostly Agree or Mostly Disagree even if it is difficult for you to decide which alternative best describes your opinion.

	Mostly Agree	Mostly Disagree
1. Only a fool would correct a boss's mistakes.	✓	
2. If you have certain confidential information, release it to your advantage.	✓	
3. I would be careful not to hire a subordinate with more formal education than myself.		✓
4. If you do somebody a favor, remember to cash in on it.		✓
5. Given the opportunity, I would cultivate friendships with powerful people.	✓	
6. I like the idea of saying nice things about a rival in order to get that person transferred from my department.		✓
7. Why not take credit for someone else's work? They would do the same to you.		✓
8. Given the chance, I would offer to help my boss build some shelves for his or her den.	✓	
9. I laugh heartily at my boss's jokes, even when they are not funny.		✓

Political Orientation Questionnaire *(continued)*

10. I would be sure to attend a company picnic even if I had the chance to do something I enjoyed more that day. _____ ✓

11. If I knew an executive in my company was stealing money, I would use that against him or her in asking for favors. _____ ✓

12. I would first find out my boss' political preferences before discussing politics with him or her. ✓ _____

13. I think using memos to zap somebody for his or her mistakes is a good idea (especially when you want to show that person up). ✓ _____

14. If I wanted something done by a coworker I would be willing to say "If you don't get this done, our boss might be very unhappy." ✓ _____

15. I would invite my boss to a party at my house, even if I didn't like him or her. _____ ✓

16. When I'm in a position to, I would have lunch with the "right people" at least twice a week. _____ ✓

17. Richard M. Nixon's bugging the Democratic Headquarters would have been a clever idea if he hadn't been caught. ✓ _____

18. Power for its own sake

Political Orientation Questionnaire *(concluded)*

is one of life's most pre-
cious commodities.   ✓   _____

19. Having a high school
    named after you would
    be an incredible thrill.   _____   ✓

20. Reading about job poli-
    tics is as much fun as
    reading an adventure
    story.   ✓   _____

                    Total   *10*   *10*

Interpretation of Scores

Each statement you check Mostly Agree is worth one point toward your political orientation score. If you score 16 or over it suggests that you have a strong inclination toward playing politics. A high score of this nature would also suggest that you have strong needs for power. Scores of 5 or less would suggest that you are not inclined toward political maneuvering and that you are not strongly power driven.

One crucial caution is in order. This questionnaire is designed primarily for research purposes and to encourage you to think about the topic under study. The Political Orientation Questionnaire lacks the scientific properties of a validated personality or interest test.

Reprinted with permission from *Fundamentals of Organizational Behavior* by A. J. Dubrin, copyright 1978, Pergamon Press.

CHAPTER 10

The Role of Communications in Organizations

As we close this section on interpersonal behavior, it is fitting that we focus on communications in organizations. It seems that every (organization has communications problems.) And it has been fairly well documented that managers spend a great deal of their time in communicating.[1] But why are communications so important to organizations and to you as a manager? And why are they so problematic?

The answer to the first question lies in the fact that (communications are the lifeblood of an organization.) Just try to imagine an organization without communications. It is impossible. Without communications there would be no way to create the coordination of effort that must be present in any organization. There would be no way for managers to lead and influence their subordinates. There would be no way to move information around in an organization. And there would be no way to achieve the wide range of goals that are present in every organization. Furthermore, a great deal of research has shown that communications have important effects on the performance and satisfaction of employees and on the cohesiveness of groups. Hence, it is typical to find managers spending up to 75 percent of their time in meetings, face-to-face communications, telephone conversation, and reading and preparing written documents.[3]

The second question—why communications are a problem in organizations—is a little more complicated to answer. In fact, it is often difficult to imagine that communications could be a problem until you have experienced working in an organization. You just say what you want to say and others understand it, right? Wrong! **Communication mistakes abound in organizations because the process of communications is quite involved and because of the many factors which can get in the way**. In this chapter, we will explore how the process of communications works. We will also discuss possible outcomes to the process, as well as factors that may inhibit the process. Finally, we will suggest a number of techniques which you as a manager can use to improve communications that affect you.

The Process of Communications

In order to understand why communications are so problematic in organizations, we must understand how the process of communications works. In its simplest form, communication occurs when information is passed from one person to another. The initiator of the communication is called the **sender.** He or she transmits a message through a **channel** to the other person, who is called the **receiver.** As shown in Figure 10.1, there are also two other important parts to the process of communications— **feedback** and **noise.**[4] Let us explore each of the these elements in turn.

First, the initiator of a communication episode, the **sender,** determines the need for information to be transmitted to or from another person. It may be that the sender needs to tell the other person to do something, must ask a question of the other person, or needs to communicate for other purposes which we will discuss later. The sender must first decide what message is to be transmitted to the receiver. The sender must then decide how the message is to be translated into a set of words, gestures, signals, or nonverbal symbols. This step in the communication process is called **encoding,** and it involves the sender's choice of media to use in transmitting the message to the receiver. The sender may choose a written message, verbal contact, telephone contact or other media which we will discuss later.

Once the sender transmits the message, it enters the **channel** which connects the sender to the receiver. Basi-

**Figure 10.1
The Process of
Communications**

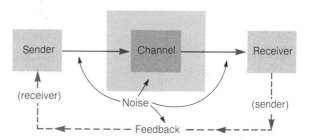

Source: Shannon and Weaver, *The Mathematical Theory of Communication* (Urbana: University of Illinois Press, 1948).

cally, this channel is the medium by which the message is carried from sender to receiver. The channel may be the air waves between you and another person as you communicate face to face. It may be the telephone lines connecting the two of you. It may be a letter or memo. It may also involve other people: for example, you as the manager give the supervisors a message, and they in turn tell the workers, who were your intended receivers.

The next step in the process is that the message reaches the **receiver.** Hopefully, the receiver is aware that the message has arrived and interprets the message in the manner intended by the sender. This interpretation part of the process is known as **decoding** the message, and **communication has not occurred until the message intended by the sender is received and understood by the receiver.** Up until that point, it is merely transmission. For example, imagine making a telephone call when the line is slightly out of order. You can hear the person on the other end of the line, but they just keep saying "Hello" louder and louder. Obviously they cannot hear you. Thus you are only **transmitting** a message; it is not being received. Hence, there is no real communication taking place. A more tragic example of this is shown in the Pan Am story in Box 10.1. Here the communications from flight tower to pilot about wind shears were sent, as the recording on the plane verified. But they were not really received and interpreted as intended. The severity of the situation was not understood, and a serious tragedy occurred.

The last step in the process of communications is **feedback.** The sender receives back from the receiver an indication of whether or not the message was received and understood as intended. Clearly, this did not occur in the Pan Am situation. Feedback may be a behavior that the receiver exhibits; it may be something said; or it may be a written message. The point is that feedback basically reverses the communication process. That is, the original receiver becomes the sender, and the original sender becomes the receiver. And in this sense, the process may go through a number of cycles of sending and receiving, as you might observe in a conversation as people talk back and forth.

This cyclical aspect of the process illustrates the devel-

Box 10.1
Pan Am Crew Voiced Worry about Wind, Jet's Weight before Crash in New Orleans

Washington—Crew members of Pan American flight 759 voiced increasing concern about their aircraft's weight and the wind direction before they crashed shortly after takeoff from New Orleans International Airport on July 9.

In the clipped language of cockpit conversation, the captain reviewed how to abort a takeoff and instructed his first officer to turn off the air conditioning to get additional power, according to the transcript of the flight recorder tape released yesterday. But 24 seconds after the captain reported that he was in a "positive climb," the Boeing 727 fell into a rain-drenched residential neighborhood, killing all 145 people on board and eight others on the ground.

With 20 seconds to go before the crash, Capt. Kenneth L. McCullers said to his first officer, Donald A. Pierce, "You're sinking, Don, come on back." Twelve seconds later the "ground proximity" alarm sounded. And in another eight seconds, the recording ends with "the sound of final impact," at 4:09 P.M. CDT according to the transcript.

Warnings Heard

The transcript confirms previous statements by the board that the crew heard three warnings about wind-shears, which are quick changes in wind direction considered very dangerous during take-off.

The crew apparently realized that wind direction might be significantly different elsewhere on the airfield. Referring to another aircraft that was asking to take off in an opposite direction, the captain said, "I don't understand why these guys are requesting Runway 28." The copilot replied: "I don't either—must be sittin' there lookin' at a windsock."

Calm Before Passengers

But the captain gave scant indication of his concern when he spoke to his passengers over the public address system. "We'll be maneuvering around, circumnavigating some, ah, some little thundershowers out there, so we would like to ask you folks to please remain in your seats," he said.

In fact, the aircraft took off into a violent thunderstorm. And although three warnings about a "low level wind-shear alert" are audible on the tape, none was specifically acknowledged by the crew. The discussion about aborting the flight, in fact, appears at least partly to be a routine discussion of federal regulations for benefit of the first officer, who had recently attended a training academy.

opmental nature of communications. As the process goes through repeated cycles, sometimes over extended periods of time, additional information is made available for each successive cycle. In Chapter 1 we pointed out how relationships develop over time, and certainly communications play an important role in this process. As you meet the new employee in the office next to yours and have your initial conversation, a relationship begins to develop. Over the next days, weeks, and months, your communications will develop so that you each know the other better and better. And your communications will develop from the superficial level to deeper and deeper levels, so long as you both feel comfortable with this growing knowledge of one another. In Chapter 4 we discussed how such feedback and sharing help to enlarge the open area in the Johari window of understanding.

The last element in the communication process is **noise.** In Figure 10.1, the arrows show that noise can enter the communications process at any point along the way. Basically noise is anything that inhibits the flow of information from sender to receiver. It can be physical noise such as you might encounter on the floor of a factory. Or time pressure can cause a sender to abbreviate the message and thus make it more difficult for the receiver to understand. It can also be something psychological. For example, the sender may have something else in mind that leads to too little focus on the preparation of the message for transmittal. Likewise, the receiver may have something else on his or her mind that decreases the receptivity to the message being sent. For example, perhaps the receiver was just chewed out by the boss and is not ready to talk with a co-worker about how to resolve the problem with a machine that is down.

In this chapter we will discuss several dimensions of this communications process—purpose, media, and direction—as well as context variables that all influence organizational communications. We will also discuss potential outcomes to communications, barriers to effective communications, and some ways of improving organizational communications. First, however, let us return to Rob of Home Computers (who we met last chapter) and delve into the communications aspects of his job as a section head—before Tom's political games led to Rob's transfer to personnel.

The Home Computers Case—More on Rob

Rob, the newly promoted section head arrived for work around 7:30 this morning. He grabbed a cup of coffee and thought about what lay ahead for him today: supervisors' meeting at 9, personnel problem to handle with one of his people, briefing meeting with his boss, and then just the regular matters of meeting production deadlines.

Shortly thereafter, he saw Jim Adams, one of the supervisors, walk by his door. Rob stepped to the door and called Jim over to discuss the production schedule for today. They stood in the hall to go over a few minor problems and try to ensure some better coordination between Jim's area and Tom's area. They ended the conversation with Rob asking Jim about the cabin he is building on a nearby lake.

Next Rob walked around to Tom's office to discuss the coordination issue with him. He was not there, so Rob left a note asking Tom to drop by his office.

Back in his office, Rob, quickly went over the morning mail. He had a couple of brochures about training programs, a quality-control report, and two memos from his boss. One of the brochures was on assertiveness training, and Rob wondered if it might help him to be a better communicator, but he did not have time to think about it then. One of the memos from his boss dealt with a coordination problem between work shifts under Rob and suggested he discuss remedies with some of the other section heads.

Putting down his mail, Rob picked up the telephone to call Hal Walker, one of the other section heads. He and Hal discussed the coordination among shifts, with Rob asking a lot of questions. Hal offered some useful ideas and said he would be willing to meet with Rob to go over some forms he had developed to help out with the coordination among shifts. But Rob wondered what Hal really felt about his inquiry. He was not sure, but he thought he sensed in Hal's tone of voice a feeling that Rob should have been able to solve such a simple problem on his own.

By now it was 8:30, and Rob began to think about the regularly scheduled supervisors' meeting at 9. He made some notes about information he wanted to share, and some evaluative comments, and then headed down the hall for the meeting. Rob opened the meeting by complimenting the supervisors on their efforts the past week. Next, he told them about a new version of the EZ2, which would soon be reaching the production stage. This new version was intended for use in schools and libraries, and it would be slightly different from the standard home and business versions of EZ2. Rob then told the supervisors that he was not happy with the increasing number of personnel problems in his section. Absenteeism was too high, work quality was beginning to suffer, and employees seemed generally dissatisfied. Rob then opened the floor for questions and brief reports from each supervisor. Surprisingly, there were no questions about the new product, and there were no ideas about the personnel problems.

As he left the meeting Rob saw several of the supervisors talking in the hall. He could not overhear what they were discussing, and they dispersed as he approached. He did catch one comment by Tom about Rob not knowing why the personnel problems were occurring. He wondered what Tom's ideas were and decided to ask him later when he responded to Rob's note.

As Rob walked through the plant, he thought about the memo from his boss about the coordination among shifts. He decided that the technology of production seemed to cut down on the frequency of communications not only between shifts, but also up and down the hierarchy. Everything was routine and highly structured. People on each shift and in each department felt a great deal of ownership for their work. They were always too busy trying to do a good job to have time to work out difficulties with other shifts and departments. Why, just last month he had had an argument with one of the design engineers about the best production method for the new version of EZ2. He had felt like he was talking to a brick wall, unable to get through to this engineer.

Rob returned to his office and decided to let his boss know about his concerns regarding the coordination problems in the plant. He was pretty clear on what was going wrong, but he was not altogether sure of why. And he did not want to come across to his boss as not knowing how to solve the problem. He contemplated whether to write a letter to his boss, to call him on the phone, to set up an appointment to talk with him, or just to let it ride for awhile.

He decided to let it ride for awhile. After a few days he realized that Tom had never responded to his note, so he tried to call him about it. Tom was not in. Rob went around to see him several times but never found him in. He finally decided to drop it since it really was not that important. Over the next several months it seemed that more and more of his communications were not received and reacted to in the fashion he desired. His supervisors started avoiding him in the hall, and the weekly supervisors' meeting was becoming less and less useful. Hardly anyone talked but Rob, and he could make no eye contact with anyone except Jim Adams. Occasionally Tom would interject some information that caught Rob totally off guard, but otherwise the meetings were pretty quiet.

Rob decided to ask Jim to come to his office for a chat.

He asked Jim what was going on in the plant. After some pushing on Rob's part, Jim reluctantly said that (Rob was not respected by the supervisors.) He knew that Rob cared about his people and worked in their behalf, but the grapevine had it that [Rob only did these things to get ahead. Rob was not well informed on matters that really counted to his people, and did not really respect their opinions. Rob was shocked, but he thanked Jim for his honesty. Jim said he liked Rob and wanted to see things get better. They shook hands as Jim walked out. Rob sat back down and gazed around his office at the diplomas and certificates hanging on the wall. He wondered what had gone wrong.

(What has gone wrong for Rob?) Several things are obvious. First, Rob (does not listen very well) to the nonverbal messages being sent, like when his people disperse as he walks up after the meeting. Also, he is (not always able to ensure that his message has gotten through as intended, as with the design engineer. Rob is not in touch with the grapevine, and he is reluctant to talk to his boss. He also (does not communicate well) with people in other departments, as with section head Hal Walker. Finally, Rob is often (unsure of the best medium to use) to send his messages. For example, his note, phone calls, and visits to Tom were ineffective. Perhaps he should have used the more (formal approach of sending a memo)for a scheduled meeting. By looking back over the case, you can probably pick out other communications problems. It is also possible to see the developmental aspects of the process, as communications degenerate and result in many undesirable outcomes. Let us now discuss the dimensions of the communications process (purpose, media, and direction) to see how they help us better understand Rob's problems.

Dimensions of Communications

There are several dimensions of communications which are important to our understanding of why communications are a problem in organizations. We will discuss the purposes of communications, the media used, and the direction of communications in an organization (vertical, horizontal, and diagonal).

Purposes

There are many purposes for which people communicate in organizations.[5] And even single messages can serve more than one function. The primary purposes of communications include: (1) control, (2) instruction, (3) motivation, (4) problem solving, (5) feedback and evaluation, (6) information exchange, (7) social needs, and (8) political goals. Let us look at each one individually.

By control we mean communications that are designed to integrate and coordinate the activities of people in an organization. Formal communication channels, as represented by the organization chart, are a good example. Another example would be the standard operating procedures that organizations use to keep records and to locate necessary facts. Such communications serve the purpose of creating order in an organization, so that multiple goals and tasks can be pursued.

Instruction communications are used to let people know what they must do in their jobs. When routine problems arise, instructions can help solve the problem. And when an employee moves to a new job or is asked to perform a new task or to do a job a different way, there is a need for instruction.

The third purpose, **motivation**, serves the function of influencing the behavior of people in the organization. This purpose is the basis for the earlier chapters on motivation and leadership. Motivation communications are used by managers to encourage and stimulate employees to work toward the accomplishment of organizational goals. Such communications may include issuing orders, making job assignments, and rewarding behavior and performance.

Problem-solving communications usually involve the asking of many questions and are used on problems that do not have an easy solution. Managers and subordinates engage in a give-and-take discussion to determine what to do in the situation. For example, the telephone conversation Rob of Home Computers had with Hal Walker was a problem-solving communication.

Feedback and evaluation communications let people

know how they are doing on the job. Often feedback and evaluation are linked together in a developmental fashion with instruction and motivation communications. For example, as a manager you explain a new procedure to an employee in your department. You then watch to see if the person does it correctly. If they do it approximately right, you may decide to praise them for their progress. And you may also evaluate their performance and explain to them what they need to do to improve. This example thus illustrates the use of instruction, motivation, evaluation, and again instruction communications in a developmental sequence.

The sixth purpose, **information exchange**, is the most basic of all communication purposes. In fact, all of the other purposes are special cases of this one. Communications always have an information purpose of some description. This category is intended for those communications which are purely informational in nature—like Rob's telling the Home Computers supervisors about the new EZ2 for schools and libraries.

Next, **social needs** communications relate to the emotional and non-task-oriented interactions that occur in every organization. Employees need to talk about the baseball game, the weather, politics, and so forth. And while such communications do not directly affect the performance of the organization's tasks, they serve the need for employees to feel a connection with others at work. And it is not uncommon for these communications to include discussions of pay, treatment on the job, what the boss is like, and so forth. Obviously, these issues are more closely related to the job than is the baseball game, though again they are not directly a part of the job. Still, we know that how employees feel about these work conditions can influence their performance on the job.[6]

The final category of communications purposes, **political goals** is a little different from the others. These communications are outside the expected range of communications. They can be positive if directed toward accomplishing organizational goals but involving non-traditional channels or media (that is, positive politics as in Chapter 9). Or they can be negative if directed toward accomplishing personal goals at the expense of organizational goals. As people strive for personal gain, they may distort information, give poor feedback, and fail to use the positive side of the communications purposes discussed above.

Media

Just as there are many purposes for which people communicate in organizations, there are also many media they can use to convey their message.[7] As we explore these media we will discuss some of the advantages and disadvantages of each one.

There are the two obvious media categories of written and verbal, but within each of these two broad categories are several different types of media. **Written** communications can, for example, take the form of a procedures manual, a report, a memo, a letter, a handwritten note, or a file. **The basic advantage to written communication is that it can be thought out to ensure better clarity.** Furthermore, you do not have to be present when the receiver reads the message. But herein lies **the major disadvantage of written communication—it is basically one-way in nature.** How can you know if the receiver interprets your message as intended?

In transmitting any written message, you will have to decide which form to use in a given situation. A letter is more formal than a memo, and something typed is more formal than a handwritten message. How you sign a letter also is an important indicator—first name only is less formal, full name is more formal. Addressing the letter "Dear Mr. Smith" is more formal than is "Dear Jim." Finally, who you carbon copy on a letter can be important. For example, copying to the addressee's boss is a subtle way of putting pressure for response or action on the person. We could go on and on about the subtleties of written communications, but our purpose here is just to make you think about these issues and to make you more aware of them as you communicate in organizations.

There are also many different types of **verbal** media. For example, there are formal and informal one-on-one conversations, formal and informal meetings, and the telephone. **The biggest advantage to verbal communications is that they allow for immediate feedback as to whether your message has been received as intended.** They allow for a two-way form of communications where the people involved are both sender and receiver. **The biggest disadvantage to verbal communications is that they may be less well-planned than written communications, and there is no record of the exchange of information.**

In deciding which type of verbal media to use in a given situation, you can consider several factors. A formal meeting with a group can be very similar to written communications in terms of preparation, but it can more easily involve several people simultaneously. A formal one-on-one meeting, such as a performance review session, can be a good way to document issues of concern and make plans for future action. Of course, formal meetings can consume a great deal of time. Informal meetings and impromptu one-on-one conversations can be used effectively to transfer information, solve problems, and stimulate action. And in fact, research suggests that such impromptu meetings are the most common form of interaction for high level managers.[8]

Finally, you have the choice of the telephone, and managers do make good use of this verbal medium.[9] The telephone can make it very easy to reach someone quickly, even though they are not in the same building, or even the same city, state, or country. And with the advent of telephone-answering machines, it has become easier to depend on reaching a person in a relatively short time period, even though they are presently out of the office. Also, teleconferencing makes meetings possible among people who are in different cities. But in using the telephone, you give up another very important medium of communications—nonverbal communications.

Nonverbal communications are all communications which do not involve the use of words. Some researchers estimate that over two thirds of our communications are via nonverbal media.[10] As we discussed in Chapter 9, ceremony, symbols, and settings are important nonverbal means of communicating.[11] In addition, nonverbal media include tone of voice, volume, gestures, body language, silence, color (for example, blushing), touch, smell, time, signals, and objects.[12] Most of these are straightforward, but several do deserve some definition.

For example, **body language** refers to signals given by standing versus sitting, crossing legs and arms, facial expressions, and eye contact. **Silence** is just that. By not answering someone's question, you convey a message.) For example, if you ask for a raise, and the boss says nothing, you have received your answer. The **color** of your office carpet and walls could convey harshness if it were red, whereas a pale blue would convey more warmth. **Smell** would include body odor or bad breath or nice cologne, each of which conveys a message you may or may not intend.)

Time can indicate your degree of interest in something. For example, if you answer a request for information the next day, as opposed to three weeks later, the time difference may suggest how you feel about the original sender or the request. **Signals** include such things as fire alarms, horns to indicate lunch break in a plant, beepers on a watch to remind you of a meeting, or the beep on a word processor to indicate you have made a mistake.) Finally, **objects** are the focus of the work, and they can convey a message. For example, if you are a dishwasher in a restaurant and the busser brings a load of dishes to your window, no words need be exchanged for you to begin washing dishes.)

Directions

When we shift to the last dimension of communications, **direction**, we are considering the people who are engaged in communication. More specifically, **directions of communications help us focus on the organizational roles of the sender and receiver.** Basically, communications can be vertical, horizontal, and diagonal, as determined by their relationship to the organizational chart.[13]

Vertical communications can be broken down into two directions: upward through the hierarchy, and downward through the hierarchy. Usually **downward communications** are used for control, instruction, motivation, and evaluation purposes.) For example, managers in organizations are expected to set priorities and tasks for subordinates, to tell people what their jobs are, and to motivate the employees. Rob was using this direction when he told his supervisors about the personnel problems in the section.

Upward vertical communications are typically used for information exchange, problem solving, and as a response to downward communications.) In a great many organizations, upward communications are not used nearly as frequently as downward communications. The primary reason is that lower-level organization members are expected to initiate these communications, when there may be no incentive, channel, or precedent for doing so. If upper-level managers would solicit and encourage an upward flow of information, this direction could become a more important vehicle for improved communications in organizations. Our case illustrates this well both with Rob's decision to delay contacting his boss about the coordination problems in the plant and with the lack of communication up to Rob from his supervisors.

Horizontal communications can also be broken down into two categories. First, there are communications with your peers in the same department and/or shift. Typically, these communications are for information exchange, minor problem solving, and social needs purposes. Second, horizontal communications may cut across department and/or shift boundaries to people at your same level in the organization. For example, Rob's contact with Hal Walker, another section head, was interdepartmental, horizontal communications. Typically, interdepartmental horizontal communications are for control, information exchange, problem solving, and social needs purposes.

Diagonal communications are like the interdepartmental horizontal communications except that they link you to people at higher or lower levels in the organization hierarchy. For example, you may need to get a particular new procedure initiated in another department of your plant. In order to do this, it might be necessary for you to talk directly with that department head, who is two levels above you in the hierarchy. Now you might wonder why you should not go up your chain of command to this department head's level and let the two department heads discuss the issue. One reason might be that it will take too long, and another may be that your boss wants you to handle this matter. Such situations occur frequently in organizations, and they point out the importance of personal power sources and politics, as discussed in Chapter 9. Furthermore, they highlight the fact that communications often do not mirror the lines connecting people on an organization chart.

And this point suggests that the **informal communication system** (or **grapevine** as it is sometimes called) is another direction of communications. The grapevine does not at all adhere to the organization chart.) There are people in every organization who always seem to have the latest news or gossip. Other people gravitate to this person instead of their boss to find out what is going on in the organization. And it is probably safe to say that organizations would be less effective without such an informal communication system(a great deal of important information is transmitted via this system)

Structural, Technological, and Historical Influences

In addition to these three dimensions of communications, it is important for us to be aware that(organizational communications occur within a **context**, consisting of organizational structure, technology, and past history.)[14] Figure 10.2 illustrates this point while also summarizing our discussion up to this point. Let us briefly explore each of the three context variables.

First, the **structure** of an organization directly influences its intended communications. People grouped into one department are thought to have a need to communicate more closely than are people in different departments. However, research has demonstrated that the organization structure may not coincide very well with the actual communication networks that emerge.[15] In fact, the(formal structure can actually inhibit the flow of necessary information.)The(structure certainly inhibited)the flow of communications at Home Computers between Rob (the superior) and Tom (the subordinate) and between Rob and all of his supervisors.

In addition to structure, the **technologies** in organizations influence the communications that emerge.[16](As the technology becomes more routine, the frequency of communications tends to decrease.) For example,(the assembly-line section at Home Computers that Rob supervises would probably have fewer communications than the research and development department.)(Communications also tend to be more horizontal and less vertical with more routine technologies.) Furthermore, (increases in technological routine tend to result in more stimulus and motivation communications and fewer problem solving communications.)

Finally, communications in organizations take place

Figure 10.2　Organizational Communications: Process, Purposes, Media, Directions, and Context

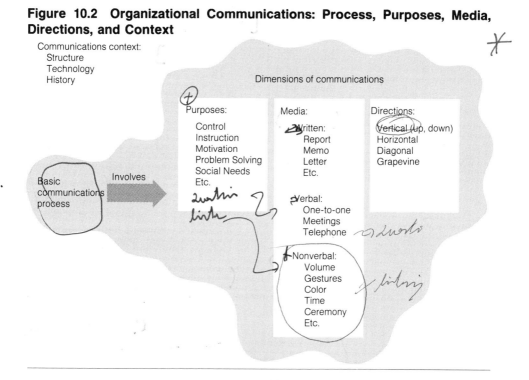

Communications context:
　Structure
　Technology
　History

Dimensions of communications

Basic communications process

Involves

Purposes:
　Control
　Instruction
　Motivation
　Problem Solving
　Social Needs
　Etc.

Media:
　Written:
　　Report
　　Memo
　　Letter
　　Etc.
　Verbal:
　　One-to-one
　　Meetings
　　Telephone
　Nonverbal:
　　Volume
　　Gestures
　　Color
　　Time
　　Ceremony
　　Etc.

Directions:
　Vertical (up, down)
　Horizontal
　Diagonal
　Grapevine

within a **historical context**. People in organizations have had an opportunity to interact over time. They have seen the power and status differences and have learned about the norms and incentives in the organization. For example, you may learn over time that you never disagree with your boss in public. Or you may learn that notes to people get a better response than do telephone calls. Your past communication experiences in the organization are thus part of the historical context. **Our point is that the pattern of communications in any organization develops over a period of time, and it will continue to evolve into the future.** As technologies, structures, and people change, so will the communications in an organization.

Outcomes Associated with Communications

Given our understanding of the communication process and the dimensions and context of communications, we can now explore some of the outcomes associated with communications. And there can be many such outcomes in an organization, some positive and some negative. As we have said, **communications are the primary vehicle by which leadership is activated, people are motivated, and relationships are developed.**

As a new member of an organization or after a departmental move, you learn through communications how to become effective in your position. That is, you become socialized. You learn the job, the norms of the organization, your peers, your subordinates, and your superiors. If communications are open with the people in your organization, it is possible to develop good relationships with these employees. A feeling of support and honesty can develop that will make working together both a pleasure and a real success in terms of organizational goals. If communications are guarded, you will not become properly socialized to the organization and will be less effective in your job.

Second, through communications it is possible to develop **liking** and **respect** for others. As a manager, you probably will want your subordinates both to like and respect you. Thus if you develop communications that convey a sense of warmth, trust, and closeness with your people, liking will tend to develop. If you convey a sense of aloofness and distance, liking probably will not develop.[17]

Of course, as a manager, you must also have the respect of your people. Indeed, respect may be more important for getting the task done than is liking. If your communications convey a sense of competence on your part and a respect for the abilities of your people, you will tend to gain their respect. If, on the other hand, you convey a sense of superiority and disrespect for the subordinates' abilities, they probably will not respect you as much, either.[18]

Closely associated with these two outcomes is the **trust** that can develop via communications. If liking and respect are present, you will probably find trust. In relationships, trust is something that develops slowly over time. Usually it requires that one or both people involved take risks with each other. For example, let one of your subordinates be responsible for a task and do not look over her shoulder. A certain level of trust is necessary for any organization to run properly, and some recent books have stressed the growing importance of trust for successful organizations.[19]

As we discussed in Chapter 3, communications can also be very important in aligning perceptions held by different people. If messages are clearly sent and received, perceptual errors are more likely to be discovered and corrected. And when perceptions are aligned, working to achieve the organization's goals will be more unified. Indeed, research has shown that accuracy of communications is associated with improved performance.[20] And research has shown that communications can increase cohesiveness and morale in a group. But if communications are not handled well in a group they can lead to increases in conflict and distrust, as we shall discuss in Chapters 11 and 12.[21]

Each of the outcomes discussed above has both a positive and negative side—and this is determined by the way in which the communication process and its dimensions are used by the people in an organization. There are many factors which can inhibit effective communications and lead to the negative outcomes. Let us now turn to these factors and then to some ways of improving communications in an organization.

Factors That Inhibit Communications

In discussing the factors that can inhibit the flow of communications in an organization, it is helpful to tie our comments to the basic model of the communications process in Figure 10.1 and the basic dimensions of communications in Figure 10.2.[22] So first let us look at the problems from the point of view of the sender.

Problems Related to the Sender

As the originator of a communication, the sender has the responsibility of ensuring that the message is transmitted so that the receiver has the greatest chance of receiving and understanding it. A primary problem is in the encoding of the message. The sender may select the wrong set of words and symbols for the receiver. For example, at Home Computers, Rob felt he was talking to a brick wall when talking to one of the design engineers about

"What do you mean, I don't communicate? Didn't you read the memo I left you at breakfast?"

From *The Wall Street Journal*, with permission of Cartoon Features Syndicate.

the best production method for the new EZ2. He was probably using different language than the design engineer typically used. This problem can also exist between different levels of an organization, as illustrated in Box 10.2.

Another problem is that managers sometimes abbreviate a message, thus making it unclear. For example, a manager may explain steps 1, 3, and 5 of a six-step process, assuming that an employee will be able to fill in steps 2, 4, and 6 to complete the required task. The manager assumes that the employee has as complete an understanding of the process as does the manager, but this may not be true.

Another reason for sending an incomplete message is that the sender is not sure of the response the receiver will send back. For example, you may be reluctant to tell your boss in great detail how you made a very costly mistake, because of what you think the response may be. Thus, you tell only part of the story and try to correct the problem before the boss finds out any more. Recall in the Home Computers case how Rob decided not to communicate with his boss about the coordination problems in the plant.

Box 10.2
Taking the Boss at His Word May Turn Out to Be a Big Mistake at a Lot of Companies

New York—If Mr. Dithers worked for Citicorp, he couldn't just summon Dagwood and say, "You're fired!" Oh, no. "Bumstead," he'd say, "you're being impacted by job discontinuance, and you're getting assigned to the mobility pool for decruitment."

Despite the best efforts of English professors, business-communications consultants and other horrified bystanders, obfuscation in business lingo appears to be a growing and troublesome phenomenon. Career counselors say that it can mean big trouble especially for inexperienced or naive subordinates who take business talk at face value. "Kids out of school are apt to take things literally," says Betty Harragan, a New York career counselor, speaking of fresh masters of business administration. Others say that women, relatively new to management and executive ranks, also sometimes fail to comprehend the overstatement, understatement and evasion that characterizes much bureaucratic talk.

"You won't succeed if you don't pick up the language," says Felice Schwartz, president of Catalyst, a New York resource center for career women. "It isn't a huge thing, but it can be a hugely important thing." Subordinates, the counselors say, should pay especially close attention to management "suggestions." When the boss says, "Please finish that job when you have a chance," more often than not he really means, "Do the job now, or else."

By Mary Bralore, *The Wall Street Journal*, June 4, 1982. Reprinted by permission of *The Wall Street Journal*, © Dow Jones & Company, Inc. 1982. All rights reserved.

This problem can often lead to the more general problem of a poor relationship between the sender and receiver. If the relationship is not good or if the status differences are too great, communications may be altered as they are transmitted from the sender. Indeed, the personalities of the sender and receiver (as discussed in Chapter 4) play an important role in the developmental aspects of communications. And they can create real barriers to the flow of information between sender and receiver. For example, we can speculate that Rob is a feeling type (as per Chapter 4), and this could be part of his communication problem with Tom, who we may speculate is a thinking type. Rob's high relationship style of leadership may come across as weak with Tom, because their past experiences have created such different personality types.

A related issue is the degree of trust that the sender

has in the receiver. If past experience has shown that the receiver seldom understands and acts on the sender's messages, a lack of trust may develop and make the sender uncertain how to ensure that communications are complete.

Finally, the sender can fail to recognize the time implications associated with a communication. For example, Rob may ask a supervisor to do something that will take more time than he has allowed in his request. The supervisor may then hear only the part of the message he or she feels can be accomplished in the allotted time. On the other side of the coin, Rob might be telling people about the new EZ2 version too far in advance to hold their interest. If he announces it six months in advance, they may not give it as much attention as if he announced it two months in advance. The point with time is that you, as a sender, must be aware of the appropriate timing of your message if you want to increase its probability of reception.

Problems Related to the Receiver

The primary problems associated with the receiver are lack of awareness of the message, misinterpretation of the message, and lack of acceptance of it. People are often bombarded with many messages and other stimuli, and they simply must ignore some messages. Suppose you come back from lunch to find six phone messages taped to your office door, three reports and three memos in your in-basket, and someone waiting to see you. While you are talking to this person, your phone rings twice, your secretary buzzes you, and you try to sneak a glance at the reports. Is it any wonder that you may miss some of the messages intended for you?

As John Naisbitt, author of *Megatrends* suggests, this problem of information overload will drastically increase in the information society of the coming years.[23] He suggests that **information float**, the time it takes for messages to be transmitted from sender to receiver, will be greatly reduced. For example, instead of taking three or four days to send a letter across country and three or four days for it to return, that week's float will be reduced to a matter of seconds with the advent of electronic mail.

Just imagine what that will do to the amount of correspondence you will have to deal with each day at work.

One way that receivers respond to this flood of communications is to use programmed responses and decision rules to determine which messages to pay attention to. And as you use such devices, you run the risk of missing important information or an important request.

The second problem revolves around decoding the message that is received. If the language used by the sender is unfamiliar to you as the receiver, you may misinterpret the message. You may also read between the lines and assume messages that were not intended. For example, at Home Computers, when Rob wondered about Hal's tone of voice and interpreted it in a defensive manner, he may have been receiving a message that Hal did not intend.

The final problem of the receiver is that he or she may not accept the message even if it is heard and understood. If a subordinate tells you of a problem with one of your decisions, you may ignore the comment because you do not want to hear criticism, even if it is accurate. Here the credibility of the sender is important. As we discussed in Chapter 9, the sender's expert power may make the difference in your acceptance of the subordinate's message. Likewise, a lack of trust that you have in the sender can be a barrier to communications.

Thus, the ego of the receiver can be an important barrier to the flow of information. If the message sent seems to create the need for the receiver to make a change or admit a mistake, the receiver's ego may make it difficult to really hear the message, understand it, and accept it. The rather powerful incident described in Box 10.3 is a good example of how ego can block communications until something harsh occurs.

Problems in the Channel

Problems in the communications channel arise when the sender chooses a medium that is inappropriate for the receiver or for the message. For example, at Home Computers Rob chose to leave a note for Tom, to call him, and to drop by his office, when maybe he should have used a more formal channel, such as a memo. Of

**Box 10.3
Sobering Method:
Firms Are Confronting
Alcoholic Executives
with Threat of Firing**

Officials of Richardson-Vicks Inc., suspecting a company executive was an alcoholic, used a new technique to deal with him: They called a surprise meeting, surrounded him with colleagues critical of his work and threatened to fire him if he didn't seek help quickly.

When the executive tried to deny that he had a drinking problem, the medical director of the big consumer-goods company based in Wilton, Conn., came down hard. "Shut up and listen," he said. "Alcoholics are liars, so we don't want to hear what you have to say." The man, then a $65,000-a-year executive, recalls the scene:

"They said I had a choice. Either they would send me to a facility for treatment or. . . . They never had to finish it. I picked up on the message immediately."

The executive, who has since joined another company, credits the office confrontation and his subsequent treatment with saving his career. "Whatever they did to me," he says, "it took."

course, sometimes the structure of the organization may dictate the choice of media. If two people are located in offices 2,000 miles apart, the only logical media may be the telephone for quick contact, at least until electronic mail becomes common.

Another problem with the channel is that it may involve several conflicting media. For example, suppose someone shouts that he is not mad at you while standing over you with crossed arms, a red face. The nonverbals clearly contradict the words—and you would probably listen more to the nonverbals, even though the person might be calming down and really mean what he says.[24]

Finally, the channel may involve more than one person in linking the originating sender to the ultimate receiver. The problem is that a message tends to get distorted as it passes through several people, all with their own biases, priorities, and communications abilities. Research has indicated that up to 80 percent of a message can be lost in communication cycles completed by five successive people.[25]

Problems Related to the Context

In addition to the barriers to communications, which deal with purpose, media, direction, and process, we must consider the **context** in which the communications occur. Because the **structure** of an organization creates status differences, authority and responsibility differences, and incentives for action, it can also create a barrier to communications. People cannot communicate simply as people; they must communicate as role occupants in the organizational structure. For example, the roles that Rob and the design engineer fill at Home Computers may create barriers to communications that might not exist if the two of them were playing golf together. And certainly, the status differences between Rob and his boss may be the factor inhibiting Rob from communicating about the coordination problems across shifts.

Another factor inhibiting the communications between Rob and the design engineer is that they are in different departments. To the degree that organizations form departments that are highly specialized and which function in a very formalized manner, communications between departments will be inhibited. As the departments become more separated in their activities, they will develop their own priorities, norms of behavior, and time frames. Thus, what may be of critical and immediate importance to Rob may be much less important to the design engineer. And this difference will make the engineer less receptive to what Rob wants.

As for the **technological** barriers, if the technology of the organization is complex and nonroutine, there will be a great chance for miscommunication, even though communications will be very frequent. On the other hand, if the technology is routine, the frequency of communications will be reduced, and the accuracy should be increased. However, over time the routine technology can lead to bored workers who get careless with their communications, thus leading to reduced accuracy.

The **history** of communications can also become a barrier to current communications. A past history of miscommunications between you as a manager and your subordinates can lead to a severe conflict. It appears that this is what happened to Rob. As he chose not to deal directly with the symptoms of poor communication in his section, they became worse and worse. A sense of distrust developed on the part of his people, and finally Rob was reassigned to another department.

Ways to Improve Communications in Organizations

With all these problems of communications, the complexity of the process, the many dimensions, and the context variables, you may be wondering if there is any way to have good communications in an organization. Or you may have already thought of some ways to improve communications, as you read this chapter. If so, let us compare ideas as we proceed to explore several ways to improve communications. To provide order to this discussion, we will use Figure 10.3 as an outline of some steps for improving communications in organizations.

**Figure 10.3
Steps to Improve
Communications in an
Organization**

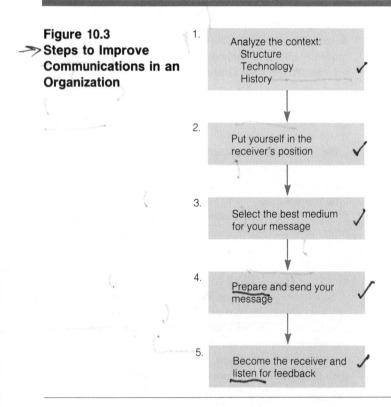

1. Analyze the context:
   Structure
   Technology
   History

2. Put yourself in the receiver's position

3. Select the best medium for your message

4. Prepare and send your message

5. Become the receiver and listen for feedback

Step 1: Analyze the Context

The first step in improving communications in organizations is to understand the context in which the communications must occur. You need to assess the technological, structural, and historical context in which the communications must occur. Changes in this context can be used to improve communications. For example, use of computer-based information systems can improve communications. As Naisbitt suggests, managers of the future will have computer terminals right on their desks, and they will know something about basic programming so they can make the computer work for them.[26] Box 10.4 explores one such example, and some potentially negative side effects. In the future, though, managers without computer skills will be lost in a sea of rapidly changing information.

A structural change is for companies to employ communication specialists and special units.[27] When the situation is very complex or is rapidly changing, the hierarchical order of communications may need to be altered. The use of task forces, special ad hoc committees, and special project groups can be especially helpful in linking departments in an organization, when strong differences make it difficult for them to communicate.

It may also be possible to link machinery to computers to reduce the need for communications among the people in an organization. The emergence of robots in the work place illustrates the potential of this device for improving communications.[28]

But as a manager, you may not always be able to use technology and structure to your advantage. They may actually be constraints on your behavior, as we noted earlier. And you need to understand these constraints in order to move in the right direction for effective communications. If you know you are in a very routine and highly structured situation, your communications will be much more controlled than if you were in an unstructured and nonroutine situation.

Another aspect to consider is the political context in which you operate, as we discussed in Chapter 9. Often decisions and other important communications are heavily influenced by the politics of the situation. The cultural network determines what type of communications will be most effective. It may be formal communications, or

**Box 10.4
Some Chief
Executives Bypass
and Irk Staffs in
Getting Information**

It's 7:30 A.M. Do you know where your chief executive is?

Managers at Thermo Electron Corp., Banco Internacional de Colombia and Northwest Industries Inc. strongly suspect that at their companies, the boss is already pecking away at a computer terminal to monitor the business and, they fear, to check up on them. Depending on their boss's style, they are beneficiaries or victims of a new wrinkle in computer technology—executive information systems.

These systems, also called decision support systems, allow an executive to bypass the usual intelligence channels and quickly discover for himself how his company or industry is faring. Depending on the system's complexity and his own needs, a boss unfazed by computers can call up information as detailed as the name of a bank officer who authorized a specific loan and as general as total corporate sales.

To most people, the ability to control what the chief executive officer sees and to influence how he sees it is power. Staff people who collect, interpret and analyze executive information therefore tend to be very powerful. So are operating executives who set plans, budgets and strategies. Executive information systems change all that.

Put more bluntly, these systems scare the daylights out of subordinates. If the chief executive has direct access to information, staff groups and data-processing managers fear that their influence will wane, and operating heads fear a loss of automony, as well as microscopic scrutiny.

Initially, all that Banco Internacional de Colombia managers knew was that at 7:30 A.M. Mr. Jensen would be at his terminal and that by 8 A.M. he would be telephoning them. "At first, there was concern," he admits. "There was the reaction: 'The boss knows more than I do, and I'm in trouble.' "

As managers scrambled to keep up with the president, concern turned into professional pride. Marketing people found clients impressed with their detailed knowledge. Managers realized that they could better monitor their subordinates. "Even people who at first resented it began to realize they can control other people with it," says Gloria Bronsema, an independent management consultant.

it may be informal, spontaneous communications.[29] The point is: **you must understand the situation if you are to communicate effectively in it.**

Step 2: Put Yourself in the Receiver's Position

As the sender, you need to understand the receiver if you wish to communicate effectively. For example, if you are dealing with a relatively uneducated worker on the shop floor, you must choose your words differently than if you are communicating with your boss. Likewise, if the receiver is very angry, you must communicate differently than when the receiver is calm. Perhaps if people are angry, you should wait until they calm down. Remember, **if you do not transmit in a language and manner, and at a time when the receiver can hear your message, the chances of communication are greatly reduced.**

Rogers and Farson talk about a process called **active listening** as a vehicle for getting inside the other person's viewpoint.[30] They suggest that you listen for total meaning. Try to get not only the content of messages, but also the sender's feelings. To do so, you must listen to all the cues being sent, especially the nonverbal ones. Then if you take into account the receiver's feelings, you are much more likely to be able to communicate your message effectively.

Step 3: Select the Best Medium for Your Message

Once you have analyzed the context and reflected on the receiver's position, you need to think about the best vehicle for transmitting your message. As we have noted, written communications have the advantage of thoughtful presentation, and the receiver can reflect on the message in privacy. On the other hand, if the message to be sent is complex, research has shown that the two-way process of verbal communications is best.[31] Of course, you can use several media together (for example, a phone call to make a request followed by a memo repeating the request).

And you must not forget the nonverbal media, since they are an integral part of any communication. For example, the timing and location of the communication are both part of the media decision. Usually the more immediate the communication, the better, though at times you may decide it is smarter to let some time pass (for example, when someone is angry).

Step 4: Prepare and Send Your Message

With all of the information in hand from steps 1 through 3, you are now ready to actually formulate and send your message. At this point it is good to rethink the message you wish to send to be sure you still want to send that message. **If you are open to the feedback received in analyzing the situation and the receiver, you may now decide to change the message you originally wanted to send.** For example, you may have intended to reprimand one of your people for poor performance. But after analyzing the situation, you now feel that the context actually created the poor performance and the receiver was doing his best in the situation. Hence you may change your message to a problem-solving session with the employee.

Such development over time is possible if you are open to the information available to you in the organization. And if you listen while also sending your message, you can make adjustments in your communications as the process unfolds. For example, in assertiveness training, people are taught to mix in understanding with their assertiveness.[3] The understanding allows them to actively pay attention to the receiver. It also allows them three distinct levels of assertiveness:

1. **Understanding-assertive**, where the focus is primarily on understanding the other person, though not to the point of being submissive.
2. **Equally assertive-understanding**, where there is a balance between listening to the other person and getting across your ideas.
3. **Assertive-understanding**, where the focus is primarily on getting across your ideas, though not to the point of being aggressive and running over the other person.

During an exchange, it is possible to shift gears through all three levels, depending on how a situation unfolds. And it is important to recognize that a situation may unfold over a few minutes in an exchange—or over several months in a series of exchanges.

Step 5: Become the Receiver and Listen for Feedback

Now that you have sent your message, you need to switch roles and become the receiver of feedback. **Listen to be sure your message got through and was understood as intended.** Part of your responsibility as the sender is to ensure that the feedback loop is completed. Such feedback may be verbal or written, as in a request for information. Or it may be behavioral. That is, when you ask someone to do something, you can watch what they do. For example, it was feedback to Rob at Home Computers when Tom did not respond to his note to come by the office. When the feedback indicates that the message was not received, you will have to go back to step 1 and begin a follow-up cycle to try to complete your intended communication.

Following these 5 steps and incorporating an understanding of the process, dimensions, context, outcomes, and inhibitors of communications can make you a better communicator, if you work at it. Remember, **as the sender, you are responsible for transmitting a message the receiver can understand and for ensuring that you receive feedback. As the receiver, you are responsible for understanding a message that is sent to you and for ensuring that feedback is received by the sender.**

Chapter Highlights

In this final chapter of the section on interpersonal behavior in organizations, we have focused on communications as a vital organizational process. **Communications are the lifeblood of any organization.** Organizations simply cannot operate without them. And communications in organizations are typically very problematic.

We then explored the process of communications. The **sender** decides what message to send, encodes the message, and transmits it into the media channel. The message then reaches the intended **receiver**, who decodes it for its intent. **Until the receiver gets the message and interprets it as intended by the sender, communication has not occurred.** In fact, this means that the last step in the process is actually **feedback**. And **it is this cyclical aspect of the communication process that makes it devel-**

opmental in nature. Finally, we pointed out the last aspect of the process—namely, **noise** that inhibits the flow of communications.

We then looked in on Rob at Home Computers. Following that, we discussed three basic dimensions of communications: **purpose, media**, and **direction**. We defined eight basic purposes for which people communicate in organizations: (1) control, (2) instruction, (3) motivation, (4) problem solving, (5) feedback and evaluation, (6) information exchange, (7) social needs, and (8) political goals.

We then discussed three basic types of media that you can use to send your message to other people: **written, verbal**, and **nonverbal**. The written category includes procedures manuals, reports, memos, letters, handwritten notes, and files. The basic advantage to written communication is that it can be thought out to ensure better clarity. The biggest disadvantage is that it is essentially one-way communication.

Verbal communications include formal and informal one-to-one conversations, formal and informal meetings, and telephone. The primary advantage to verbal communication is that it is essentially two-way. The disadvantage is that it may be less well planned, and there is no record of the communication.

Nonverbal communications include tone of voice, volume, gestures, body language, silence, color, touch, smell, time, signals, objects, ceremony, symbols, and settings. Some researchers estimate that over two thirds of our communications are via the nonverbal media.

The last dimension of communication that we discussed was direction: **vertical, horizontal, diagonal**, and the **grapevine**. Vertical communication can be upward and downward. Horizontal communication can be within a department or between departments at the same level. Diagonal communications are also interdepartmental, but they are links to people at higher or lower levels in other departments. Finally, the grapevine does not follow the organizational chart. **Each direction serves particular purposes, and you must be skilled at using each direction to be an effective manager**.

In the next section, we discussed the context in which communications occur. The context is influenced by the organization's **structure**, **technology**, and **history**. Furthermore, each of these contextual factors will change over time and create forces for change in the communications of the organization. Thus, the communications of an organization will develop over a period of time.

We then discussed several outcomes associated with communications in organizations, some positive and some negative. Through communications you become socialized to the organization; develop liking and respect for others; develop trust or distrust; develop more, or less, closely aligned perceptions. The quality of communications determines whether the outcomes are positive or negative.

We then explored a number of factors which can inhibit communications and yield negative outcomes. First, there can be problems related to the sender. The sender can encode the message improperly or send an incomplete message. A poor relationship between sender and receiver can inhibit communications. The sender can also fail to recognize the time aspects of communications.

There can also be problems related to the receiver. The receiver may not be aware of the message, may misinterpret it, or may not accept the message as sent. There can also be problems in the communications channel: the sender can choose the wrong medium; the sender may send conflicting messages through different media; and the message may have to travel through several people.

Finally, there can be problems in the context of the communication. The organizational structure creates different statuses, authorities, responsibilities, and incentives, and it can inhibit communications for people who are performing their organizational roles. The structure places people in different departments, which can also inhibit communications. And the technology and history of the organization can also create barriers in the communications process.

The final section of the chapter explained five steps to improve communications in organizations. First, analyze the context. Second, put yourself in the receiver's position. Third, select the best medium for your message. Fourth, prepare and send your message. And fifth, become the receiver and listen for feedback. By using these five steps and applying the understanding of process, dimensions, context, and inhibiting factors set forth in this chapter, you will be in better shape to deal with the problematic nature of communications in organizations. Indeed, you must if you want to be an effective manager in the long run.

Review Questions

1. Why are communications so important in organizations?

2. What are the main reasons why communications in organizations are so problematic?

3. Explain why we say that communications have not occurred until the message is received and understood by the receiver.

4. Why do we say that communications are developmental in nature?

5. Explain the basic purposes for which people communicate. Why are some more positive than others in terms of organizational goals?

6. Explain the advantages and disadvantages of each of the three basic types of communication media.

7. What purposes are typically associated with the basic directions of communications?

8. How do the context factors of communications suggest that communications are developmental in nature?

9. What communication outcomes develop over a period of time, again supporting our contention that communications are developmental in nature?

10. What are the factors that tend to inhibit communications, as related to the sender, the receiver, the channel, and the context?

11. Explain the steps you can use to improve communications in an organization. Can you explain the cyclical aspect to these steps?

Notes

1. H. Mintzberg, *The Nature of Managerial Work* (New York: Harper & Row, 1973); and J. P. Kotter, *The General Managers* (New York: Free Press, 1982).

2. C. A. O'Reilly and L. R. Pondy, "Organizational Communication," in *Organizational Behavior*, ed. S. Kerr (Columbus, Ohio: Grid Publishing, Inc., 1979), pp. 119–50.

3. Mintzberg, *The Nature of Managerial Work*, and Kotter, *The General Managers*.

4. C. Shannon and W. Weaver, *The Mathematical Theory of Communication* (Urbana: University of Illinois Press, 1948).

5. This section draws primarily from W. G. Scott and T. R. Mitchell, *Organization Theory: A Structural and Behavioral Analysis* (Homewood, Ill.: Richard D. Irwin, 1976), chap. 9; and L. Thayer, *Communications and Communications Systems* (Homewood, Ill.: Richard D. Irwin, 1968), pp. 187–301.

6. Scott and Mitchell, *Organization Theory*.

7. W. V. Haney, *Communicational and Interpersonal Relations* (Homewood, Ill.: Richard D. Irwin, 1979).

8. Mintzberg, *The Nature of Managerial Work*, and Kotter, *The General Managers*.

9. Mintzberg, *The Nature of Managerial Work*.

10. R. G. Harper, A. N. Wiens, and J. D. Matarzzo, *Nonverbal Communication: The State of the Art* (New York: John Wiley & Sons, 1978).

11. J. Pfeffer, *Power in Organizations* (Marshfield, Mass.: Pitman Publishing, Inc., 1981).

12. D. Fisher, *Communication in Organization* (St. Paul, Minn.: West Publishing Co., 1981).

13. This section draws primarily from D. Katz and R. L. Kahn, *The Social Psychology of Organizations* (New York: John Wiley & Sons, 1966), ch. 9.

14. O'Reilly and Pondy, "Organizational Communication."

15. T. Allen and S. Cohen, "Information Flow in R&D Laboratories," *Administrative Science Quarterly* 14 (1969), pp. 12–20.

16. W. A. Randolph and F. E. Finch, "The Relationship Between Organization Technology and the Direction and Frequency Dimensions of Task Communications," *Human Relations* 30 (1977), pp. 1131–45; and W. A. Randolph, "Organization Technology and the Media and Purpose Dimensions of Organization Communications," *Journal of Business Research* 6 (1978), pp. 237–59.

17. W. Bennis, D. Berlew, E. Schein, and F. I. Steele, *Interpersonal Dynamics*, 3d ed. (Homewood, Ill.: Richard D. Irwin, 1973).

18. Bennis et al., *Interpersonal Dynamics*.

19. W. Ouchi, *Theory Z: How American Business Can Meet the Japanese Challenge* (Reading, Mass.: Addison-Wesley Publishing, 1981); and T. J. Peters and R. H. Waterman, Jr., *In Search of Excellence* (New York: Harper & Row, 1982).

20. For example, see C. A. O'Reilly and K. H. Roberts, "Task Group Structure, Communication and Effectiveness in Three Organizations," *Journal of Applied Psychology* 62 (1977) pp. 674–81.

21. O'Reilly and Pondy, "Organizational Communication."

22. This section draws primarily from H. Guetzkow, "Communications in Organizations," in *Handbook of Organizations*, ed. J. G. March (Skokie, Ill.: Rand McNally, 1965) pp. 534–73; L. W. Porter and K. H. Roberts, "Communication in Organizations," in *Handbook of Industrial and Organizational Psychology*, ed. M. D. Dunnette (Skokie, Ill.: Rand McNally, 1976), pp. 1553–89; and O'Reilly and Pondy, "Organizational Communication."

23. J. Naisbitt, *Megatrends* (New York: Warner Books, 1982).

24. A. Mehrabian, *Silent Messages* (Belmont, Calif.: Wadsworth, 1971).

25. I. J. Lee and L. L. Lee, *Handling Barriers in Communication* (New York: Harper & Row, 1968), p. 69.

26. Naisbitt, *Megatrends*, p. 35.

27. J. Hage, *Communications and Organizational Control* (New York: John Wiley & Sons, 1974).

28. Naisbitt, *Megatrends*, p. 29.

29. T. E. Deal and A. A. Kennedy, *Corporate Cultures* (Reading, Mass.: Addison-Wesley Publishing, 1982), ch. 5.

30. C. R. Rogers and R. E. Farson, "Active Listening," in *Organizational Psychology: A Book of Readings*, 3d ed., ed. D. A. Kolb, I. M. Rubin, and J. M. McIntyre (Englewood Cliffs, N.J.: Prentice-Hall, 1979), pp. 168–79.

31. For example, see J. Short, "Effects of Medium of Communication on Experimental Negotiation," *Human Relations* 27 (1974), pp. 225–34.

32. W. M. Morgenroth and W. A. Randolph, *Assertiveness Training: A Workshop for Leaders* (Columbia, S.C.: The Daniel Management Center, University of South Carolina, 1983).

Resource Readings

Fisher, D. *Communication in Organization*. St. Paul, Minn.: West Publishing Co., 1981.

Haney, W. V. *Communicational and Interpersonal Relations*. Homewood, Ill.: Richard D. Irwin, 1979.

Harper, R. G., A. N. Weins, and J. D. Matarzzo. *Nonverbal Communication: The State of the Art*. New York: John Wiley & Sons, 1978.

Mintzberg, H. *The Nature of Managerial Work.* New York: Harper & Row, 1973.

O'Reilly, C. A., and L. R. Pondy. "Organizational Communication." In *Organizational Behavior,* ed. S. Kerr. Columbus, Ohio: Grid, 1979, pp. 119–50.

Porter, L. W., and K. H. Roberts. "Communication in Organizations." In *Handbook of Industrial and Organizational Psychology,* ed. M. D. Dunnette. Skokie, Ill.: Rand McNally, 1976, pp. 1553–89.

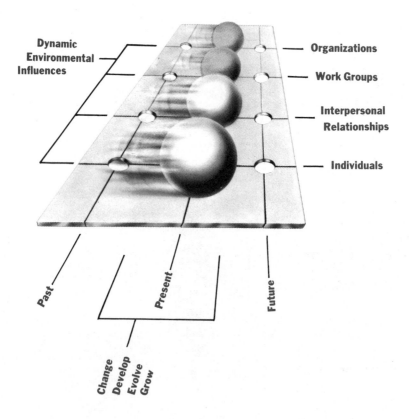

Dynamic
Environmental
Influences

Organizations

Work Groups

Interpersonal
Relationships

Individuals

Past

Present

Future

Change
Develop
Evolve
Grow

Work Teams in Organizations

Having now completed our analyses of both individuals and interpersonal relations in organizations, we will explore the behavior of groups of people in organizations. Chapter 11 will look at why groups are so important to you as a manager in an organization. And we will examine a number of individual and situational inputs to the behavior of groups. Overlaying this discussion will be an explanation of the developmental aspects of groups.

Chapter 12 will explore the emergent structural and process elements of groups in organizations. You will learn how norms, status and power relationships, cohesiveness, communications, leadership, decision making methods, and roles of group members help define the behavioral patterns, daily operation and effectiveness of groups. It will become clear that these emergent elements are essential factors for you to manage if you are to lead or belong to an effective work group. In essence, the input variables discussed in Chapter 11 form the context in which the structural and process elements in Chapter 12 must be managed.

The final chapter in this section (Chapter 13) will deal with the interactions among different groups that make up an organization. As a manager, it is not enough to manage only the group of people who report to you. You must also be concerned with other groups to which you belong and those with which your group must interact to accomplish its work. Chapter 13 will deal with managing the inevitable conflicts and problems of coordination that develop among groups in organizations.

Throughout these three chapters, it will be important for you to remember the material covered in Sections II and III of the book, "Individuals in Organizations" and "Interpersonal Relations in Organizations." Also, you need to recall the model of organizations presented in Chapter 1 as the guiding framework for our analysis. It is repeated on the following page for your reference, with the focal points of this section highlighted. People are the basic building blocks of any organization, and along with interpersonal relations, they form the basis for this section on group behavior.

A Developmental Framework for Studying Organizations

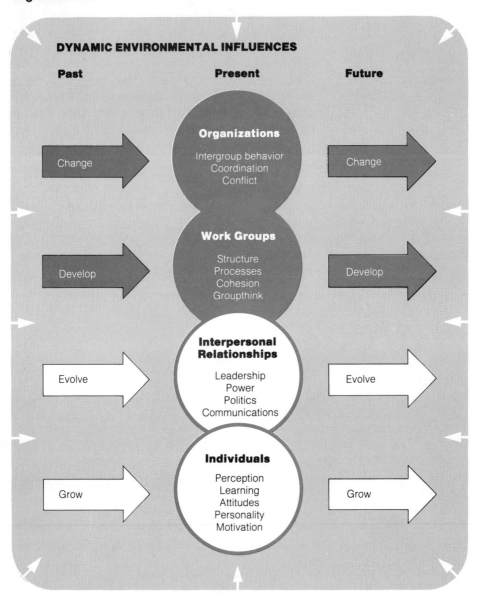

DYNAMIC ENVIRONMENTAL INFLUENCES

Past   Present   Future

Organizations
Intergroup behavior
Coordination
Conflict

Change   Change

Work Groups
Structure
Processes
Cohesion
Groupthink

Develop   Develop

Interpersonal Relationships
Leadership
Power
Politics
Communications

Evolve   Evolve

Individuals
Perception
Learning
Attitudes
Personality
Motivation

Grow   Grow

Understanding Groups of People at Work

Just as people and their interpersonal relations are always unique and developing, so too are groups. **Each group in an organization will have a unique character, and this character will have developed over time and will develop into the future.** As we move into a discussion of group behavior, think about various work groups, study groups, committees, church groups, and so forth, to which you have belonged. By applying what we discuss to your own experiences, you will benefit more from the material presented in this chapter.

The Importance to a Manager of Understanding Groups

If you are to learn to be an effective manager, you must be able to work with and in groups of people. This statement is an extension of the one made in introducing Chapter 7, that **the very essence of managerial work is to do things through other people**. The difference is that by focusing on groups we realize that "doing things through other people" takes place in a collective atmosphere. In an organization we cannot work with people in a one-on-one fashion. We must work with a group of people who also interact with each other. Indeed, one way of viewing an organization is as a collection of groups, rather than as a collection of individual people.

Few jobs in an organization can be done alone. We need other people to assist with our work and to ensure that the total job gets done. Hence, **groups are a fact of life in organizations.** Unlike the school atmosphere, where we depend primarily on ourselves, and our grades are individually determined, our performances in a work organization are highly dependent on other people. Organizations simply could not exist without groups that divide the labor and coordinate individual effort. And groups are becoming even more important with the advent of quality circles, worker participation in management decisions, and entrepreneurial ventures in large companies. For example, Box 11.1 illustrates how groups have been involved in many of the advances in the computer field.

As another example, the early Hawthorne studies clearly established the importance of groups in affecting

Box 11.1
Large Computer Firms
Sprout Little Divisions
for Good, Fast Work:
Convergent
Technologies Let a
Group Have Free Rein
to Build a New Machine

Santa Clara, Calif.—*About a year ago, Matt Sanders got kicked out of his office.*

His belongings were packed in boxes, and two new workers moved into the space at Convergent Technologies Inc., a Silicon Valley computer maker. Mr. Sanders hung around the building for a few days, borrowing desks, without a phone to call his own.

"If you get into trouble, call me," said his boss, Allen Michels, "and if you get some goods news, call me, too. But I ain't calling you." Mr. Michels adds: "Let me tell you he was scared."

Mr. Sanders wasn't being fired, and he wasn't in trouble with his boss. On the contrary, he had been named leader of what Mr. Michels calls a "strike force" to build a new computer that would enable Convergent, which makes high-priced business computers, to enter the market for lower-priced personal computers in just one year. The idea was to tap into the entrepreneurial forces that energize so many Silicon Valley start-ups by cutting Mr. Sanders loose and letting him form his own "company-within-a-company." It's an approach that several large or maturing technology companies are turing to.

Quicker Reflexes

Companies say that small groups, given great freedom, can react better and more quickly to the abrupt changes in electronics technology that constantly buffet the valley. Unlike industries where change is more gradual, computer makers must regularly come up with new products or enhancements of the old, and for ever-lower costs. An electric-toaster model might sell for years, but a computer, particularly at the lower-priced end of the market, might have a life span of only 18 months before technology passed it by.

Apple Computer Inc. turned to a small group to help develop its Lisa, a $10,000 easy-to-use machine for business people. Timex Corp. did likewise to get into the computer business quickly with its Timex Sinclair 1000. Daniel Ross, the vice president and chief operating officer of the Timex Computer unit, says one virtue of the small-group approach is that responsibility gets pushed to lower-level employees. Also, he says, small groups can better focus their energies on a single goal. "Creativity is fostered in this kind of organization," he says.

individual behavior.[1] As the researchers increased lighting levels, rest periods, and incentives, performance improved. But it continued to improve even as the lighting levels, rest periods, and incentives were decreased. The group impact on individual performance was more important than the external factors. Throughout history, there have been many instances where workers have held back on production because of group pressure, even though it cost them money to do so. On the other hand, group pressure can cause people to perform at peak levels of performance if the group accepts the organizational goals. A good example is an athletic team with less talent beating a stronger team. As a manager, **you must realize that the work group you supervise is a potential competitor with your leadership in influencing the behavior of group members; it can also be your ally in influencing the group members**. You need to understand groups so you can achieve the positive outcome.

Another reason why groups are important to you as a manager is that you will simultaneously belong to several groups within an organization. You will supervise one group of people. You will also belong to a group consisting of your peer managers and your boss. In addition, you may belong to a special committee or project group or to a task force with people from various parts of the organization. And you might also belong to groups based on common interests or friendship that cut across both departmental and hierarchical lines in the organization. Furthermore, you will no doubt belong to groups outside the organization, such as a family, club, or church. Our focus, however, is on groups within an organization. As a member of multiple groups in an organization (as summarized in Figure 11.1), you will encounter many forces that affect your behavior. You must know how to deal with these often conflicting forces if you are to be successful both as a manager and as a member of groups.

Finally, groups are important to understand because they are complex entities. Many factors influence whether or not a group will be effective. The remainder of this chapter and the next will be devoted to these factors, but let us briefly preview them here. Groups both influence and are influenced by the behavior of individuals. Further, the context in which the group operates influ-

Figure 11.1 The Multiple Groups of an Organization

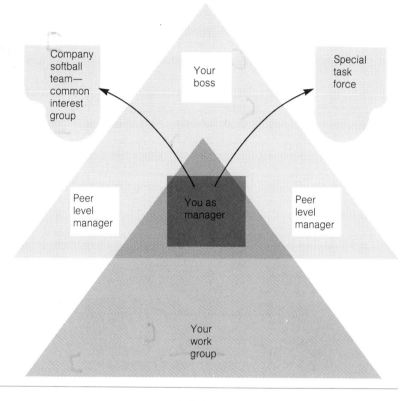

ences its development and effectiveness. Over time, groups develop particular norms, role relationships, power relationships, and internal status differences, and they use various communication, leadership, and decision-making processes. Because all of these elements are constantly changing and interacting, your job as a group member or group manager is very difficult.

Our job in this and the next chapter is to provide a model to help you understand and analyze groups. We also share some ideas on how to effectively manage and work as a member of groups in organizations. Let us begin by exploring the definition of groups, their advantages and disadvantages, some important types of groups, and the developmental stages that groups go through.

The Definition of a Group

The literature on groups has been fairly consistent in defining the term. A **group in an organization is a collection of two or more people who, over a period of time, develop shared norms of behavior, are interdependent, and interact with each other for the purpose of achieving some common goal or set of goals.**[2]

Group **norms** provide a sense of identity. The **interactions** of group members reinforce the group as an entity, while also helping the group achieve its purposes. The **interdependence** of group members on one another for achieving the group goals helps define different roles for the members. For example, a task force assigned to solve a quality control problem at Home Computers may divide this task into various parts for different group members: research the technical design, look into the production process, interview customers, prepare a written report. Finally, the **time dimension** of groups has not often been made explicit in the definition, but it is important from a developmental perspective. And its importance will become even clearer as we proceed in our discussion of groups.

Unfortunately, the definition of a group does not really help us understand **why** groups are formed in the first place. Basically, **groups are formed because they have the potential to accomplish more than would the same number of people working alone.** Groups allow for specialization of function by its members. They also permit a synergistic effect, where the whole is greater than the sum of its parts. However, the reverse can also occur: groups can result in the whole being **less** than the sum of its parts. For example, as mentioned earlier, we can all think of athletic teams with excellent talent at every position losing to a less talented team that played well together. The point is that **groups are an essential part of every organization, but it is very difficult to make them work effectively over time.**

Types of Groups

To further understand the definition of groups we need to look at the two basic types of groups: formal and informal. **Formal groups** are those prescribed by the organization. Within the departments of any organization, groups of people (often called sections or units) are assigned particular tasks to perform. Management might also assign you to a project group, committee, task force, or quality circle. Project groups are typically formed to accomplish a particular short-range task—for example, to design the modifications on Home Computers' EZ2 for the school and library markets. Committees and task forces are usually formed to manage either ongoing or problem-solving issues within the organization. Quality circles are problem-solving groups of workers within the production sector of our society. Typically, they meet once a week for an hour or so to try to solve production problems. Effective use of such groups has led to the implementation of many successful solutions.

Informal groups are not prescribed by the organization, but develop because of proximity, common interest, and individual need satisfaction. For example, a car pool group may develop among several people who live in the same neighborhood. And they may not even work for the same organization, just ones in close proximity. Company baseball teams or bridge groups form because of the common interest in those activities. Groups may also form at break and lunch times as people come together to complain about things in the company—for example, pay and working conditions. You can probably think of many other examples of informal groups that connect organizational members outside of their formal work groups.

Each type of group serves particular needs, and each will develop its own personality. To be an effective member of these groups, you need to understand how groups operate. Furthermore, since you will belong to more than one such group at the same time, it is important to recognize the conflicting demands they may place on you. An informal group sometimes opposes the goals of the organization and has a big negative impact on people in the group. But informal groups can also help the organization if they accept the organizational goals. **As with formal groups, informal ones can either help or hinder the organization; which result occurs depends in part on what you as a group member or manager do.**

Group Development Stages

To truly understand and manage groups, though, you must learn to recognize the developmental stages they go through. Since the late 1940s there have been a number of group development models proposed by various authors. Indeed, the very number of models (almost 20) suggests the strong support for the conclusion that groups do move through stages of growth in a developmental process. In Chapter 1 we discussed the model proposed by Schutz with the three stages of inclusion, control, and affection.[3] A more complete model for our purposes here was proposed by Tuckman in 1965.[4] The two models are very similar in the basic stages defined, but Tuckman's model (shown in Figure 11.2), defines stages in terms of both interpersonal relations and task functions that are essential concerns of any group. Any group must manage both task and interpersonal relations to be effective over the long run.

As we discuss Tuckman's stages of group development, you must recognize that the length of time spent in each one can vary greatly. **Each stage lasts until its paramount issues are essentially resolved.** **The group then moves on, but the stages are not so clearly marked that there is no overlap between them.** As always, models of behavior are much neater than the actual behavior. Groups really operate to varying degrees in all of the stages all of the time. The issues of one stage will, however, usually be primary at any one point in time as the group evolves.

Figure 11.2   The Process of Group Development

Stage 1	Stage 2	Stage 3	Stage 4
Testing and orientation	Conflict and organization	Cohesion and information exchange	Interdependence and problem solving

Source: B. W. Tuckman, "Developmental Sequence in Small Groups," *Psychological Bulletin* 63 (1965): 384–99. Copyright 1965 by the American Psychological Association. Adapted by permission of the author.

Groups also sometimes regress to earlier stages of development. The addition of new members, a change in the group's task, and other factors can cause this backtracking. In other words, the process of group development is ongoing and complex. With this background, let us now review each of the four stages of Tuckman's model.

Stage 1: Testing and Orientation

In Stage 1, group members try to determine what behaviors will be acceptable to the group, what skills and resources each member brings to the group, what goals and motivations each member has, and who will really psychologically commit to the group. In this stage, people are becoming acquainted with one another and want to know what is expected of them. Group members depend on the leader to set the rules, establish an agenda, and make sure things happen. Likewise, they depend on the leader to define the task, establish group goals, and basically be responsible for the task accomplishment. This stage is consistent with the leadership situation where the subordinates are not capable or motivated enough to be productive and where the leader must provide a great deal of structure.

Stage 2: Conflict and Organization

As a group moves into Stage 2 of development, conflicts tend to emerge. Often, the group members begin to doubt the leader. Other members begin to exert influence on the group, and a fight over control of the group can follow. A group in this stage may have difficulty in making decisions and communicating effectively.

Coupled with these interpersonal conflicts are the task functions of really becoming organized. A leader must have followers, and the group must determine who will be responsible for what. Norms of expected behavior, standards, and work rules start to develop during this phase. And as the conflicts are resolved, some dissident group members may leave the group, either physically or psychologically. If a group gets through Stage 2 successfully, it is well on the way to becoming an effective group. However, it is often difficult to fully resolve the leadership and organizational conflicts of this stage—especially if there is much turnover in the group or many changes in the task and situation of the group.

Stage 3: Cohesion and Information Exchange

During Stage 3 a real sense of cohesion and teamwork begins to emerge. Group members feel good about each other and really identify with the group. They share feelings, give and receive feedback, and begin to share a sense of success. It is during this stage, however, that a group runs the greatest risk of falling into "groupthink."[5] **Groupthink** occurs when the feelings of cohesion override the realistic appraisal of alternative courses of action. Groupthink makes a group think of itself as invulnerable, and group members tend to censor any thoughts that are not consistent with the group consensus. Groupthink can lead to carelessness which yields mistakes and a drop in productivity.

But groupthink does not have to occur. The other choice for Stage 3 groups is to develop the potential for exchanging all kinds of information relevant to their task. With the group oriented and organized, it is primed for the exchange of information that will help them accomplish their task effectively. If group members focus on information that is necessary rather than just on what people want to hear (as with groupthink), Stage 3 can

"Rose colored glasses in place?"

be marked by a conflict over ideas, which is not the kind of conflict that attacks egos and personalities. By arguing over ideas while supporting each other as people, a group can avoid groupthink, maintain cohesiveness, and be very productive. Stage 3 is a junction point. If the issues of the first two stages have not been settled, the group will tend either to erupt into serious conflict or fall prey to groupthink. If the group has resolved those issues, the conflict level will rise slightly as ideas are exchanged and groupthink is avoided.

Stage 4: Interdependence and Problem Solving

Stage 4 of development is difficult to achieve for most groups. The interpersonal relations in this stage are marked by a sophisticated level of interdependence. Group members can now work well with all other group members. Everyone can and does communicate with everyone else. Decisions are made with full agreement by everyone and after a comprehensive discussion of all alternatives. Group members understand the roles they need to perform if the group is to be highly effective. The group is very much oriented to maintaining good relationships among its members and to getting its task accomplished.

Indeed, the task function side of the ledger suggests that the group has matured into a real team. It can solve complex problems and implement the solutions. There is commitment to the task and to experimentation in problem solving. This stage is really an extension of Stage 3. Cohesion has progressed to the point of collaboration of effort, and information exchange has advanced to real problem solving. People in the group really care about each other, but they are also not afraid to speak their minds. Confidence reaches a high level for the few groups who reach this stage.

Unfortunately, even if a group reaches Stage 4, they still face the difficult job of staying there. Many factors can force the group back to earlier stages. For example, I have seen some very well-respected and successful groups of Organizational Behavior faculty revert to Stage 1 when one member of the team moves to another university. Such breakups can create real havoc for a group and lead to poor performance. If a group gets a new leader, it must deal again with many of the issues of Stage 2 (conflict and organization). The addition of a new member raises many of the issues of Stage 1 again. And any major change in the technology or task of the group raises issues on task development that were encountered in Stages 1 and 2. For example, as offices are becoming automated, work groups are being forced to relearn their jobs and the nature of their interrelationships. Indeed, as the arrows in Figure 11.2 indicate, (the **group developmental process is a never-ending process.**) Groups never reach a position where they can simply sit back and continue to be effective.

In the remainder of this chapter and Chapter 12, we will develop a model of group behavior that will help you be a better group manager and member. But first, let us look at some groups at Home Computers. As you read the case, think about the developmental stages and how you would analyze and work with these groups to achieve effectiveness.

Quality Circle Groups at Home Computers

Harvey, the president of Home Computers, has been exploring a number of personnel and production problems with the help of a consultant. Their focus has been primarily on the Dayton plant, which was the original Home Computers plant in 1977. Over the years this plant has become very routine in its operation: assembly lines are the primary form of production, workers are paid by the hour, and most decisions are made by the plant manager. Somehow, this highly structured approach is not working well. The workers say they do not feel like they belong; they have no sense of achievement in their jobs. A number of the original Home Computers people have left the company, and many of those remaining are very unhappy with their jobs. Production at the plant is starting to suffer in terms of quality and quantity. Harvey knows something must be done, because demand for the computers is growing rapidly and he is considering opening a third plant.

The consultant suggested that they start up some quality circles including people from different shifts and different departments. His suggestion was to get the workers and lower-level supervisors involved in solving the problems of morale and production plaguing the Dayton plant. Harvey had some doubts, but decided to give it a try. The consultant suggested that they use the Denver plant as a comparison to determine if the changes in Dayton have a positive effect.

Shortly after this discussion three quality circles were begun in Dayton, one for each of the three product lines—home use, schools and libraries, and small businesses. Each quality circle was made up of three people from production, three from sales, and two from personnel. A couple of different levels of the hierarchy were represented, and all shifts were represented. Since there were many indicators of friction between sales and production, a personnel person was appointed to head up each circle. Each circle was given a meeting room and an appointed time to meet each week. One-and-a-half hours was allocated for each meeting. In addition, the members were encouraged to meet informally during the week on their breaks or at meal time to keep ideas and energy flowing on the task.

Harvey was present at the first meeting of each group to explain the purpose of the quality circle. He asked them to come up with recommendations which would help solve the production and personnel problems of the plant. He assured them that their ideas would be implemented if at all possible, and that they would get a response to every suggestion. He told them that this was their plant to make successful or unsuccessful. He also said he had confidence in them or he would not even try this quality circle approach. The consultant then worked with each circle to help the members become acquainted with each other and to help them determine how their strengths and resources could help the circle. The consultant also worked with the circle leaders on agenda setting and how to run an effective meeting. This process went on over several months until each circle and leader felt comfortable in their roles.

In two cases it became clear that the circle leader had a great deal of expertise about the Home Computers operation. Furthermore, the status of these two leaders was enhanced by their being from the neutral personnel area rather than either production or sales. Both of these groups developed norms of hard work and commitment to the goals laid out by Harvey. There were some conflicts between production and sales about whose fault the problems were, but the circles were able to overcome these and to become well organized within about three months. Cohesion and a sense of teamwork were strong in both groups, and they moved quickly into providing problem definitions and solutions which were useful to plant management.

In the other group, however, the appointed leader from personnel was not as experienced, and problems developed soon after the consultant pulled out. Some of the team members were higher in the hierarchy than the leader, and several constantly vied with him for the leadership of the group. They tried to coordinate and summarize the actions of the circle, and they often disagreed with the leader on important decisions. Instead of moving into a sense of teamwork and cohesion, this circle became mired in conflict and disorganization. The meetings were difficult and unproductive. Some members even began to avoid the circle members. Finally, the team leader went to the consultant to ask for additional help.

What would you suggest if you were the consultant? What has gone wrong with this group? Could something still go wrong with the other two groups? Let us deal with some of these questions as we develop our model of group behavior.

A Model of Group Behavior

As you try to analyze what is happening with the quality circles at Home Computers, it would help to understand some basics principles of groups. For example, how do groups operate? What factors influence their behavior? We will explore such questions as we discuss the model presented in Figure 11.3, which summarizes the aspects of group functioning. This model draws on a number of theories related to groups. In the remainder of this chapter we will deal with the two sets of input variables— individual and situational—and their impact on group structure and process, and outcomes such as performance, satisfaction, and turnover. In Chapter 12 we will explore the structure and process elements shown in Figure 11.3. The end result will be to provide you with a better understanding of how to be an effective manager and member of groups. Let us begin this journey with a quick overview of the model presented in Figure 11.3.

The individual and situational input variables form a context within which you, as a manager, must work with a group of people. In Section II of this book, we dealt extensively with understanding the individual as the basic building block of an organization. Because groups are made up of individuals, **individual variables** (discussed

Figure 11.3 A Model of Group Behavior

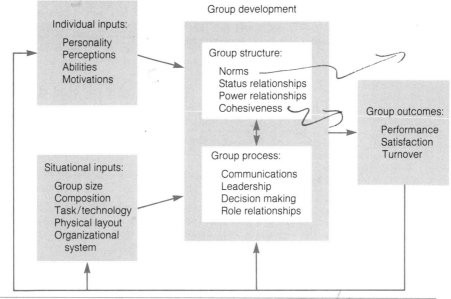

in Chapters 3 through 6) are inputs to a group since they are brought in by each member of the group. How people learn, their attitudes, perceptions, abilities, personalities, and backgrounds, and what motivates them, all impact on the group and its ability to function effectively.

Likewise, the **situational variables** form part of this context for the group. The size of the group, as well as its composition of people (for example, a homogeneous group of engineers or a heterogeneous group of engineers, accountants, marketers, and production people) affect the way a group operates and how effective it is. In addition, the type of task that the group must accomplish and the physical layout of the group also affect its functioning. For example, an assembly-line operation where the work is routine and people are spread out over a long, noisy distance will be different from a problem-solving committee where people sit around a table to discuss a complicated situation. Finally, the other groups in a department—and even the entire organization—form a part of the context which will affect the group's functioning.

Once these inputs come into play, the group begins the developmental process we discussed earlier. Through the operating processes and structure that emerge over time, the group develops a character of its own that ultimately affects the outcome variables. By **group structure** we mean the norms, status and power relationships, and cohesiveness that develop as a group operates. And by **group process** we mean the communications, leadership, decision making, and role relationships that are a part of the group's activities.

All of these factors converge to yield the outcomes of a group, as shown in Figure 11.3. Is the group effective in accomplishing its task? Are the group members satisfied with being a part of the group? Is there a great deal of absenteeism and turnover in the group? These outcomes serve as feedback to both the group development and inputs parts of the model, as a group moves forward in its developmental process. A successful group will receive reinforcement for its structure and processes; an ineffective one may feel pressure to make changes, even in the input variables.

With this introduction, let us now explore in detail the two sets of input variables. We will save the structure and process variables for Chapter 12.

Individual Inputs

All of Section II of this book dealt with understanding individuals. Thus, we will only briefly mention these inputs here and will refer you to Chapters 3 through 6. **Remember that each person will bring to a group a unique set of characteristics, and each person can potentially be in a different stage of personal development.** As these unique people come together to form a group, the interaction among these characteristics can influence both positively and negatively the group's processes, structure, and performance.

The quality circles in our case may be made up of people representing several of the 16 personality types we described in Chapter 4. The impact of this can be seen in the way the group functions.[6] For example, extroverts and feeling types could be expected to talk more than introverts and thinking types. Thinking types, however (along with sensing types) may be able to analyze situations in greater detail than either feeling or intuitive types. If the appointed leader happens to be an introvert, it may be difficult for him or her to effectively lead extroverts. The variety of personality types allows group members to enhance each other's strengths by compensating for the weaknesses. In other words, the combination of different types can result in either positive or negative outcomes, but the major impact will be on the group processes and interactions.

In addition, the backgrounds of the group members, as reflected in their perceptions and abilities (discussed in Chapter 3) can be unique. Indeed, such differences are one of the strong points of groups. One person may perceive the situation incorrectly or may not have the ability to perform a task that is necessary. Through interaction and group development, a group of people can learn to use their differences to achieve a high level of effectiveness. For example, in a student work group only one person may really know how to use the computer to analyze data. Another person may know how to write well and type. Either person working alone would have a hard time completing the task, but together they can complete an excellent report. At Home Computers, the successful quality circles may be successful partly because they use the differences in the individual members, while the unsuccessful circle lets these differences destroy it.

Finally, each group member may be motivated by something different. In Chapters 5 and 6 we discussed many things that can motivate people. Some of the group members may be motivated by the feeling of belonging that they get from the group interactions. In the unsuccessful group, people may be motivated by power and the desire to influence. Still others may be motivated by the challenge of the task. These different motivations can create problems for the group if they lead to conflict rather than cohesion as the group develops. But they can also lead to a real synergy of effort if directed toward the goals of the group. Indeed, different motivations, perceptions, and abilities can help the group avoid groupthink if they are directed toward the goals of the group.

Overall, the point is that individuals make up a group, and individuals are all different. **To be an effective member or manager of group interactions and outcomes, you need** to appreciate the potential effects of individual inputs. You must learn to manage the differences in your group to capitalize on the mix of people in the group. Otherwise, you could find yourself in the position of the unsuccessful circle leader at Home Computers.

Situational Inputs

Our model also includes several situational factors which influence both group development and performance: size, composition, task/technology, physical layout, and the organizational system. As we will discover, the group's task/technology may be the most critical input variable in terms of impact on the group—but let us explore each variable in turn.

Group Size

Size is simply the number of people constituting a group. Its effects on several other group variables have been widely researched.[8] Small groups (two to four people) tend to be characterized by greater tension and greater seeking of harmony and agreement than larger groups.[9] The logical reason for this is that people in a small group must be more intimate with one another. In larger groups (five or more), more interactions will be directed toward releasing tension and toward getting information out on the table for discussion. Thus larger groups may take longer to move through the developmental stages.

Size has also been found to affect the satisfaction, level of absenteeism, and turnover of group members. Given the greater degree of involvement in smaller groups, it is not suprising that people in small groups tend to be more satisfied and have less absenteeism and turnover. As our understanding of motivation from Chapters 5 and 6 suggests, there would appear to be more motivating factors present in small groups than in larger groups. For example, people in a small group more easily identify with the whole task and feel a sense of belonging. On the other hand, there appears to be no direct relationship between group size and **performance.** As we will explore shortly, the nature of the group task tends to dictate the group size. Certain complex tasks simply require more people to be involved. Still, a number of successful, large U.S. companies are working hard to keep work units small and to make workers feel involved, as described in the Minnesota Mining & Manufacturing Company example in Box 11.2.

Finally, group size is a variable that can change over time. Changes in the group task, which necessitate changes in group personnel, as well as people leaving or joining the group, can easily cause changes in group size. And these changes then affect the other variables we have just discussed.

Group Composition

Group composition focuses our attention on the combined effects of the individuals in a group.[10] **Each person brings a unique character to the group, but once the group has formed, we become concerned with the particular combination of people that makes up the group**. In particular, are the group members alike in many ways—a **homogeneous** group—or are they different in many ways—a **heterogeneous** group?

If a group is homogeneous, communications should be enhanced and conflict reduced. The group should move rather quickly through the first three stages of group development. If the group's task is quite routine—for example, on the assembly line for a simple product—homogeneity of the group can lead to increased performance and satisfaction. However, too much homogeneity can cause a group to overlook good alternatives and miss out on vital pieces of information when problem solving.

At Home Computers, the quality circles were heterogeneous, and the differences in the people probably caused the development of the groups to proceed slowly. With people from several different departments, the potential for conflict was increased, and communications were made more difficult by the various backgrounds of the people. (Recall our discussion in Chapter 10 on how communications can be inhibited between people from different parts of an organization.) The advantages of heterogeneity are that it broadens the perspective of the group and should lead to better solutions when dealing with complex tasks. Indeed, that is Harvey's hope in forming the three quality circles at Home Computers.

Box 11.2
Some Firms Fight Ills of Bigness by Keeping Employe Units Small

*S*t. Paul, Minn.—*For a company with some 87,000 employes and annual sales in excess of $6 billion, Minnesota Mining & Manufacturing Co. spends a lot of time "thinking small."*

"We are keenly aware of the disadvantages of large size," says Gordon W. Engdahl, the company's vice president for human resources and its top personnel officer. "We make a conscious effort to keep our units as small as possible because we think it helps keep them flexible and vital," he says. "When one gets too large, we break it apart. We like to say that our success in recent years amounts to multiplication by division."

Mr. Engdahl's comment is no conceit. 3M's average U.S. manufacturing plant employs just 270 people, and management groups as small as five guide the fortunes of the company's numerous household, industrial and scientific products. In the 1970s, its sales and earnings grew almost fourfold, while its U.S. work force increased by 40%.

In light of the attention given in recent years to "alienated" workers in big companies, firms have been seeking ways to ameliorate the effects of bigness. Some have adopted programs to make work groups smaller, to improve communications between workers and supervisors, and to give rank-and-filers more say over the way they do their work.

Worker Involvement

3M uses a broad array of worker-participation devices, including regular work-crew and management-group meetings and voluntary "quality circles" that assess work procedures.

3M's exhortations to its workers are relentlessly upbeat. At a multipurpose company plant in Menominee, Wis., cartoon figures mouth safety slogans from the walls, and posters proclaim "Safety Day" records instead of injury counts.

Many of the plant's employes have small radios on their workbenches, quietly playing the music of their choice. The radios replaced a plant-wide system of piped-in music that workers complained was too bland. Informality is the rule; not only does everyone go by his first name, but nicknames such as Bob, Jerry and Joe adorn managers' doorplates.

Marge Froeschle has worked at the plant for six years. She is a "group leader," a sort of assistant foreman in work crews that range in size from two or three to a dozen employes. This is her first factory job, and she likes it. "I get to do different things around the plant, and I can put in my two cents' worth whenever I want," she says. "It's not at all what I thought working for a big company would be like."

Task/Technology

The **task and technology** of a group are important factors in determining the effects of other situational variables. Indeed, they, along with the individuals in the group, may be the most important input variables. We can think of different task types and their potential effects on groups.[11] **Simple tasks** require simple and routine technologies. They can be highly structured, with very few exceptions to the work and only simple problems to solve. In addition, simple tasks require only low-level technical and interpersonal skills. On the other hand, **complex tasks** require nonroutine and complex technologies. There are many alternatives, many exceptions to the work, and very difficult problems to solve. In addition, complex tasks require high levels of both technical and interpersonal skills. Information needed to complete the task tends to be spread among many people. Obviously, the issue of task/technology is more complicated than this analysis, but this level of detail serves our purpose here.

When a group deals with simple tasks, group structure and process can develop in straightforward ways. Group satisfaction and performance can be expected to be high, turnover to be low, if the group members do not desire challenging work (as we discussed in Chapters 5 and 6 on motivation). With simple tasks, smaller groups can be expected to be more successful than larger groups, and homogeneous groups will tend to outperform heterogeneous ones.[12] In other words, there must be a match between the people and the task/technology if effectiveness is to result.

When a group must deal with complex tasks, such as the one facing the quality circles at Home Computers, the development of group structure and process will be more problematic. For one thing, the group will tend to be larger (8 people in the case) and more heterogeneous (three departments represented in the case). Increased size and diversity in the group means more difficult communication and more conflict, and a probable slowdown in the developmental process. There is a greater likelihood that status differences and power differentials will be larger, thus slowing down the development of norms and cohesiveness. Still, because of the complex task, larger, more heterogeneous groups should be more effective in terms of performance. And if the group members desire challenging work, then satisfaction should also be high and turnover low. As we shall see in Chapter 12, a critical factor in achieving these results with a complex group task is the type of group process that develops. And the members of the group are the keys to how group process develops.

Physical Layout

One of the other situational inputs, **physical layout**, is closely associated with the task/technology input. If the physical layout of a group places people close together, interactions tend to increase, unless noise or other factors inhibit them. And **increased interaction among group members should lead to quicker development of the group.**[13] It should also lead to faster development of group norms and cohesiveness. If a group is spread out along an assembly line, the individuals are less likely to become a cohesive group as quickly as a group of office workers working at adjacent desks with no partitions between them. In the Home Computers case, the physical layout is constantly changing. The quality circle members work in their own departments with some members seeing each other more frequently than others. Then once a week they sit down around a table for a meeting. It is quite likely that such an arrangement might slow down the group development and make it more difficult for the groups to perform effectively.

But physical space can change over time, with continuing effects on a group. With the advent of automated offices, floor designs are changing. Some companies are going from a large open space with nothing separating the desks to partitions separating the employees. Likewise, automated office equipment is changing the task/technology of work groups, moving things toward the complex end of the continuum. The primary point to remember is that task/technology and physical layout are important influences on a group, and both are highly subject to change. As a manager, you need to be aware of the effects brought on by such changes. You need to manage these changes if your groups are to be effective. For example, in the Home Computers case, understanding these issues might help you resolve the problems encountered by one of the quality circles.

The Organizational System

The final situational input is the **organizational system** surrounding a particular group. Our guiding analytical framework (Figure 11.1), emphasizes the importance of the remainder of the organization. Other groups with which a group must work are an important influence, as we will discuss in Chapter 13. The culture and norms of the organization also influence a group.[14] It is difficult for a group to have norms and power relationships that run counter to the overall organization. For example, the takeover of Conoco by DuPont has created many cultural adjustments for the groups of employees at Conoco (see Box 11.3).

In any organization, there are a number of factors which define its culture—for example, rules, roles of people, provisions for training, and the reward system. And certainly one of the most important of these factors is the reward system. In many organizations, the reward system encourages individual behavior from people who must work in groups. Is it any wonder that groups sometimes have internal conflicts in these situations? In other organizations, the reward system is based on group behavior, and highly effective work teams often result.[15] To be an effective group member or manager, you must work with these situational inputs—by adjusting to them and to their impact on your groups. Then too, you may sometimes be able to alter the situational inputs to yield a more favorable effect on your groups.

Overall, then, we can say that situational and individual factors are important for you to understand as a manager. They do appear to have an impact on **performance** of a group, but perhaps even more important, they have an impact on the development of a group's **structure** and **process** (elements we will discuss in Chapter 12). And in turn, group structure and process directly influence the performance of the group and satisfaction of its members.

Furthermore, the performance of a group serves as feedback to affect the input variables. If a group is successful, new people may desire to join it and thus alter the

Box 11.3

Honeymoon's End:
Du Pont, Once a Hero,
Has Become a Bother,
Many at Conoco Feel

Less than a year ago, Du Pont Co. was a hero to most of Conoco Inc.'s employees. The chemicals giant rescued the coveted oil company from two unwanted suitors—Mobil Corp. and Seagram Co.—and promised there would be no bloodbath, no major shake-up.

But after eight months of living with Du Pont, some Conoco people believe that the $6.8 billion takeover—the biggest ever—has turned out to be a mixed blessing. They tell of anxiety over what Du Pont has in mind for its new subsidiary, of squabbling over who moves into whose office and of more serious conflicts involving corporate style and strategy.

Constructive Relationships

Du Pont says it hasn't been callous in its treatment of Conoco. Rather, it says, it has purposely been making changes slowly to ease the adjustment pains. "All things considered, I'm pleased with the response from the Conoco side of the house," says Du Pont Chairman Edward Jefferson, who has been mingling with Conoco employees in their plants and offices, at Christmas parties and on golf-course fairways. "For every difference of opinion," he says, "I think there is an example of a constructive relationship."

The major culture shock for some Conoco people is Du Pont's financial conservatism. Used to the fast-paced, wheeling-dealing nature of the oil business, they are a bit confounded to find that some Du Pont executives value restoring the company's triple-A credit rating more than making a big oil discovery. "Conoco wasn't nearly as conservative about debt. Their attitude was you borrow like hell to search for oil," says Harold May, a Du Pont man who was appointed vice president of corporate studies this year to help map strategies.

Not as Much Fun

Some chemical workers say they are having fits adjusting to Du Pont's bureaucratic management and its emphasis on paper work. "It was really fun at Conoco Chemicals," an employee says. "You could make mistakes—not the same one twice—and it felt like you really made a difference. But the merger has knocked a lot of that out." He says he recently was called to task for taking the initiative of writing a letter expressing his views on some environmental legislation. Du Pont executives didn't disagree with him. They were just miffed, he says, because he hadn't cleared the letter with them.

By Ronald Alsop, *The Wall Street Journal*, June 16, 1982. Reprinted by permission of *The Wall Street Journal*, © Dow Jones & Company, Inc. 1982. All rights reserved.

group slightly (for example, size increases and composition changes). And if a group is not successful, some members may leave the group while others join, again affecting the composition and perhaps size. Certainly, too, poor performance may lead to changes in physical layout, technology, rewards, and so forth. What you need as a manager or group member is to learn how to improve group effectiveness by managing the input variables. So let us look into some ways to better design groups.

Improving Group Effectiveness by Managing the Input Variables

Perhaps the first step in understanding how to more effectively manage and belong to groups in organizations is to accept the fact that groups are a way of life in organizations. As a manager you must get work done both through formal and informal groups of people. Synergy of effort is the desired goal, in addition to effort directed toward accomplishment of organizational goals. Both informal and formal groups can improve communications and enhance interpersonal relations that are beneficial to the organization, as long as they accept the goals of the organization. Beyond this first step, it is important to recognize that group effectiveness involves many factors. Up to this point we have focused only on the input variables which can be used to design a work group. In Chapter 12, we will focus on the emergent structure and process variables that characterize the daily operation of a group.

For now we need to place the input (design) variables in a framework which will make managing them more understandable. As we pointed out in Chapter 1, managing a group is similar to putting together the pieces of a puzzle—except for three points:

1. There is no guarantee that all the pieces will be present.
2. There is no guarantee that the pieces will fit together.
3. The pieces continue to change through growth and development.

Still, by understanding the variables that must fit together in the puzzle, you will become both a better manager and a better member of groups. The framework we propose is shown in Figure 11.4. It is based on the same

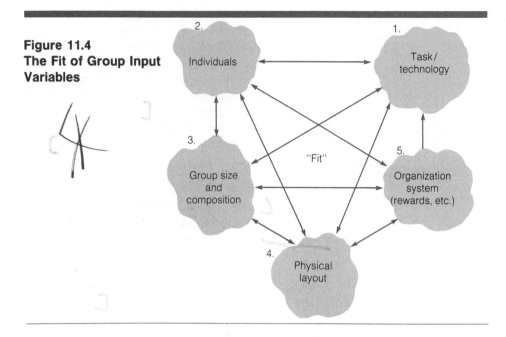

**Figure 11.4
The Fit of Group Input
Variables**

2.
Individuals

1.
Task/
technology

3.
Group size
and
composition

"Fit"

5.
Organization
system
(rewards, etc.)

4.
Physical
layout

concept of congruence that we defined in Chapter 6 in talking about the fit of variables which determine the motivation of an employee. A good fit, or match, between the variables shown in Figure 11.4 should lead to higher group effectiveness. And a continuing fit over time, as these inputs develop, should lead to both long-term and short-term effectiveness.

In using the framework in Figure 11.4, the place to start is with an analysis of the **task/technology** variable. As we have pointed out earlier, the nature of the task/technology seems to influence the effect that other input variables have upon group performance. And the task/technology variable determines the type of people who would best fit in a group. The more complex the task/technology, the more highly skilled people are needed. We should point out that although the technology often cannot be altered by you as the manager, sometimes you can make important changes in the task. As we discussed in Chapter 5 on motivation you can alter the task to make it more intrinsically motivating. Some of these same variables (skill variety, task significance, task identity, autonomy, and feedback) can make the job more or less complex to better fit the people available to the group.

Thus, the second critical variable from Figure 11.5 is the **individuals** who make up the group. As a manager, you need to work toward understanding the personalities, perceptions, abilities, and motivations of the group members. In fact, this information will be useful whether you are the leader of the group or simply a group member. Perhaps through selection or training you can find people who are best suited for the type of task the group must do. Or by understanding the people, perhaps you can alter the task or other variables to fit the people you have. It really does not matter. **The key point is to achieve as good a fit as possible between the people and the task.**

The next fit variable to consider is the **group size and composition**. Usually smaller groups perform better than larger ones. One reason is that the number of interpersonal connections grows rapidly as size increases. And this makes it harder to work out all of the conflicts and communication problems necessary to achieve cohesion. For the same reason, homogeneous groups are easier to manage than heterogeneous groups. Of course, if the group task is complex, group size will need to increase, and the composition will need to be heterogeneous to cope with the task. And in such a case, larger, heterogeneous groups will outperform smaller, homogeneous groups, providing their interactions are well managed. Again, **the fit between size/composition and the task and people is the critical issue to manage**.

In considering the **physical layout** as an input variable, we are essentially returning to the task/technology variable. Often the physical layout will be largely determined by the task/technology, but then too, there is usually some room for adjustment. Usually you want people in a group to be close to one another so they can easily interact, since interaction will help move them through the stages of group development. And interaction also leads to greater cohesion and hence greater effectiveness. But again, the physical layout must be consistent with the other input variables. If people must perform different aspects of the task and the technology suggests that these aspects be performed in different ways, the physical layout of the group may have to separate people. The key then becomes the use of certain group members as links between the different subgroups that will form in each physical space.

Finally, to the greatest extent possible, you should use the **organizational system** (such as rules, procedures, rewards, and goals) to emphasize the group effort. Establish individual jobs which are clearly linked to group goals that have been spelled out to the group members. And then reward behaviors which are consistent with these goals and group effectiveness. A real-life example occurs in a grocery store chain in North Carolina. All departments in each store receive a bonus each month based on the sales of their department—group cooperation is very high. Without group-oriented systems, the situation described first in Box 11.4 can easily occur.

Your actions as a manager, plus the organizational system will determine if a heterogeneous group that may be physically spread out working on unique aspects of the group task will pull together or pull apart. In the Home Computers case, the organizational systems input will be very important in moving the quality circles through the group stages and making them effective in both the short and long term. When a group is homoge-

---

**Box 11.4
Rewarding Groups**

Management consultant Reed Whittle sees significant drawbacks in automatically pushing promising employees to compete. "The idea is to put them all in a dark room with a knife, and the guy who comes out is the best guy," he says. But "while they're in there slicing each other up, the competition is out there slicing you up."

To head off problems from competition, consultants recommend issuing formal performance evaluations regularly and rewarding all producing employees in some way. Thomas Peters, a management professor at Stanford University, cites the reward and evaluation system of Tupperware International, a subsidiary of Dart & Kraft Inc. The sales agents who host Tupperware parties, where the company's household containers are marketed, meet to compare results every week. Mr. Peters says that "unless you're sick, lame, lazy or drunk on the job, you get a ribbon or a prize." The system, he says, "works like a charm; Tupperware is coining the bucks." In 1981, Tupperware earnings accounted for 28% of the parent's pretax profit of $862.8 million.

The Wall Street Journal, July 19, 1982. Reprinted by permission of The Wall Street Journal, © Dow Jones & Company, Inc. 1982. All rights reserved.

neous, small, close together, and working on a simple task, your emphasis on these organizational issues can probably be reduced. However, we would argue that these issues are always important for a manager and a group, given the cultural orientation in our society toward individual performance.

The final point to be made in using Figure 11.4 is for you to manage the developmental aspects of each of the fit variables. Each fit variable can and will change over time.[16] To the degree that you keep the fit variables matched, your group will move through the stages of development more quickly. In starting up a new group, if the input variables are properly matched, the group will move rapidly through the early stages of group development. And to the extent you keep the inputs in congruence, the group will continue to be effective and move toward the final, desirable stage of development.

For example, technology/task variables tend to move from the complex toward the simple over time. At the same time, individuals tend to develop from lower to higher levels of skill. Thus, at the early stages of a group, the technology may be more complex than the people can effectively handle. This means that you as the manager will have to provide skill training, structure, procedures, and rewards to compensate for this mismatch. Over time, the group's skills may surpass the demands of the technology. When this happens, you will need to loosen up on the structure and encourage greater innovation on the part of the group. Again, the point is continuous management of the group input variables discussed in this chapter.

Once the group is set up with the input variables and starts to operate, the emergent structure and process variables in Figure 11.4 come into play. In Chapter 12 we will deal with those issues in detail as we expand your understanding of what you can do to help make work groups effective.

Chapter Highlights   This chapter has marked our shift from the interpersonal level of organizational behavior to the group level.

In introducing this section of the book, we stressed the importance of building upon the interpersonal and individual behavior material discussed in the previous two sections of the book. Furthermore, we pointed out that just like individuals and interpersonal relations, groups move through developmental stages.

We then dealt with the importance to you as a manager of understanding groups. The main reason is that **the essence of management is doing work through groups of people**. Indeed, groups are an essential fact of organizational behavior. And you as a manager, and your people, will belong to several groups within an organization. **Groups are very complex entities to understand**, and our goal in this chapter has been to begin the process of helping you to understand groups.

In the next few pages of the chapter, **we defined a group as a collection of two or more people who exist over some period of time, develop shared norms of behavior, are interdependent, and interact over time for the purpose of achieving some shared set of goals**. To further elaborate the definition, we discussed several types of groups and their developmental stages. We mentioned formal and informal groups, both of which can be a help or a hindrance to an organization. As a manager, your job is to ensure the positive outcomes.

In discussing group development, we presented Tuckman's four-stage model. It was chosen because of its focus on both interpersonal and task elements of development. The first stage of development is called **testing and orientation**. It is the stage where the group members become acquainted with one another and also learn what is expected of them on the task.

The second stage is called **conflict and organization**. In it group members begin to have conflicts over who is the real leader of the group. It is also the time when the norms, standards, and work rules emerge to give the group a sense of organization. Stage 3 is called **cohesion and information exchange**. In this stage group members begin to feel really comfortable with each other. It is at this time that groups are most vulnerable to **groupthink** where they let cohesiveness override analytical processes. But in this stage a group can also become good at exchanging information relevant to the task.

The final stage of group development, which is not reached by many groups, is called **interdependence and problem solving**. At this stage a group works like a team, both in terms of interpersonal and task issues. **This group developmental process is a never-ending process; many factors can cause groups to slide back into previous stages of development.**

We then checked in on Home Computers to give you a chance to look at a real group situation. We then introduced you to a model of group behavior consisting of individual and situational inputs, structure, process, and outcomes (shown in Figure 11.3).

In terms of individual inputs, we stressed how the personalities of different group members might influence, either positively or negatively, group interactions and performance. Perceptions, abilities, and motivations of the group members were also discussed as important inputs. **In order to be an effective manager of a group, you need to manage the potential effects of individual inputs.**

We then went through a more lengthy discussion of the various situational inputs in Figure 11.3. **Group size** was mentioned as an important situational input which affects the interactions of a group. A larger group moves more slowly through the stages of group development.

Group composition, that is the particular combination of people comprising the group, was categorized as either homogeneous or heterogeneous. Homogeneous groups communicate more easily and have fewer conflicts. They work best on simple tasks. But with complex tasks, heterogeneous groups tend to do better.

The task/technology input variable tends to moderate the relationships between the other input variables and group outcomes. When dealing with a simple task/technology, smaller, homogeneous groups can be expected to perform better and to move rapidly through the stages of group development. With complex task/technologies, more effective groups will tend to be larger and more heterogeneous.

Physical layout was treated briefly as a variable closely connected to the task/technology. **The key point was that people who work in close proximity interact more frequently and should be expected to develop as a group more rapidly.**

The final situational input variable we discussed was the **organizational system**. Other groups, as well as rules, procedures, and reward systems are important factors that can affect a group.

In Figure 11.4, we presented a framework for managing group behavior based on a proper fit between all of the individual and situational inputs. In essence, we talked about the process of designing groups for high performance. But because of the developmental aspect of groups, we were also discussing a continuing process of assessment and adjustment among the inputs for a group to have continued high performance.

In using the framework in Figure 11.4, we suggested that the place to start is with an analysis of the task/technology of the group, since it seems to influence the relationship between the other inputs and performance. The next fit variable to consider is the people. By understanding your people, you can work toward a good fit between task/technology and the members of a group.

Next you should consider the size and composition of the group to be sure you design a fit between size/composition and task and people. To the extent that physical layout can be altered, it too should be congruent with the other input variables. Finally, you need to be sure that the design of the group is consistent with the organizational system, in terms of norms, rules, procedures, and rewards.

With the basic understanding you now have of groups and group development, and how to manage the group input variables, we are ready to deal with the action phase of managing group structure and process. And it is to that task we turn in Chapter 12.

Review Questions

1. Why is it important to keep in mind the material we have discussed in Sections II and III of this book (individual and interpersonal behavior) as we explore group behavior in organizations?

2. Why is it important for you as a manager to understand about groups in organizations?

3. Why is the developmental aspect of groups so important in the definition of a group?

4. Why is it important for you as a manager to understand the individual and situational inputs to group behavior shown in Figure 11.3, even though they may be difficult for you to influence?

5. Explain the four stages of group development presented in this chapter. Does this developmental process make sense when applied to groups to which you have belonged?

6. Why do we say that the group development process is a never-ending process?

7. Which aspects of individuals would be most important for you to consider as inputs for understanding group behavior?

8. What are the impacts of group size and composition on the interactions and performance of a group? Why do we say that these two situational inputs are perhaps less important than the task/technology input variable?

9. Explain what is meant by the task/technology input variable and how it impacts on the size, composition, and physical layout input variables.

10. Which aspects of the surrounding organization have influence on group behavior and performance?

11. Explain how Figure 11.4 can be used to help you in the design process for input variables to group behavior and performance?

Notes

1. E. Mayo, *The Social Problems of an Industrial Civilization* (Boston, Mass.: Harvard University, Graduate School of Business, 1945).

2. For example, see M. E. Shaw, *Group Dynamics: The Psychology of Small Group Behavior,* 2d ed. (New York: McGraw-Hill, 1976).

3. W. C. Schutz, "Interpersonal Underworld," *Harvard Business Review,* July–August 1958, pp. 38–56.

4. B. W. Tuckman, "Developmental Sequence in Small Groups," *Psychological Bulletin* 63 (1965), pp. 384–99.

5. I. L. Janis, "Groupthink" *Psychology Today*, November 1971.

6. R. W. Napier and M. K. Gershenfeld, *Groups: Theory and Experience*, 2d ed. (Boston: Houghton Mifflin, 1981), pp. 214–15.

7. Shaw, *Group Dynamics*.

8. This section draws primarily from L. L. Cummings and C. J. Berger, "Organization Structure: How Does It Influence Attitudes and Performance?," *Organizational Dynamics* 5 (1976), pp. 34–49, and R. M. Steers, *Introduction to Organizational Behavior* (Glenview, Ill.: Scott, Foresman, 1981).

9. R. F. Bales and E. F. Borgatta, "Size of Group as a Factor in the Interaction Profile," in *Small Groups*, ed. A. P. Hare, E. F. Borgatta, and R. F. Bales (New York: Alfred. A. Knopf, 1956).

10. This section draws primarily from A. P. Hare, *Handbook of Small Group Research* (New York: Free Press, 1962).

11. This section draws primarily from D. M. Herold, "The Effectiveness of Work Groups," in *Organizational Behavior*, ed. S. Kerr (Columbus, Ohio: Grid, 1979), and W. A. Randolph, "Matching Technology and the Design of Organization Units," *California Management Review* 23 (1981), pp. 39–48.

12. Hare, *Handbook of Small Group Research*, p. 201.

13. D. Cartwright, "The Nature of Group Cohesiveness," in *Group Dynamics*, 3d ed., ed. D. Cartwright and A. Zander, (New York: Harper & Row, 1968), pp. 91–109.

14. T. E. Deal and A. A. Kennedy, *Corporate Cultures* (Reading, Mass.: Addison-Wesley Publishing, 1982).

15. R. E. Walton, "Establishing and Maintaining High Commitment Work Systems," in *The Organizational Life Cycle*, ed. J. R. Kimberly and R. H. Miles, (San Francisco: Jossey-Bass, 1980), pp. 208–90.

16. Walton, "Establishing and Maintaining."

**Resource
Readings**

Hare, A. P. *Handbook of Small Group Research*. New York: Free Press, 1962.

Shaw, M. E. *Group Dynamics: The Psychology of Small Group Behavior*. New York: McGraw-Hill, 1976.

Tuckman, B. W. "Developmental Sequence in Small Groups." *Psychological Bulletin* 63 (1965), pp. 384–99.

Walton, R. E. "Establishing and Maintaining High Commitment Work Systems." In *The Organizational Life Cycle,* ed. Kimberly, J. R. and R. H. Miles. San Francisco: Jossey-Bass, 1980, pp. 208–90.

Managing Group Structure and Process

In the preceding chapter we began our exploration of groups in organizations. Besides stressing the importance of groups to you as a manager, we explained the developmental stages that groups pass through. We focused on your understanding and managing the input variables that create the context for the development of group structure and process. With that background, we are now ready to go inside the operation of a group to study the emerging structure and process and to learn how to manage these key group variables. For your convenience, we repeat our model of group behavior from Chapter 11 and highlight the parts of the model which will be our focus in this chapter (see Figure 12.1).

Once a group has been designed by determining the individual and situational input variables, the group begins to function, and the structure and process variables determine just how successful the group will be. Indeed, **getting the most out of a group depends heavily upon**

Figure 12.1   A Model of Group Behavior

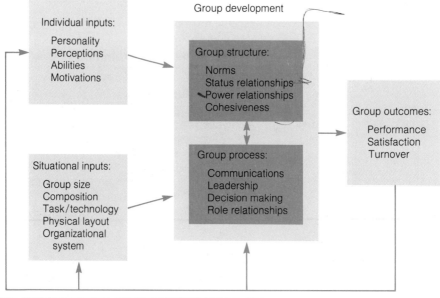

the group structure and process that emerge during the
developmental stages. And as a group manager or member, you will have more direct influence over these variables than over the input variables. In many ways, the
input variables are givens that you work with; they are
constraints on your own and the group's actions (especially when you must work with a preexisting group).
Thus, the structure and process variables become the key
variables for you to understand and learn to manage.
That is our challenge in this chapter.

The Group Structure Variables

As our model in Figure 12.1 reflects, once a group begins
to operate and develop over time, a group structure and
process begin to emerge. Also, the group outcomes serve
as feedback to the emergence of structure and process.
In this section we will explore group structure and how
it develops over time. **Group structure is the pattern of
relationships that develops among group members and
influences the group's outcomes.** As shown in Figure 12.1,
group structure consists of: (1) norms, (2) status relationships, (3) power relationships, and (4) cohesiveness. Each
of these is influenced by the individual and situational
inputs and the group outcomes, and they emerge in a
developmental fashion. Let us review each one in turn.

Norms

**Norms are the rules of behavior that are developed
by group members and which provide guidance to group
activities.** They are present in every group, and in fact,
without norms it would be difficult for a group to exist.
Norms direct the behaviors of individual members toward
the group's goals. As a manager, you must be concerned
that group norms are consistent with the goals of the
organization, because norms are a powerful influence on
group member behavior. If, for example, a group develops
a norm of restricting performance to the minimum re-
quirement, it can be very difficult for you, the manager,
to achieve a higher level of performance.

In a group context, norms usually develop and change
gradually. As group members learn what behaviors are
really important for the accomplishment of group goals,
they develop expected standards for those behaviors. Of

course, it is possible for groups to set norms quickly by verbally agreeing to a particular guiding behavior. For example, a group might decide that everyone on a committee is expected to come to the meetings on time and prepared.

And there are consequences associated with violation of group norms. As a group member, you are expected to adhere to the norms that are developed. But what happens to someone who deviates from the group norms? At first, other group members usually communicate more frequently to try to bring the deviate back into the group. But if the deviate continues to ignore the group norms, a time will come when this person is rejected by the group. Other members may stop talking to, and psychologically withdraw from the deviate. For anyone who saw the movie or read the book, *Lords of Discipline*, the drumming of a cadet out of the military school is a vivid reminder of what can happen to one who deviates from accepted norms.[3] Because he stole gas from a fellow cadet, one of the cadets was forced to walk out of the school down a path lined, on either side, by his peers. As he passed each one, they turned their backs on him, vowing never to speak his name again. (Honesty was a strong norm which this cadet violated.) It is true that such stringent measures are rare in the business world. In fact, having a deviate around may enable a group to more clearly identify group norms for new members.[4] When the deviate person is disciplined by the group, the contrast between the deviate's behavior and that of other group members makes the norms much clearer.

However, all norms do not apply equally to all people in a group. High-status members can ignore group norms more easily than lower-status members. But, even the high-status person must be careful of the side effects of ignoring group norms. As the manager, you might, for example, ignore a norm of being on time for meetings with your work group. In turn, they might not work as hard for you as they would if you respected their norm, or they might be less punctual in coming to work each day.

The Development of Group Norms

With regard to the development of group norms, we can anticipate that different types of norms would be associated with the four stages of group development.[5] During the **testing and orientation stage**, norms develop around who is and who is not a member of the group, attendance, and commitment. Once these issues are basically settled, the group develops norms about leadership, status, ways of doing work, and organization as they move into the **conflict and organization stage**. If the group succeeds at this stage and moves into the **cohesion and information exchange stage**, norms about relationships among group members, ways of showing caring in the group, and the balance between task and interpersonal relationships will develop. During the final stage, **interdependence and problem solving**, a group can be expected to develop norms which relate to how much experimentation will be present, adaptation, and ways of maintaining a highly cohesive group.

Like the group development stages, the focus on norms does not proceed in a highly orderly fashion. There are many factors which influence the development of group norms.[6] Let us briefly comment on how the input variables in Figure 12.1 impact norms. First of all, different individuals respond differently to norms. The more intelligent group members are, the less likely they are to develop and conform to norms. The same is true for people who are authoritarian in nature. For example, a group of research scientists is unlikely to develop norms of behavior as easily as a group of assembly line workers in an auto manufacturing plant. This is because the scientists see themselves more as unique individuals with different values, personalities, and motivations, as we discussed in Chapters 3 through 6.

The size and composition of a group can also influence the development of norms. Larger groups tend to have a stronger sense of norms—perhaps they have to in order to create cohesion among the larger number of people. Homogeneous groups tend to develop norms more rapidly than heterogeneous groups.

As for the task/technology input, the more routine and well defined the task, the quicker norms will develop. But once norms are developed, new, ambiguous tasks may cause groups to fall back on established norms, as a form of security. Indeed, this may be one reason groups tend to resist change so strongly. The physical layout of a group can affect norm development because groups that interact more frequently develop stronger norms, and groups that are in close proximity tend to interact more frequently.

The norms of the larger organization will also influence the development of group norms. Most group norms will be consistent with the organization's norms. If, however, the organization's norms are considered highly unfavorable to the group, the group can develop strong norms that run counter to the organization. A good example of this is the union action that occurs in some organizations.

The group process variables of communications, decision making, leadership, and member roles that emerge also have an impact on group norms (see Figure 12.1). Likewise, the performance, satisfaction, and turnover of the group members will influence group norms. A successful group will tend to maintain existing norms and develop only those new norms that are consistent with existing ones. On the other hand, an unsuccessful group may feel the need to alter the status quo and develop new norms which it hopes will lead to better outcomes.

Status and Power Relationships

Status and power relationships are treated together in this section because of their similarity. Status is the importance ranking that is associated with each of the group members. Not all members will have the same status, and hence, a set of status relationships will develop in a group. These differences in status can be based on individual characteristics, job title, level of authority and responsibility, and possessions, among other things.

For example, in considering group composition as an input, you, as department manager of data processing, might be in a group along with the plant manager and two section heads from accounting, working on an accounting project for the plant. The plant manager would have a higher status than you, but you would have a higher status than the accounting section heads. It is easy to imagine how communications and decision making, for example, might be influenced by this configuration of status relationships.

In addition to these status differences, we might expect power differences, as well. In Chapter 9 we discussed several bases of power: referent, expert, reward, coercive, legitimate, information, connection, and resource. In our example, the accounting section heads may have more expert power than you or the plant manager, since the task is to solve an accounting problem. But you have the resource that they need—namely, your computer system and analysts. Hence there are both power and status differences in this group.

With these differences, inconsistencies that will create conflicts in the group can emerge easily. No one group member has all the status and power variables in his or her favor. Indeed, this may be one of the primary reasons for forming a group in the first place. But these inconsistencies can create problems. During the conflict and organization stage of development, for example, conflicts may be more heated when there are inconsistencies in status and power, and the group might be expected to develop more slowly. However, these differences may also help to clarify the roles for group members and ultimately lead to a very effective group.

What, then, affects the status and power relationships in a group? Individuals bring various status and power bases with them as inputs to a group. Thus, there is an initial set of status/power relationships that already exist when a group is formed. The larger and more heterogeneous the group, the greater the chance of status inconsistencies. The same is true for a complex task/technology and a physical layout that spreads people out. These cases invite status/power differences. But such differences do not always have negative effects on a group. If properly managed, they can be helpful to a group. Take a look at Box 12.1. Do you feel that the power/status differences in the meetings at Corning Glass Works are properly managed? It may be that Mr. Houghton's use of power will crush others in the top management group. Or, will the culture of the organizational system, as discussed in Chapter 11, win out?

As a group begins to develop, the process variables will influence the emergent status/power relationships. While some differences and inconsistencies in status and power may not be apparent during the design of a group, they will become obvious as the group begins to operate. And the performance and satisfaction of group members will feed back into the development of these relationships. A successful group will move forward with the status

Box 12.1
With New Chairman,
Corning Tries to Get
Tough and Revive
Earnings

Corning, N.Y.—Corning Glass Works' management-training program, so the joke on Wall Street goes, consists of three weeks of polo, three weeks of squash and three weeks of platform tennis.

Corning clearly has a reputation for a laid-back management style—a reputation that observers inside and outside the company say is deserved. They blame the company's 41% drop in net income since 1979 partly on management's unwillingness to make difficult, but necessary, decisions on cost cutting, acquisitions and divestitures.

Last week, Corning decided to try to change course. Amory Houghton Jr., Corning chairman and chief executive for almost two decades, stepped down at age 56, and was replaced by his 47-year-old brother, James R. Houghton. The new boss, who had been vice chairman, has a reputation for toughness and is the chief architect of strategy, including management reorganization and extensive writeoffs, that Corning hopes will revive its sagging fortunes.

"I'm viewed around here as a little bit of a hard-ass," says the new chairman, who confesses to having just reread Machiavelli's "The Prince." "I have a reputation for asking hard questions and sometimes not being very nice in meetings. I guess I don't put up with too much explanation for lots of problems."

Changing a Culture

Still, most people believe he won't have it easy. It is hard to change a corporate culture, and the one at Corning has been around a long time.

Moreover, that culture of paternalism and an easy-going, risk-averse style has been provided by the Houghton family, which started Corning 130 years ago here in upstate New York.

and power relationships that were prescribed in designing the group and that emerge during group development. An unsuccessful group will encounter much greater conflict in determining the relationships which will develop.

Cohesiveness

Group cohesiveness is one of the most researched of the group variables. In some ways it is an outcome variable, but most researchers agree that cohesiveness is a property of a group that affects both performance and satisfaction. Hence, it is usually referred to as a group structure variable. **Cohesiveness is the degree to which members of a group are attracted to one another and motivated to work together.**[7] In simpler terms, it is the degree to which a group feels it is a team. As we discussed in Chapter 11, the development of cohesiveness marks one of the four stages of group development. Indeed, without cohesiveness, a group of people cannot really be referred to as a group.

Since group cohesiveness develops over time, it is influenced by the group process variables we will shortly be discussing. In fact, frequency of communications, a process variable, is a key factor influencing the development of cohesiveness. More frequent interactions lead to greater cohesiveness.[8] Frequency of interactions will be influenced by the status/power relationships that develop in the group, by group size, and by the task/technology. Status/power relationships must be resolved during the conflict and organization stage of development for cohesiveness to develop in the group. Internal conflicts can cause problems in developing a sense of cohesiveness for a group.

As group size increases, interactions per person will be more limited because of the finite amount of time for communication. And with the decrease in interactions, cohesiveness will develop more slowly. Increased size also makes it more difficult to agree on common goals and activities. Finally, increases in group size bring about the need for subgroups to form to get the work done. This division of labor is another obstacle to the development of cohesiveness.[9]

With regard to task/technology: The more complex it is, the more interaction is necessary within the group and this should lead to increased cohesiveness.[10] However, the complexity of the task could also make it more difficult for the group to achieve cohesiveness, unless they can agree on some common goals and activities. What this usually means is the group needs an overall goal that everyone in the group wants to achieve.[11]

Of course, agreement on group goals is, at least, partially dependent on the people who make up the group. Compatibility of personalities, perceptions, motivations, and abilities can make the development of cohesiveness easier. Thus, the composition of the group is really the key variable affecting the interpersonal attraction among group members, and the cohesiveness that develops. Research has consistently shown that groups of people who are attracted to one another tend to be become a cohesive group more quickly than if interpersonal attraction is low.[12] But as we discussed in Chapter 11, too much cohesiveness can lead to errors of groupthink. Thus, as a manager you want to consider the personalities, motivations, and attitudes of people making up a group. You must try to form a group in which the people are compatible and can develop cohesiveness. But you must also recognize that some heterogeneity can help avoid excessive cohesiveness, which may lead to groupthink.[13]

Another important factor in the development of cohesiveness is the performance and satisfaction that the group achieves. And this feedback loop reinforces the developmental aspect of the group structure variables. A group that is successful in achieving its goals will develop cohesiveness more quickly than a group that is unsuccessful.[14] Success makes the group members feel good about each other and their efforts to date. It may also make them feel good compared to less successful groups—a sense of superiority that leads to better feelings about each other. On the other hand, failure can lead group members to throw the blame at each other as they search for a scapegoat. It is not hard to see how such conflict could lead to decreased cohesiveness, and perhaps dissolution of the group.

The final factor that can affect cohesiveness is the organizational system input variable. If a group is in an organization that encourages group performance through its reward structure, cohesiveness will tend to increase. Cohesiveness may not increase if the reward system encourages individual performance. Likewise, the greater the resources of the organization, the better chance cohesiveness has to develop. When resources are abundant, little differences can often be overlooked, but when things are tight, little disagreements tend to become magnified and inhibit cohesiveness.

Effects of Cohesiveness

It should be obvious that a cohesive group can accomplish more than one that is not cohesive. The question is, what goals are they working toward? A very cohesive group that sets performance goals consistent with the organization's goals can be very productive. But one that decides to go counter to the organization can be a very powerful negative force. **As a manager, you must work to ensure a compatibility between group and organization goals so that cohesiveness can work for you.** If you do not, you could encounter problems like those described in Box 12.2. Cohesive groups that do not accept the goals of the organization can be very problematic, indeed.

Cohesiveness provides greater satisfaction for the group members, and membership in the group becomes very valuable. Group members want to participate in the group and exhibit great loyalty to it. Cohesiveness also leads to greater communication among the group members and stricter adherence to group norms.

In fact, herein lies the groupthink pitfall. Cohesiveness is an illusive quality for a group, and once it is achieved, groups do not want to give it up, even at the risk of making mistakes and performing poorly. Deviance may not be tolerated in a group that is too cohesive, for fear of rocking the boat. Conformity becomes more valuable than achieving high performance. Your goal as a manager, or as a group member, is to help move the group into the fourth stage of development (interdependence and problem solving) where cohesiveness is high but internal conflict is viewed as a positive norm that will help the group continue to be successful.

Group Process

Now that we have completed our discussion of group structure, we are ready to explore the very important group process variables. **Process variables are the daily interactions that occur as a group works together to accomplish its tasks; they relate to how the group works together.** As such, they represent variables you can influence on a regular basis. Furthermore, you can influence these variables whether you are the group manager or a member of the group. They relate very closely to some of the leadership material we discussed in Chapters 7 and 8.

To explore this point a little further, researchers of

Box 12.2
In an Era of Givebacks,
Members of One Union
Are of No Mind to Give

The more things change, the more the United Electrical, Radio and Machine Workers Union stays the same.

Other unions these days are negotiating contract concessions and persuading members to give back wage and benefit increases in order to save jobs. But to the UE, givebacks will only "leave workers with fewer crumbs than they have now."

Other unions are cooperating with industry in so-called quality circles, or discussion groups in which workers and plant managers try to solve job problems. But the UE calls quality circles "a new tactic for old-fashioned union busting." What's needed is "fewer labor leaders who go to bed with companies" and "more solidarity among workers and standing up to bosses."

If all this sounds like unionism of another era, UE leaders don't think so at all. "The reason for unions hasn't changed since we began"—back in 1937—"and neither have our principles," says Boris Block, the UE's secretary-treasurer, who helped to organize some of the UE's first members.

Aggressive Struggle

In its constitution, the UE pledges to "pursue at all times a policy of aggressive struggle to improve our conditions." And the union still engages in the same kind of militant strikes it was known for in its early days.

Today the UE is a fraction of its World War II-era size. Union officials say membership in the U.S. and Canada totals about 160,000, but outside observers say there probably aren't more than 50,000 dues-paying members in the U.S.

But what the UE lacks in numbers it has in spirit. On picket lines and at labor rallies, UE members are visible and vocal. Many wear jackets stamped with the slogan "The Workers Run This Union," and they lock arms to sing such old labor songs as "Solidarity Forever" and "Which Side Are you On?" "They have more positive feelings about their union and more spirit than a lot of us bigger unions combined," says an official at the 1.2-million-member United Steelworkers Union.

The UE has resisted Westinghouse's efforts to enlist workers in quality circles. The company already has established nearly 1,000 circles, but not at UE-organized plants. "They say we're just one big happy family, but if that's so I have to ask who is the father," says Hugh Harley, UE's director of organizing. "Workers have never run quality circles."

groups make a distinction between group **process** and group **content.** [**Content is the task that group members work on.**] Are they solving a budgeting problem? Are they trying to decide about the introduction of a new product? Are they trying to complete a difficult task in a short period of time? Often, academic training focuses on the content aspects of group work. You learn in courses and seminars what analytical techniques best apply to a given problem. And you learn to make rational decisions. What you often do not receive enough training in is [**group process, which is how a group works together in trying to achieve a quality solution that can be implemented.**] As is pointed out in the best-seller, *In Search of Excellence*, analytical techniques are necessary but not sufficient for solving the often irrational problems you will encounter as a manager.[15] Furthermore, they do not help that much in ensuring that good decisions are implemented. And what good is an excellent decision that is never properly implemented? Since the process aspects of group work deal with these issues explicitly, it is very important that you grasp the concepts that are explored in the following pages. They will be extremely useful to you whether you are the group manager or simply a group member.

Member Participation

As a manager or member of a group, one of the first things you can observe is the participation level of group members. Usually, some people speak up more than others, and some group members have very little at all to say. And there may be shifts in these involvement patterns. Some people may have a great deal to say when information is being shared and less and less to say as decision time approaches. For others the pattern may be just the reverse. What is important for the group is that people participate in a manner appropriate to their ability to contribute.

Over time we would expect group member involvement to even out so that no one member dominates the group, but there will still be differences in involvement level. As we discussed in Chapter 4, some people are just more extroverted than others, so we would expect them to be more involved. **The key concern for you as a manager** is to avoid too much participation by people who really have little to contribute at a particular time and to avoid too little participation by people who are holding back valuable information. People who are not participating need to be drawn into the group; people who tend to dominate need to be toned down. As we will discuss later, there is ample opportunity for all group members to become involved. True group cohesiveness, as well as high performance, are both dependent on active involvement by all group members.

Group Communications

Communication in a group is also one of the easiest of the process variables to observe. Yet, it is extremely important, for it relates to other process variables which we will shortly discuss. As we explored in Chapter 10, communication is the means we have for moving information from one person to another, and it is an extremely complex process to understand fully. However, in a group we can observe who communicates with whom. Seldom do people communicate with the entire group. They tend to make eye contact with people they respect or like, even if their words may be spoken for all to hear. But people may also selectively communicate with only some members of the group, and by noting the communication pattern that emerges, you can better understand the dynamics that are unfolding.

If you were to step back and observe a group of people communicating over a period of time, there are a variety of communication patterns which you might witness. And a number of these patterns have been analyzed in terms of their impact upon various group outcome variables. Let us explore five of these patterns, shown in Figure 12.2.[16]

The first pattern is called the **wheel or star** and looks very much like we might envision an organizational chart. As is shown in Figure 12.2, the wheel is very clear that person X is the leader of the group. Unfortunately, the lack of opportunity for communication for the other group members leads to low levels of member satisfaction. Only the leader is really satisfied in this pattern. And even that may be short lived if the group is working on a complex task, since this pattern is associated with low performance on such tasks. It can, however, be very effec-

Figure 12.2   Five Possible Group Communication Patterns

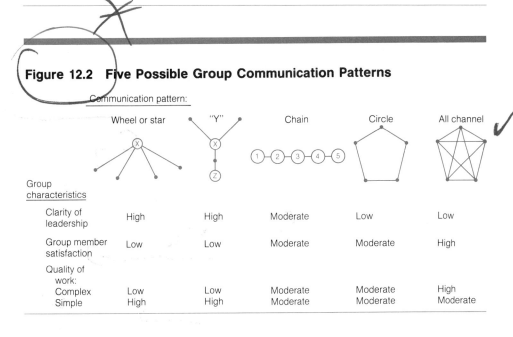

Communication pattern:	Wheel or star	"Y"	Chain	Circle	All channel
Group characteristics					
Clarity of leadership	High	High	Moderate	Low	Low
Group member satisfaction	Low	Low	Moderate	Moderate	High
Quality of work:					
Complex	Low	Low	Moderate	Moderate	High
Simple	High	High	Moderate	Moderate	Moderate

tive on simple tasks where the group members accept the leader's authority. The Y pattern is very similar to the wheel. Indeed, the only real difference is that the person at the bottom of the Y (person Z) is one person further removed from the leader (person X).

The **chain** pattern of communications results when people communicate only with some people in the group but everyone is somehow connected with someone else in the group. Who the leader is is unclear. A variation of this pattern that may be more common in organizations is the formation of cliques within a group. For example, persons 1 and 2 in the chain talk to each other but not to the other three people. And persons 3, 4, and 5 communicate with each other but not with the other two people. It is as though the chain is broken between persons 2 and 3. In such situations, it is also unclear who is leading the group. In fact, with cliques there may be two or more leaders. Member satisfaction tends to be better than the wheel but not as high as some of the other patterns. In terms of performance, these patterns tend to work moderately well for both simple and complex problems. The biggest problem facing groups with these patterns is a lack of coordinated effort. They do not function much like a team, and leadership is also weak.

The **circle** pattern is quite similar to the chain pattern;

the only difference is that the two end people are now connected. And as shown in Figure 12.2, the results associated with the circle are very similar to the results with the chain, including the lack of clear leadership.

The final pattern we will discuss is the **all-channel** pattern. At first glance this network looks like chaos, with everyone talking at once. And indeed, if no one is listening to other group members, it would be chaos. But to depict chaos, we would draw lines from each group member but not connect them to other group members. In other words, ideas would die on the table. With the all-channel pattern, everyone in the group can talk to everyone else, and over time they do. The result is that leadership is unclear because it is shared by all members. As we will discuss later, this is possible because of the many functions that must be performed in a group that exhibits sustained high performance. With the all-channel pattern, group satisfaction tends to be quite high, as does performance on complex tasks. One might even argue that this type of interaction is essential for dealing with complex tasks. On the other hand, if the task is simple, the performance of such a group will be only moderate, primarily because it will take longer than the wheel pattern. And since time is such a valuable resource, it might be better to use the wheel pattern for solving simple tasks, unless you are also concerned with developing your people for long-term effectiveness—as we discussed in Chapters 7 and 8 on leadership.

It should be clear from Figure 12.2 that each communication pattern has strengths and weaknesses. As a manager or group member, you must weigh these trade-offs, remembering both **solution quality** and **implementation** as critical criteria. Later we will provide more guidance for making a decision about the appropriate network. For now, it is enough to recognize the effects of the patterns and to think about how you might alter the pattern as necessary. For example, as a manager in a wheel group, if you feel that pattern is not working, you might consider charging the group with a goal and then leaving the room so that a more all-channel pattern can emerge. For example, President John Kennedy used just such a maneuver to arrive at a decision about how to handle the Cuban missile crisis, when missile sites aimed at the United States were being built in Cuba by the Soviet Union.[17] This tactic helped avoid groupthink and a confrontation with Russia.

Group Decision Making

The missile crisis leads us nicely into the next process variable. Often groups are confronted with problems to solve or decisions to make. How should they deal with a new vacation plan? How should they solve a production problem which is resulting in too high a defective rate? **Decisions which are high in quality (that is, their implementation will resolve the problem) and to which everyone in the group can commit themselves must be made**. As we have pointed out before, a good decision that is not implemented is worthless. But how do groups make decisions? There are several ways, each with its own set of strengths and weaknesses. These decision methods are summarized in Figure 12.3 and explained in the following paragraphs.[18] As you read through this section, think about which of these decision-making approaches best describes the Frito Lay situation described in Box 12-3.

The first method of making a decision is what we might call "decision by default" or **lack of response**. In essence, a group member's idea is decided upon because no one speaks either for or against it. It is simply ignored. In such cases it is difficult to determine either the quality or acceptance of the decision. It may be a good idea that gets ignored or maybe it was ignored because it was

---

Figure 12.3   Ways Groups Make Decisions

	Decision Characteristics			
	Quality			
Decision Method	Complex	Simple	Group Acceptance	Group Time Needed
1. Lack of response	?	?	?	None
2. Authority rule	Bad	Good	?	Very little
3. Minority rule	Bad	Good	Poor	Little
4. Majority rule	OK	Good	Fair	Moderate
5. Consensus	Good	Good	Good	Great deal
6. Unanimous	Good	Good	Good	Very great deal

Source: Edgar Schein, *Process Consultation*, © 1969, Addison-Wesley, Reading, Massachusetts. Pages 53–57 (adapted). Reprinted with permission.

**Box 12.3
The Public Doesn't Get
a Better Potato Chip
without a Bit of Pain**

Dallas—*Twenty managers at Frito-Lay Inc. sit at a conference table, nibbling thick, white tortilla chips. The chips taste good, but the managers aren't here for idle munching.*

Small tortilla-chip makers in the West have been winning customers who like corn chips to eat with meals, rather than just as a snack. Their paler, blander chips are hurting sales of two Frito stars, Doritos and Tostitos. The chips the Frito managers are sampling, a proposed new offering called Sabritas, are supposed to put a stop to that.

But there are problems. The marketing people want Sabritas to be made only of white corn so they will be pale, but Frito-Lay plants now use yellow corn or a yellow-white mix. Will a new grain bin have to be built for the white corn?

Another thing: The competing chips have a twist tie around the top of the bag. Twist ties are expensive and are a bother to put on. But shoppers might not think of Sabritas the way they do the others if Sabritas' bag doesn't look the same.

Wayne Calloway, the company's president, gives the objectors a meaningful look. "Jerry, Jim, we need to get with this one," he says. "We're already late." A committee is formed to solve the problems so that test marketing can begin. The product manager for Sabritas has scored a small victory.

In the Chips

This may seem like a rather elaborate approach to a commodity most people just crunch absent-mindedly. But Frito-Lay didn't get to where it is by taking tortillas for granted. The PepsiCo Inc. subsidiary takes in $2 billion on snack food a year, easily topping big rivals like Nabisco and Borden, not to mention the regional makers. Frito-Lay's earnings from operations have been growing an average of 23% a year, though the pace slowed a bit in recent months. The $311 million Frito earned last year made it the biggest contributor to PepsiCo's profits.

Coming up with new products is essential to keeping this lead, and Frito-Lay is good at it. Company managers consider hundreds of suggestions each year, but their screening process is so tough that only five or six get much past the idea stage. To go from being a gleam in the eye to a bag on the shelf, a new chip has to make it through the test kitchen, consumer taste testing, naming, package design, ad planning, manufacturing and test-marketing. A poor grade on one of the tests—or a poor decision about the name or ad theme—can kill a new product.

A successful one, though, can be worth $100 million or more a year in added revenue. So, although Frito-Lay develops certain products to meet specific competitive threats, its researchers are constantly trying to dream up new ideas simply in hopes of selling more snacks.

By Janet Guyon, *The Wall Street Journal*, March 25, 1983. Reprinted by permission of *The Wall Street Journal*, © Dow Jones & Company, Inc. 1983. All rights reserved.

a bad idea. Who can say? In some cases one such idea is plopped on the table only to be followed by another lack of response decision, and another. The group members are simply not communicating with each other, and nothing can happen. The group is stuck. Perhaps you have been in such a situation and left a meeting feeling that nothing happened.

The second decision form, and one that requires a little more time, is **authority rule.** Here the leader makes the decision for the group. Referring back to the leadership material, the leader is using a directive style. Such decisions can be either good or bad, depending on whether or not the leader has all of the information and skill necessary to make the best decision. In a simple situation, such as having people in the group complete an activity report, you as the leader may have all of the information to make a good decision. The only question may be whether you can get the group to accept the decision and properly implement it. Will they start completing the reports as you desire? A lot will depend on your position power, your relationship with the group, and your presentation of the idea. If, on the other hand, you must decide on a complex matter, such as cutting down on waste in the production process of the group, it may be difficult for you to have all of the information necessary to make a good decision. And the acceptance of an authority rule decision in this situation may be more difficult because there will be many different opinions about how to solve the problem.

The third decision method, **minority rule** (commonly called railroading), involves a little more time and yields about the same results as authority rule. Essentially, a few people in the group make the decision for the group as a whole. If these people have all of the relevant information and a good relationship with the other group members, this method can work very well. But often this is not the case, especially with complex problems, and some group members wind up feeling coerced and are reluctant to accept the "group" decision. Often this results in problems in implementing the decision. For example, the solution to the waste problem mentioned is decided by the minority to be a rotation of jobs so that people can check up on each other and not become bored with a particular task. But some people who were left out of the communication clique that made the decision feel that will just make the situation worse, since people will constantly be adjusting to a new task. Hence, they half-heartedly work through the task changes, making many mistakes and demonstrating how bad the decision was.

The same potential exists with the next decision method, **majority rule**. This method involves voting on the best method for solving the waste problem. Now you may be thinking, what could be wrong with this method? Is this not how all important issues are decided in our democratic society? The possible solutions are presented and discussed until people are ready to vote. Then after the vote everyone accepts and works with the majority decision. This process does result in better quality decisions and greater acceptance than any of the methods discussed so far, but think for a moment about the voting process. Suppose two solutions are being considered. When the vote is taken, five people in the group are for solution 1 and three people are for 2. Thus, you go with solution 1. But what about the commitment of those three people who lost the vote? They lost, and they may not at all like the solution that was chosen. The question is whether they will be able to psychologically commit to implementing a solution they so clearly opposed. Thus we say acceptance may only be fair (see Figure 12.3).

On the quality issue, majority rule has the potential for reasonably good decisions in complex situations. The biggest problem lies with the question of whether all really useful solutions are adequately discussed and presented. The politics of the situation (as discussed in Chapter 9) can enter and affect the rational process of majority rule. People may be tempted not to bring up a solution because of who might be against it. And furthermore since people get labeled both with solutions they suggest and with solutions for which they vote, they will be cautious if there are potential political repercussions. Group members may feel they cannot vote against another group member who is more powerful than they are. Or they may vote for the solution of one group member in order to get something from that member later on. One final point with regard to majority rule; it does take a moderate amount of time, and with the potential problems just mentioned, one can only wonder about our tendency to place so much faith in this method. But what else is left?

Consensus decisions, which we will come back to in a minute, and unanimous decisions still remain to be discussed. In **unanimous decision**, everyone in the group feels a particular solution to the waste problem is the best one. Naturally, this means that acceptance will be high and implementation will be much easier. Clearly, this decision process would be very desirable. The problem is that in order to get a unanimous decision, a great deal *tIne* of discussion must take place, even for relatively simple problems. Perhaps you have been involved in meetings where a "simple" matter seemed to take up a great deal of time. For a complex problem, the discussion to reach a unanimous decision may take far too much time to be practical. There is, however, one exception to this conclusion, and one which you as a manager or group member should monitor. Sometimes groups make a unanimous decision rather quickly because they fall into the groupthink trap, which we have discussed before. What appears to be a unanimous decision is actually a disguised disagreement. People appear to agree when in fact they have reservations. And these reservations come out during implementation or when the group later discovers that a bad decision has been made. Have you ever been in a meeting where everyone seems to agree, but afterward in the hall people begin to raise all sorts of questions about the decision and how it will not work? If so, you have probably been through groupthink.

In order to avoid groupthink, the last decision method, **consensus**, can be utilized. In essence consensus decisions are a cross between majority rule and unanimous decisions. They are like majority rule in that, if people were asked to vote, they might still have their preferences for how to solve the waste problem. But at this point they are also willing to commit to a particular solution and do their best to make it work, which is like unanimous decisions. The psychological commitment is there, even though the analytical process still leaves some questions. In complex situations, the consensus method may be the best you can hope for, since unanimous decisions take too long or may never be achieved. In fact, with complex issues, consensus decisions also take up a great deal of time—but they tend to be worth it in terms of good decision quality and acceptance by group members. Furthermore, the time spent to ensure acceptance may result in a better relationship both among group members and with the leader so that down the road an authority rule decision will have a greater chance of acceptance. This developmental aspect of consensus decisions makes them especially useful for developing a group into a high performing team.

Leadership in a Group

We will be brief here, since we have already spent two chapters on leadership and will return to this variable as we later discuss group member roles. In observing a group to which you belong, you should be aware of who is leading the group. Is it one person, two people, or several group members? As we discussed in Chapter 11, one of the central issues in the conflict and organization stage of group development is: who is the leader? Especially important is whether there is conflict between the appointed group leader and another member of the group who wants to be the leader.

But one of the key aspects of group involvement is that it is possible for there to be more than one leader in a group; in fact, everyone in the group can be a leader. There are many aspects that contribute to the effective functioning of a group, and different group members can exert influence in different areas, thus making everyone a leader. One might even argue that a group which operates like a team will exhibit such leadership by all group members. It will, however, be well coordinated so that conflicts are not dysfunctional. We will return to this point in more detail when we discuss the roles that people can play in a group.

A final point for now on leadership is to observe the methods of influence that group members use in exerting leadership (as discussed in Chapters 7, 8, and 9). Do they use coercive power, expert power, position power—or another base of power? Is their style of leadership directing, coaching, supporting, or delegating? Do the group members' methods vary from time to time as the group moves through its developmental stages and deals with different problems? As we will soon see, answering such questions will help you to better understand what is happening in a group to which you belong.

As a way of integrating some of the group process variables discussed thus far, let us take a look at Figure 12.4. Here we show what leadership style and decision making method is most likely with each of the five communication patterns from Figure 12.2. As the figure shows, the wheel pattern is most likely to be associated with authority rule decisions and directive leadership. The leader is clearly in command in this case. In moving across to the right, the communication patterns open things up for the group members and allow first minority rule and coaching leadership and then majority rule and supporting leadership. And consensus decisions and supporting leadership are most likely with the all-channel communication pattern. With these associations, you might think about which of the three process variables (communications, decision making, or leadership) would be easiest to observe in a group setting. Probably communications, would you agree? Thus, as a group leader or member, if you pay attention to the communications in the group you can learn a great deal about how decisions will be

Figure 12.4   Integrating Communication Patterns with Decision-Making Methods and Leadership Style

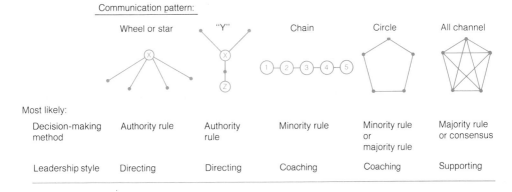

Communication pattern:					
	Wheel or star	"Y"	Chain	Circle	All channel
Most likely:					
Decision-making method	Authority rule	Authority rule	Minority rule	Minority rule or majority rule	Majority rule or consensus
Leadership style	Directing	Directing	Coaching	Coaching	Supporting

made and about the leadership that will be exercised. As we said in Chapter 10, communications are the life-blood of an organization. This statement applies equally well to a group. Let us now turn to the final group process variable, group member roles.

Group Member Roles

In observing a group over time it is possible to see many types of behaviors exhibited by the group members. Three categories of behavior, which we will call **roles**, are particularly important as they relate to group effec-tiveness: self-oriented roles, task roles, and maintenance roles. Some examples of these types of roles are shown in Figure 12.5. In almost any group to which you belong, it is possible to see people performing all three types of roles. **Self-oriented roles** are behaviors that are self-serv-ing and actually hinder the performance of a group. A **blocker** is someone who always seems to get in the way of group progress toward completion of its task. The **rec-ognition seeker** tries to gain personal distinction, even at the expense of the group. Such people are not team players. A **dominator** tries to run everything, whether it is best for the group or not. And an **avoider** just does

Figure 12.5   Three Categories of Group Member Roles

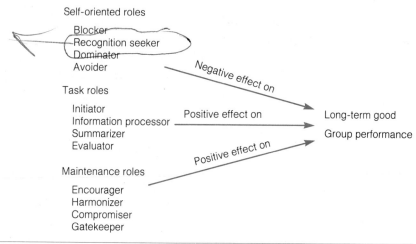

Self-oriented roles

Blocker
Recognition seeker
Dominator
Avoider

Task roles

Initiator
Information processor
Summarizer
Evaluator

Maintenance roles

Encourager
Harmonizer
Compromiser
Gatekeeper

Negative effect on

Positive effect on

Positive effect on

Long-term good

Group performance

not contribute to the group and cannot be counted on. As we might expect, research has shown the presence of these roles in a group to be associated with poor performance.[19]

We now turn to the more positive side of the group-roles picture as we look at **task** and **maintenance** roles. And these types of activities in a group should ring a bell for you. They are essentially the same as the two key dimensions of leadership which we focused on in Chapters 7 and 8. **Every group must not only get the task done, but also maintain itself over time as a group**. And the task and maintenance roles shown in Figure 12.5 are instrumental in accomplishing these two ends. Research has found support for a positive relationship between the performance of task and maintenance roles and group effectiveness.[20]

Let us look into the task roles. An **initiator** is someone who offers many ideas and suggestions to a group. The **information processor** both seeks and gives information that will be useful to the group in performing its task. The **summarizer** restates, clarifies, and organizes the information and ideas which are offered and helps the group remain clear about its goals. The **evaluator** helps the group test its ideas and problem solutions against logical and rational benchmarks, and also helps select the best alternative decision from among several choices.

As for the maintenance roles, the **encourager** praises the ideas and contributions of others and supports the efforts of other group members. The **harmonizer** acts to resolve differences of opinion and reduce tension that may develop in a group. Similarly, the **compromiser** tries to help group members locate an acceptable middle ground which everyone can support. This function is invaluable in helping the group achieve a consensus in a complex situation. Finally, the **gatekeeper** ensures that everyone gets a chance to speak openly by drawing out people who sit back or toning down the dominators in the group.

These task and maintenance roles are important for a group to perform in order to be effective. Which roles are most vital will vary as the group works through a problem, and even from one group development stage to another. For example, during the testing and orientation stage, the gatekeeper and initiator roles would prove helpful in providing the group with the guidance and involvement that is needed to get off to a good start. During the conflict and organization stage, the summarizer, information processor, harmonizer, and compromiser roles can help a group resolve the inevitable conflicts and move into the productive stage of cohesion and information exchange. During this and the final stage of interdependence and problem solving, almost all of the roles are important if the group is to maintain a record of high performance. In the ebb and flow of daily activities, the emphasis on particular roles may be high or low, but over time, an effective group will take care of both task and maintenance needs, while avoiding the self-oriented roles.

We can summarize this point by looking at Figure 12.6. As with the leadership material we place the performance of task roles on the horizontal axis and the performance of maintenance roles on the vertical axis. Then, by observing which roles are present and which are absent, we can categorize a group into one of the four cells in Figure 12.6. A group which has many of the task roles present but few of the maintenance roles could be called a **task-oriented group**. In the short run, this might be

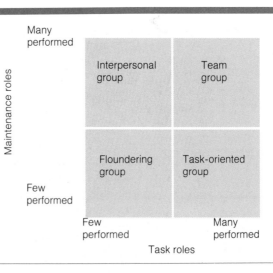

**Figure 12.6
Types of Groups
Based on
Performance of Task
and Maintenance
Roles**

appropriate to meet a deadline or with a temporary committee, but over the long haul, such a group will tend to die from the inside out. As a leader or member of such a group, you could be of most help by performing some of the maintenance roles to help move the group into the team category.

The **team group** is one with both task and maintenance roles performed; **the team group should be the best performing group over the long run.** If you are the leader of such a group, you can delegate much of the work to the group and free yourself to work more with your peers and superior. If, however, your group is high on the maintenance roles, but low on the task roles, we call this an **interpersonal group.** Here, you as the manager need to provide the task roles so the group will not love itself to death and ignore the task that must be performed.

Finally, the **floundering group** has neither task nor maintenance roles. It is probably not very effective and needs both task and maintenance roles performed. But can you as manager do both simultaneously? Probably not. Hence, drawing upon the leadership material from Chapters 7 and 8, we suggest that a directing style focusing on the task roles should be applied first. Then as the group experiences some success, you can back off the task roles and focus more on the maintenance roles. Or perhaps someone in the group will start to take up this slack. **The key point here is that leadership style and group roles are quite interconnected.** To positively influence a group, you need to determine which roles are missing that would be present in a team group. Then you can try to perform those roles to help the group move toward a team. And in this case, you can use Figure 12.6 to help you exercise this kind of influence in a group even if you are not the appointed leader. As a way of further focusing your attention on these roles, turn now to the end of the chapter and complete the Group Roles Survey—what roles do you feel you usually perform in a group?

Now let us turn to the Home Computers case to see how our knowledge of group structure and process can help us better understand what is happening in the problematic quality circle from Chapter 11.

Application to the Home Computers Case

One of the quality circles started by the consultant encountered problems as soon as the consultant left. Many conflicts surfaced, the group was very disorganized, meetings were difficult and unproductive, and people began to avoid the meetings of the circle. A <u>norm</u> seemed to develop rather quickly that the meetings <u>were not important</u> and you should go only if you had nothing else to do. Jim Andrews, the leader of the team, was <u>outranked in the organizational hierarchy</u> and in terms of experience, and could not seem to get the team members to follow his lead. The group just was not very cohesive and looked like it would soon self-destruct. Wisely, the leader went to the consultant for help.

Jim's first questions dealt with why he had been placed in such a difficult situation. He did not have either the status or the power to influence the group in the desired direction. The consultant's answer was that Jim was the only person for the job. This quality circle was in the relatively new schools and libraries product area, and most of the people available were excellent technically, but <u>lacked the managerial expertise</u> needed. On the other hand, while Jim was young and relatively new with the company (two years), he did have a Master's degree in Business Administration, as well as an engineering degree. Unfortunately, the group was developing in the wrong manner. The consultant told Jim she would work with him to teach him how to better manage the group by understanding the communications, decision-making, and leadership aspects of the group. Then they would work with the entire group on the same task. Jim agreed, though he had his doubts.

Sally Barnes, the consultant, began to explain the process side of group development to Jim. She also explained the stages of group development. Together, Sally and Jim determined that the group was stuck in the conflict and organization stage of development. After explaining the process variables of communications, leadership, decision making, and roles, Sally helped Jim analyze the quality circle in terms of these variables in hopes of gaining an understanding of how to correct the situation.

First they looked at the communications in the group. Sally asked Jim who did most of the talking. Jim said he did. Sally asked if people in the circle listened to Jim. His response was, "I am not sure." Sally decided to attend the next meeting of the quality circle to explain how she wanted to help them become a real team and to observe the group in action. Jim was right; he did most of the talking but few people really listened. At times, the group would override Jim and make decisions. Things were really out of hand.

After the meeting, Sally and Jim discussed what had happened. She told Jim that he was running the group in a very directive manner. The communications mostly came from Jim, and sometimes the others did not listen to him too well. She said that a particular clique of engineers railroaded a number of decisions.

Sally then explained how consensus decisions can be used to achieve high quality decisions to which everyone is committed. She suggested that Jim did not have all of the information needed to make a high-quality decision. And he did not have the power or status to get the group to accept his decision. Yet, their acceptance of a high quality decision was critical for implementation that would solve their problems. Sally suggested that Jim needed to use a more participative style of leadership to provide structure and also get everyone involved.

"But how can I do that?" asked Jim. "The group does not seem to respect me. How will I be able to get them involved?" Sally showed Jim a diagram similar to Figure 12.6. She explained about the task and maintenance roles, and they identified the group as being an interpersonal group—high on maintenance roles and low on task roles. What the group needed was someone to perform some task roles to help push them toward the team group. "Of course," said Sally, "you will have to carefully select the roles to play to avoid coming across as too directive." Jim suggested that perhaps he could be more of an information seeker and summarizer of the ideas of others. By using this approach maybe he could get others to initiate ideas and could draw out Sam and Mary, who were excellent at evaluating solutions to problems. They also decided that while the group was high on some maintenance roles, it lacked a harmonizer and compromiser. People encouraged each other in their cliques and communicated freely in the cliques, but the conflicts between cliques, and between the group and Jim were ignored. Thus, Jim decided to speak to Harold in private to encourage him to serve these roles. Harold seemed to have the respect of most of the circle members.

Jim immediately put his plan into action. Sally continued to observe and to help Jim and others play their roles effectively. Gradually, the group became more cohesive and productive. People attended meetings more regularly, as a new norm of interest in the group developed. The circle gained a new respect for Jim and his ability to bring the group together. Finally, the group began to come up with some good solutions to the problems confronting them. Within about six months, this quality circle was operating as an effective team.

What can we learn from this episode from Home Computers? First, we can see the need for you, as a manager in such situations, to be a problem solver. This means that you must collect facts on group process (communications, decision making, and leadership), determine what the group's problems are, and determine solutions which will hopefully solve the problems. A recognition of the power/status differences, norms, and cohesiveness (group structure variables) will certainly be helpful in this process. By observing the communications in the group, the consultant was able to determine a great deal about both Jim's style of leadership and the decision making approach of the group. This analysis helped Jim determine the leadership/decision making approach which seemed best for this quality circle.

The second point to be emphasized is that Jim still needed some guidance as to how to be the kind of leader that the group needed. By analyzing the roles being performed in the group, he and Sally were able to determine some specific actions which Jim could engage in to implement the chosen leadership/decision-making approach. In other words, the role analysis helped make Jim's job a lot more explicit. Also, by taking the perspective of analyzing the roles performed in the group, Jim had something he could monitor as the group progressed.

And progress they did. As the case ends, we see that this quality circle has become both cohesive and quite productive. If we could now observe this group, we would probably find a good balance between the task and maintenance roles. Furthermore, this should free Jim from having to shoulder the entire burden of the group. He can delegate responsibility to the group and work with them to achieve positive ends. And as long as the group can keep focused on the goals of the organization, they should be very productive as a quality circle.

However, we must give several caveats here. If there is much turnover of personnel in the circle, some of the cohesiveness could be decreased, and the group could slide back into previous stages of development (such as conflict and organization). Second, if new procedures, techniques, or tasks are introduced for the group to deal with, this too could bring about the need for reanalysis and adjustment to the new situation. Third, other groups in the organization, with which this group must interact, could create forces for change in the quality circle. For example, the production department could make some changes which would affect the engineering department. And this is the topic we will discuss in the Chapter 13. But first let us summarize what we have learned about groups in these last two chapters.

What a Manager Should Know about Groups

If you are about to take over a group at work or join one as a member, the first thing you should do is to analyze the people who make up the group and the situational aspects of the group. What kind of task does the group have to perform? What is the size and composition of the group? What are the people like in terms of personality, abilities, and motivation? By drawing on the material from Chapter 11, you can then determine whether there is a fit between the people and the situation. Are the conditions ripe for a successful group? If not, maybe you can alter something about the people or the situation to achieve a better fit. And of course, if you are starting up or joining a new group you have the opportunity to more immediately influence these factors.

The second thing to do is to determine the stage of group development. What are the problems facing the group currently? By analyzing the group structure that exists and the nature of group processes, you can determine the stage of group development. And knowing this, you can better predict where the group is headed next. The process variables, especially, can be helpful in analyzing where a group is and where it is headed. They are relatively easy to observe, and they clearly affect the emerging structure variables. And if problems are developing with norms, cohesiveness, and power and status relationships, the process variables serve as early warning signals.

Conversely, the structure variables for an existing group may help you understand why the process variables are problematic. A group that has status and power problems, for example, will probably exhibit communications and decision making difficulties. And a group with strong cohesiveness and norms that conflict with the organization may be using their process variables to work against the organization. Your analysis of these variables can prove most useful in determining what you can do to help get the group on the right track. And, you may say, "What is the right track?"

A group that is functioning well will exhibit several key properties, aside from good performance. And problems in these areas may foretell problems in the group's performance down the road. First, **group members should be willing to argue with one another about ideas and opinions without the argument becoming too personalized.** They should avoid arguing just to win an argument. The goal should be the best for the group. Second, group members take the responsibility for **both hearing what others say and for getting their ideas across.** Closely tied in here is the fact that group members are willing to change their minds. They want the best for the group, not just to get their own ideas across. Third, **all members of the group perform roles which are important for the group (that is, task and maintenance roles)** and avoid performing self-oriented roles. In other words, they all serve as leaders of different functions which the group must have performed. Remember, the reason for having a group in the first place is to achieve a whole which is greater than the sum of the parts, that is, synergy. **Groups are difficult to run effectively over time, and if synergy is not achieved, the group may not be worth the trouble.** We believe that if you make the effort to use the material covered in these last two chapters you can be both a good group leader and a good group member.

Chapter Highlights

In this chapter we have completed our analysis of what happens inside groups in organizations. Having looked at the design aspects of groups in the last chapter, we focused on the emergent properties of groups in this chapter. We first looked at group structure variables and then at process variables.

Group structure is the pattern of relationships which develop in a group over time and influence outcomes. It consists of norms, status relationships, power relationships, and cohesiveness. **Norms** are the rules of behavior which provide guidance to group activities. They develop over time and provide a basis for determining what is expected of people in a group. **Each group will develop its own unique set of norms in its own unique way.**

We then treated **status and power relationships** together because of their similarity. **Status** is the importance ranking associated with each group member, while **power** relates to the sources of influence that each group member has to draw on. Both variables relate to the different group members' abilities to influence the behavior of other group members. Status/power differences also help us understand some of the conflicts which arise in a group. People bring to the group varying positions in an organization and varying bases of power, but the emergence of relationships is influenced by the group processes which transpire over time.

Next we dealt with one of the most heavily researched group variables—cohesiveness. **Cohesiveness** is the degree to which group members are attracted to one another and motivated to work together. Cohesiveness develops over time and is influenced by input variables, group process, **and group performance**. To the extent that a group performs well together, they tend to become more cohesive. We mentioned two important negative effects of cohesiveness for you as a manager to keep in mind. First, a cohesive group that does not accept the organization goals can be a serious problem. And second, a cohesive group can fall prey to groupthink, resulting in serious mistakes affecting their performance.

Next we looked at **group process variables which are some of the most important variables for you to understand in working with and in groups.** We say this because they occur every day and because you can start to change these variables more quickly than the other group variables we have discussed. We made a distinction between group content and group process. **Content** is what the group is doing, while **process** is how the group is doing it. Process includes member participation, communications, decision making, leadership, and group member roles.

We first discussed **member participation** as a vehicle for you to focus on whether all of the group's resources are being utilized. Next we discussed one of the key process variables because of its relationship to all of the other ones. **Communication** is an easy variable to observe. We discussed five patterns of communications: wheel, Y, chain, circle, and all channel. The wheel pattern seems to be most effective with simple tasks and problems, though it tends to result in low group member satisfaction. At the other extreme, all-channel communication seems to work best with complex problems and tends to also result in high member satisfaction.

Then we turned to group **decision making** and made the point that group decisions must not only be of high quality, but also acceptable to those who must implement them. We discussed six approaches to decision making: lack of response, authority rule, minority rule, majority rule, consensus, and unanimous. Each of these approaches was described and related to time needed, quality of decision and acceptance.

We then discussed leadership in a group. The key point here was that **it is possible to have more than one leader in a group; indeed, everyone in an effective group can be a leader if it is handled properly**. We also pointed out how communication, decision making, and leadership are interrelated. The wheel pattern of communication is often seen with authority rule and autocratic leadership. On the other hand, the all channel pattern is often associated with consensus decisions and participatory leadership.

The final process variable we discussed was group member roles. There are three types of roles: self-oriented roles which are dysfunctional for the group, and task and maintenance roles, both of which serve useful purposes for the group. After defining a number of these roles, we defined four types of groups depending on the presence of these roles: task-oriented group, interpersonal group, team group, and floundering group. And we talked specifically about how you can use this grid (Figure 12.6) to be a better group member or manager.

We then went back to the Home Computers quality circle, mentioned in Chapter 11 as having some problems, and explored the group using some of our new tools.

In closing the chapter, we summarized what a manager should know about groups. First determine if there is a fit between the people and the situation. Second, determine the stage of group development. And third, study the group's structure and process to determine what actions you can take to improve performance. The final paragraph then summarized what a well-functioning group should look like to achieve the synergy that justifies the effort it takes to make a group work.

Review Questions

1. What is group structure and why do we say that it develops over time?

2. What kinds of norms might we expect to be associated with each of the four stages of group development?

3. Why do status and power differences develop in a group? What effects can these differences have?

4. Why do we say that cohesive groups can create problems for managers?

5. Why is it important for you to understand group process variables in addition to analytical aspects of content?

6. Why are different communication patterns effective when dealing with complex tasks as opposed to simple tasks?

7. In deciding which of the six decision-making approaches to use, what factors should you as a manager keep in mind?

8. How do leadership, communication, and decision making interrelate in the functioning of a group?

9. How can you use group member roles to help you determine the leadership needs of a group?

10. What are the characteristics of a group that is functioning well?

Notes

1. R. W. Napier and M. K. Gershenfeld, *Groups: Theory and Experience,* 2d ed. (Boston: Houghton Mifflin, 1981), p. 122.

2. L. Berkowitz and R. C. Howard, "Reactions to Opinion Deviates

as Affected by Affiliation Need and Group Member Interdependence," *Sociometry* 22 (1959), pp. 81–91.

3. P. Conroy, *Lords of Discipline* (Boston: Houghton Mifflin, 1980).

4. R. A. Dentler and K. T. Erikson, "The Functions of Deviance in Groups," *Social Problems* 7 (1959), pp. 98–107.

5. D. A. Nadler, J. R. Hackman, and E. E. Lawler, *Managing Organizational Behavior* (Boston: Little, Brown, 1979), pp. 124–26.

6. This section draws primarily from H. T. Reitan and M. E. Shaw, "Group Membership, Sex Compositions of the Group, and Conformity Behavior," *Journal of Social Psychology* 99 (1969), pp. 45–51.

7. M. E. Shaw, *Group Dynamics: The Psychology of Small Group Behavior* (New York: McGraw-Hill, 1976).

8. G. C. Homans, *Social Behavior: Its Elementary Forms* (New York: Harcourt Brace Jovanovich, 1961).

9. E. J. Thomas and C. F. Fink, "Effects of Group Size," *Psychological Bulletin* 60 (1963), pp. 371–84.

10. W. A. Randolph and F. E. Finch, "The Relationship Between Organization Technology and the Direction and Frequency Dimensions of Task Communications," *Human Relations* 30 (1977), pp. 1131–45.

11. M. Sherif, *Group Conflict and Cooperation: Their Social Psychology* (Boston: Routledge & Kegan Paul, 1967).

12. A. J. Lott and B. E. Lott, "Group Cohesiveness as Interpersonal Attraction: A Review of Relationships with Antecedent and Consequent Variables," *Psychological Bulletin* 64 (1965), pp. 259–309.

13. N. R. F. Maier, "Assets and Liabilities in Group Problem Solving: The Need for an Integrating Function," *Psychological Review* 47 (1967), pp. 239–49.

14. M. Sherif and C. Sherif, *Groups in Harmony and Tension* (New York: Harper & Row, 1953).

15. T. J. Peters and R. H. Waterman, Jr. *In Search of Excellence* (New York: Harper & Row, 1982).

16. This section draws from H. J. Leavitt, "Some Effects of Certain Communication Patterns on Group Performance," *Journal of Abnormal and Social Psychology* 46 (1951), pp. 38–50; H. Guetzkow and H. Simon, "The Impact of Certain Communication Nets upon Organization and Performance in Task-Oriented Groups," *Management Science* 1 (1955), pp. 233–50; and A. Bavelas, "Communication Patterns in Task-Oriented Groups," in *The Policy Sciences,* ed. D. Lerner and H. D. Lasswell (Palo Alto, Calif.: Stanford University Press, 1951).

17. I. L. Janis, *Victims of Groupthink* (Boston: Houghton Mifflin, 1972).

18. E. Schein, *Process Consultation* (Reading, Mass.: Addison-Wesley Publishing, 1969), pp. 53–57.

19. W. A. Randolph and S. A. Youngblood, "An Analysis of Group Processes: The Relationship Between Performance of Group Roles and Task Effectiveness of Interacting, Problem-Solving Groups" (paper presented at the National Academy of Management meeting, Atlanta, 1978).

20. Ibid.

**Resource
Readings**

Dyer, W. G. *Team Building: Issues and Alternatives*. Reading, Mass.: Addison-Wesley Publishing, 1977.

Homans, G. C. *Social Behavior: Its Elementary Forms*. New York: Harcourt Brace Jovanovich, 1961.

Janis, I. L. *Victims of Groupthink*. Boston: Houghton Mifflin, 1972.

Napier, R. W., and M. K. Gershenfeld, *Groups: Theory and Experience*. 2d ed. Boston: Houghton Mifflin, 1981.

Schein, E. *Process Consultation*. Reading, Mass.: Addison-Wesley Publishing, 1969.

Group Roles Survey

Think about past times when you have participated in group work. Perhaps it was a task group or committee at work or a student project group. Did you:

	Never	Seldom	Often	Frequently
Task Behaviors				
1. Initiate ideas or actions	1	2	3	4
2. Facilitate introduction of facts and information	1	2	3	4
3. Clarify issues	1	2	3	4
4. Evaluate issues	1	2	3	4
5. Summarize and pull together various ideas	1	2	3	4
6. Keep the group working on the task	1	2	3	4
7. Ask to see if group is near decision (Take consensus)	1	2	3	4
8. Request further information	1	2	3	4
Maintenance Behaviors				
1. Support and encourage others	1	2	3	4
2. Reduce tension	1	2	3	4
3. Harmonize (Keep peace)	1	2	3	4
4. Compromise (Find common ground)	1	2	3	4
5. Encourage Participation	1	2	3	4
Self-oriented Behaviors				
1. Express hostility	1	2	3	4
2. Seek Recognition	1	2	3	4
3. Avoid Involvement	1	2	3	4
4. Dominate Group	1	2	3	4
5. Nitpick	1	2	3	4

Now look at which roles you feel you frequently perform. Are they mostly task, maintenance, or self-oriented roles? Which of the four group types discussed in the chapter (task-oriented, team, interpersonal, or floundering) do you encourage with your actions?

Source: Adapted by permission from *Organizational Behavior*, Third Edition, by Hellriegel, Slocum and Woodman; copyright © 1976, 1979, 1983 by West Publishing Company. All rights reserved. Page 216.

Managing Intergroup Conflict and Coordination

In this chapter we shift our focus to the interactions that occur between groups in an organization—that is, to intergroup behavior. As we have discussed in the last two chapters, groups are an important element in the makeup of any organization. As organizations grow, managers break down tasks for groups of people to perform. And if there are several groups working on different tasks related to the overall organizational goal, then there will have to be interactions among these groups, just as there are interactions among the people in the organization. It is important to you as a manager to learn to manage these intergroup interactions. You must learn to manage the conflicts that arise and achieve a coordinated effort.

The Importance of Understanding Intergroup Behavior

As we turn our attention to intergroup behavior, we are actually beginning to look at the organization as a whole. This chapter is a bridge between the behavior of people in organizations and the behavior of organizations. As we proceed, it is important for you to understand that we are building on all the material on individuals, interpersonal behavior, and group behavior that we have discussed in the first 12 chapters. Effective management of intergroup behavior is contingent on using this previous material as a basis. And you must learn to deal with the dynamics of intergroup behavior if you aspire to upper management levels. A look at any organization chart makes it clear that, as you move up the hierarchy, you move from managing people to managing groups of people. For example, Figure 13.1 depicts career situations where you might find yourself over time. As a young production manager, you are responsible for the seven workers below you, that is, for one group of people. But later in your career, as product manager, you are responsible for the four groups under the two subassembly managers.

Even at relatively low levels of an organization, you and your group are affected by the actions of other groups in the organization. For example, in Figure 13.1, as production manager you may manage the first-shift operation, while manager A manages the same work on second shift. If A's people leave the machines in a broken-down state, that will create problems for you. But if A warns

Figure 13.1   A Typical Organization Chart

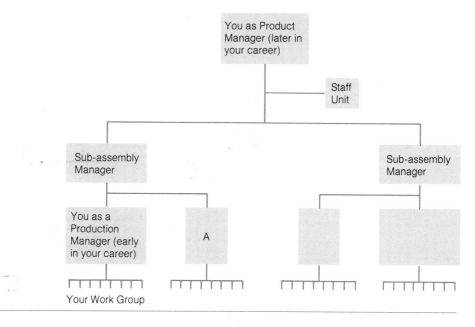

you about a problem they had on second shift, you may be able to avoid a downtime loss. As we shall explore, these intergroup interactions can make the difference between your success and failure as a manager.

In many ways, the management of intergroup interactions is really a balancing act. Will the interactions result in conflict or in coordinated effort? When groups of people are placed in a situation where each group develops a unique culture because of the different tasks they must perform, where groups must compete for scarce resources, and where interaction must take place, it is not surprising that there is a potential for conflict. Yet these same factors can help to create needed specialization within a well-coordinated, whole organization. Unfortunately, the rational behavior choices intended by top management are not always possible between groups. Sometimes, the ambiguity of a situation or the desires of one individual or group may make political actions (such as those discussed in Chapter 9) necessary. For these reasons, the task of managing and living with intergroup behavior is difficult.

You may ask, "why are organizations made up of interacting groups with different goals and different perspectives?" The answer has to do with the growth of an organization. As we saw with the Home Computers case in Chapter 1, the starting organization consisted of only two people. But as the company grew, and more and more people were added, it was not possible to run the company as one big group. Some people had to sell the product while others produced it and still others designed it. Such specialization is necessary for organizations to deal with the uncertainty that always exists in running a business. By breaking the organizational task into parts, each part of the overall task can be better managed. The problem is that this division of labor creates problems of coordinating the efforts of different organizational subunits. It also creates the potential for intergroup conflict that develops over time as an organization grows and adjusts to technological and product changes.

Our focus in this chapter is on how to achieve the coordinated effort that is necessary among groups in an organization if success is to be achieved. To do this, we want to explore why there is the potential for conflict among groups. We also want to explore both the positive and negative aspects of intergroup conflict. Yes, there are some positive aspects. Finally, we want to explore both ineffective and effective ways to manage conflict in an organization and thus create coordinated intergroup effort. However, before we embark on these tasks, let us visit Home Computers to gain a more realistic perspective on the topic for this chapter.

Intergroup Behavior at Home Computers

As Home Computers has grown from a fledgling company operating out of a garage, it has developed specialization along several functional lines. Production is handled primarily out of two plants (one in Denver and one in Dayton). Attached to each plant are salespeople, accountants, and design engineers. As the largest and oldest plant for Home Computers, the Dayton plant is looked upon as the guiding light for the company, especially since the corporate offices are also there.

Over the years, the Dayton plant moved into assembly-line production and became very bureaucratic. Some of the original employees left during this transition, feeling that the company had become too rigid. But production had to become more highly structured, since the plant was using three shifts. Furthermore, production errors were very costly, and not every computer that went out the door could be completely tested for defects. Production quantity fell off and product quality became an issue as customers complained to the salespeople.

Further, the salespeople were constantly complaining about the slowness and poor quality coming out of the plant. The home computer industry was fast moving, and people expected machines that worked right all the time and for a long time, too. The salespeople had to focus on short-term goals and problems, and they knew that their pay depended directly on the volume of sales they could generate.

To deal with the frustration of the production problems, the salespeople often distorted information sent to production on their sales orders. Primarily they indicated a deadline earlier than was actually needed. They complained to management that production would not cooperate with their needs. And they also restricted their contact with the production people as much as they could. They drew together as salespeople and worked hard to outsmart the production people. One sales rep was even heard to say, "We have to do everything we can to protect ourselves and our customers from the problems in production."

On the other hand, the people in production felt the salespeople were unorganized and made impossible demands. As a result, production would also distort information about meeting the sales deadlines. Even when it was possible to meet the deadlines, they gave reasons why they could not get the job done as requested. In fact, some production people would do things to put production behind schedule just to hurt the salespeople. If confronted with these problems, the production people would refer the problem up the hierarchy, saying that if they had better lead time and planning from sales, they could do their job right. But if they were rushed, quality problems were likely to occur.

As Harvey met with the consultant to discuss the problems between sales and production, he was hoping she would have some ideas about what to do. How could he keep his very successful organization from going down the tubes because of the conflict and lack of coordination between sales and production?

Intergroup Conflict as a Developmental Process

Imagine yourself as the consultant to Home Computers. What would you tell Harvey? How would you analyze the situation to determine the causes of the problems facing the company? It is clear that there is conflict between sales and production when there needs to be cooperation. Why does this happen? What is causing the groups to be in conflict? How could they avoid conflict and achieve coordination? The issues of conflict and coordination in intergroup behavior are crucial for you to learn to manage, as your career develops. So let us explore answers to these questions.

In beginning to answer the questions, let us define intergroup conflict. **Intergroup conflict exists when one group attempts to achieve its goals at the expense of the goal attainment of another group in the organization.** Thus conflict is the opposite of the desired cooperation and coordination between groups in an organization, and unfortunately it is all too common. To complete the definition of conflict, we need to recognize that **intergroup conflict is a cyclical process involving four repeated steps: frustration, conceptualization, behavior, and outcome.** Figure 13.2 illustrates the process of conflict and its cyclical nature.[1]

The first step in the conflict process is the **frustration** which develops when a group feels blocked from achieving a goal. Examples might include blockage from a performance goal, from the completion of a task, from information that is needed, or from financial or personnel resources. Such frustration can create negative attitudes toward the other group, since they are seen as the cause of the blockage.

The second step in the process is **conceptualization** of the conflict. By this we mean the group members attempt to understand why they are frustrated and who is responsible. In addition, they begin to plan a reaction to the frustration and may even anticipate the subsequent reaction from the group responsible for the frustration. Conceptualization is the problem-solving and strategy stage in the process that precedes actual behavior in response to the conflict situation. Sometimes it is a subconscious step that is influenced by the past history and attitudes of the groups involved.

Behavior is the third step in the conflict process. As we shall discuss in detail later, there are many possible behaviors that a group can use in reacting to a conflict situation. It can give in to the other group; it can fight with the other group; it can hope the conflict will go

**Figure 13.2
The Process of
Intergroup Conflict**

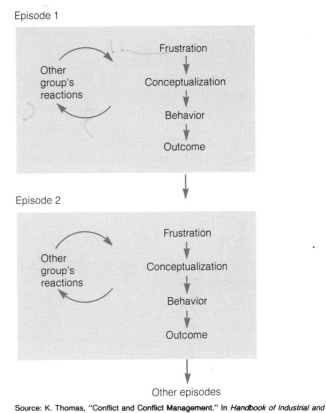

Episode 1

Frustration

Other group's reactions

Conceptualization

Behavior

Outcome

Episode 2

Frustration

Other group's reactions

Conceptualization

Behavior

Outcome

Other episodes

Source: K. Thomas, "Conflict and Conflict Management." In *Handbook of Industrial and Organizational Behavior,* ed. M. D. Dunnete. Copyright © 1976 John Wiley & Sons. Reprinted by permission of John Wiley & Sons, Inc.

away, or it can try to work out a compromise or joint solution to the problem.

As a result of the choice of behavior and the reaction of the other group, the outcome of the conflict is determined. By *outcome* we mean the satisfaction, attitudes, goal attainment, and intergroup relations of the two groups involved. Unless both groups are really satisfied with the resolution, the seeds for future episodes of conflict are sown. Hence, the second conflict is often an outgrowth of an unresolved conflict in the first episode.

Thus, the definition and process of conflict make clear that intergroup conflict and lack of coordination do develop over time. Past episodes in the relationship between two departments—just as with two people in interpersonal relations—are a big factor in determining what will happen next. This developmental aspect of intergroup behavior also suggests that problems cannot be solved overnight. It takes time for problems to build up, and it takes time for them to be resolved. The Home Computers case and Box 13.1 about Apple Computer provide excellent examples of how conflicts develop over time. They also suggest that it will take time to work through these conflicts. With these examples and the definitions in hand, let us now turn to the task of developing a model of intergroup conflict, including causes and outcomes.

Box 13.1
Growing Pains: Once All Alone in Field, Apple Computer Girds for Industry Shakeout

Capertino, Calif.—Apple Computer Inc. is growing up. And for the first time, the growing isn't so easy.

Mr. Wozniak one of the cofounders of Apple sees a basic clash between engineers and marketers. An engineer, he says, thinks that if you build a good machine, people will buy it. He cites the Apple III, a machine with a current basic price of $2,695 that dealers say could have seriously challenged the IBM PC directly but was introduced too hurriedly, with too many flaws.

Users now give the machine excellent reviews, and it is the preferred machine inside Apple.

Poor First Impression

"To the engineer, that's an incredibly functional machine that should have done so well, Mr. Wormiak says. It should be outselling IBM. Engineers don't understand what it does to sales if the first impression of a product is bad. And they don't understand what those three letters (IBM) mean."

Apple is far quicker now to recognize and correct its marketing mistakes, Mr. Jobs says. Apple, for example, originally planned to sell Lisa for $9,995 directly to major corporations when it became available in June, and to limit retail sales to a few dealers. "We got a little too much Fortune 500-itis," he says. The corporate sales didn't come, and retail sales were healthier than expected.

Apple quickly cut the price of the Lisa to $8,190 and also began selling it without all its powerful software for $6,995. It increased advertising and realized it had to step up efforts to produce products that will let Lisa communicate with big IBM computers. At the lower price, dealers and analysts say, Lisa's *sales may double or triple. Some also say they told Apple the price was too high long ago.*

More Meetings

In addition to focusing Apple's marketing, Mr. Sculley (Apple's new president) is trying to open up internal communications. Apple now holds meetings among its general managers once a week, rather than once a quarter. Mr. Sculley also insists that memorandums be one page or less. He has made videotapes for dealers outlining the company's strategies and directions. "You keep them well-informed, because they can't build their business on surprises," he says.

Dealers say the change is evident. In the past, says Charlie Auger, the president of Computer Solutions Inc., of Oklahoma City, "we found out an awful lot of things by the grapevine and in the newspapers." Steven Hawley, a San Diego dealer, says Apple now is more responsive to dealers' needs. "They were a very egotistical company, especially during the last year. They thought, not unjustifiably, that they were the best."

So Apple is maturing. But at nearly $1 billion in annual sales, can Apple retain its culture? It is trying. Mr. Jobs wore jeans to an interview for this article. Mr. Sculley says Apple's opulent executive offices in its new headquarters building—dubbed "The Big Pink" for the color of some interior walls—will be replaced soon by more humble offices to preserve "Apple values."

Still, some past employees wonder how long Apple can go on being Apple. Scott Love, a product marketing engineer who left in April, says, "You never know about Apple. It's a rarity. Maybe it only happens once in a lifetime."

By Erik Larson and Currie Dowin, *The Wall Street Journal*, October 4, 1983. Reprinted by permission of *The Wall Street Journal*, © Dow Jones & Company, Inc. 1983. All rights reserved.

A Model of Intergroup Conflict

As we develop a model of intergroup conflict, we will first explore some of the causes of conflict. We will then look at both negative and positive potential outcomes, and explore both ineffective and effective strategies for dealing with conflict. As we proceed, think about how the model can be applied to the Home Computers case and what suggestions you might make to Harvey if you were the consultant.

Causes of Intergroup Conflict

The first step in developing our model is to explore the causes of intergroup conflict. How many times have you heard the comment, "It was a personality clash that created the conflict?" Certainly, some conflicts are truly the result of a personality clash. But we believe that **most conflicts between people in an organization are really conflicts between the jobs and departments that the people represent.** Some form of conflict would be likely no matter which two people were in the positions, though the intensity of conflict will be influenced by the particular people involved. Two points are important for you to understand here. First, intergroup conflict involves conflict between **people.** In groups and organizations people are the actors who create the dynamics we experience. Second, however, even though intergroup conflicts involve people, the people are only actors in **roles** that are in conflict with one another. As we explore the causes of conflict, see if you do not agree.

In the next few pages we will explore eight different causes of intergroup conflict:

1. Task interdependence.
2. Different goals, norms, and time frames.
3. Ambiguity of roles.
4. Limited common resources.
5. Reward systems.
6. Communication obstacles.
7. Status and power differences.
8. Personnel skills and traits.

These causes are summarized in Figure 13.3, which indicates their effect on the conflict process. These causes set up the conditions for conflict, and the intensity of conflict is then determined as the conflict process unfolds. Let us explore each of the eight causes in turn.

Task Interdependence

A primary cause of intergroup conflict is that one or both of the groups in question cannot do their work unless the other group also does its work. For example, at Home Computers, the salespeople cannot sell the computers on any reliable basis unless production gets the product out in a timely manner. Likewise, production needs to pro-

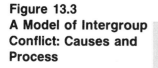

**Figure 13.3
A Model of Intergroup
Conflict: Causes and
Process**

duce computers only if sales can effectively sell them. In an organization, all groups are at least minimally interdependent or they would not be part of the same organization. The question is, how interdependent are they? Three basic types of interdependence have been identified by researchers: pooled, sequential, and reciprocal.[2] They are depicted in Figure 13.4 and described below.

Pooled interdependence between two groups in an organization means that they can perform their tasks at the same time with very little need for interaction. For example, the accounting group in the Home Computers plant in Dayton is essentially independent from the production group there. The only interdependence comes from the fact that they are both part of the Home Computers company.

Sequential interdependence means that the outputs from one group are the inputs to the other group. In other words, there is a one-way type of interdependence. In Figure 13.4, group B is dependent on group A finishing its work so that group B has some work to do. On the other hand, group A is not dependent on group B, unless group B is so slow in its work that inventory backs up thus blocking group A's output. At Home Computers the salespeople are sequentially interdependent with the production people. They cannot sell the computers until they are produced. Production is dependent upon sales only in a more limited and long term fashion.

Figure 13.4   Types of Task Interdependence

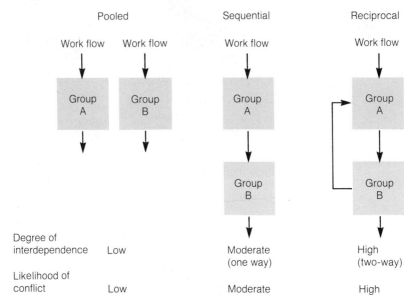

The most highly interdependent situation is **reciprocal interdependence**. Outputs from each group can serve as inputs to the other group. In other words, there is a two-way type of interdependence. If either group has problems, they will be felt by the other group. For example, in Home Computers, research and development and market research must work hand in hand to come up with a computer that is technically sound and will sell. Otherwise, both groups and the company as a whole will suffer.

The type of interdependence that exists between two groups does not guarantee more or less conflict. It simply sets up a condition which can make conflict easy and coordination of effort difficult. Pooled interdependence creates the least potential for conflict, except perhaps at budget time. Sequential interdependence creates more potential for conflict, and reciprocal interdependence creates the most potential for conflict.

Differentiation

Another extremely important cause of coordination problems among groups is the **differentiation** that occurs in the design of the groups. As we have said, organizational growth results in the need to create different functional work units in an organization. And the logical way to divide up the work in an organization is to create work groups with different responsibilities and specialties.[3] At Home Computers it makes sense for one group to be concerned with selling the computers—the salespeople—and another group to be concerned with manufacturing them—the production people. The results of this specialization are twofold. First, they allow people to become experts and to develop a sense of identity with their tasks. But over time these groups learn to do things differently, and this can create coordination problems for the organization.[4]

This differentiation can be summarized in four major areas for the groups:

1. Goal orientation.
2. Time orientation.
3. Formality of structure.
4. Nature of interpersonal relationships.

With the different groups there will obviously be different **goal orientations**. Production groups focus on goals related to cost control and utilization of manufacturing technology. Sales groups focus on goals related to consumer response to the product and generation of sales revenue. Research and development groups focus on contributions to science and applications of science to new products. Such different goal orientations can lead to conflicts in the priorities of certain activities. For example, when I worked as a marketing analyst for Exxon, my need for information to complete an analysis was often my number 1 priority. But the salesperson from whom I had to get this information sometimes considered this task a number 10 priority. You can imagine the potential for conflict that existed.

Closely associated with the goal orientation that results from differentiated work groups is a difference in **time orientation**. Because of the particular goals assigned, some groups may develop long-term orientations while others develop short-term perspectives. For example, at Home Computers we can imagine that the salespeople have developed a short-term orientation, since they must respond to a rapidly changing and demanding marketplace. On the other hand, production people have developed a somewhat longer-term perspective. They must be concerned with the costs of changing setups from manufacturing one product to another—and long runs of the same product are cheaper than short runs and frequent changes. If we think about the research and development department at Home Computers, we might anticipate an even longer-term orientation, since their endeavors are scientific in nature. These differences in time orientation can obviously create tension between sales (which wants the new product on the market) and research (which wants to develop a product that will perform well) and production (which must produce a reliable product and keep costs down).

The third effect of differentiation is a difference in the **formality of the structure** that develops in the different groups. Some groups may develop a great many rules and paperwork procedures to guide their work, such as you might expect in the production group at Home Computers. But others may do things more informally by word of mouth and with very few rules, such as you might find in sales at Home Computers. In addition, the clarity with which with roles within the groups are defined may vary substantially. Closely associated with the formality of structure is the **nature of interpersonal relationships.** Some units develop norms of behavior that are very task oriented, while other groups tend to be more relationship oriented. As just noted, these differences tend to make it more difficult to coordinate activities that cut across group lines.[5]

Ambiguity of Roles

The effects of differentiation and task interdependence are both influenced by the degree of ambiguity and task uncertainty that exists. When the tasks assigned to the different groups are not clearly defined, ambiguity about responsibility can result. In some cases, this ambiguity can result from top management not doing their homework in setting up the groups, but it can also result from a technology that is uncertain and nonroutine in nature. If the company works in a rapidly changing and complex industry like the home computer industry, defining clear tasks can be difficult.[6] And if the technologies used in the company are characterized by many exceptions to the work plan and difficult problems in the sequencing of work, it will be difficult to clearly define group tasks.[7] Regardless of the reason, task uncertainty for groups and ambiguity about group roles open the door for conflict. And they also open the door for responses that are politically determined and are dysfunctional for the organization.

Resources and Rewards

Two additional causes of intergroup conflict and politically oriented responses are **limited common resources** and **reward systems**. When two groups are both dependent upon the same set of resources—be it people, machinery, or dollars—and when these resources are limited, there is potential for conflict over their distribution. The typical reaction is competition for the scarce resources. The same potential exists where rewards are limited and associated with comparative performance. For example, if two shifts at Home Computers are rewarded on how many nondefective computers they turn out compared to the number turned out by the other shift, destructive competition may result. Each shift may do things at the end of the shift to make it difficult for the following shift to get started quickly. A well-known example of this type of competition has been the subject of a popular television show, "Dallas." As J. R. and Bobby Ewing competed for the right to run Ewing Oil alone (determined by which one could generate the most profit in their half of the company), they resorted to actions which have helped themselves but hurt the company. Box 13.2 relates other examples of how reward systems have encouraged destructive competition. A relevant question here is, "What good is it to be the best group in a company that is out of business?" **So long as resources and rewards are allocated based on individual group criteria, as opposed to criteria based on contribution to intergroup success, conflict will almost be inevitable**.

Communication Obstacles

Another factor that relates to intergroup conflict is **communication obstacles**. These may be: (1) physical bar-

**Box 13.2
Pitting Workers
against Each Other
Often Backfires, Firms
Are Finding**

To prod branch managers to perform better, a European bank encouraged them to compete against each other to produce the most improved results.

The winner was promised a bonus. But the outcome was disappointing. The bank discovered that a greedy officer had steered a customer to a rival bank rather than help another branch manager win the bonus.

Companies often pit manager against manager in the hopes that the race will bring out the best in both. When monitored properly, internal competition can boost employees' egos and help them feel they control their own destiny. "It's healthy," says organizational psychologist Raf Haddock. "There's a human drive to compete and to strive." But the competition can get out of hand when the stakes are too high or supervisors get careless.

Sales Contests

Chase Manhattan Bank hoped to create healthy competition between divisions by linking employees' bonuses to the fees their divisions generated. But the bonus plan encouraged employees to aim for high-volume customers rather than good credit risks. One group built a huge portfolio with a tiny new company called Drysdale Government Securities Inc. In May Drysdale defaulted on interest payments on securities it had borrowed through Chase. Chase forecasts it will take an after-tax write-off of $117 million in the second quarter as a result.

What Works?

Just posting performance rankings hurt the efficiency of a Los Angeles-based workman's compensation insurance company. It ranked offices according to how frequently they distributed disability payments on time. But a former employee recalls that when one office got a claim that was meant for another, workers frequently used the mail rather than the telephone to reroute the information in an attempt to lower the rankings of the competitors.

riers, such as geographical separation; ② time barriers, such shift work; ③ information barriers, such as when one group knows something the other group does not know; and ④ semantic barriers, such as engineering jargon versus sales jargon versus accounting jargon.[8] In general, when different groups lack information about the work, goals, and priorities facing other groups, communications will be difficult.

Status and Power Differences

Another factor that can create intergroup problems is the **difference in the status and power of groups**. For

"IT'S NOT SURPRISING THE PRODUCTION DEPARTMENT IS IN SPAIN, THE WAREHOUSE IS IN KOREA, THE ACCOUNTING DIVISION IS IN BOLIVIA, THE BOARD OF DIRECTORS IS IN CANADA..."

© 1985 Sidney Harris.

example, if Home Computers is a market-oriented company, the salespeople may be viewed as more important than the production people. The salespeople may be responsible for **absorbing the uncertainty** from the Home Computers' markets. By this we mean the salespeople use their abilities to satisfy customer demands while allowing production and research and development the time needed to create a viable new product. Of course, production and R & D may see things somewhat differently, but to the extent that sales can handle this uncertainty for the company, they are in a more powerful position than the other two groups. Closely associated with this basis of status difference is the **substitutability** of each group. If the salespeople at Home Computers are viewed as indispensable, while production is viewed as something that could be subcontracted out, sales is going to have greater status and power in the organization.

Such status and power differences between groups create the potential for intergroup conflict. Furthermore, the weaker group often feels it must give in to the more powerful group, and this can lead to decreased satisfaction and lower overall performance.[9] To achieve the greatest degree of coordination in an organization, it is desirable for groups to be essentially equal in status and power.

Personnel Skills and Traits

The final cause of intergroup conflict we will discuss is the **skills and traits of the personnel** in the groups. As we mentioned earlier, even though intergroup conflict involves the groups, the **people** in the groups are the actors in the situations. Hence, the extent to which the people are domineering, aggressive, and tolerant of ambiguity determines the potential for intergroup conflict.[10] Different personality types, as we discussed in Chapter 4, deal with conflict in different ways. For example, we might imagine that **thinking** types would be more conflict oriented than **feeling** types, since they like things handled in a logical fashion and can get along without harmony. And **judging** types might be more conflict oriented than **perceptive** types, since they like to get things settled and finished. In addition, communication skills and problem solving skills of the people might be important predictors of the potential for intergroup conflict.

Summarizing the Causes of Intergroup Conflict

In thinking over the eight causes of intergroup conflict in Figure 13.3, we can note that all but the last of them are situational in nature. That is, the people in the situation are not a factor in these causes. **People come into play as the conflict process unfolds. The causes of conflict merely create conditions which are ripe for conflict.** True, the causes create some base level of conflict. The question is, how severe will the conflict be. Will conflict win out in a destructive manner, or will coordinated intergroup effort win out? Here is where the people come into play. **The actions of people determine whether negative or positive outcomes will result as the conflict process unfolds.**

Conflict Outcomes

Let us now turn our attention to the possible outcomes of the conflict process. Figure 13.5 extends Figure 13.3 to include the negative and positive outcomes to conflict. We will first explore the negative outcomes, since they are probably the most familiar to you. Then we will explore the often surprising positive outcomes to intergroup conflict.

Negative Outcomes to Intergroup Conflict

Think back to times when you have been in situations where conflict existed between two groups. One good example, and one where conflict is supposed to occur, is in a football game between two college fraternity teams. In this situation it is easy to recall some of the negative outcomes shown in Figure 13.5.[11] Information was concealed—your team did not let the other team know its plays. You obviously felt concern only for your own team, and you may have been unconcerned when one of the other team's players went down hurt. You felt distance between your team and the other team; you did not interact with the other team until the game was over. A climate of distrust, and a "we-they" attitude developed. In short, it was a conflict situation full of negative outcomes, as competitive sports are supposed to be.

But imagine how these negative outcomes might develop in Home Computers between sales and production, and further, imagine the effects on the company as a whole. What will happen since sales and production have

Figure 13.5   A Model of Intergroup Conflict: Causes, Process and Outcomes

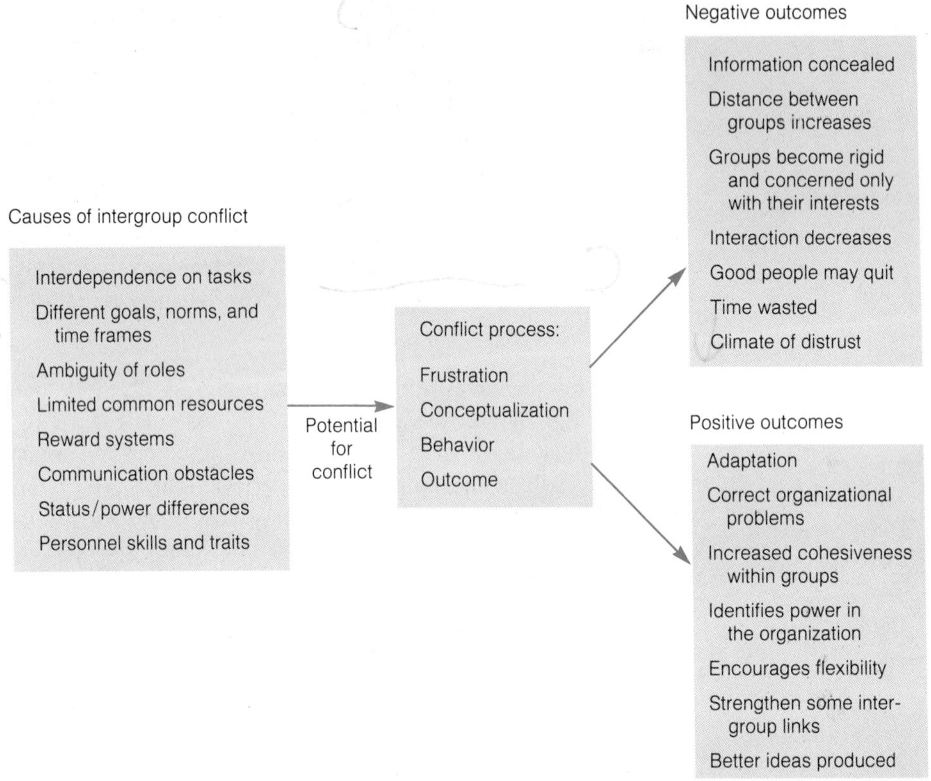

Negative outcomes

Information concealed

Distance between
  groups increases

Groups become rigid
  and concerned only
  with their interests

Interaction decreases

Good people may quit

Time wasted

Climate of distrust

Causes of intergroup conflict

Interdependence on tasks

Different goals, norms, and
  time frames

Ambiguity of roles

Limited common resources

Reward systems

Communication obstacles

Status/power differences

Personnel skills and traits

Potential
for
conflict

Conflict process:

Frustration

Conceptualization

Behavior

Outcome

Positive outcomes

Adaptation

Correct organizational
  problems

Increased cohesiveness
  within groups

Identifies power in
  the organization

Encourages flexibility

Strengthen some inter-
  group links

Better ideas produced

started concealing information from one another? Will that help sales and production do their jobs in the long run? No. And as they operate this way over time, the distance between the groups will increase. Sales and production may each become more concerned with only their own goals and objectives, and pressures will develop within each group to do things for itself and against the other group.

As these pressures mount and result in decreased interaction between sales and production, distrust will run rampant. Sales will imagine that production is doing even more things than they are to hinder the work of the sales people, and production will exaggerate in the same way about sales. A great deal of energy in each group will be directed toward the conflict instead of toward cooperative work that is productive for the organization. In time, the productivity of both groups will suffer. Good people may quit to get out of this destructive situation. The negative outcomes that are expected and accepted on the football field are not helpful in Home Computers or any other organization. What good will it do for sales or production to win the conflict if Home Computers goes out of business in the meantime?

Positive Outcomes to Intergroup Conflict

Believe it or not, there are positive outcomes that can occur as a result of intergroup conflict. Indeed, some degree of conflict in an organization is inevitable and desirable. You may find this hard to believe; and, in fact, not long ago management literature suggested the elimination of all conflict in organizations.[12] But since the 1940s, the literature has shown more acceptance of the fact that intergroup conflict is inevitable given the divisionalized design of organizations. More recently, researchers have recognized that elimination of all conflict may be as bad for an organization as having too much conflict. As we have noted in earlier chapters, groupthink and lack of conflict can cause a group to make serious mistakes. The same rationale applies to intergroup behavior. As we shall discuss in the next paragraphs, and as shown in Figure 13.5, **intergroup conflict can serve as a signal that problems exist and as a motivator to correct these problems.** In other words, conflict can be viewed as a way of questioning the status quo and motivating improvements. Let us explore this point further as we look at several positive outcomes of intergroup conflict.[13]

Intergroup conflict can have very positive effects **within the groups** that are involved. Internal cohesiveness typically increases for groups in conflict, and interpersonal conflicts within the groups tend to be overlooked in light of the larger intergroup conflict. A good example of this would be the New York Yankees baseball team of a few years ago. While they were winning the World Series, they were able to put aside their differences and play as a team to win. But after the intergroup conflict was over (that is, the World Series), the conflicts among the Yankees and their manager and owner boiled over. This example also points out the tendency for intergroup conflict to make the groups attend more carefully to the tasks they are assigned to perform. It makes the groups adapt more readily internally to do a better job. Of course, as we stated before, extreme amounts of intergroup conflict can absorb so much energy that group tasks and adaptability can be hindered.

At the **organizational level**, intergroup conflict can make people aware of the problems that exist in terms of the variables that cause conflict. For example, a reward system which encourages competition rather than collaboration among the groups may become obvious as a result of conflict. Or power differences that are dysfunctional for the organization may come into view as a result of intergroup conflict.

As a result of highlighting problems and making people uncomfortable, intergroup conflict can also **motivate people to find solutions to problems causing the conflict**. It can strengthen linkages between certain groups by forcing their interaction to resolve the problem. In a manner of speaking, the conflict is a force for growth for the groups. As such, it can increase flexibility in the way the groups interact, result in the generation of better ideas for their interaction, and lead to structural and power changes that reduce the negative impacts of conflict. For example, at Home Computers, sales has greater status and power than production. The conflict that this produces could be reduced if Harvey were to start emphasizing quality and cost as much as he emphasizes meeting customer delivery demands. Or perhaps less conflict would result if some of the production work were subcontracted. The point is that intergroup conflict can motivate action to resolve the difficulties between sales and production. Some organizations thrive on conflict which helps them solve problems more effectively—recall the New York Yankees example.

Now that we have discussed both positive and negative outcomes to conflict, you may be wondering what determines which set you will see in an organizational setting. Naturally, the causes shown in Figure 13.5, that we discussed earlier, play an important determining role, but there are also management strategies which have a great deal to do with the conflict outcomes. Let us turn now to a discussion of those strategies.

Strategies for Managing Intergroup Conflict

The causes of conflict shown in Figure 13.5 have a great deal to do with creating the conditions for conflict. Indeed, they may determine the first episode in the process of conflict. But whether conflict escalates to the dysfunctional level and results in the negative outcomes or is maintained at a healthy level and results in the positive outcomes depends on the **behaviors** in the first and subsequent conflict episodes. There are both ineffective and effective strategies for managing intergroup conflict. **The ineffective strategies try to suppress the conflict; the effective strategies accept it and try to keep it under control or alter its causes.** The effective strategies do not always work well, and the ineffective ones sometimes work out all right, but you can better manage intergroup conflict if you understand the differences between the two sets of strategies. Before discussing a number of specific strategies for managing conflict, let us distinguish among some basic dimensions of the conflict management process.

Actions designed to deal with intergroup conflict fall into one of three categories: (1) win/lose, (2) lose/lose, and (3) win/win.[14] In **win/lose** one group gains a goal at the expense of the other group. In **lose/lose** the conflict results in both groups being denied their goals. And in **win/win** both groups manage to achieve their goals. We might also think of these categories along the two dimensions of **cooperativeness** and **assertiveness**. And we can then use these two dimensions to define 5 ways of dealing with conflict, as shown in Figure 13.6.[15]

In the upper left-hand corner of Figure 13.6, **competing** is a win/lose strategy. A competing group asserts its position and tends to ignore the position of the other group. In some cases this may be the right approach if a group feels very strongly about its position. But in such situations, we might expect to see some of the political behaviors we discussed in Chapter 9, and we question the effects of this approach in the long run. Also, if both groups employ this strategy, it can turn into a lose/lose situation when two equally strong combatants tangle.

In the lower right-hand corner of the figure, **accommo-**

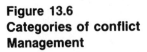

Figure 13.6
Categories of conflict
Management

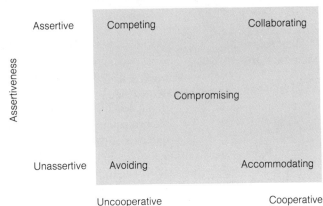

Source: K. Thomas, "Conflict and Conflict Management." In *Handbook of Industrial and Organizational Behavior.* Ed. *M. D. Dunnette.* Copyright © 1976 John Wiley & Sons. Reprinted by permission of John Wiley & Sons, Inc.

dating is also a win/lose strategy. This time, however, the accommodating group gives in to the other group, probably because of a large power difference or because the issue at stake is not too important to the group. In such cases, accommodating might be the best strategy to follow. But accommodation in the short run may be a political strategy to win in the long run—sort of a lose-the-battle-to-win-the-war strategy. Such behaviors can result in long-term problems for the organization, so again we question the wisdom of this strategy in most cases. And if both parties employ an accommodating strategy, the result may be a lose/lose situation. The parties are so cooperative that they fall prey to an intergroup type of groupthink.

In the lower left-hand corner of Figure 13.6, **avoiding** is a strategy where a group takes no action and hopes the conflict will go away over time. If this group encounters a competing group, the result will probably be win/lose, with the avoiding group losing. Or the avoiding group could wind up winning if they are dealing with an accommodating group. Sometimes, avoiding may be the best strategy, especially if the issue is unimportant to the group, but avoiding usually just delays the negative outcomes associated with intergroup conflict. From this discussion, we can see that **the behavior of one group is important only in relation to what the other group does.** The outcomes of a conflict depend on the behaviors of both groups.

In the upper right-hand corner of the figure, **collaborating** is a win/win strategy. The collaborating group is concerned with the goals of both groups and those of the larger organization. Thus, even if this group encounters a competing, accommodating, or avoiding group, the potential is still there for a win/win resolution, so long as they maintain their collaborating behavior. The **compromising** behavior in the center of Figure 13.6 is a middle ground; each group may give up something in order to gain something else. We might refer to this as a half win/win and half lose/lose situation, since each group asserts itself on some points and cooperates on others.

These general conflict management strategies provide us with a framework for understanding some specific ineffective and effective strategies for dealing with intergroup conflict, as shown in Figure 13.7.

Ineffective Management Strategies

In Figure 13.7, we show seven ineffective strategies for managing conflict. **These strategies are ineffective because they attempt to ignore the conflict in hopes it will go away or because they are too much oriented toward group goals as opposed to organizational goals.**

Avoiding strategies. The first three strategies fall into the category of avoiding, which we identified in Figure 13.6. **Nonaction/avoidance** is rather straightforward in meaning, but administrative orbiting and due-process nonaction deserve further comment.[16] **Administrative orbiting** is more commonly called "buck passing." Rather than making a decision, a manager will refer the issue to a higher manager or form a committee to study the situation. As the process continues, the conflict simply goes on unresolved and worsens. **Due-process nonaction** is an extension of administrative orbiting. It involves setting up a procedure for handling conflicts that is so cumbersome or risky that groups are reluctant to use it. Or

Figure 13.7   A Model of Intergroup Conflict: Causes, Process, Management Strategies and Outcomes

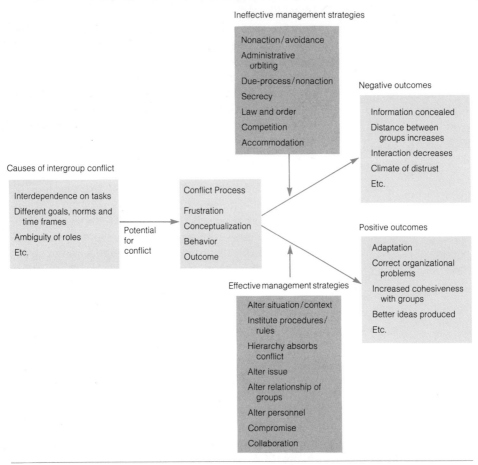

if they do use it, they become mired in the details of the process.

Competing strategies.   Secrecy and law and order-strategies could most easily be classified as competing strategies. They are actions which try to ensure that one group's goals are achieved even at the expense of the other group's goals. Indeed, **secrecy** involves the concealing of information, which we identified as a negative outcome of intergroup conflict. When groups which must work together withhold information from each other, the outcome will at best be win/lose, and over time it is most likely to be lose/lose and dysfunctional for the organization as a whole. Likewise, the **law and order** strategy is an implementation of the Golden Rule: "He who holds the gold makes the rules." The group with the greatest power will attempt to discredit or stigmatize the other group in the name of organizational security or the status quo. It is also possible on some occasions for a low-power group to use this same strategy to gain the upper hand with a more powerful group, but usually the organization will suffer from this process.

As we have suggested, **open competition** between two conflicting groups is usually an ineffective strategy because in competition there is at least one loser, and sometimes two. The hostilities that can result from competition often lead to attitudes which create long-lasting problems between groups in an organization. And such negative attitudes and behaviors can become a natural part of the groups involved, lasting far beyond the tenure of the present members of the group. Indeed, the socialization processes for the groups can grow to include the establishing of a we-they attitude for new members of each group.

In many ways, the **accommodating** strategy can be almost as bad. This strategy ensures some problems for the group using it and perhaps for the organization as a whole. The accommodating group may fail to achieve a goal that is really just as important to the organization as the goals of the other group. And such behavior may be a smoke screen for long-term competitive behavior. Thus, the accommodating strategy only prolongs the conflict and allows it to smolder, only to burst into a raging fire at a later date.

In summary, the ineffective strategies tend to ignore conflicts in hopes they will disappear, or to create win/lose situations. Sometimes these strategies do result in positive outcomes, but usually they only delay the surfacing of conflict and allow it to grow worse without being resolved. Fortunately, there are better alternatives, so let us explore those now.

Effective Management Strategies

In Figure 13.7, we show eight effective strategies for managing conflict. **These strategies are effective because they focus on altering the causes of intergroup conflict or on collaboration.**[17] The eight effective strategies in Figure 13.7 fall into one of three basic categories: structural, process, and mixed approaches.[18] Let us explore the strategies within each of these in turn, recognizing that no strategy works every time.

Structural Approaches. These approaches focus on altering some of the causes of intergroup conflict. The first effective strategy—**alter the situation/context**—is clearly a structural approach. Perhaps goals of the organization and the various groups can be made more clear. Perhaps rewards can be devised to promote intergroup cooperation. Another possibility would be to alter the tasks assigned the two groups so that interdependence is reduced toward the pooled end of the continuum. Probably the simplest way to alter the situation is to help the groups focus on goals they have in common rather than on those where they have conflict. If a common goal can be identified and the goal will last over time, this strategy can go a long way toward bringing the intergroup conflict under control. For example, if the sales and production people at Home Computers can be made aware of the threats from other computer firms, especially larger more established companies, the goal of beating these competitors could help sales and production work together more effectively.

Another structural strategy is to **institute particular rules and procedures** for handling conflicts that are bound to arise. A good example of such a strategy is a procedure to handle employee grievances. When an employee has a complaint that is not satisfactorily handled by the boss, the employee and the boss know the procedure that is to be followed. Rules serve the same type of function by specifying behaviors that must be carried out by each of the groups involved in a conflict situation. For example, at Home Computers, rules could be established setting the lead time sales must give production to fill an order. This should eliminate the fighting over the timing of an order. As you might imagine in the situation of a home computer company, one disadvantage of rules and procedures is that they reduce flexibility and are not easily changed to fit rapidly changing situations. And, groups must be careful to use rules and procedures to help manage conflict, rather than let them become due-process nonaction tools.

Two other structural approaches can be mentioned, but they are clearly less effective and may not be possible in a given situation. First, it may be possible to **separate the groups** so that they do not have to have much contact. Second, it may be possible to **relocate particular individuals** who are intensifying the intergroup conflict. Transfers, job rotation between groups, and promotions are all possibilities. But as we have said, many "personality conflicts" are much more than that. And by moving people around, you may only temporarily cover up the **role** conflict.

Process Approaches.   Process approaches involve-changing the behaviors and attitudes of the people in the conflicting groups. They focus on collaboration and compromise. The primary means for accomplishing these changes fall under the approach called **altering the relationship of the groups** in Figure 13.7. Through confrontation among the groups involved, compromise and/or collaboration can be accomplished. One strategy involves holding direct negotiations between the groups: Let them sit down and talk about the problems facing them. Often, such negotiations will also involve a third party who acts as a mediator. And a strategy commonly used by such third parties is called "image exchange."[19] For example, sales and production at Home Computers get together in a neutral place to work out their differences. Each group is asked to write down perceptions of their own group and of the other group, focusing on both pros and cons. These lists are then shared in an open meeting. Next, the sales and production people return to their separate groups to discuss what they have learned and how they can use this information to improve the relationship between the two departments. The groups then get back together to share and discuss their ideas on how to work together more effectively. The focus in this process is on beginning the development of a feeling of collaboration, for one half-day or all-day meeting of this sort will not immediately erase years of conflict behavior between sales and production.

This strategy can lead to another process strategy, which is to **require regular and extended interaction between groups** to resolve the conflicts that exist between them. Frequent and regular meetings between sales and production can lead to changes in attitude and behavior that will benefit the company as a whole.

Another process strategy closely related to the two above is to **alter the issue in dispute.**[20] Often when groups are brought together for image exchange, they begin to see the issue of conflict in a different way. The issue of conflict can be broken down into parts and dealt with one part at a time. The hope is to reduce the issue to manageable size. Alternatively, sometimes the issue can be dealt with more effectively if it is expanded. By expanding the conflict issue, it may be possible to find areas of common concern that can serve as the basis for beginning coordination between the groups. For example, sales and production at Home Computers might define their ordering conflict as a conflict between customer needs and Home Computers' capabilities. This new definition may make it possible for them to agree on a plan to better meet customer needs, without arguing over the timing of orders in relation to production. The objective in expanding or breaking down a conflict is to search for common concerns and manageable conflict issues. Other aspects of altering the issue include removing issues that are a matter of principle and limiting the scope of precedents set in resolving conflicts. In matters of principle and precedent, groups are more likely to hold strongly to their position, since the stakes seem so high. If you can reduce the stakes in the conflict, you will more often be able to achieve the desired reduction in conflict.

The final process-oriented strategy falls under the **alter-the-people** category. To change attitudes and behaviors, we can provide training to equip people to deal more effectively with intergroup conflicts. People can be taught better communication, assertiveness, and negotiating skills. They can also be cross-trained for jobs in both groups. An interesting example of this is how some physicians are now getting law degrees (see Box 13.3). Finally, the groups themselves can also be trained in intergroup

Box 13.3
Some Doctors Are
Picking up Law
Degrees to Cope With
Legal Disputes and
Red Tape

Dr. Jerry Zaslow, a surgeon in Elkins Parks, Pa., recently advised the wife and children of a terminally ill, comatose patient to forgo further life-sustaining treatment. With their consent, he then authorized that the patient not be resuscitated if he stopped breathing.

The looming threat of malpractice claims makes most doctors shy from such decisions, but Dr. Zaslow has the advantage of also being an attorney.

The estimated 650 professionals with degrees in both medicine and law represent a growing alliance between two fields that traditionally have recognized few shared interests. A number of issues are now bringing them together, says Robert Burt, a Yale Law School Professor: "At the heart of the matter . . . are the ethical issues that have to do with expanded technological capacities."

Ethics and Red Tape

With medicine's ability to sustain life increasing, says attorney Alexander Capron, "life and death are becoming much more a matter of human choice and agency, and much less a matter of just standing by." The change requires more communication between the professions. "There are real quandaries here," says Mr. Capron. "It's no longer just a question of the lawyer learning a few basic rules or the scientist a few facts."

Doctors also need to know how to work with regulations. A study by the Hospital Association of New York State, which stirred controversy when released in 1978, found that 164 regulatory agencies have some jurisdiction over the state's hospitals. The study said about $1.1 billion a year, or 25% of hospital costs, is spent on complying with regulations, adding about $40 a day to a patient's bill.

In addition to the problems of ethics and red tape, there also is "a growing litigious consciousness" among physicians, says Mr. Capron. Malpractice claims have more than tripled over the past 10 years, insurers say.

"Many physicians are feeling insecure," says Dr. Zaslow, "and so they're saying, 'My God, I'm going to go to law school and learn what it's all about.'" A physician since 1940, Dr. Zaslow got a law degree in 1971 after attending night school. He was the only doctor in his law class; a few years later, there were a couple of doctors in almost every class, he says.

team building. Such alteration of the people can be expensive—but then, so is conflict and lack of coordination between groups in an organization.

The key point of process strategies for dealing with intergroup conflict is to accept that the basic causes of conflict cannot be substantially changed and to deal with the reactions of the people involved. Where possible, structural strategies for conflict management are probably the most effective, since they deal directly with the causes of conflict. But in some cases, structural changes are not practical, and process changes offer a viable alternative. For example, you might like to reduce the interdependence between sales and production at Home Computers or expand the size of the common resource pool that is being used. But these changes would not be likely given the nature of the product and the competitiveness of the industry.

Mixed Approaches. Mixed strategies for intergroup conflict management are just that—a mixture of structural and process elements. When the **hierarchy absorbs the conflict** by a manager's decision, the structural aspect of the manager's power and authority to make such a decision comes into play. The manager would have responsibility over both of the conflicting units. But the manager's style in handling the conflict (as we discussed in the two chapters on leadership) would also enter the process. Such a strategy can be effective in the short run, but to use a manager on a long-term basis for this purpose can be dysfunctional to the organization. The use of rules and procedures or some of the other mixed approaches discussed below would be preferable for the long run.

There are several mixed approaches which fall under the category of **altering the relationship of the groups**. First, the groups can appoint liaison or boundary-spanning people. Such people would provide lateral communications which are needed to improve the interactions of the two conflicting groups. Liaison people at Home Computers could interact daily between sales and production to make sure that both units can respond to customer demands in a timely manner and still maintain cost and quality goals. If the liaison people are versed in both sales and production responsibilities, they effectively keep the channels for coordination open between the two groups.

Second, if the problems between sales and production are more complex, it might be necessary to use a **temporary task force**, that is, a group of people working on the problem to find solutions. Task forces are especially useful when more than three groups are involved in the conflict. For example, if the research and development department was also involved in the conflict between sales and production at Home Computers, it might be useful to form a task force of people representing each group to work on the problem. When the problem is resolved to the point that a liaison or other strategy can handle the coordination, the task force members return to their respective jobs full time. A task force, then, is a temporary group that deals with the process of solving a coordination problem in an organization.

Third, if the coordination is extremely difficult, it may be desirable to form a permanent **integrating department**. The integrating department may consist of only one person, or of several people. It would function much like the temporary task force, but it would be viewed as more permanent. The department's sole responsibility would be to enhance the coordination between groups which are by nature in conflict. Integrating departments usually have real authority and responsibility for the groups they work to coordinate. They may report to a manager who is above both of the groups, or they may have an impact on the budgets of the two groups. Either way will give them some clout, but they must also depend on some intangible factors as well. They must be viewed by the two conflicted groups as neutral but also skilled in the specialties of both groups.[21] Further, they must be viewed as having skills which can help the groups achieve the desired goal of coordination. Thus, we have a mixture of the structural aspects of formal assignment and authority and the process elements of skill and impartiality.

In summary then, we have discussed a number of effective strategies for dealing with intergroup conflict. In most cases, the structural approaches will probably be the most effective, since they deal directly with the causes of the conflict.[22] Still, the process and mixed approaches can be very effective when they are used properly. But in order for any of these strategies to be successful, you will have to analyze the causes of intergroup conflict. Also, you will have to deal with the actors in the conflict. Thus, both behaviors and attitudes must often change in order to manage intergroup conflict and achieve the desired coordination of effort.

Chapter Highlights

In this chapter we have actually begun to integrate organizational behavior and what researchers call organization theory. As we stated early in the chapter **understanding intergroup behavior is vital for you as a manager if you are to manage effectively in an organizational context**. The goal of intergroup behavior is to achieve coordination of group efforts so that organizational goals are achieved. The problem is that **group** goals can become so important to the groups that conflict arises between the groups and begins to hurt the organization. Our objective has been to help you understand why this happens, and how to deal effectively with intergroup conflict.

After looking in on Home Computers to illustrate intergroup conflict, we gave a definition of it: **Intergroup conflict is the situation where one group attempts to achieve its goals at the expense of another group in the organization**. Furthermore, intergroup conflict is a process consisting of a series of episodes, each made up of four steps: (1) frustration, (2) conceptualization, (3) behavior, and (4) outcome. The outcome of one episode leads to the frustration which begins the next conflict episode. From this definition, it is clear that **intergroup conflict is a developmental process that builds up over time, and it also takes time to bring conflict under control**.

In order to better understand intergroup conflict and how to manage it, we then began exploring a model. First, we looked at eight causes of conflict (shown in Figure 13.3), which set up the conditions where conflict is likely. **The primary cause of conflict among groups appears to be the interdependence that is necessary for the groups in doing their tasks**. We discussed three types of task interdependence: (1) pooled, (2) sequential, and (3) reciprocal.

Probably **the second most important cause of conflict is the differentiation which occurs as a result of the specialization among task groups**. The different goal and time orientations, formalities of operation, and interpersonal relationships in various groups create problems in coordinating their efforts without conflict.

Further complicating the matter can be several other causes of conflict—**ambiguity of roles, common limited resources, and reward systems**. If groups are unclear about their responsibilities in relation to those of other groups, coordination efforts become difficult. If the people, equipment, and financial resources are also limited, the groups can easily feel the need to compete. And often, **reward systems encourage competition by rewarding each group based upon how they perform compared to other groups**.

Finally, we discussed three other causes of conflict. To the extent that there are **communication obstacles** and **differences in status and power** between groups, coordination will be made more difficult. And if the **people in the groups lack conflict management skills**, the groups will have greater difficulty in their interactions.

Having discussed the causes of conflict, we turned our attention to the potential outcomes of intergroup conflict, as shown in Figure 13.5. We talked about **negative outcomes**, such as concealing information, increasing distance between the groups, increasing self interest of the groups, decreasing interaction among the groups, wasting energy, loss of good people, and the development of a climate of distrust.

And while you may be quite familiar with these negative outcomes, you are probably less familiar with the **positive outcomes. Intergroup conflict can serve as a signal that problems exist in the organization and as a motivator to correct these problems**. Furthermore, intergroup conflict leads to increased cohesiveness within the conflicted groups and can strengthen certain intergroup linkages. It can also encourage adaptation and flexibility in solving problems, and thus lead to better ideas produced by the groups. And it can lead to the identification of power differences among groups in an organization.

What really determines, over time, whether the negative or positive outcomes of conflict result, are the strategies which people use to manage the intergroup relation-

ship. Thus, we next discussed various strategies for managing conflict. We identified three general categories of behavior: (1) win/lose, (2) lose/lose, and (3) win/win. And we further defined five basic strategies based on the degree of cooperativeness and the degree of assertiveness of a group: (1) competing, (2) accommodating, (3) avoiding, (4) collaborating, and (5) compromising.

We then moved to a more specific discussion of both ineffective and effective strategies for managing intergroup conflict, as shown in Figure 13.7. The first three ineffective strategies (nonaction/avoidance, administrative orbiting, and due-process nonaction) are basic **avoiding** strategies, which are used in hopes the conflict will go away. The next four (secrecy, law and order, competition, and accommodating) are all basically **competing** strategies. They are geared toward win/lose and usually result in long run increases in conflict.

As Figure 13.7 shows there are also a number of effective conflict management strategies. **Structural approaches** are geared toward altering the causes of conflict. You can alter the situation or context that the groups must manage, or you can institute rules and procedures. You can also separate the groups or transfer particular people to reduce the conflict. The **process** approaches are geared toward changing the behaviors and attitudes of the people without changing the situation. For example, you can alter the relationship among the people through negotiation or confrontation, or you can alter the issue in dispute, or you can provide training for the people to enable them to better handle conflict situations. The third category is a **mixture of structural and process approaches**. For example, the hierarchy can absorb the conflict, liaison or boundary spanner personnel can be appointed, task forces can be formed on a temporary basis, and integrating departments can be put into place.

Structural strategies are probably the most effective, but they may not always be possible. And in such cases the process and mixed approaches can be very effective, if both the behaviors and attitudes of the group members are altered. Your long-term effectiveness, especially as you move up the corporate ladder, will be enhanced if you become skilled in using the strategies which lead to positive outcomes from intergroup conflict.

Review Questions

1. Why is it important for you as a manager to understand how to manage intergroup conflict and coordination?

2. What is intergroup conflict, and why do we say it is a developmental process?

3. How might task interdependence and differentiation together create a great deal of potential for intergroup conflict?

4. How do resources and rewards, as well as status differences, ambiguity of roles and communication obstacles, help to create the potential for intergroup conflict?

5. How are people skills and traits important in the level of conflict that develops between two groups in an organization?

6. Discuss both negative and positive outcomes to intergroup conflict.

7. How is the ultimate level of intergroup conflict determined? Can you distinguish among the five categories of conflict behavior that are determined by the levels of cooperativeness and assertiveness that groups exhibit?

8. What are the common factors among the various ineffective conflict management strategies that we discussed in this chapter?

9. What are the structural approaches to conflict management, and how do they differ from the process approaches? Which ones tend to be more powerful?

10. Why are some approaches to conflict management called "mixed approaches"? What are some of these approaches and how effective are they?

Notes

1. K. W. Thomas, "Conflict and Conflict Management." In *Handbook of Industrial and Organizational Psychology*, ed. M. D. Dunnette (Skokie, Ill.: Rand McNally, 1976), pp. 889–935.

2. J. D. Thompson, *Organizations in Action* (New York: McGraw-Hill, 1967).

3. D. Katz and R. L. Kahn, *The Social Psychology of Organizations,* 1st ed. (New York: John Wiley & Sons, 1966).

4. P. R. Lawrence and J. W. Lorsch, *Organization and Environment: Managing Differentiation and Integration* (Homewood, Ill.: Richard D. Irwin, 1967).

5. This paragraph draws primarily from Lawrence and Lorsch, *Organization and Environment*.

6. W. R. Dill, "Environment as an Influence on Managerial Autonomy," *Administrative Science Quarterly* 2 (1958) pp. 409–43.

7. C. Perrow, *Organizational Analysis: A Sociological View* (Belmont, Calif.: Wadsworth, 1970).

8. R. H. Miles, *Macro Organizational Behavior* (Glenview, Ill.: Scott, Foresman, 1980), ch. 5.

9. R. E. Walton, *Interpersonal Peacemaking: Confrontation and Third Party Consultation* (Reading, Mass.: Addison-Wesley Publishing, 1969).

10. Miles, *Macro Organizational Behavior*.

11. This section draws primarily from R. E. Walton and J. M. Dutton, "The Management of Interdepartmental Conflict: A Model and Review," *Administrative Science Quarterly* 14 (1969) pp. 73–84.

12. S. P. Robbins, *Managing Organizational Conflict: A Nontraditional Approach* (Englewood Cliffs, N.J.: Prentice-Hall, 1974).

13. The following section draws primarily from Miles, *Macro Organizational Behavior*, ch. 5.

14. A. Filley, *Interpersonal Conflict* (Glenview, Ill.: Scott, Foresman, 1975).

15. K. Thomas, "Conflict and Conflict Management."

16. Miles, *Macro Organizational Behavior*.

17. This section draws largely from Miles, *Macro Organizational Behavior*, and R. Likert and J. G. Likert, *New Ways of Managing Conflict* (New York: McGraw-Hill, 1976).

18. D. A. Nadler, J. R. Hackman, and E. E. Lawler III, *Managing Organizational Behavior* (Boston: Little, Brown, 1979).

19. E. H. Schein, *Organizational Psychology,* 2d ed. (Englewood Cliffs, N.J.: Prentice-Hall, 1970).

20. Miles, *Macro Organizational Behavior*.

21. P. R. Lawrence and J. W. Lorsch, "New Management Job: The Integrator," *Harvard Business Review* 45 (1967), pp. 142–51.

22. Nadler, Hackman, and Lawler, *Managing Organizational Behavior*.

Resource Readings

Lawrence, P. R., and J. W. Lorsch. *Organization and Environment: Managing Differentiation and Integration*. Homewood, Ill.: Richard D. Irwin, 1967.

Likert, R., and J. Likert. *New Ways of Managing Conflict*. New York: McGraw-Hill, 1976.

Miles, R. H. *Macro Organizational Behavior*. Glenview, Ill.: Scott, Foresman, 1980, ch. 5.

Robbins, S. P. *Managing Organizational Conflict: A Nontraditional Approach*. Englewood Cliffs, N.J.: Prentice-Hall, 1974.

Thomas, K. W. "Conflict and Conflict Management." In *Handbook of Industrial and Organizational Psychology,* ed. M. D. Dunnette. Skokie, Ill.: Rand McNally, 1976, pp. 889-935.

Walton. R. E. *Interpersonal Peacemaking: Confrontation and Third Party Consultation*. Reading, Mass.: Addison-Wesley Publishing, 1969.

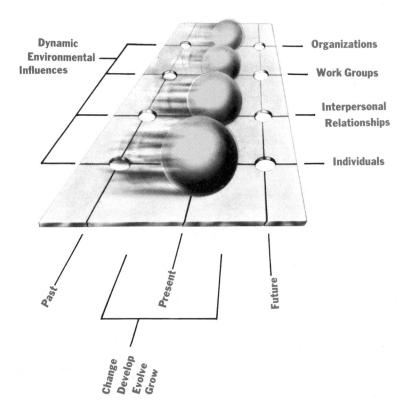

Dynamic Environmental Influences

Organizations

Work Groups

Interpersonal Relationships

Individuals

Past

Present

Future

Change Develop Evolve Grow

Conclusion
and Recap

Chapter 14
**Understanding and Managing
Organizational Behavior**

As we close this book, it is helpful to think back to the first chapter where we stated the purpose of the book. **Our purpose has been to help you gain an understanding of the dynamics of behavior in organizations and to help you learn to manage people in organizations effectively.** These were ambitious objectives, for, as we stated in Chapter 1, it is difficult to live either with or without organizations. To be an effective manager, it is important that you understand the many elements of an organization that operate in a dynamic and interactive manner.

In this book we have focused on understanding and managing the people element in organizations. This means that people must be understood and managed as individuals, as interpersonal relationships, as groups, and as multiple, interacting groups. But they also must be understood and managed within the dynamic context of the tasks they perform, the technologies and structure of the organization, and the environment facing the organization. Throughout the book, we have referred to a developmental framework for analyzing and studying organizations, as repeated here for your reference. Managing all of these components of organizational behavior is indeed a difficult job, but we believe this book has provided a great deal of information and a number of models to make your job as a manager easier. Chapter 14 concludes and recaps our developmental perspective of understanding and managing organizational behavior.

**A Developmental
Framework for
Studying
Organizations.**

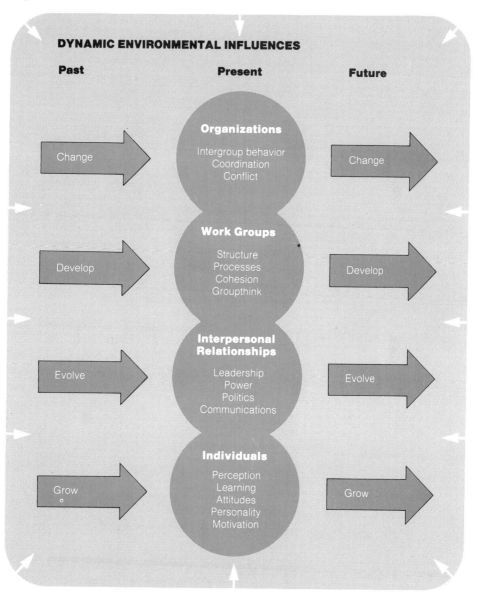

DYNAMIC ENVIRONMENTAL INFLUENCES

Past   Present   Future

Change

Organizations

Intergroup behavior
Coordination
Conflict

Change

Develop

Work Groups

Structure
Processes
Cohesion
Groupthink

Develop

Evolve

**Interpersonal
Relationships**

Leadership
Power
Politics
Communications

Evolve

Grow

Individuals

Perception
Learning
Attitudes
Personality
Motivation

Grow

C H A P T E R 14

Understanding and Managing Organizational Behavior

501

A s a way of reviewing and integrating the key concepts of our book, let us imagine that you are walking into Home Computers or some other company today to begin work as a lower-level manager. What would you do? What questions would you ask? What elements of the organization would you explore? What would you find out about the organization's past? What about its expected future? How would you decide what actions to take to be an effective manager? Think about it for just a minute before we proceed. What are your thoughts? Now let us compare ideas.

Analysis and Action in Organizations

In analyzing your situation and developing action plans, it is important for you to do two things. First, you should use a developmental analysis/action model to guide you in a general sense. Second, you should use the material from this book to provide detail to your analysis and help you decide on your action plan.

A Developmental Analysis/Action Model

Overall in this book, we have outlined a number of issues which you must analyze as you enter your position as a new manager, if you wish to be an effective manager. Indeed, this entire text might be viewed as a developmental analysis/action model of organizational behavior. The headings and subheadings in this final chapter provide you a fairly good checklist for analyzing your new situation. But a general framework for analysis and action would be most helpful. We suggest the model shown in Figure 14.1.

The first step you need to take in your new job is to diagnose and analyze the situation to understand the factors that are operating. In the terms of this text, you would include in this analysis the individuals, their interpersonal relationships, groups, intergroup behavior, and the overall organization and its environment. The next step in the model is to develop a plan for action. What actions might help you become an effective manager and have a successful career? Then comes the point at which you implement your plan for action. This is a critical

Figure 14.1   A Developmental Analysis/Action Model of Organizational Behavior

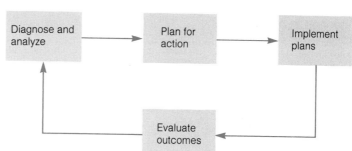

point for you as a manager. You must go beyond analysis if you are to be effective—**you must act**. And as you move into action, you move forward historically; your actions now become part of the situation. Hence, the important next step in the model is to evaluate the outcomes associated with your plan. In conducting this evaluation, you also begin the cycle in Figure 14.1 over again, since evaluation means the collection of data which must be diagnosed and analyzed. And **this process should continue over and over again in a never-ending series of cycles as you work as a manager and move through your career**. By doing this, you are explicitly dealing with the developmental aspects of organizations. If your analysis misses a critical factor at one point in time, or if a critical factor changes, this repeated process helps you make valid analyses over time.

Let us further emphasize the point about taking action. As we have noted many times throughout this text, managers are action-oriented people. Indeed, they must be. **Throughout your managerial career you must be willing to take action, to try new things, and to take risks, if you are to be really successful**. As Box 14.1 indicates, some companies value mistakes that managers make. However, we might add that superiors also value managers who **learn** from their mistakes. The point here is that you must be willing to try new things, to make mistakes, and then you must learn from your mistakes. Recall the

**Box 14.1
Quaker Oats Chairman
to Continue to Make
Changes in New
Position**

*Chicago—To inspire managers at Quaker Oats Co., Chairman
William Smithburg tells them about his mistakes—the 1982 acquisition of a small video-games business that he has since closed
or the French pet-accessory business he bought, then wrote off.*

*"I want you to take risks," he recently told 60 food-products
marketers at a meeting. "There isn't one senior manager in this
company who hasn't been associated with a product that failed,
or some project that failed. That includes me. It's like learning
to ski. If you're not falling down, you're not learning.*

*Mr. Smithburg has taken plenty of risks in reshaping Quaker,
and he has had more successes than failures. In the past, the
century-old food company had a patrician image and unaggres-
sive manner. Since Mr. Smithburg became chief executive officer
two years ago, Quaker has closed or sold weak businesses, improved marketing and introduced more products. And this summer he engineered Quaker's biggest acquisition ever, its purchase
of Stokely-Van Camp Inc.*

*If you're in a mature business and you stand still, you will
definitely lose," Mr. Smightburg says.*

learning model we discussed in Chapter 3. One important
step in the learning cycle was "concrete experience." You
must learn from experience, just as we hope you have
learned from this book, if you are to be an effective manager over your career.

The comments recently made by a very successful manager highlight this point very well. The manager indicated
that his success could be attributed to "making right decisions." When asked how he had learned to make right
decisions, his reply was, "Experience." And when some
brave soul in the audience pressed him on how he had
gained all this experience which now helped him make
right decisions, his reply was, "Wrong decisions."

With the model in Figure 14.1 now in hand, you can
begin to use the material from this book to help you analyze and take action in your new managerial job. If you
think back over this book as a whole, we have explored

individuals, interpersonal relationships, group behavior, and intergroup behavior, all in a dynamic, organizational context. Furthermore, in Chapter 1 we suggested that task, technology, structure, and environment are important contextual elements to understand if you want to be an effective manager. So let us suppose that you want to be effective, to get promoted, and to have a successful career. Where would you start your analysis? Would you start by analyzing the larger contextual issues, over which you may have limited control? Or would you start by analyzing the individual behavior of your people?

Individuals and Their Behavior

We believe you should begin your analysis by assessing the individuals with whom you must work, including yourself. As we have noted repeatedly throughout the book, people are the keys to getting work done in an organization. They are the essential building blocks for organizational behavior. And **to the extent that you know your people, your peers, your bosses, and yourself, you will know what actions to take to be a more effective manager and will have a more successful career.**

Perception and Personality

In Chapters 3 and 4 we provided a great deal of information about understanding people as dynamic beings. In Chapter 3 we focused on the important and difficult process of perception. **Probably next to the process of communications, perception is the most underestimated process in organizational behavior. We all seem to fall into the trap of thinking that what we see is what others also see.** We hope that Chapter 3 made you aware of just how unlikely that occurrence is in organizations. And we hope you learned some ideas to help you deal with the problems of perception. Furthermore, perception was important to our understanding the developmental aspects of people, since it is so dependent on past experiences. You must not underestimate the importance of perceptions of people as they affect behavior. People always behave according to their perceptions. And to the extent that you as manager can create consistent perceptions between yourself and others, your job will be easier.

For example, if your perceptions of your job match

those of your boss, you are more likely to perform well in that job. The key is to clarify with your boss any aspects of your job you do not understand. And it is easier to do this early in a job than later when everyone assumes you understand the job. And in addition, you need to clarify with your people what you want them to do in their jobs, if you expect them to perform well.

In Chapter 4, we extended your understanding of people by focusing on the development of personality. If you are to truly understand your people, you will have to learn about their personalities. Focusing on each individual employee you can determine: Is he or she an extrovert or an introvert? A sensing or intuitive type? A thinking or feeling type? A judging or perceptive type? By knowing the personality types of the people around you in the organization, you will better understand how to lead them effectively. Recall how much we learned by studying the personalities of Steve and Louise in the Home Computers case excerpt in Chapter 4. We were able to understand how Louise had been so successful, and why Steve's career progress had been slower. You can develop the same understanding of your people if you take the time to know them. And this knowledge will help you know what actions to use in motivating and leading your people to high performance.

In essence, we are advocating that the open area of the Johari Window be large (compared to the other three cells in the window) for yourself and for your people. If it is, the work group and organization should be much more effective. And because stress, socialization, and other organizational factors can cause changes in the personalities of employees, it will be necessary to continually share things about yourself and receive feedback to keep the open area large. Likewise, you will need to encourage the same from your people. This developmental aspect of personality means it takes time to develop a large open area in the first place. For example, imagine going on a date with someone for the first time. If you share all about yourself on the first date and expect the same from them, you may not have a second date. Getting to know people must take time and must continue indefinitely, if a good relationship is to develop and last. Take the time to know your people, peers, and managers—it will make you a more effective manager.

and your work group. As we stated in earlier chapters, these interpersonal behaviors will clearly influence the performances of you and your people. In Chapters 7 through 10 we discussed several important components of interpersonal behavior—leadership, power, politics, and communications. Which leadership style should you use with the work group you must manage? What power bases and political behaviors should you use? How should you manage the critical communications that exist within your group? Answers to these questions followed by implementation of the appropriate decisions can indeed make you a more effective manager and lead to a successful career.

Leadership

A vital question for most managers, especially young managers, is how to get work done effectively through other people. How do you ensure high-quality work delivered on time? As you know from earlier chapters, this is a leadership question. Once you understand your people and their tasks you must begin to work through them to accomplish the job. Leadership is one of the key variables affecting performance that we have discussed in this book. It deals directly with issues of being an effective manager.

In Chapter 8 we provided a process for analyzing leadership situations to determine the appropriate leadership style to use both now and later. We indicated that by analyzing the fit between task and subordinate characteristics you could determine the best style of leadership for the current situation—directing, coaching, supporting, or delegating. But we pointed out that you would have to continue to monitor the situation, since either the subordinates or task could change, thus altering the desired leadership style. In fact, if you are an effective leader, you will see the group grow in ability and motivation, and you will have to change your leadership accordingly.

But the analytical process is not over at this point. You also need to analyze the context and leader characteristics. What is your position power? What was the style of the previous leader? What are other leaders in the organization like? What are your power needs? What power bases do you have at your disposal? What are your work relations with the subordinates? What kind of experience do you have? Based on your assessment of answers to these questions, you may have to alter your style of leadership. And again, you must continue to assess these variables as time passes.

A key to your success as a lower-level manager may be to learn from more experienced managers what you can and cannot do at your company. You need to develop your relationships with others in the company, and a mentor can really help with this process. So too can your thoughtful analysis of the situation and careful use and monitoring of the leadership style that seems best. Recall how Louise in Chapter 8 used many of these leadership ideas in dealing with the programmers in Phoenix, as well as with her boss, John Wood. If you analyze the situation and act in accordance with the leadership model in Chapter 8, we believe you can be an effective manager.

Power and Politics

As mentioned above and discussed in Chapter 9, you need to know what your power bases are, as well as those of others with whom you will work. Does your position as manager give you very much legitimate, reward or coercive power? And do you, in this new job, have very much referent or expert power? And what about information, connection, or resource power? And perhaps equally important is for you to think about how you can develop those power bases that are lacking and how you can use those you do have. As you probably recall, **power is the resource that allows you to be a leader. Leaders must use power, ideally in a positive way, if they are to have influence over other people.** Again, the mentor we mentioned above can help you move from analysis to action, but **you** really determine what happens in this first job at your company.

Equally important to you will be to gain an understanding of the political behaviors that are available and acceptable in your company. In particular, are negative politics used in the organization? And does your situation seem to necessitate the use of positive political behaviors? By reviewing the political behaviors in Chapter 9 and learning why people engage in politics in your company, you will be in a much better position to be an effective manager. For example, if Rob at Home Computers in Chapter 9 had recognized the negative politics of Tom, he probably could have dealt effectively with them using positive politics. He might have been able to retain his job as section head, while revealing what Tom was trying to do. If you are to be an effective manager, you will have to understand political behaviors and learn to use positive politics when they are appropriate.

Communications

Finally, with regard to interpersonal behavior, **communications are the lifeblood of an organization**. As you analyze your people and the relationships that you will encounter as a manager, and as you start to operate as a manager, communications are vital for you to understand. And as we noted in Chapter 11, communications within a group give you many clues about the decision-making and leadership styles that are being used.

Furthermore, as noted in Chapter 10, the process of communications has many dimensions which make it difficult to perfect. Indeed, communications in organizations are usually far from perfect. There are many purposes for which people communicate, many media that they use, and many directions that communications can flow. And there are also many factors that can act as noise and inhibitors of communications between people. It is critical for you as a manager to remember that **a message you send is not a communication until it is received and understood as you intended**. In order to aid you in this difficult process, we provided you with five steps to improve communications: (1) analyze the context, (2) put yourself in the receiver's position, (3) select the best medium for your message, (4) prepare and send your message, and (5) become the receiver and listen for feedback. If you follow these simple steps, you will find yourself becoming a better communicator—both sending and receiving.

If Rob had used these steps in the Chapter 10 Home Computers segment, he might have improved communications and avoided the negative impact of Tom's political behavior. Rob just did not read all the signals that were coming to him, and he did not act to correct the communications problems he saw. It is critical for you as a manager not only to analyze situations but also to act on your analysis. Without action, your analysis will be worthless —managers must be action oriented. And communications are a natural vehicle for moving from analysis to action.

Analyzing Your Work Group

Once you have gained an understanding of the people and interpersonal relationships in your organization, you are ready to analyze as a whole your first work group in the organization. You know that these people can most quickly break you or start you on the road to a good future in the company. What would you want to find out about this important group of people? Let us compare notes.

Group History

As pointed out in Chapter 1 and elaborated in Chapter 11, **the history of a group is important for you to understand if you are to effectively manage it**. What has been the past performance record of the group? Has performance been on the rise or on the decline? How much turnover has the group been experiencing? Is that on the rise or the decline? And what is the stage of group development?

For example, if your group is in Stage 1 (testing and orientation) and has not been performing well, we can draw on the leadership model in Chapter 8 to learn that you should use a directing style. Once the group has moved into Stage 2 (conflict and organization), you can become a more participating leader. As you recall, we found just that situation in the quality circles at Home Computers in Chapter 12. Jim, the leader, had to provide more structure in order to move the group out of the conflict/organization development stage. But he had to carefully select the way to be directive and also provide for supportive behaviors—in this case from another person. But this participating style did produce results. And over about six months, the group moved into Stage 3 (cohesion and information exchange) and was performing well. Jim could then use supporting or delegating leadership styles. But should the circle start to decline in performance, he could move back to participating leadership. The point is that you, like Jim, must determine where the group is now in relation to where it has been. And you must continue to monitor the situation as the group develops.

Input Variables

Another important way to analyze a group is to assess the state of fit between the group members and the situational variables discussed in Chapter 11 (task/technology, organizational system, physical layout, group size, and composition). If performance is not up to par, an analysis of the fit among these variables may reveal the problem. For a group that has been performing well and has begun to decline of late, we need to ask if there have been any changes in these fit variables. Perhaps changes in the technology or physical layout or rewards have thrown the fit among the variables out of balance. It is easy to forget that a change in any one variable will create the need for changes in **all** of the other variables. For example, a change in technology may make people much more interdependent, but the rewards and group composition have always been geared toward jobs with very little interdependence. Or as Box 14.3 demonstrates, changes can make people less interdependent. The question is how such changes will affect the fit variables and hence, performance over time. As the new manager, you will need to analyze the fit among variables and any changes that have occurred in any of the variables in order to determine what you should do. **It is tough, but the group input variables described in Chapter 11 must achieve and maintain a degree of fit if the group is to be effective.**

Group Structure and Processes

In addition to analyzing the input variables, you will also need to analyze group structure and process in order to really understand your work group. What norms prevail in the group? What status and power relationships exist within it? Is the group cohesive, too cohesive? The material we discussed in Chapter 12 will be most valuable as you analyze the past, present, and future of these group structure variables.

As you direct your attention toward the group pro-

**Box 14.3
Faced with a Changing
Work Force, TRW
Pushes to Raise
White-Collar
Productivity**

Redondo Beach, Calif.—*When Dennis E. Hacker moved out of the crowded computer room where he and other TRW Inc. software designers hammered out computer code, two things happened. He felt isolated, and his productivity soared.*

TRW put Mr. Hacker and 34 of his colleagues into private, windowless offices wired with state-of-the-art computer equipment: terminals that talk to the company computer network, electronic mail, teleconferencing facilities and sophisticated programs that help write programs. The company expected the programmers to become more productive, but it didn't anticipate an increase of as much as 39% in the experiment's first year. "The results were so good we were reluctant to believe them," says Robert Williams, vice president of systems information and software development.

Particularly surprising were the reasons the programmers gave for their increased output. Predictably, they loved their electronic gadgets, but simple changes such as quiet, privacy, and comfortable chairs also helped a lot.

Mr. Hacker says he missed the friendly chaos of the bullpen during his first few days in solitary. "I didn't feel like part of the team any more," he recalls. But he soon came to like his new surroundings. "I'd close the door and grind away at my work, and the next thing I knew I was getting hungry. I realized it was 6 p.m. and I'd worked right through the day."

The lesson for productivity, says Mr. Williams: "Don't overlook the simple things."

But psychologists warn about the long-term effects of such changes in the quality of people's work lives. Optimistic projections such as TRW's can be dashed in the long term if care isn't taken to measure human factors as well as product output, says Alexandra Saba, a Los Angeles industrial psychologist. Miss Saba worked on a study of similar work place changes for Verbatim Corp., a supplier of magnetic storage media. She says the study found that depriving workers of face-to-face contact could be damaging.

"If you stick people into little cubicles they start suffering psychological effects and physiological effects of worker alienation," she says. "In the long term, productivity can actually go down."

Mr. Hacker says that isn't his experience. He had to leave the experimental offices when a code-writing project he was working on ended. Back in the old offices, surrounded by the press of humanity, he says he felt "an immediate decrease" in his productivity. He says he has learned to prefer a conference call on a computer screen to a casual chat in the corridor.

cesses that are at work in the group, you can also draw from Chapter 12, as well as from Chapters 7 and 8 on leadership and Chapter 10 on communications. What are the communication patterns that characterize the group as you observe it over time? Is it the wheel, the Y, the chain, the circle, or the all-channel? Or perhaps it varies depending on the issue being handled or even among the stages of handling an issue. For example, everyone may enter into the discussion in the early stages (all-channel). But when decision time comes, all of the communications are funneled through one person (wheel).

And as we discussed in Chapter 12, your analysis of the communication patterns in the group will tell you a great deal about the decision-making and leadership styles in the group. For example, recall how Jim and his quality circle at Home Computers in Chapter 12 used the wheel pattern, as observed by the consultant. Jim did most of the talking. And with the wheel pattern, the decisions are probably made by authority rule and the leadership is directive. These may be appropriate for the situation, but they were not for Jim's situation, partly because of his low status/power in the group. The material in Chapter 12 on decision making and the two chapters on leadership will help you determine which leadership style is appropriate in your work group. It helped Jim determine that he needed to be more participative. In order to analyze your situation and then put a plan into action, you will have to use the material from Chapters 7, 8, and 12.

In addition to communications, decision making, and leadership, your analysis of the work group should include an assessment of the roles being played by the members. Are any of the self-oriented roles we discussed in Chapter 12 present and hindering the group? And in terms of the task and maintenance roles, what type of group are you walking into—task oriented, team, interpersonal, or floundering? As we saw in Chapter 12 in the Home Computers case, such an analysis helped Jim determine which leadership roles to perform to help the group. The group was interpersonal (high on maintenance roles and low on task roles); hence, he needed to perform some of the task roles to move toward the desired team group. A present and continuing analysis of your group, followed by appropriate action, is vital to your success as a manager. We believe that the assessment of roles provides clear direction as to what you need to do. And remember, action is the name of the game as a manager, but if you make it analysis first, then action, your chances of success go up greatly.

In Chapter 12, we also pointed out that you must conduct this type of analysis of other groups to which you belong. This is especially important for the group which includes your peers (who manage other groups), and your immediate boss. As a subordinate in this group, you can still have—indeed you **must** have—influence on what the group does. Your assessment of the group roles from Chapter 12 and of the politics of the group (Chapter 9), can enable you to be an influential member of that group. And finally, these same analysis points will apply to your performance in ad hoc groups, committees, and other groups to which you will belong over your career.

Intergroup Relationships

It will also be important for you to analyze the other groups in the organization with which your work group must interact. As we discussed in Chapter 13, work groups in organizations do not work in isolation. To varying degrees, they must interact with other work groups in order to complete their task and for the organization to be successful. The essential question is: will there be conflict or coordination between the groups in an organization. As we found in the Home Computers segment in Chapter 13, conflict between sales and production was hurting the company. By analyzing the causes of conflict and exploring some effective strategies for managing conflict, we were able to identify a number of ways to improve the coordination between sales and production. As the new manager of a work group, you too will need to explore the history of relations between your group and the other groups that they must interact with in doing their job. Has the history of these relationships been one of conflict or cooperation? What is the future likely to hold for your group in its relations with other groups? By delving further into these questions using the material from Chapter 13, you will be able to analyze the causes of any conflict that exists. And you will be able to determine how to move the situation toward collaboration, regardless of whether the solution is structural or process oriented. And you will be able to do this without stifling positive conflict that is needed to keep the organization alive and adaptive to change.

The Larger Organizational Picture

Once you have analyzed your situation in terms of people, interpersonal relations, group behavior, and intergroup relations, you need to consider the larger organizational picture—the environment, technology, structure, and culture. These variables form the context of your managerial behavior and of the people and groups you will work with. As we suggested in Chapter 1, this larger picture is not a primary focus of our book, but you must consider it in general terms if you are to conduct an adequate analysis of your new position and determine the actions needed to be effective. At first, you might think that environment, technology, structure, and culture are beyond your concerns as a lower-level manager. But we believe that they can strongly influence the success of your actions. Thus, even if you cannot change these variables from your lower-level management position, you need to act in accordance with these constraints on your behavior.

The Environment

As Box 14.4 shows, the industry in which the organization is located can have both a dynamic and dramatic effect on the organization. Only a few years ago, people were falling all over themselves to get into the home computer business. Now however, a shakeout of grand proportions is occurring, and many recently prosperous companies are suffering greatly. It would be important for you to gather some information about your company's industry, both its past and its anticipated future.

In addition, it is important for you to learn about the environment in a more general sense. What are the immediate and long-term prospects for the United States and world economies? Will our society continue to become more and more legalistic?[1] Will robotics, computers, lasers, and other such high technology industries be the growth industries of the future? If so, how might that

Box 14.4
With 'Peanut,' IBM
Plans Attack on Low-
Priced Computer
Market

Here comes Big Blue. Again.

International Business Machines Corp., which set the higher-priced end of the small-computer market on its ear when it introduced the IBM Personal Computer in 1981, is now poised to attack on the lower-priced portion of that market. Anytime within a day to 9 months—no one is quite sure, and IBM isn't talking—the company will introduce Peanut.

According to competitors, analysts with IBM contacts, dealers, and other industry sources, Peanut will sell for $600 to $750, perhaps less, and will consist of a keyboard and a computer plugged into a home television set. Analysts say it will be sold through outlets including such mass marketers as Sears, Roebuck & Co., J.C. Penney Co. and K mart Corp.

Peanut would mark IBM's entry into a market segment it has ignored before, and throw the company's weight against Commodore, Atari and Texas Instruments computers. That market is already huge, and growing bigger with amazing speed; analysts estimate that over 2 million home computers were shipped last year and that in 1983 the number will nearly triple.

In the market for computers costing less than $1,000, Atari is the current leader, though Commodore is expected by many to take over the lead in 1983 with Atari slipping to third behind Texas Instruments. Tandy Corp., which sells through its Radio Shack chain, and Sinclair, which pioneered the under-$100 computer marketed in the U.S. by Timex, are other major players.

PC II and Rover

All that, however, reckons without IBM's production and marketing power when it enters the lower-priced arena. In the past five years it has added more than 20 million square feet of production-plant capacity; that, along with its heavy spending on research and development, have given the computer giant the ability to expand quickly into any market it decides is attractive.

Next month it is expected to introduce PC II, an upgraded version of its hot-selling personal computer that has an improved color monitor as an option and much more storage capacity in the form of a hard disk drive built into the memory core. Another imminent product, according to analysts: Rover, an add-on to the company's 3270 "dumb" terminal that would turn it into a personal computer and still let the user tap into big mainframe computer units if he chose. Analysts estimated that about 1.5 million 3270s and other compatible terminals have already been installed.

But most of the industry's attention is fixed on Peanut, which could help alter the character of the whole home-computer market. Despite the popularity of these machines, they are still viewed *mainly as gadgets that let the user play video games without paying a quarter every time. The potential of home computers to perform some of the functions of more costly personal computers, such as word-processing and use as educational tools, hasn't been fully realized despite producers' promotional efforts.*

IBM could change that. Its no-nonsense, businesslike image could induce use of home computers for less frivolous purposes, like controlling lighting or burglar-alarm systems, and actually helping educate the children instead of just teaching them to score high on video games. Computer programs already exist to dream up recipes for leftovers in the icebox and help people with home budgeting and accounting.

The industry is buzzing with speculation about when IBM will choose to introduce Peanut. Insiders at Apple Computer, trying to fight off inroads by IBM in the personal-computer market, suspect that Peanut will be introduced immediately to steal Apple's thunder when it unveils its new personal computer, Lisa, later this week.

By Susan Chace, *The Wall Street Journal,* January 18, 1983. Reprinted by permission of *The Wall Street Journal,* © Dow Jones & Company, Inc. 1983. All rights reserved.

affect your company? And what if the answer is no? What will be the growth industries of the future, and how do they relate to your company? Such environmental factors as these may influence the growth potential of your company, and hence, the growth potential for your career. They may also suggest changes in the direction the company will take. Perhaps it will alter its product or service to take advantage of changes in the environment. These factors will have a direct impact on your career and the directions it takes. As we discussed in Chapter 2, your career will go through a number of stages, as you also go through a number of life stages. It is thus important for you to think about the dynamic environment of your company and its current and future impact on you and your career. You need to start a life-long process of asking and answering these general questions that will ultimately affect your career.

The Technologies

At a level which more directly affects you as a manager on a daily basis, the larger picture consists of the technologies in your company, the structure of the company, and the corporate culture. In short, what is the situation you will find as a new manager? As we have discussed in earlier chapters, your organization will have developed technologies for making its products or providing its services. And it will be important for you, as a lower-level manager, to understand the tasks and technologies of your work group, as well as possible future changes in them if you are to be an effective manager.

For example, you may recall how we analyzed the task characteristics of your subordinates in Chapter 8 on leadership. The degree of task structure and task variability are important for you to understand when determining the appropriate leadership style to use. As we saw in the Home Computers case in Chapter 8, Louise faced a situation with an unstructured task and high variability. Hence, she had to use a directing leadership style to get things moving. But as the leadership model in Chapter 8 suggested, as the technology becomes more routine over time, you will need to alter your leadership style to fit a situation which has become easier for your people.

Likewise, we discussed in Chapter 6 how technological changes in the job can create both problems and opportunities for motivation. As jobs become more and more routine, people tend to become bored, and this can create motivation problems. On the other hand, automation can take over many boring jobs and thus create opportunities for people to perform more challenging jobs.

We could go on by recalling the impact technology has on communications in an organization, as discussed in Chapter 10. Or we could recall its impact on group behavior, as discussed in Chapter 11. But the key point to be made is that **technology is a powerful force that affects many aspects of your job as a manager**. You must make it part of your present and continuing analysis of the situation into which you are walking, if you are to perform effectively in your job.

The Structure

Another important aspect of the larger organizational context is the structure of the organization and of the department in which you will work. It creates part of the context that can help or hinder you as a manager. You need to know: Is the structure relatively rigid and bureaucratic, or is it loose and flexible? The more bureaucratic it is, the more clearly defined your role will be, but it will also be constrained. Furthermore, what has been the history of the organization structure, and where can it be expected to go in the future? For example, Home Computers has moved rapidly from a loose and flexible structure to one that is quickly becoming bureaucratic. And as we saw in Chapters 5 and 6, this has created motivation problems in the plants. The employees felt the company had become too bureaucratic, and they were not as excited and motivated about working there any more. Early in the company's life, (note the time aspect) the employees had been very enthusiastic and excited about their work, but that has changed as the company has grown more bureaucratic over time.

Also, as the organization has grown, it has become necessary to create a number of different departments and plant sites. As we discussed in Chapter 10, the creation of different departments, while necessary, creates barriers to effective communications in the organization. In addition, such differentiation can lead to increases in organizational politics (as discussed in Chapter 9). It can also lead to status differences between departments, which will inhibit their necessary interaction (as discussed in Chapter 13). If you are to perform your best as a manager, you must recognize and act in a manner consistent with the context imposed by the structure of your company.

The Corporate Culture

As you analyze these aspects of your new organization, it is also important to assess the more subtle aspects of organizational culture and climate if you want to be effective. What are the norms of behavior in the organization? What are the rituals and symbols that are important for you to understand? For example, your predecessors may have taken the secretary out to lunch when they first came into the position. To ignore such a ritual could produce problems for you, as a new manager. So ask other managers about these norms and other expected behaviors. You will also need to gain an appreciation for the political processes that characterize the organization. In Chapter 9, we discussed a number of elements comprising the power and political components of an organization. You can use these ideas to help you understand the power bases that people have and use. And you can use them to help you understand the political behaviors that are predominant in the organization. Watch, observe, and ask people about these issues. Then you can work to develop your power bases and learn to use political behaviors to help you succeed in your organization's culture.

Conclusion and Challenge

Throughout this text, our challenge has been to help you understand the people element of organizations within the dynamic context of task, technology, structure, and environment. And it has also been our task to help you understand people as dynamic beings who exist in evolving relationships and groups. As we have noted, and as you now appreciate, this is not a simple task. **In order to truly understand the elements of an organization, it is necessary to analyze their history, as well as their present status. This analysis then determines what you as a manager should do to be effective.**

Your job is not done at this point. **You must then manage people as they and their context develop over time.** The job of an effective manager is one of analysis, action, evaluation and action again in a never-ending cycle. We feel this book can help you in this task. And we hope that you will accept the challenge to try the things suggested throughout the book, even if they are hard or do not work for you the first time. Becoming a successful manager and staying one over a career is a job that must be tackled with great fervor and with the expectation that you will make mistakes. Just remember to learn from your mistakes and to continue learning about management as you progress through your career as a manager. If you use the ideas from this book, you can become an effective manager and turn "wrong decisions" into "right decisions." Good luck, and enjoy yourself!

Notes

1. J. Naisbitt, *Megatrends* (New York: Warner Books, 1982).

Index

This book has been set VideoComp in 10 and 9 point Times Roman, leaded 2 points. Section and chapter numbers are 18 point Spectra Bold, section and chapter titles are 30 point Spectra Bold. The size of the type page is 30 by 47 picas.